Japanese Modality

Japanese Modality

Exploring its Scope and Interpretation

Edited by

Barbara Pizziconi

and

Mika Kizu

Department of Japan and Korea
School of Oriental and African Studies
University of London

First published 2009 by
PALGRAVE MACMILLAN

Palgrave Macmillan in the UK is an imprint of Macmillan Publishers Limited,
registered in England, company number 785998, of Houndmills, Basingstoke,
Hampshire RG21 6XS.

Palgrave Macmillan in the US is a division of St Martin's Press LLC,
175 Fifth Avenue, New York, NY 10010.

Palgrave Macmillan is the global academic imprint of the above companies
and has companies and representatives throughout the world.

Palgrave® and Macmillan® are registered trademarks in the United States,
the United Kingdom, Europe and other countries.

ISBN-13: 978–0–230–57632–2 hardback

This book is printed on paper suitable for recycling and made from fully
managed and sustained forest sources. Logging, pulping and manufacturing
processes are expected to conform to the environmental regulations of the
country of origin.

A catalogue record for this book is available from the British Library.

A catalog record for this book is available from the Library of Congress.

10   9   8   7   6   5   4   3   2   1
18   17   16   15   14   13   12   11   10   09

Printed and bound in Great Britain by
CPI Antony Rowe, Chippenham and Eastbourne

Contents

v

List of Figures

List of Tables

Preface

Introducing a book on modality is not an easy task. As a cursory look at the content of this volume concisely demonstrates, the concept of 'modality' is relevant to very many aspects of language, and is an object of interest to a broad range of disciplinary fields. But the very definition of modality is a contentious issue, which reflects the plasticity (and therefore the vagueness) of this 'umbrella' term, and at the same time, the elusiveness and huge variety of the phenomena that research aims to capture. The editors of this volume do not intend to 'take sides'. Instead, we wish to present a non-dogmatic overview of modality studies, to put this very diversity on display, provide food for thought, and let readers make up their minds as to the most effective and fruitful approach, to pursue much needed further research.

But this book, the first collection on Japanese modality (or rather 'Japanese *Modariti'*) in the English language, also intends to be a display of modality research on Japanese, a considerable amount of which has only appeared in Japanese, and is unknown or little known to the worldwide academic community. Some of the chapters in this collection not only reference but address issues emerging from the traditions of *Nihongogaku* ('Japanese linguistics') or *Kokugogaku* ('Japanese philology'), which we hope will provide a glimpse of their very rich landscapes.

This volume is the offspring of the international conference *Revisiting Japanese Modality*, held on 24 and 25 June 2006, at the School of Oriental and African Studies, University of London. Two of the most prominent authorities in the field, professors Takashi Masuoka and Yukinori Takubo, provided thoughtful and thought-provoking plenary sessions. Over 50 participants from Japan, America and other European countries contributed to two days of insightful and constructive discussion across disciplinary borders. The chapters in this volume (with the exception of those of the editors, which are later additions) represent a selection of the conference papers, and we thank all the contributors for their continued enthusiasm and collaboration throughout the serpentine journey to publication.

The success of the conference led to an additional workshop on Japanese modality for Japanese language teachers held in London in October 2007, and eventually to this publication. Our project would not have materialized without the generous financial support of the Japan

Foundation, the Great Britain Sasakawa Foundation and the Daiwa Anglo-Japanese Foundation, whom we thank sincerely.

We also wish to acknowledge our gratitude to David Bennett, Giovanna Ceroni, Aki Hedigan and Peter Sells for reviewing and assisting with the editorial work.

BARBARA PIZZICONI
MIKA KIZU

Notes on the Contributors

Setsuko Arita is Professor in the Department of Japanese Language and Literature, Osaka Shoin Women's University, Japan. She has published articles on Japanese conditional constructions and a single-authored book: *Japanese Conditionals and Tensedness* (2007). Her research interests include conditionals, topicality, modality, aspect and temporality, in semantic theory and cross-linguistically.

Kaoru Horie is Professor of Linguistics at the Graduate School of International Cultural Studies, Tohoku University, Sendai, Japan. His numerous publications include 'The grammaticalization of nominalizers in Japanese and Korean: a contrastive study', *Rethinking Grammaticalization* (2008), and an edited volume *Complementation* (2000). He specializes in linguistic typology, cognitive-functional linguistics, and Japanese/Korean contrastive linguistics.

Noriko Iwasaki is Lecturer in Language Pedagogy in the Department of Linguistics at SOAS, University of London, UK. Her current interests are psycholinguistics, second language acquisition and foreign language pedagogy. Her publications include 'Style shifts among Japanese learners before and after study abroad in Japan: Becoming active social agents in Japanese' to appear in *Applied Linguistics.*

Mika Kizu is Lecturer in Japanese in the Department of Japan and Korea, SOAS, University of London, UK. She has been working on Japanese syntax and published *Cleft Constructions in Japanese Syntax* in 2005. She is also interested in the syntax–pragmatics interface and second language acquisition in Japanese.

Lars Larm is Senior Lecturer in Japanese Linguistics at the Centre for Languages and Literature, Japanese Studies, Lund University in Sweden. He completed his doctorate on Japanese modality at the University of Oxford in 2006. His research interests are semantics, pragmatics and Japanese linguistics.

Takashi Masuoka is Professor in the Department of Japanese Language and Culture, Kobe City University of Foreign Studies, Kobe, Japan. He has published influential articles and books, including: *Nihongo Modariti Tankyu* [Investigations of Japanese Modality] (2007), and *Nihongobunpoo no Shosoo* [Aspects of Japanese Grammar] (2000). His research interests are Japanese syntax and semantics, and Japanese grammatical description.

Tetsuharu Moriya is Professor of English Linguistics at the School of Teacher Education, Kanazawa University in Japan. He has published articles with Kaoru Horie such as 'Negation of ability in Korean and related languages', in W. O'Grady et al. (eds), *Inquiries into Korean Linguistics II* (2006). His research interests are cognitive-functional linguistics, grammaticalization, and Japanese/Korean contrastive linguistics.

Heiko Narrog is Associate Professor at Tohoku University, Sendai, Japan. He has published numerous articles on Japanese language history and semantics, as well as a book in German on morphological change in the Japanese verb phrase. His monograph: *Modality in Japanese: the Layered Structure of the Clause and Hierarchies of Functional Categories* has just appeared (2009). His research interests include the Japanese language, diachronic change, semantics and typology.

Barbara Pizziconi is Senior Lecturer in Applied Japanese Linguistics in the Department of Japan and Korea, SOAS, University of London. Her research output includes studies on Japanese linguistic politeness, pragmatic, cognitive and sociocultural aspects of native and non-native language use, and Japanese language acquisition.

Teruko Shin'ya is Professor at J.F. Oberlin University, Tokyo, Japan. Her publications include the co-authored book: *Nihongo Zuihitsu Tekusuto no Shosoo* [Aspects of Japanese Essays] (2007) and *Nihongo Un'yoo Bunpoo* [Japanese Grammar in Context] (2003). Her research interests are grammar/syntax and contrastive linguistics.

Yukinori Takubo is Professor of Linguistics at the Graduate School of Letters, Kyoto University, Japan. He has published a number of influential single- and co-authored articles and books, including *Hukubun to danwa* [Compound Sentences and Discourse], Vol. 4 in the series *Nihongo no Bunpoo* [Grammar of Japanese] (2002). His research interests are Japanese syntax, Korean syntax, discourse theory, pragmatics, and the syntax–semantics interface.

Suwako Watanabe is Professor of Japanese at Portland State University in Portland, Oregon, USA. Her research interests are discourse analysis, Japanese sociolinguistics, language pedagogy and assessment. Her publications include 'Analyzing discourse in group discussion', in *Pragmatics in 2000: Selected Papers from the 7th International Pragmatics Conference 2*, Nemeth T. Eniko (ed.) (2001).

Introduction

Barbara Pizziconi and Mika Kizu

Several decades of linguistic inquiry into various linguistic phenomena labelled 'modal' by researchers have not managed to achieve an uncontroversial definition of 'modality', nor a consensus about its nature or its boundaries. Multiple terms adopted in the Japanese literature on the subject have possibly compounded the problem (Nakau 1999: 28, Kurotaki 2002: 87), referring to modality either through Sino-Japanese compounds like *hoosei* (法性) or *johoosei* (叙法性, Kudoo 2005), and its association with 'mood', or the loanword *modariti* (モダリティ, first coined by Nakau 1979), with its deceiving lexemic equivalence.

The lack of terminological or even notional correspondence across studies that claim to investigate modal phenomena no doubt depends, in part, on language-specific discourses about it. Different grammatical categories identified as 'prototypically' modal in different languages have to a large extent determined the make-up and trajectories of this field of studies in different traditions, with considerable consequences that even contemporary researchers still have to grapple with.

The thorny ontological question of what is meant by 'modality' and how it can be best characterized is an obvious concern in most of the volume's contributions. Contemporary research in Japanese modality undoubtedly keeps an eye on its own history, but also shows a palpable aspiration to dialogue with the wider linguistic community and sensitivity to the achievements of other linguistic traditions.

Heiko Narrog's opening chapter tackles and contextualizes this question from a sociocultural/historical point of view. In his overview of the development of Japanese modality studies, he notes how each tradition produces particular 'framings' of the subject matter in ways that cannot be entirely explained on the basis of the scientific rigour or explanatory power of this or that model. Rather, he submits that not only historical,

1

but importantly, also sociopolitical factors led Japanese modality scholarship to be driven mostly by its understanding of modality as an expression of the speaker's 'subjectivity'. Several of this volume's contributors directly confront themselves with this 'heritage', and elaborate on the ontological and epistemic consequences of the choice of 'subjectivity' (rather than, for example, 'factuality', 'necessity/possibility', 'speaker commitment', etc.) as a heuristic notion.

Narrog himself argues against the use of subjectivity as a suitable parameter, on the grounds that this does not discriminate between modals and other grammatical and functional categories such as sentence-final particles or illocutionary force, and maintains that the notion of 'factuality' (or the opposition between worlds of *realis* and *irrealis*) is both a more reliable and a cross-linguistically generalizable discriminator.

This position is also maintained in the chapter by Takashi Masuoka, who also links the notion of factuality with the concepts of *teigen/kakugen*, or 'assertive/probable', already familiar to Japanese scholars from the work of some of the most authoritative voices in the Japanese linguistic school, such as Hideo Teramura and Akira Mikami. Masuoka too notes the greater explanatory power of the notions of *realis/irrealis*, which allows cross-linguistic comparisons, but maintains that 'subjectivity' must nevertheless be considered as an intrinsic feature of modal markers. The opposite, however, i.e. that 'subjectivity' confers modality to a marker, does not invariably hold: distinguishing 'compositional' and 'non-compositional' subjectivity, he claims that the latter (including for example, propositional honorifics and directional verbs, that is, lexicalized evaluative judgements and deictic terms) does not qualify as modal indicator.

Incidentally, the dialogue between the Japanese and other linguistic traditions is evident also in the way Masuoka conceptualizes the 'layering' structure attributed to Japanese, inspired by Fujio Minami. While adhering to such a 'layered' view of utterance structure with his 'semantic layer structure model', Masuoka's original take emerges in his positing semantic-compositional, rather than sentence-structural layers, which not only deftly avoids the dangers of assuming functional uniformity in individual linguistic forms, but also allows cross-linguistic comparisons by assuming different surface realizations in otherwise commensurate semantic domains.

Lars Larm's chapter similarly acknowledges that modality has to do with the dimension of *irrealis*, but claims that also the distinct dimension of subjectivity, insofar as it can be linguistically 'encoded' in a specific form (but compare this with Pizziconi's take below), has to be taken into account in order to yield a precise semantic description of a modal marker. For Larm, subjectivity/objectivity are matters of 'degrees', and he proposes a battery of tests, based on criteria derived from both Japanese and non-Japanese analyses, to establish such degrees empirically.

Tetsuharu Moriya and Kaoru Horie address the theme of 'subjectivity' not as a product but as a process, i.e. 'subjectification' – a progressively abstract and subjective construal of the world. They argue that, contrary to Traugott's thesis, although a process of subjectification is involved in the genesis of Japanese modal auxiliaries, the type of grammaticalization process involved is arguably very different from that of English. In other words, grammaticalization should not be considered as governed by a set of unique rules (such as the metaphorical mapping of the logic of the external world onto the internal world, arguably responsible for the development of epistemic meanings from deontic meanings in English), but should be seen as an epiphenomenon derived from several independent laws. A unidirectional model that prescribes a linear development from deontic to epistemic modality (assumed by some to be universal) shows little explanatory adequacy for the features of Japanese, in which modern epistemic and deontic markers are formally distinct and extremely specialized.

A process of subjectification can indeed be invoked to describe the historical development of the synthetic/polysemous modal expressions of Old Japanese into the current system, but their development is marked by the emergence of periphrastic forms (with both epistemic and deontic meanings), equidistant from an original *irrealis* meaning. Hence the notion of *irrealis* turns out to be the most powerful characterizing trait of modality, as it can be used to describe a 'core' trait present in polysemic markers, a constant feature in the development of epistemic from deontic meanings in English, as well as a common feature of both epistemic and deontic markers in Japanese, regardless of developmental paths. A further comparison with Korean, which like Japanese exhibits many periphrastic constructions, allows the authors to argue that cultural/typological factors play a role in developmental pathways.

Setsuko Arita's chapter explores the dimension of (non-)factuality through the semantic notion of 'settledness' in the antecedents of 'epistemic' conditionals (whose truth value is held to be 'objectively settled' but not necessarily known to speakers, as distinct from 'predictive' and 'counterfactual' conditionals whose antecedent is respectively 'unsettled' or 'settled'). Unlike English, Japanese displays grammaticalized epistemic conditionals, and Arita submits that the notion of 'settledness' of the antecedent (roughly, that 'a proposition is settled when its truth value is determined at the time of speech') can explain distributional differences between tensed (-*nara*- and -*n(o)nara*) and non-tensed (-*eba* and -*tara*) conditional clauses in a way that previous analyses, based on causal relations, cannot.

Conditional modality is also discussed in the chapter authored by Yukinori Takubo. Takubo argues that the traditional distinction of epistemic and evidential modals (as instances of propositional modality) based on the presence or absence of overt evidence for a speaker's inference can be reconceptualized in terms of type of inference involved. Epistemics and evidentials differ in terms of the specific direction of inference in conditionals (i.e. deduction for epistemics, and abduction, its inverse, or induction for evidentials), and he argues that these two inference types correlate with different scope properties. Takubo too looks back to traditional Japanese linguistics in his acknowledging 'true' and 'pseudo'-modality uses for the same linguistic form; however, departing from such traditional approaches, he develops his analysis on a semantic and cognitive basis, supported both empirically and theoretically.

The chapter by Mika Kizu concludes the foray into formal linguistic analyses. Kizu overviews some of recent syntactic analyses proposed for Japanese modal predicates. She introduces a phrase structure based on the theory of fine-grained CP structure, in which two types of modal predicates, epistemic and utterance modals, are represented in Japanese. Focusing on the phenomena of person restrictions, she explores to what extent syntax can deal with Japanese modality. Kizu points out that the person restriction phenomena do not fall into the common type of syntactic agreement system, and argues that although the 'person information' might be represented in the syntax in these phenomena, the conditions on which 'person' is required are rather semantic/pragmatic, and are not directly encoded in the syntax.

Predicates (and predication) have been central in studies of modality and Japanese modality, in spite of the established fact that modality is not an exclusive property of the verb. The chapter by Teruko Shin'ya makes the point that modality needs to be analysed beyond its typical instantiation in unmarked full sentences, and looks instead at 'minor' sentences, or predicateless utterances, which are nevertheless taken to be self-sufficient functional units in discourse. Shin'ya argues that the speaker choice between an unmarked and a marked construction can be seen as an instantiation of the speaker's attitude (i.e. that a marked construction conveys an additional expressive meaning) and therefore (following Maynard) that marked constructions should be seen as discourse modality indicators. While noting their semantic incompleteness, she argues that they achieve a communicative function thanks to co-textual and contextual elements, and then examines various patterns in the internal structure of NP utterances that are responsible for their enhanced expressive function.

The chapter by Suwako Watanabe and Noriko Iwasaki explores modality in the field of language learning – an applied dimension that is still under-researched. While the earlier chapter by Moriya and Horie looked at the phylogenetic development of epistemic/modal meanings, this chapter looks at its ontogenesis in English-speaking learners of Japanese. If it is the case, as has been suggested, that the modal systems in these languages are likely to derive from different prototypes (deontic for English and possibly epistemic for Japanese), it could be assumed that learning how to use modal markers appropriately represents a considerable challenge. Data from oral interviews with learners at various proficiency levels before and after a period of study in Japan are used to explore three types of modality: epistemic, discoursal and interactional. The study suggests that the type of modality more likely to benefit from exposure to the target language/culture depends on the learner's proficiency level, that is, it varies with the learner's degree of awareness of the different functions of utterances in discourse.

Barbara Pizziconi's final chapter attempts to flesh out the implications of a conceptualization of modality as a fundamentally deictic system, i.e. one that indexes the speaker's position towards the information and the participants' knowledge thereof. The first implication is that the functional meanings achieved in interaction cannot be thought of as 'encoded' in a specific modal marker but they are rather contingent and 'emergent': they are derived from the combination of a marker's indexical meaning with contextual (i.e. discursive and interactional) factors. They are therefore volatile, and never entirely predictable. The second implication is that, since issues of knowledge are never socially neutral, the speaker's orientation toward the information is of significant interactional importance and the use of a modal is likely to be sensitive to social positioning in discourse. Pizziconi suggests that the study of modality in actual interaction benefits from, and at the same time provides a test for, other types of analyses, and that research from an interactional perspective can shed light on the communicative role of modal markers in the construction of cognitive, affective and ultimately sociocultural stances.

This collection offers a window on the variety of disciplinary, methodological and ontological angles that have been brought to bear in an effort to elucidate the nature and operating mechanisms of the elusive notion of modality in Japanese, and the socio-historical context in which they have emerged. Since the boom of Japanese modality studies of the late 1980s, the engagement of scholars of Japanese with other linguistic traditions has markedly intensified, and we believe that the contributions in this volume are a testimony to this dialogue. We hope this glimpse on *modariti* will stimulate it even further.

References

Kudoo, H. (2005). Bun no kinoo to johoosei [The function of sentences and modality]. *Kokugo to Kokubungaku* 82(8): 1–15.

Kurotaki, M. (2002). Nichiei-taishoo – ninshikiteki modariti no kenkyuu dookoo [Comparative studies on epistemic modality between English and Japanese]. *Gengo-bunka to Nihongo-kyooiku* [Language and Culture, and Japanese Language Teaching] – Special Edition: The State of the Art in Second Language Acquisition and Instruction Research – a Guidepost to Japanese Language Education for the New Century. Tokyo: Bonjinsha: 87–101.

Nakau, M. (1979). Modariti to meidai [Modality and proposition]. In: Hayashi Eiichi Kyooju Kanreki Kinen Ronbunshuu Henshuu Iinkai (ed.), *Eigo to Nihongo to* [Japanese and English]. Tokyo: Kuroshio: 223–50.

Nakau, M. (1999). Modariti o doo toraeru ka [How do we capture modality?]. *Gekkan Gengo*, 28(6): 26–33.

Part I

Contextualizing and Defining Japanese Modality

1
Modality, *Modariti* and Predication – the Story of Modality in Japan

Heiko Narrog

1.1 Introduction

Since the 1990s, publications on Japanese modality, especially those written in Japanese and published in Japan, abound. There are more than a dozen book publications alone with 'modality' (*modariti*) in their title, in addition to countless papers and articles. Although it is difficult to provide exact numbers for comparison, it can hardly be doubted that this has been *the* most popular research topic in Japanese linguistics for the past 15 years. However, this surge of research interest seems to come out of nowhere. Until the mid-1980s, very little had been written on 'modality'. The two most influential reference volumes on Japanese linguistics of the time, the *Research Dictionary of National Language Studies* (Satō 1977) and the *Great Dictionary of National Language Studies* (Kokugo Gakkai, 1980) do not even have an entry for either 'modality' or 'mood'.

Based on these facts, one might suspect that around 1990 in Japan the concept of modality was newly discovered or newly imported from general linguistics. However, a close investigation reveals that nothing could be further from the truth. It is merely the case that modality studies in Western linguistics in the 1970s and 1980s, which themselves surged around that time, helped to contribute to the increased interest in the topic in Japan. In fact, all the important elements of modality theory as known in current Japanese linguistics were already in place in the 1950s. However, research on them was simply known under a different labelling. That is, it was not the concept that was newly discovered and adopted around 1990, but the labelling. Conversely, the dominant concept of *modariti* in Japan is not the same as the mainstream concepts

9

of modality in Western linguistics. It is only the labelling which suggests identity (or close similarity).

The goal of this chapter is to inform, within the limitations of its format, about the development of *modariti* concepts in Japan from their beginnings to the present, and to unravel the mystery of how they relate to *modality* in Western linguistics. I will try to take into account not only the linguistic ideas as such, but also their social and political–historical background. I will start by introducing the dominant concept of modality in current Japanese linguistics, which is represented mainly by two scholars, namely Takashi Masuoka and Yoshio Nitta (section 1.2). I will then go back into the history of Japanese linguistics and show how these concepts developed and where their sources can be found (sections 1.3 and 1.4). These sections are followed by a short evaluation (section 1.5) and an exposure of contemporary alternative concepts of modality in Japanese linguistics (section 1.6), before a conclusion follows in section 1.7.[1]

1.2   Establishing the concept in Japan – Takashi Masuoka and Yoshio Nitta

At present, a large number of linguistic researchers in Japan are concentrating their activities on the field of modality. Some of them have been more influential and prolific than others. It is fair to say, however, that the modern study of modality in Japan is first and foremost identified with the work of two scholars, namely Takashi Masuoka and Yoshio Nitta. Not that they were the first to use the label 'modality' for Japanese. In fact, it is generally believed that the first use of the term goes much further back, namely to a dissertation by Uyeno (1971). However, they were the first to come up with the term in major publications in Japanese (Nitta and Masuoka 1989; Masuoka 1991; Nitta 1991), and the concept of modality that they moulded at that time has become the model for most of the subsequent research that has been carried out within the domestic field of Japanese language studies (*nihongogaku*). An understanding of their concepts of modality is essential to an understanding of contemporary writing on modality in Japan. Masuoka's and Nitta's concepts are close but not identical and shall be introduced here concisely.

Masuoka has the following basic view of modality: 'Proposition and modality are the two big elements that make up a sentence. I define them as the element that expresses objective facts, and *the element that expresses subjective judgements and attitudes*, respectively'[2] (Masuoka 1991: 6, 1999: 46; emphasis added). This definition crucially refers to two factors. One is a bipartition of the sentence into proposition and modality, that is, essentially a syntactic factor. The other is the identification of one part of the bipartition with the expression of the speaker's judgements and attitudes. This is a semantic–pragmatic factor. Research that builds on Masuoka thus has to assume that:

1. Every sentence can be divided into proposition and modality, and there is a criterion (or criteria) for such division. Masuoka originally named a whole set of criteria (interrogation, nominalization, past tense) as the dividing line (Masuoka 1991: 34–6).
2. The dividing line between proposition and modality that was set in (1) coincides with a semantic division between objective and subjective sentence elements.

If this definition is taken seriously, the dividing line between proposition and modality becomes a crucial issue, and Masuoka has indeed repeatedly spent time on this issue and revised his position (e.g. Masuoka 1987: 9, 1991: 34–6, 1999). Given the obvious fact that many linguistic expressions are neither clearly objective nor subjective, Masuoka introduced the terms of 'primary modality' (*ichijiteki modariti*) for always subjective expressions and 'secondary modality' (*nijiteki modariti*) for expressions that can be both subjective and objective (Masuoka 1991: 36). For most researchers, however, Masuoka's definition has only served as a starting point to investigate (and describe) a number of linguistic categories in Japanese that are saliently associated with some measure of subjectivity. Masuoka himself distinguished nine types of modality (Masuoka 1991: 47–59):

1. Modality of speech attitude (incl. sentence-final particles etc.)
2. Modality of politeness (incl. politeness markers)
3. Expression pattern modality (refers to sentence mood)
4. Modality of truth judgement (refers to epistemic modality)
5. Modality of value judgement (refers to deontic modality)
6. Modality of explanation (incl. the sentence nominalizer *no(-da)* and *wake*)
7. Modality of tense (refers to tense)
8. Modality of polarity (refers to negation)
9. Modality of topic and focus (incl. topic- and focus-marking like *wa*, etc.)

This is an extraordinarily wide array of linguistic categories. Many of them, such as tense or topic and focus, in fact, would not be recognized as part of modality in most linguistic theories, but are recognized as grammatical categories in their own right. In contrast, dynamic modality (ability, circumstantial possibility, volition and so on), which is often viewed as part of modality in English and Western linguistics is, in keeping with the Japanese linguistic tradition, not viewed as modal. Masuoka later slightly revised his position and narrowed down somewhat the scope of modality. Specifically, in 1999, he shifted to complementation with *koto* as the dividing line between modality and proposition (Masuoka 1999: 47). This leads to the exclusion of at least tense and polarity from the list above. Overall, however, it is fair to say that researchers (primarily descriptive linguists) who are indebted to, or sympathize with, Masuoka's notion of modality have not been much concerned with the problematic aspects or the faithful application of this concept. They have rather focused on the aspect of subjectivity and concentrated on the description of categories that are at the core of other Japanese modality concepts as well.

Nitta's concept of modality has from the beginning been narrower, more traditional and more focused. He defines modality as follows: 'Real typical modality is the *linguistic expression of the speaker's psychological attitude* towards the verbalized state of affairs or towards the utterance and the communication itself at the time of speech' (Nitta 1989: 34; cf. also Nitta 1989: 2, Nitta 2000: 81; emphasis added). In this definition we can find the same two elements of both modality vs something and subjectivity, but the idea of a bipartition of the sentence is assigned less prominence, since in Nitta's view modality does not necessarily modify the proposition but can also modify an utterance, or even something else. Therefore, the element of subjectivity takes the spotlight.

However, modality as a semanto-syntactic component still plays a significant role for Nitta. He has recourse to the most popular model of syntax in traditional Japanese linguistics, the layering model (for example Minami 1964, 1974), and locates modality in this model by dividing the sentence in Japanese into a layer of 'expressed situation' (*genpyō jitai*) and a layer of 'expressed attitude' (*genpyō taido*) (Nitta 1989, 1991). The sentence model is represented graphically in Figure 1.1. The 'expressed situation' layer comprises the situation core, as well as aspect, voice and tense. The 'attitude' layer consists of modality and politeness (Nitta 1991: 18). These layers roughly correspond to proposition and modality in models such as Masuoka's. Furthermore, according to Nitta, a sentence is only formed when the proposition (expressed situation) is enwrapped by modality (Nitta 2000: 81). That is, modality is seen as an indispensable semantic element of sentence formation.

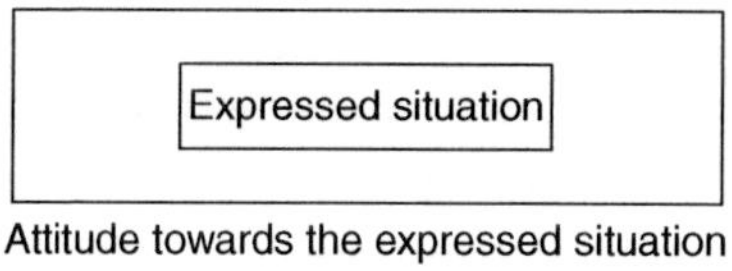

Figure 1.1   Modality in Japanese sentence structure, according to Nitta (1989: 1)

Since Nitta's concept of modality is narrower than Masuoka's, it is not surprising that he distinguishes fewer subcategories. Specifically, Nitta proposes two bipartitions of modality, which do not totally overlap with each other (Nitta 1989: 2, 34–40). First, he distinguishes 'contents-directed modality' (*genpyō jitai meate no modariti*) and 'utterance/communication modality' (*hatsuwa, dentatsu no modariti*). The former includes expressions of volition and desire on the one hand and epistemic modality on the other (Nitta 1989: 41). The latter refers mainly to sentence moods, such as declarative, imperative, etc. (Nitta 1989: 41). Second, he distinguishes 'true modality' (*shinsei modariti*), which can take neither past tense nor negation, and must always be associated with the first person (speaker), from 'pseudo-modality' (*giji modariti*). This distinction, which corresponds to Masuoka's 'primary' vs 'secondary' modality, is a consequence of the identification of modality with subjectivity. Presumably, past tense, negation and non-first person signal a distancing from the speaker, and thus non-subjectivity. 'True modality' includes linguistic forms that are not subject to past, etc. marking; for example, imperative inflectional endings or the inferential *daroo*. 'Pseudo-modality' markers include most deontic and boulemic (volitional) modal expressions (Nitta 1989: 34–8).

1.3   Roots of the concept I: Western linguistics

As the emergence of 'modality' as a major research topic in Japan is so recent, it would only be reasonable to assume that its roots lie in Western linguistics. Indeed, it is not difficult to find direct equivalents to Masuoka's 'subjective judgements and attitudes' and Nitta's 'speaker's psychological attitude' in Western linguistic writing. Lyons (1968: 308) defined 'modalities' as the grammatical marking of the 'attitude of the speaker', and later described sentence adverbs, including epistemic adverbs, as expressing '[the speaker's] opinion or attitude towards the proposition that the sentence expresses or the situation that the proposition describes' (Lyons 1977: 452).

Lyons' idea itself is much older. In modern linguistics, it can be traced back at least to the German Indo-Europeanists Hanns Oertel and Karl Brugmann (cf. Noreen 1923). Oertel spoke of 'the attitude of the speaker toward the utterance' (Oertel 1901: 287), and identified verbal moods ('modes') as a salient form of its expression, while Brugmann defined moods as 'a statement about a mental mood of the speaker, a subjective state with respect to which the [verbalized] event constitutes the determining objective side element to which the state is related' (Brugmann 1970 [1904]: 578). This concept was further popularized by Karl Jespersen, who wrote that moods 'express certain attitudes of the mind of the speaker towards the contents of the sentence' (Jespersen 1992 [1924]: 313). However, Oertel, Brugmann and Jespersen apparently did not attempt to define modality but simply to characterize Indo-European verbal moods.

For the bipartition of the clause into proposition and modality, a different possible model can be identified. Charles Fillmore saw modality as a complementary constituent to the proposition in sentence structure. He defined the proposition as the 'tenseless set of relationships involving verbs and nouns' (Fillmore 1968: 23). All other elements of the sentence, that is negation, tense, mood and aspect, would accordingly belong to modality. He thus offers the following formula to define the constituency of a sentence:

(1) Sentence → Modality + Proposition (Fillmore 1968: 24)

This is almost exactly the kind of bipartition of the sentence that we find with Masuoka (1991), and Masuoka does acknowledge Fillmore's influence (Masuoka 1991: 45). On the other hand, it should be taken into account that Fillmore was not researching modality: his goal was to clarify the concept of proposition on the way towards introducing his theory of case grammar, and not the concept of modality itself. As Fillmore himself admitted, 'the exact nature of modality may be ignored for our purposes' (Fillmore 1968: 24).

1.4 Roots of the concept II: *Chinjutsu-ron* 'Predication theory'

1.4.1 The development of the concept – Yamada Yoshio

We saw in the preceding section that the modality concept in Japanese linguistics could indeed be thought of as an offspring of its Western counterpart, or, to be more precise, a very particular choice among the many concepts of modality available in Western linguistics. However, under closer scrutiny it turns out that this is a rash conclusion. In fact, all the elements of the Japanese linguistics *modariti* concept as espoused by Masuoka and Nitta were already in place much earlier. Beyond that, although the term *modariti* was virtually unknown until recently, a lot of research was done in the same area, but under a different label, namely *chinjutsu-ron* 'predication theory'.

The term *chinjutsu* ('predication') was coined by one of the great founding figures of modern Japanese linguistics, Yamada Yoshio (1873–1958). He was strongly influenced by state-of-the-art English and German grammars of his time, in particular J. C. A. Heyse's *Deutsche Grammatik*, which appeared in numerous editions from 1814, and Sweet's *New English Grammar* appearing in 1891. These scholars were concerned with the nature of the sentence (or clause) as a unit of thought, and grammatically as the linking of two major obligatory elements, the subject and the predicate. Heyse identified the verb as the centre of the sentence/clause (the German term *Satz* has both meanings). The most important function of a sentence/clause is predication (*Aussage*), and the element of the sentence/clause that bears the predication is the verb (Heyse 1868: 248f.). This understanding of *Aussage* 'predication' is the basis for Yamada's term *chinjutsu*. Sweet defined the sentence as 'the expression of a complete thought or meaning' (Sweet 1900 [1891]: 155), and Heyse likewise viewed a sentence/clause as 'a complete, coherent and independently understandable predication or utterance of a thought' (Heyse 1868: 248). Yamada, in principle, agrees when he writes: 'A clause is a thought that presents itself by borrowing the outer shape of language' (Yamada 1908: 1187; cf. also ibid.: 1165–6 discussing Sweet and Heyse).

Yamada, however, could not be satisfied with the idea of a sentence/clause that strictly presupposes a subject and a predicate, since in Japanese subjects are simply too frequently omitted, and there are many sentences consisting of only one word. He thus felt the need to add a different, psychological dimension to the definition of sentence and he sought it in the theory of Wilhelm Wundt (1832–1920), the first psycholinguist. There Yamada found a psychological concept applied to grammar, namely that of 'apperception' (cf. Eschbach-Szabó 1989). For Wundt, sentences/clauses are 'the linguistic expression of the willful structuring of a total conception into units which stand in logical relationships to each other' (Wundt 1900: 240). Apperception (which, from a subjective perspective, is equal to 'attention' (*Aufmerksamkeit*)) is the psychological process responsible for the integration and structuring of various elements that make up conceptions (Wundt 1900: 244f.). This 'apperception' can then operate in all kinds of sentences, even if superficially incomplete, as long as they form a complete thought. Following this idea, for Yamada, *chinjutsu* ('predication') is the apperceptive role of predicates (verbs and adjectives) in predicative (declarative, interrogative, imperative) clauses (cf. Yamada 1908: 1238f.). Sweet, on the other hand, saw moods as forms expressing relations between subject and predicate in sentence formation. He defined 'moods' as 'forms expressing different relations between subject and predicate' (Sweet 1900 [1891]: 105). Here we might construe a connection between apperception, predication and modality (moods), but Yamada himself did not make this connection. For Yamada, the fundamental question related to 'predication' (*chinjutsu*) was how clauses are formed.

Yamada's concept was eagerly taken up by other linguists and shifted in diverse directions. Miyake (1934) distinguishes himself from many other scholars that have explored *chinjutsu* through his relatively scientific approach to the description of the Japanese language, which is based on phonological analysis. Like Yamada, he also sees *chinjutsu* in predicative clause types, but unlike Yamada, Miyake essentially sees it as an element at sentence level and not at clause level (adnominal clauses, for him, have no *chinjutsu*; cf. Miyake 1934: 18). Thus, for Miyake, *chinjutsu* is what makes a sentence a sentence. Also, in an innovative step that is more advanced than even many of his successors in *chinjutsu* theory, he sees the locus of *chinjutsu* ('predication') not in the (lexical) verb itself, like Yamada, but in the inflectional endings of the verbs, in sentence-final particles and in sentence intonation (Miyake 1934: 23f.). Mio (1939) raised awareness of the fact that Yamada's *chinjutsu* concept may be too broad and unspecific. He suggested dividing it into 'clause integrating function' (*tōitsu sayō*) and 'judgement function' (*dantei sayō*), which operates on top of the 'clause integrating function', thus creating two layers. It is the latter which is the true *chinjutsu* ('predication') (Mio 1939: 77f.). With this division between 'clause integration' and 'judgement', Mio already indicates what would be the main point in Watanabe's *chinjutsu* theory (see below).

1.4.2   The Tokiedan turn towards subjectivity

The *chinjutsu* concept of Yamada and his pre-war successors was concerned with what makes a clause a clause, and later, a sentence a sentence. It is thus related to sentence moods, but hardly to a specific grammatical category. It was Motoki Tokieda and his successors who gave the concept an entirely new twist and who, still under the name of *chinjutsu* ('predication'), moulded the concept of *modariti* in current Japanese linguistics which is fundamentally based on the idea of subjectivity.[3]

Tokieda (1900–67), who is often viewed as one of a triad of the most influential scholars in the history of National Language Studies together with Yamada and Hashimoto Shinkichi, came forward with a new subjectivized view of language as a process which, in principle, can only be investigated through introspection. He strongly opposed objectivist Western linguistics, and revealed a fervent nationalism in his writings. Although it may be possible to interpret his theories purely from a linguistic viewpoint, they can arguably only be fully understood against the political and social milieu of his time. As the Japanologist Günther Wenck once put it,

> The Japanese nationalism of the later 1930s, which was not a political movement only, could not be content without some substantial connection between the Japanese language and the Japanese mind. The objective of Japanese language studies had to shift from linguistic structure [with Hashimoto] to the psychological and cultural character of the language, and it seems to have been on this tide that arose Tokieda's theory of language as a process. (Wenck 1989: 10)

Tokieda saw language primarily as the activity of the speaking subject (Tokieda 1950: section 1.3). He divided all morphemes (*go*) into 'objective' *shi* (contents words) and 'subjective' *ji* (function words). The subjective *ji* express the speaker's judgement, while the *shi* express objective conceptual contents of things and states of affairs (Tokieda 1950: ch. 2). In the structure of clauses, a *shi* is always followed by a *ji*, thus forming 'nested boxes' structures. If no overt *ji* is given, a zero-*ji* has to be posited (Tokieda 1950: ch. 3). For him, it is the subjective *ji* that have the predicative (*chinjutsu*) function, and not the predicates, which represent objective material (Tokieda 1941: 334). That is, *chinjutsu* can, in principle, be identified with subjectivity.

Note that for Tokieda, unlike Yamada, *chinjutsu* is not important to explain what makes a clause a clause, or a sentence a sentence (he has a different term for that element, namely *kanketsusei* ('completion'). The concept is about the speaker's expression in the sentence. While the idea of predication itself goes back to Yamada, the idea to identify predication with a specific set of dependent morphemes, and at the same time to identify those morphemes with subjectivity is clearly not something intended by Yamada. However, this idea has become the most fundamental idea behind the concept of *modariti* in modern Japanese linguistics. In this sense, the representative concepts of modality in modern Japanese linguistics, as espoused by Masuoka and Nitta, can be labelled appropriately as Tokiedan.

From a purely linguistic point of view, the attraction of Tokieda's model of language structure rests both in the elegance of its simplicity and in its theoretical consequence. The price that is paid for these merits is counterintuitive analyses and the apparent mismatch with actual language data. Tokieda's language model is therefore often compared to generative grammar in its earlier stages. Representative examples for problematic analyses are the so-called zero-*ji*, which the theory requires when no overt *ji* appears in the actual clause structure. Also, the idea that the subjective expression of the speaker is tied up with specific morpheme classes was controversial from the outset (cf. e.g. Mikami 1972 [1959]: 115f.).[4]

1.4.3   *Chinjutsu-ron* at its height

Despite obvious shortcomings, the 'predication theory' of the Tokiedan brand continued its advance. Watanabe Minoru set an influential milestone in 1953 when he differentiated *chinjutsu* as a subjective and communicative (hearer-oriented) function expressed mainly by sentence-final particles and concluding a sentence, from *jojutsu* (also 'predication') as clause integration expressed mainly by the predicate. Grammatically speaking, it is *jojutsu* which is closer to Yamada's original *chinjutsu*, since Yamada's *chinjutsu* is identified with the predicate in the (potentially subordinate) clause. Watanabe thus liberates *chinjutsu* from its predicative function for purer subjective expression in the Tokiedan sense. Watanabe, while Tokiedan in principle, also brings about a synthesis between Yamada and Tokieda, since he articulates the syntactic role of *chinjutsu* in sentence formation in the sense of the former and simultaneously emphasizes its subjective nature in the sense of the latter.

While the mainstream of Japanese linguistics and most scholars working on 'predication theory' at this time had strong nationalistic leanings, and seemingly developed their ideas independent of Western linguistics, other scholars framed the same or a similar idea in terms of concepts developed by the Swiss linguist Charles Bally. Bally, a scholar of French language, advocated the bipartition of sentence elements into *dictum* and *modus*. The former is the sentence contents, the latter the expression of the speaking subject. It should be noted, however, that this concept of *modus* does not bear much similarity to modality in the modern sense and is also not exactly identical to the Japanese *chinjutsu* concept. Bally primarily identifies the locus of the *modus* in a sentence with verbs of emotion and judgement and their overt and covert subjects (Bally 1965 [1932]: 36f.). Bally's linguistic thought was introduced to Japan through translations and articles from the late 1920s on by Hideo Kobayashi, and is widely cited by some of the authors associated with *chinjutsu-ron* ('predication theory'). However, his ideas were not read and adopted in any detail, and those who cite Bally make it clear that they have learned about his ideas not from his original writings but through the filtering of these by Kobayashi. One of the major scholars who cited Bally in the *chinjutsu* debate in fact made the embarrassing mistake of identifying *modus* with the objective component and *dictum* with the subjective component (Kindaichi 1953: 34). It appears that the reference to Bally mainly fulfilled two functions. First, it served as an inspiration, as Bally seemed to confirm that the Japanese intuitions about objective vs subjective contents in the language have a broader foundation in linguistics. Second, it allowed those scholars who did not identify with the nationalistic linguistic tradition of Tokieda and Watanabe (such as Mikami and Kindaichi; see below) to use different terminology for the same or similar concepts, thus indicating a more open- or internationally minded approach.[5]

Important scholars referring to Bally in their concept of *chinjutsu* include Yasushi Haga and Akira Mikami. Mikami adopted the *dictum* vs *modus* bipartition (1972 [1953]: 20; 1972 [1959]: 116) and related the *modus* part to 'moods' (a term rarely used in Japanese linguistics until then). The moods, such as finite mood or imperative mood, are identified with specific inflectional verb forms and particles (Mikami 1972 [1959]: 123–7). Mikami also pointed forward to Masuoka's *modariti* concept by including topics in the *modus* part of the sentence. Haga (1954, 1982) also adopted the *dictum* vs *modus* bipartition, but most importantly he distinguished two types of 'predication', judgemental predication (*jutteiki chinjutsu*) and communicative predication (*dentatsuteki chinjutsu*) (Haga 1954: 58; he later also used the terms 'modus' of judgement and 'modus' of communication, Haga 1982: 44–6). Both *modi* (or types of predication) are associated with specific sentence types. Haruhiko Kindaichi (1953) proposed a different classification of objective vs subjective linguistic expressions from Tokieda when he acknowledged subjectivity only for non-inflecting suffixes. He identified his new classification with Bally's *dictum* vs *modus*, as filtered by Kobayashi.

Crucially, at this point in time, and specifically with Haga (1954), all the fundamental elements of modality in modern Japanese linguistics as represented by Masuoka and Nitta are already in place. There is the bipartition of the clause, in which one part is identified with the expression of the speaker's attitude. Furthermore, there is the distinction between contents-oriented elements and hearer-oriented elements within the elements expressing the speaker's attitude, corresponding to Nitta's *contents-directed modality* and *utterance/communication modality*. The only element that is still missing now is the very label *modality* to replace the older labels *chinjutsu* and *modus*.

1.4.4   The turn towards *modariti*

The last links to modern *modariti* can be found in the linguistics of the 1960s and 1970s. First, models of a layered structure of a clause, as the one used by Nitta, were espoused by the likes of Shirō Hayashi (1960) and Fujio Minami (1964, 1974). Thus it was made explicit that *chinjutsu* or *modus*-type of sentence elements form an outer layer to the contents-oriented elements (in principle, this was already implied by Tokieda and Watanabe). Uyeno (1971), as mentioned above, was probably the first to use the term *modality* for Japanese (Yamaoka 2000: 73). She did so in an English piece of writing, but the understanding behind it is in the Japanese tradition, since she uses the term very broadly for particles, sentence types, modal suffixes and so on, without providing a definition. Suzuki (1972: 44) is the first to use the term in Japanese. He defines it as 'the attitude of the speaker towards reality and the hearer'. Okuda (1985: 240) similarly uses *modus* as the speaker's expression of the relationship between sentence contents and reality; according to him, *modus* is obligatory for every sentence. The idea of the relationship of sentence contents to reality as a central part of modality is neither original nor home-grown in Japan. It goes back to Vinogradov's writings from the 1940s and 1950s, and was expounded in detail in the Russian academy grammar of 1980 (cf. Kristophson 1994). Okuda and Suzuki were central members of the Linguistic Study Group (*Gengogaku Kenkyūkai*). This group, being originally Marxist and oriented towards Soviet linguistics, only had outsider status within the social dynamics of the field of National Language Studies, which has always had a diametrically opposed political orientation. Their studies of the Japanese language were groundbreaking but can hardly be called representative of the field, because they were shunned and until recently did not earn full recognition.

In contrast, Hideo Teramura is a scholar who, although coming from English linguistics, in hindsight formed part of the mainstream of Japanese linguistics. He is also the one scholar who had the most direct influence on Masuoka and Nitta. Teramura, in keeping with Japanese tradition, espoused a bipartition of the clause into objective and sub-jective elements, labelled as *koto* 'things' and *mūdo* 'mood' respectively (Teramura 1982: 51). He further divided *mūdo* into contents-oriented and hearer-oriented (ibid.: 60). Probably the first person to use the very term *modariti* in the current sense as related to a bipartition of the clause was Nakau (1979). In the 1980s, a build-up towards the explosion of publications from 1989 on is visible, including papers by Masuoka and Nitta. At this stage, the terms *mūdo* 'mood' (Teramura) and *modariti* 'modality' (Nakau) still vary with each other.

Conversely, the concept *chinjutsu* recedes into the background. In 1990, traditionally minded Keisuke Onoe bemoans: '*Chinjutsu-ron*, which was a hot commodity until just 12 or 13 years ago is lying unsold on the shelves now for no apparent reason. Even if it is still sometimes touched upon, its original spirit is forgotten, and it is reduced to the discussion of modality, or to a practical means to arrange sentence-final word forms' (Onoe 1990: 16).

Having all elements so clearly already in place from the early 1950s, one may justifiably ask: 'What was new, after all, with the *nihongo-gaku* approach and *modariti* in the late 1980s? How could it cause such an explosion in research activities?'

As argued above, contents-wise the concept of modality brought to the fore in the 1980s by Masuoka, Nitta and others could hardly be called revolutionary. The reason for its success instead can only be sought in social and psychological factors. The act of establishing a new English category labelling indicated a shift towards an international attitude towards research and the opening-up of an academic field that until then had been exclusive and narrow in many respects. This alone may have been enough to set free new energies. Also, the recognition of grammatical categories as such was not common in Japanese linguis-tics, which tended to focus on the study of individual morphemes and, with the notable exception of the Linguistic Study Group centring on Okuda and Suzuki, mentioned above, even to deny the existence of cat-egories such as tense, aspect and mood for Japanese (note that *chinjutsu* is not a grammatical category). The notion of grammatical categories only started to become mainstream in the 1980s with papers such as Nitta (1985).

The most decisive factor, however, appears to be the overall social situation surrounding Japanese language studies. Until the 1970s this was a mostly self-contained field preoccupied with theoretical issues and with strong conservative, if not nationalist, leanings. The field itself was called *kokugo-gaku* or 'National Language Studies', and many scholars of the field strictly distinguished themselves from 'linguists'. Yamada was a key figure in the nationalistic education policies of the 1930s and 1940s, while Tokieda repeatedly repudiated Western linguistics and provided the ideological basis for the linguistic colonialization of Korea (the imposition of the Japanese language on the Korean people) in wartime (cf. Yasuda 1997). Even after the war, this did little harm to their reputation in the field, showing that their ultranationalistic leanings were potentially shared by a large majority of scholars devoting themselves to the same field of study.

However, new challenges arose in the 1980s with the increasing influx of foreign students into Japan who were in need of Japanese language education. 'Internationalization' (*kokusaika*) was one of the most significant keywords in Japanese politics and society of the 1980s and 1990s. The 'National Language Studies' tradition, with its indifference towards language description and its low regard for modern language as opposed to classical language, was simply unable to respond to the practical needs arising then. The new generation of *nihongo-gaku* 'Japanese Language Studies',[6] as represented by Masuoka and Nitta, not only used new, internationally oriented category labels, but were also committed to a decidedly descriptive orientation and to modern language. The area of modality, in turn, as conceptualized by Masuoka and Nitta, and in keeping with Japanese tradition, is so large that it comprises a wide area of grammar that is highly important for language description, and also highly relevant to language teaching, especially a language teaching which has to deal not only with rules of grammar but also with actual language use.

1.4.5   Conclusion of the historical overview

As conclusion of the preceding two sections, it should have become clear that the concept of *modariti* in Japanese language studies is in fact the product of an original development. The biggest influences from outside are not Lyons and Fillmore, as it might seem superficially, but rather Sweet, Heyse, Wundt and Bally. Their concepts were, however, not simply imported, but transformed in a way that would help Japanese scholars to formulate intuitions that they shared about their own language.

Furthermore, although not explicitly discussed so far, it should have become clear that *modariti* in Japanese language studies cannot be equated with *modality* in modern general linguistics. A different spelling appears to be not only justified but also appropriate. *Modariti* to a large extent is the continuation of the 'predication' (*chinjutsu*) concept (Tokieda's, not Yamada's) formed within Japan. *Chinjutsu* is probably the most important concept in the history of Japanese grammar studies. As Onoe (2001: 265) writes, 'One can say that grammar theory in National Language Studies was developed around the concept of and from the perspective of [*chinjutsu*].'

The current *modariti* concept is therefore a mixture of the concept of a grammatical category, namely one which supposedly serves the expression of the speaker's attitude, and the answer to the question of what makes a sentence a sentence. This view is motivated by facts pertaining to Japanese language structure, where particles expressing the speaker's attitude and her or his orientation towards the hearer feature prominently. It is quite different indeed from most concepts of modality in general linguistics. Prevalent concepts of modality in general and English linguistics, where notions such as necessity and possibility, or factuality, or *realis/irrealis* are often central, have played little role in *modariti* studies. Arguably, in English linguistics, consciously or unconsciously, the modals have served as the model, or the prototype, for the linguistic expression of modality. Japanese also has linguistic expressions that correspond to the modals, and at least some of them are also viewed as being part of *modariti*. However, it is the illocutionary force-modulating sentence-final particles which appear to be grammatically more salient and to which definitions of Japanese modality apply best. Thus, there is a clear discrepancy between the focal points of the *modariti* concept in Japanese and modality in general linguistics.

1.5 Merits and problems of the dominant model

The preceding sections discussed the dominant concept of *modariti* in modern Japanese linguistics and its roots in Japanese and Western linguistic traditions. The merit of this concept, which is represented by Masuoka and Nitta, is already documented by its huge success. This success is mainly due to the fact that despite its English name, it seamlessly continues the linguistic traditions of Japan and it matches intuitions that many native-speaker scholars share about their language. Also, while in Western linguistics emphasis is usually placed on a certain rigour of definition and analysis, the *modariti* concepts are decisively vague, leaving room for various interpretations. Thus, while Masuoka and Nitta both understand modality in terms of speaker's attitude, the actual linguistic categories that they believe to be part of the expression of the speaker's attitude differ to an extreme degree. Arguably, then, the success of the model can be ascribed exactly to the fact that this vague concept of modality places few constraints on scholars with respect to the subject or the methods of research. It is, so to speak, a big house in which everybody can live.

Arguably, this vagueness and vastness of the dominant *modariti* concept is at the same time its biggest shortcoming as well. It is highly questionable whether a linguistic category or a set of specific linguistic forms can be defined through subjectivity or speaker's attitudes (cf. Harada 1999, Onoe 2001, Narrog 2002). Research in many languages, including Japanese, shows that the speaker's attitude is expressed throughout the sentence, and not confined to specific form classes or grammatical categories (cf. Narrog 2005b). Furthermore, *modariti* conflates various categories that are treated separately in general linguistics (modality, illocutionary force modulation, politeness, tense, information structure and so on). The broader the category is defined, encompassing a large number of different subcategories that have little in common with each other, the more meaningless it becomes as a category label. Finally, it is at least dubious whether there is a specific layer in the sentence that can be identified with a specific category 'modality'. Modal markers occupy at least two or three positions in sentence structure, interspersed by other categories, such as tense and negation (Narrog 2009).

These and some other problematic aspects of the dominant model have been noted by many scholars inside and outside Japan. The following section is devoted to research that takes a different approach to modality in Japanese.

1.6 Alternative approaches

So far in this chapter, the dominant approach to modality in Japanese linguistics, which is based on the concept of subjectivism, as developed in the *chinjutsu* theory up to the 1950s, has been identified with only the work of two scholars, Masuoka and Nitta. Of course, this is a gross simplification. Other scholars who have shared essentially the same view, although from different perspectives, and who have contributed substantially to *modariti* research from early on, include Takurō Moriyama, Hisashi Noda or Kazuhito Miyazaki. In a closer study of contemporary modality research, their contributions would merit broader exposition than can be given here. The following sections instead briefly introduce the contemporary work of a number of scholars inside and outside Japan who take a critical stance towards the dominant Tokiedan subjectivity-based *modariti* concept and espouse alternative theories. They can be divided into those who work within the framework of traditional Japanese linguistics (section 1.6.1), and those with a general linguistic orientation (section 1.6.2).

1.6.1 Alternative approaches informed by the Japanese tradition

Ever since the new descriptively and practically oriented movement that can be identified with the label of *nihongo-gaku* ('Japanese language studies') started to conquer the field in the 1980s, the traditional National Language Studies have receded into the background. However, individual scholars with a more explicitly tradition-conscious stance have still remained influential. In their view, the descriptive approach that has nowadays virtually monopolized the field of modality is theoretically dissatisfying, if not simply superficial. Keisuke Onoe is a scholar who prominently not only has given a voice to such dissatisfaction, but who has also come up with an alternative model, namely that of *johōron* ('modal theory') (Onoe 2001). He is followed by some other scholars, such as Kawamura (2002).

Onoe, in criticizing *modariti* theory, points out that the equation of modality with subjectivity is highly problematic. First, this use of the term of modality is not compatible with 'modality' in general linguistics, and second it is impossible to divide linguistic forms into objective and subjective ones (Onoe 2001: 432, 445, 485). Also, *modariti-ron* is unable to explain in a systematic way the polysemous behaviour of modal markers that may have meanings stretching across different semanto-syntactic layers (ibid.: 437f., 483f.; Onoe 2004: 51f.).

Onoe himself defines modality as 'the meanings expressed by predicative forms (*juttei keishiki*) that describe an irrealis state of affairs' (Onoe 2001: 454). Onoe's definition thus contains two major elements. The first is *irrealis* meaning. The idea that *irrealis* is central to modality is not uncommon in general linguistics, in contrast to Japanese linguistics. Onoe in particular identifies himself with the cognitive grammar approach of Langacker, and Langacker indeed also shares the view that modality is defined by *irrealis* meaning.[7] The second element central to Onoe's definition, the 'predicative forms', are peculiar to his own theory. They refer to so-called auxiliaries (*jodōshi*) in Japanese school grammar and complex endings (*fukugobi*) in Yamada's grammar. According to Onoe, these predicative forms correspond to certain basic types of predication (*nobekata*) and express various meanings in correlation to the syntactic position in which they are used. They can be identified with 'mood' in the Western sense (cf. Onoe 2001: 439). Crucially, while the mainstream approach sees modality as an element outside the proposition, wrapped around the proposition like layers of an onion, Onoe, in a shift back to Yamada's idea of predication, sees the locus of modality within the predicate, the auxiliaries (or complex endings) being part of the predicate.

Onoe's critique of the mainstream approach is fully appropriate. His idea of locating modality again in the predicate is intriguing, and the observation that modal forms take different meanings in correlation to syntactic functions is important. As a theory of modality however, Onoe's *johōron* is not yet fully developed. One major issue that still has to be dealt with is the relationship between the supposed mood forms and modality as a whole, since modality can also be expressed outside the predicate, for example in adverbs. The second problem is how Onoe's predicative forms can be identified morphosyntactically. Onoe seems to identify them with the *jodōshi* in traditional grammar, but the morpheme analysis on which terms such as *mizenkei* or *jodōshi* are based has long been shown to be linguistically unfounded (cf. Suzuki 1978, Narrog 1998, and others). It is also not clear how periphrastic forms such as *ka-mo shirenai* (epistemic possibility) are to be integrated into the predicative forms, if at all.

The names of two scholars should be mentioned who, in principle, share the same critical stance towards the mainstream from a tradition-conscious perspective, but who in their argumentation remain independent of Onoe. Nomura (2003) critically focuses on the concept of subjectivity. He rejects the equation subjectivity = modality on the grounds that subjectivity is an epistemological category and not a grammatical one. He thus maintains that subjectivity and modality are mutually independent categories. For him, there are both objective and subjective types of modality, which is defined as the expression of the relationship between sentence contents and reality (cf. also Nomura 2004). Ōshika (1999, 2004) views modality from the perspective of sentence formation. For him, epistemic modality lies at the core of the category, and he sees the possibility of interrogation as the most fundamental criterion for the classification of moods.

The scholars mentioned above all have one thing in common, namely that they see themselves in the tradition of Yamada and his predication theory, as opposed to the dominant Tokiedan approach. However, one can also take the opposite direction, and take the Tokiedan tradition of equating modality with subjectivity to its full consequence. This is what Senko Maynard did when she coined the term 'discourse modality' and defined it as 'the speaker's subjective, emotional, mental or psychological attitude toward the message content, the speech act itself or toward his or her interlocutor in discourse' (Maynard 1993: 38). Final particles and discourse markers constitute the core of discourse modality. Maynard thus manages to solve the contradiction that mars the mainstream approach, which includes in its notion of modality both discourse markers and equivalents of modal verbs, mixing up a wide range of categories of various and unclear degrees of subjectivity.

1.6.2 Alternative approaches informed by general linguistics

Besides the mainstream in Japanese linguistics, and a smaller group of scholars who firmly identify themselves with the Japanese tradition but are critical of the mainstream, some scholars inside and outside Japan take a third stance by orienting themselves towards general linguistics. One group of such scholars has already been mentioned, namely the Linguistic Study Group (*Gengogaku Kenkyūkai*) centred around Okuda, who oriented themselves towards Soviet linguistics. With respect to modality, their tradition has been continued mainly by Hiroshi Kudō, who identifies himself less specifically with Soviet linguistics than with traditional European grammar in general (e.g. Kudō 1989, 2005) as well as Mayumi Kudō (e.g. Kudō 2004, 2006), who presents herself as a direct successor of the linguistics of Okuda, but also takes into account recent research in English-language linguistics. The stance towards modality of Hiroshi Kudō and Mayumi Kudō is very similar. Both see modality as part of a broader concept of 'predicativity' (*chinjutsu-sei*), which also includes other categories such as temporality. They follow Vinogradov's concept of modality as 'the grammatical expression of the relationship between the sentence contents, reality, and the relationship [of the speaker] to the hearer from the speaker's point of view', as also adopted by Okuda (cf. Kudō 1989: 14, Kudō 2004: 3, 15). The central concern in this view of modality is the interface between grammatical form, semantic contents and communication that is found most saliently in different sentence types. Therefore, the notion of *chinjutsu*, in Yamada's sense of what makes a sentence a sentence, or what integrates a sentence, is also highly relevant for this approach (cf. Kudō 1989: 16f.). Unlike the dominant approach to *chinjutsu* and *modariti* in the Tokiedan tradition, a broad range of lexical, syntactical and morphological devices are identified with the expression of modality, including 'objective' modality (for example, alethic and deontic modality), emotive expressions and evidentials. Thus, in a sense different from the mainstream approach, the Kudōs also espouse a broad view of modality that is characterized primarily by its deliberate lack of distinction between grammar and pragmatics.

Harada (1999) and Johnson (2003) define Japanese modality in terms of traditional logically oriented English linguistics, that is with the axes of necessity and possibility on the one hand, and epistemicity and deonticity on the other. Johnson also integrates a specific notion of 'degree of modality' into the dimension of epistemic modality. For her, the lower the degree of the speaker's conviction (weak possibility), the higher the degree of modality. That is, epistemic necessity is lower in modality than epistemic possibility (Johnson 2003: 105, 116f.). Within Japanese linguistics in Japan, however, approaches like this, based on the approach to modality in English linguistics, have struggled to take hold.

Another possible way to investigate Japanese modality is from a cross-linguistic or typological perspective. This assumes that it is more profitable to investigate Japanese with a model that is valid for as many languages as possible, also allowing for comparison across languages, than to adhere to a peculiar concept developed specifically for Japanese, or to apply a concept that is particularly suitable for English. Definitions of verbal categories in typological research can only be based on semantics, and not on syntax. Subjectivity, which is a pragmatic rather than semantic concept, is certainly not an appropriate candidate to define a category cross-linguistically, since it is extremely difficult, if not impossible, to identify subjectivity with a particular set of linguistic expressions even in a single language (cf. above). Much better candidates are the concepts of factuality or validity, or actuality of the proposition (Chung and Timberlake 1985, Kiefer 1987, 1997, Narrog 2005b). This concept allows modality to be confined to a specific area of grammar, distinguishing it from illocutionary force (cf. Dik 1997, Van Valin and LaPolla 1997), tense, politeness and so on, which are viewed as categories in their own right. Narrog (2005a) proposed a cross-linguistic model for modality for the formulation of which Japanese data play an important role. He set up two dimensions along which modality differs. One dimension is volitivity (cf. Jespersen 1992 [1924], Heine 1995). Modal categories are categorized by the presence (e.g. deontic modality) or absence (e.g. epistemic modality) of it. The other dimension is event orientation vs speaker orientation (comparable to (inter)subjectivity in the sense of Traugott (1989) and Traugott and Dasher (2002)), a dimension that is crucial for diachronic change, which always goes in the direction of speaker orientation. Note that (inter)subjectivity is taken as a descriptive dimension of modality but not as its defining element. This model has been applied to both the synchrony (Narrog 2009), and diachronic change of modal markers in Japanese (Narrog 2007).

1.7 Conclusion

In this chapter, an overview was given about the historical development of modality studies in Japan and the current state of affairs. It was pointed out that the concept of *modariti* in Japanese linguistics cannot be equated with modality as a grammatical category in general linguistics. The currently dominant concept is the result of a unique development within Japan which reflects both the tradition of linguistic discussion within Japan and the intuitions of many Japanese scholars about what is salient in their language. At the same time, the problematic equation of modality as a grammatical category with subjectivity, which forms the basis of the *modariti* concept, has repeatedly led to criticism and to the development of alternative approaches, both from within the Japanese tradition and from more general linguistic points of view.

As was already mentioned above, the issue of *chinjutsu* 'predication' and its successor *modariti* in the conscience of many scholars is *the* defining issue in the history of Japanese grammar studies. An important point that has emerged here, although it could not be fully developed, is that the history of these concepts (and possibly of important ideas in linguistics in general) cannot be completely understood without reference to their social contexts, both inside and outside academia. The concept of *chinjutsu* 'predication' and its successor *modariti* would be excellent material for a case study in linguistic politics, especially in the light of its importance for the Japanese linguistic community. The same philosophically laden concept that was at some point associated with an anti-rationalistic and intensely nationalistic language ideology (note that Tokieda used his own 'language as process' language

theory in his ideological writings to justify the linguistic colonialization of Korea (cf. Yasuda 1997: ch. 5)), was reformulated and relabelled[8]
as *modariti* at times when the needs of society and academic life
demanded 'internationalization' and down-to-earth language description and teaching. It is certainly tempting, and entirely possible, to
describe these developments purely as a history of linguistic ideas, but
on a deeper level such an approach cannot explain why these ideas
and the way they are formulated emerged and succeeded (or failed).
From a purely scientific point of view, it is hard to see why Tokieda's
concept of *chinjutsu* should be superior to Miyake's, or why the current mainstream approach to *modariti* should be superior to that of
Okuda/Kudō. On the contrary, in describing sentence-final predication
Miyake is more scientific than Tokieda, and as a notion of 'modality'
as a grammatical category Okuda/Kudō's concept is more appropriate
than Masuoka/Nitta's. Arguably, the most successful linguistic concept
at each time in history is not necessarily the one that is scientifically
most outstanding, but rather the one that suits best the social and academic climate in the communities where it evolves and thus finds the
strongest resonance.

Nowadays, the field of modality studies is vast in Japan and, as was
shown in this chapter, scholars of different persuasions and with different backgrounds participate in it and influence it from outside the
mainstream. More and more scholars are both willing and able to seriously confront domestically grown ideas with general linguistic ideas.
Masuoka, who is one of the pioneers of the opening-up process from
the 1980s and who has been portrayed in this chapter as a representative of the current dominant approach, has recently taken his concept of
modality in a direction that is more compatible with general linguistic
concepts (Masuoka 1999, 2002, this volume). Thus, borderlines crumble,
and it is easy to foresee that in ten years from now it will be much more
difficult to identify distinct schools of thought and track down their
roots. The publication and conference project of which this chapter is
a part, by presenting research on Japanese modality in an international
context, both documents and promotes this development.

Acknowledgements

I wish to thank the editors of this volume for their support and encouragement and Hiroshi Kudō for valuable suggestions concerning the
history of Japanese linguistics.

Notes

1. The romanization system used in this chapter is Hepburn.
2. All quotes from Japanese, German and French are translated into English by the author.
3. It should be noted that the term 'subjectivity' here comprises both 'subjectivity' and 'intersubjectivity' in the modern sense of Traugott and Dasher (2002). In Japanese linguistics, sometimes 'subjectivity' and 'intersubjectivity' are clearly distinguished (Yasushi Haga was presumably the first to do so; see below), and sometimes they are treated under the same label of 'subjectivity' or 'speaker's attitude'.
4. Larm (2008) offers a detailed analysis of the *chinjutsu* concept with Yamada, Mio, Miyake and Tokieda.
5. There are at least two good indications for this assumption. First, Mikami and Kindaichi used the terms *dictum* and *modus* at points in their argumentation where they criticize the concepts of Tokieda and/or Watanabe. Second, Mikami and Kindaichi were at least temporarily associated with the Marxist Linguistic Study Group, indicating a completely different (and possibly internationalist) academic orientation from the more famous proponents of *chinjutsu-ron*.
6. The concept of 'Japanese Language Studies' as opposed to 'National Language Studies' is not a novelty. It goes back to the 1930s (cf. Yasuda 2006: ch. 3). However, from the 1980s *Kokugo-gaku* has started to be absorbed into *nihongo-gaku*.
7. 'A modal indicates that the profiled process is not accepted as part of reality' (Langacker 2003: 12). The connection of modality with *irrealis*, instead of subjectivity, is also emphasized in Japanese linguists' interpretation of Langacker (cf. Tsuboi 2004: 247–8).
8. It was not claimed in this chapter, however, that *chinjutsu* and *modariti* are identical. It is only a specific concept of *chinjutsu* which was transformed into the concept of *modariti* in the 1980s. Some scholars still use both terms simultaneously.

References

Bally, Charles (1965) [1932]. *Linguistique Générale et Linguistique Française*, 4th edn. Berne: Francke.

Brugmann, Karl (1970) [1904]. *Kurze Vergleichende Grammatik der Indogermanischen Sprachen*. Berlin: Walter de Gruyter.

Chung, Sandra and Alan Timberlake (1985). Tense, aspect and mood. In: Shopen, Timothy (ed.), *Language Typology and Syntactic Description*, vol. 3. Cambridge: Cambridge University Press: 202–58.

Dik, Simon C. (1997). *The Theory of Functional Grammar – Part 1: The Structure of the Clause*, ed. by Kees Hengeveld. Berlin: Mouton de Gruyter.

Eschbach-Szabó, Viktoria (1989). Wilhelm Wundt und Yamada Yoshio über die Definition des Satzes [Wilhelm Wundt and Yamada Yoshio on the definition of the clause]. In: Hijiya-Kirschnereit, Irmela and Stalph, Jürgen (eds), *Bruno*

Lewin zu Ehren Festschrift aus Anlaß seines 65. Geburtstages, vol. 1. Bochum: Brockmeyer: 67–79.

Fillmore, Charles (1968). The case for case. In: Bach, E. and Harms, R.T. (eds), *Universals in Linguistic Theory*. New York: Holt, Rinehart and Winston, Inc.: 1–88.

Haga, Yasushi (1954). 'Chinjutsu' to wa nani-mono? [What is 'chinjutsu'?]. *Kokugo kokubun* 23(4), 47–61.

Haga, Yasushi (1982). *Shintei Nihon Bunpō Kyōshitsu* [Newly Edited Japanese Language Classroom]. Tokyo: Shinkōsha.

Harada, Tomi (1999). Modariti-ron shōkō – modariti o meguru nihongo kenkyū no futatsu no dōkō [Thoughts on modality theory – two tendencies in Japanese modality research]. *Gengo to Bunka* 3, 123–36.

Hayashi, Shirō (1960). *Kihon Bunkei no Kenkyū* [Research on basic language patterns]. Tokyo: Meiji tosho.

Heine, Bernd (1995). Agent-oriented vs. epistemic modality: some observations on German modals. In: Bybee, J. and Fleischman, S. (eds), *Modality in Grammar and Discourse*. Amsterdam: Benjamins: 17–53.

Heyse, Johann Christian August (1868). *Deutsche Schulgrammatik oder kurzgefasstes Lehrbuch der deutschen Sprache*, 21st edn. Hannover: Hahn'sche Hof-Buchhandlung.

Jespersen, Otto (1992) [1924]. *The Philosophy of Grammar*. Chicago: University of Chicago Press.

Johnson, Yuki (2003). *Modality and the Japanese Language*. Ann Arbor: The University of Michigan.

Kawamura, Futoshi (2002). Johō to imi – kodaigo beshi no baai [Modality and meaning – the case of Classical Japanese beshi]. *Nihongogaku* 21/2, 28–37.

Kiefer, Ferenc (1987). On defining modality. *Folia Linguistica* 21(1), 67–94.

Kiefer, Ferenc (1997). Presidential address – modality and pragmatics. *Folia Linguistica* 31(3–4), 241–53.

Kindaichi, Haruhiko (1953). Fuhenka jodōshi no honshitsu (1, 2). Shukanteki hyōgen to kyakkanteki hyōgen no betsu ni tsuite [The essence of uninflecting auxiliaries (1, 2). About the distinction between subjective and objective expressions]. *Kokugo Kokubun* 22(2), 1–18; 22(3), 15–35.

Kokugo Gakkai (ed.) (1980) *Kokugogaku Daijiten* [Great Dictionary of National Language Studies]. Tokyo: Tōkyōdō Shuppan.

Kristophson, Jürgen (1994). Zur Geschichte der Modalitätsforschung in Russland [The history of modality research in Russia]. In: Jachnow, Helmut H. et al. (eds), *Modalität und Modus. Allgemeine Fragen und Realisierung im Slavischen*. Wiesbaden: Harrassowitz: 37–51.

Kudō, Hiroshi (1989). Gendai nihongo no bun no johōsei – joshō [The modality of the modern Japanese clause – a prologue]. *Tōkyō Gaikokugo Daigaku Ronshū* 39, 13–33.

Kudō, Hiroshi (2005). Bun no kinō to johōsei [The function of sentences and modality]. *Kokugo to Kokubungaku* 82(8), 1–15.

Kudō, Mayumi (2004). Mūdo to tensu, asupekuto no sōkansei ni tsuite [On the interrelation between mood, tense and aspect]. *Handai Nihongo Kenkyū* 16, 1–17.

Kudō, Mayumi (2006). Bun no taishōteki naiyō, modaritī, temporaritī no sōkansei o megutte – *rashii* to *yooda* [On the interrelation between the contents of a sentence, modality, and temporality – *rashii* and *yooda*]. In: Gengogaku Kenkyūkai (ed.), *Kotoba no Kagaku* 11, Tokyo: Mugi Shobō: 139–82.

Langacker, Ronald (2003). Extreme subjectification. English tense and modals. In: Cuyckens, Hubert et al. (eds), *Motivation in Language. Studies in Honor of Günter Radden*. Amsterdam: Benjamins: 3–26.

Larm, Lars (2008). Early uses of the term *chinjutsu*. Lund University, Dept. of Linguistics and Phonetics Working Papers 53, 97–115.

Lyons, John (1968). *Introduction to Theoretical Linguistics*. Cambridge: Cambridge University Press.

Lyons, John (1977). *Semantics*, vol. 2. Cambridge: Cambridge University Press.

Masuoka, Takashi (1987). *Meidai no Bunpō* [The Grammar of the Proposition]. Tokyo: Kuroshio.

Masuoka, Takashi (1991). *Modariti no Bunpō* [The Grammar of Modality]. Tokyo: Kuroshio.

Masuoka, Takashi (1999). Meidai to no kyōkai o motomete [Searching for the borderline between (modality) and proposition]. *Gekkan Gengo* 28(6), 46–52.

Masuoka, Takashi (2002). Handan no modariti – genjitsu to higenjitsu no tairitsu [The modality of judgement – the opposition between realis and irrealis]. *Nihongogaku* 21(2), 6–16.

Maynard, Senko K. (1993). *Discourse Modality. Subjectivity, Emotion and Voice in the Japanese Language*. Amsterdam: Benjamins.

Mikami, Akira (1972) [1953]. *Gendai Gohō Josetsu. Shintakusu no Kokoromi* [Introduction to the grammar of the modern language. An attempt at syntax]. Tokyo: Kuroshio.

Mikami, Akira (1972) [1959]. *Zoku Gendai Gohō Josetsu* [An Introduction to Modern Grammar (continued)]. Tokyo: Kuroshio.

Minami, Fujio (1964). Jutsugobun no kōzō [The structure of sentences with a predicate]. Kokugo kenkyū 18, reprinted in Minami, Fujio (1997). *Gendai Nihongo Kenkyū* [Research on Modern Japanese]. Tokyo: Sanseido: 37–57.

Minami, Fujio (1974). *Gendai Nihongo no Kōzō* [The Structure of Modern Japanese]. Tokyo: Taishūkan shoten.

Mio, Isago (1939). Bun ni okeru chinjutsu sayō to wa nani zo ya [What is predicational function in the sentence?]. *Kokugo to Kokubungaku* 16(1), 66–78.

Miyake, Takeo (1934). *Onsei Kōgo-hō* [Phonetics of the Spoken Language]. In: Hashimoto, Shinkichi (ed.), *Kokugo-hō* (Kokugo Kagaku kōza 6). Tokyo: Meiji shoin.

Nakau, Minoru (1979). Modariti to meidai [Modality and proposition]. In: Hayashi Eiichi Kyōju Kanreki Kinen Ronbunshū Kankō Iinkai (ed.), *Eigo to Nihongo to*. Tokyo: Kuroshio: 223–50.

Narrog, Heiko (1998). Nihongo dōshi no katsuyō taikei [The inflection system of Japanese verbs]. *Nihongo kagaku* 4, 7–30.

Narrog, Heiko (2002). Imironteki kategorii to shite no modariti [Modality as a semantic category]. In: Ōhori, Toshio (ed.), *Ninchi gengogaku II: kategoriika* (Shirīzu gengo kagaku 3). Tokyo: Tokyo University Press: 217–51.

Narrog, Heiko (2005a). Modality, mood, and change of modal meanings – a new perspective. *Cognitive Linguistics* 16(4), 677–731.

Narrog, Heiko (2005b). On defining modality again. *Language Sciences* 27(2), 165–92.

Narrog, Heiko (2007). Modality and grammaticalization in Japanese. *Journal of Historical Pragmatics* 8(2), 269–94.

Narrog, Heiko (2009) *Modality in Japanese – the Layered Structure of Clause and Hierarchies of Functional Categories*. Amsterdam: John Benjamins.

Nitta, Yoshio (1985). Bun no honegumi [The frame of a sentence]. In: Hayashi, Shirō (ed.), *Nihongo no Kyōiku*. Tokyo: Meiji shoin: 64–86.

Nitta, Yoshio (1989). Gendai nihongo-bun no modariti no taikei to kōzō [System and structure of modality in modern Japanese sentences]. In: Nitta, Yoshio and Masuoka, Takashi (eds), *Nihongo no Modariti*. Tokyo: Kuroshio: 1–56.

Nitta, Yoshio (1991). *Nihongo no Modariti to Ninshō* [Japanese Modality and Person]. Tokyo: Hitsuji shobō.

Nitta, Yoshio (2000). Ninshiki no modariti to sono shūhen [Epistemic modality and its periphery]. In: Moriyama, Takurō, Nitta, Yoshio and Kudō, Hiroshi, *Modariti* (Nihongo no bunpō 3). Tokyo: Iwanami: 81–159.

Nitta, Yoshio and Takashi Masuoka (1989). *Nihongo no Modariti* [Japanese Modality]. Tokyo: Kuroshio.

Nomura, Takashi (2003). Modariti keishiki no bunrui [On the classification of Japanese modal forms]. *Kokugogaku* (National Language Studies) 54(1), 17–31.

Nomura, Takashi (2004). Jutsugo no keitai to imi [Form and meaning of predicates]. In: Onoe, Keisuke (ed.), *Bunpō II* (Asakura Nihongo Kōza 6). Tokyo: Asakura shoten: 81–104.

Noreen, Adolf (1923). *Einführung in die wissenschaftliche Betrachtung der Sprache. Beiträge zur Methode und Terminologie der Grammatik* (Partial translation of the 9 volume work *Vårt Språk*, published 1903–19). Saale: Niemeyer.

Oertel, Hanns (1901). *Lectures on the Study of Language*. London: Edward Arnold.

Okuda, Yasuo (1985). *Kotoba no Kenkyū, Josetsu* [Language research. An Introduction]. Tokyo: Mugi shobō.

Onoe, Keisuke (1990). Bunpōron: Chinjutsu-ron no tanjō to shūen [Grammar: the birth and the death of predication theory]. *Kokugo to Kokubungaku* 67(4), 1–16.

Onoe, Keisuke (2001). *Bunpō to Imi I* [Grammar and Meaning I]. Tokyo: Kuroshio.

Onoe, Keisuke (2004). Shugo to jutsugo o meguru bunpō [The grammar of subject and predicate] In: Onoe, Keisuke (ed.), *Bunpō II* (Asakura Nihongo Kōza 6). Tokyo: Asakura shoten: 43–57.

Ōshika, Tadahisa (1999). Johō shōkō [Miscellaneous thoughts on modality]. *Nihon Bungei Kenkyū* 50(4), 35–45.

Ōshika, Tadahisa (2004). Modariti o bunpōshiteki ni miru [Modality in the history of grammar]. In Onoe, Keisuke (ed.), *Bunpō II* (Asakura Nihongo Kōza 6). Tokyo: Asakura shoten: 193–214.

Satō, Kiyoji (1977) *Kokugogaku Kenkyū Jiten* [Research Dictionary of National Language Studies]. Tokyo: Meiji Shoin.

Suzuki, Shigeyuki (1972). *Nihongo Bunpō, Keitairon* [Japanese Grammar, Morphology]. Tokyo: Mugi shobō.

Suzuki, Shigeyuki (1978). Yo-dan katsuyō no seiritsu [The coming-into-being of the four-graded inflection]. In: Matsumoto, Taijō (ed.), *Nihongo Kenkyū no Hōhō*. Tokyo: Mugi shobō: 125–51.

Sweet, Henry (1900) [1891]. *A New English Grammar. Logical and Historical. Part I.* Oxford: Clarendon.

Teramura, Hideo (1982). *Nihongo no Shintakusu to Imi I* [Japanese Syntax and Meaning 1]. Tokyo: Kuroshio.

Tokieda, Motoki (1941). *Kokugogaku Genron. Gengo Kateisetsu no Seiritsu to sono Tenkai* [Principles of National Language Studies. The Formation of Language Processing Theory and its Expansion]. Tokyo: Iwanami shoten.

Tokieda, Motoki (1950). *Nihon Bunpō Kōgo-hen* [Japanese grammar – the spoken language]. Tokyo: Iwanami shoten.

Traugott, Elizabeth Closs (1989). On the rise of epistemic meanings in English: an example of subjectification in semantic change. *Language* 65(1), 31–55.

Traugott, Elizabeth and Richard Dasher (2002). *Regularity in Semantic Change.* Cambridge: Cambridge University Press.

Tsuboi, Eijirō (2004). Jutsugo o meguru bunpō to imi. Ninchigengogakuteki kanten kara [Grammar and meaning of the predicate – from a cognitive linguist view]. In: Onoe Keisuke (ed.), *Bunpō II*. Tokyo: Asakura shoten: 235–56.

Uyeno, Tazuko Yamanaka (1971). A study of Japanese modality – a performative analysis of sentence particles. PhD thesis, University of Michigan.

Van Valin, Robert D. and Randy J. LaPolla (1997). *Syntax: Structure, Meaning, and Function.* Cambridge: Cambridge University Press.

Watanabe, Minoru (1953). Jojutsu to chinjutsu. Jutsugo bunsetsu no kōzō [Internal and external predication. The structure of predicative phrases]. *Kokugogaku* 13(14), 20–34.

Wenck, Günther (1989). Japanese language studies since B.H. Chamberlain. In: Wenck, Günther, *Pratum Japanisticum. Exemplifizierender Entwurf einer 'Japanistik'*. Wiesbaden: Harrassowitz: 1–16.

Wundt, Wilhelm (1900). *Völkerpsychologie. Untersuchung der Entwicklungsgesetze von Sprache, Mythus und Sitte. Die Sprache. Zweiter Theil.* Leipzig: Engelmann/ Stuttgart: Kröner.

Yamada, Yoshio (1908). *Nihon Bunpōron* [Japanese grammar theory]. Tokyo: Hōbunkan.

Yamaoka, Masaki (2000). *Nihongo no Jutsugo to Bun-kinō.* Tokyo: Kuroshio.

Yasuda, Toshiaki (1997). *Shokuminchi no Naka no 'Kokugogaku'* ['National Language Studies' in the Colonies]. Tokyo: Sangensha.

Yasuda, Toshiaki (2006). *'Kokugo' no Kindaishi. Teikoku Nihon to Kokugo Gakushatachi* [Modern History of the 'National Language'. Imperial Japan and National Language Scholars]. Tokyo: Chūō kōronsha.

2
Modality from a Japanese Perspective*

Takashi Masuoka

2.1 Introductory remarks

2.1.1 The objective of this chapter

The grammatical category 'modality' has been one of the most popular topics dealt with in grammatical research in Japan. Since the 1980s numerous papers and monographs on Japanese modality have been published.[1] Unfortunately, however, a wealth of research – written in Japanese and circulated domestically – has remained beyond the reach of Western linguistic circles. This chapter is presented with the intention of making these research results accessible to a wider overseas readership.

The objective of this chapter is thus to offer a general view of Japanese modality on the basis of previous research in Japan – particularly, research by Akira Mikami, Hideo Teramura and Fujio Minami, all of whom have had a great influence on grammatical analyses of Japanese modality. More specifically, this chapter will argue that a proposed model, called the 'semantic layer structure model', can account for such linguistic facts as observed in Japanese conditional constructions, and that the concept of modality of judgement can be meaningfully defined in terms of *realis/irrealis*. It is our belief that the following view has important implications for the study of modality in general.

2.1.2 The concept of modality

How can we look at the concept of modality? One plausible view is that this concept is defined as the expression of the speaker's attitude. Lyons is one of the linguists who define the concept of modality in this manner, as illustrated in the following quote: 'If we turn now to other modalities, apart from command and interrogation, we find a large variety of ways in which the "attitude" of the speaker is grammatically marked in different languages' (Lyons 1968: 308).

2.1.3   A characteristic of Japanese sentence structure

Lyons' view of modality is highly transparent in Japanese, because it is a language in which speaker- and context-related meaning is overtly expressed in the sentence structure. Let us consider the following sentences:

(1) *Kokoro kara no keii o   hyoosuru <u>sidai-dearu</u>.*
    heart from respect express
    'I hereby express my deep respect.'

(2) *Seido no seibi   nado   hituyoona sesaku o   kooziru <u>mono to suru</u>.*
    system buildup and so on necessary measures   take
    'Necessary measures such as building up new systems shall be taken.'

The underlined parts, that is *sidai-dearu* ((lit.) these are the circumstances) and *mono to suru* ((lit.) this is my stance), express the speaker's attitude, whereas the other parts state the objective content considered to carry propositional truth.

As a consequence, it is quite natural for Japanese grammarians to adopt the view that the sentence is composed of two parts: the objective content part and the speaker-related/context-related part.

2.2   Japanese grammarians' analyses[2]

2.2.1   Mikami and Teramura

The above-mentioned view was propounded by Akira Mikami (1942) in his first paper. In it Mikami claims that the sentence is composed of *huteihoo-bubun* (infinitival part) and *kimari* (determinant), later called *koto* (objective content) and *muudo* (modality). Notice that Mikami conceives of *muudo* (modality) as a component of the sentence, just as *koto* (objective content) is a compositional concept.

Mikami's idea is reminiscent of Fillmore's contention. Fillmore (1968) argues that the sentence is made up of 'proposition' and 'modality'.[3] It is to be noted, however, that Mikami paid equal attention to *koto* and *muudo*, in contrast to Fillmore, who restricted his analysis to proposition and developed a grammatical research model called 'case grammar'.[4,5]

Inheriting Mikami's view of sentence structure, Hideo Teramura, in his monographs (Teramura 1982, 1984), divided *muudo* into two types:

taiziteki muudo (expression of the speaker's attitude towards *koto*) such as epistemic modality, and *taizinteki muudo* (expression of the speaker's attitude towards the hearer) such as politeness. Thus, Teramura posits a sentence structure composed of three parts: *koto*, *taiziteki muudo* and *taizinteki muudo*.

Teramura's idea is similar to Lyons' view. Lyons (1977) argues that the logical structure of utterances is made up of three components: the 'phrastic' ('propositional content'), the 'neustic' ('that part of the sentence which expresses the speaker's commitment to the factuality, desirability and so on of the propositional content'), and the 'tropic' ('that part of the sentence which correlates with the kind of speech act that the sentence is characteristically used to perform'). It is interesting to note that a Japanese grammarian and a British linguist independently came up with a similar sentence structure model in almost the same period.

2.2.2 Minami

Independently of Mikami and Teramura, Fujio Minami, in his papers and monographs (e.g. Minami 1974, 1993), presented a four-layer structure model (or four-level structure model), stressing the hierarchical nature of sentence structure.[6] Minami developed this hierarchical sentence structure model, based mainly on his detailed analysis of complex sentences, that is an analysis on the basis of the distribution of elements appearing in subordinate clauses.

Minami refers to the four layers (or four levels) as 'A', 'B', 'C', and 'D'. The elements of 'A', 'B' and 'C' are claimed to be those appearing in clauses of simultaneity (such as the *nagara* (while)-clause), clauses of causality (such as the *node* (since)-clause) and clauses of concession (such as the *ga* (although)-clause). The remaining elements are analysed as those belonging to 'D'. Roughly speaking, 'A' and 'B' correspond to the notion of proposition, while 'C' and 'D' correspond to that of modality, although Minami himself does not employ the terms 'proposition' and 'modality'. In the Japanese grammatical tradition, Minami's model is highly valued as an original and well-organized sentence structure model.

2.3 Our proposal

2.3.1 The outline of our structure model

Building on Mikami's, Teramura's and especially Minami's view of sentence structure, I propose a model called the 'semantic layer structure model'. This is designated as 'semantic' so as to indicate that this structure, which characterizes a sentence in terms of four semantic layers, is a semantic composition structure. Although Minami's model also recognizes four layers, it is not semantically based, but rather is constructed on the basis of the distribution of subordinate-clause elements, as stated above.

Now, let me describe how the semantic layer structure is conceived.[7] I will illustrate the model by use of the following sentence:

(3) *Nee,   dooyara   sakuya   hagesiku yuki   ga   hutta   yooda yo.*
    you know apparently last night heavily   snow   fell   seem Modal Prt
    'You know, it looks like it snowed heavily last night.'

The component describing the objective content is *sakuya hagesiku yuki ga hutta* (it snowed heavily last night), leaving behind the component *nee, dooyara...yooda yo* (you know, it looks like), which describes the speaker's attitude. I refer to the former component as the 'propositional domain' and the latter component as the 'modal domain'.

In the propositional domain, the core component expressing the event type (in this case, the event of heavy snowfall) is *hagesiku yuki ga huru* (it snows heavily), whereas the component *sakuya* (last night)... *ta* (Past Tense) describes the spatio-temporal situation of the event in question. The former component, which corresponds to Fillmore's (1968) proposition, is referred to as the 'domain of core proposition', and the latter as the 'domain of spatio-temporal situation'.

As for the modal domain, the component expressing the speaker's attitude towards the proposition is *dooyara* (apparently)... *yooda* (seem), leaving behind the component *nee* (you know)... *yo* (modal particle), which describes the speaker's mode of utterance. I call these components the 'domain of modality of judgement' and the 'domain of modality of utterance', respectively.

With this, we have four semantic domains: the domain of core proposition, the domain of spatio-temporal situation, the domain of modality of judgement and the domain of modality of utterance. These are related in a hierarchical manner: the domain of core proposition is included in the domain of spatio-temporal situation, which in turn is included in the domain of modality of judgement, which is further included in the domain of modality of utterance.

The hierarchical relation as found in sentence (3) is represented as in:

(4) [nee [dooraya [sakuya   [hagesiku yuki ga huru] ta] yooda] yo]
    [you know [apparently [last night [it heavily snows] Past Tense] seem] Modal Prt]

Let us characterize the four semantic domains in terms of hierarchical relations and call them the 'layer of core proposition' ('P1'), the 'layer of spatio-temporal situation' ('P2'), the 'layer of modality of judgement' ('M1'), and the 'layer of modality of ttterance' ('M2'), respectively.[8]

It is to be noted that each layer can be realized as a sub-part of a sentence, as shown below:

(5) a. *Kono atari de wa, hagesiku yuki ga huru koto wa mezurasiku-nai.* (P1)
    this   area   in   heavily snow   fall   rare-not
    'In this area, heavy snowfall is not a surprising thing.'

   b. *Sakuya   hagesiku yuki ga hutta koto wa   tasikada.* (P1 + P2)
      last night heavily snow   fell   certain
      'It is certain that it snowed heavily last night.'

   c. *Dooyara   sakuya   hagesiku   yuki ga   hutta   yooda kara,   sibaraku*
      apparently last night heavily   snow   fell   seem   since   for a while
      yoozin-sita   hoo ga yoi. (P1 + P2 + M1)
      take precaution better
      'Since it looks like it snowed heavily last night, it would be better to take precaution for a while.'

   d. *'Nee,   dooyara   sakuya   hagesiku yuki ga hutta yooda yo.' to*
      you know apparently last night heavily   snow   fell   seem Modal Prt
      yuuzin ga   itta. (P1 + P2 + M1 + M2)
      friend   said
      'My friend said, "You know, it looks like it snowed heavily last night." '

The underlined parts in (5a), (5b), (5c) and (5d), respectively designate the component P1, the combination of components P1 and P2, the combination of components P1, P2 and M1, and the combination of components P1, P2, M1 and M2. Note that P1 and P2 (but not M1 and M2) appear in *koto*-clauses, which are considered indicators of propositional content in Japanese.

In terms of the above semantic layer notions, (4) can be represented as follows:

(6) [M2 [M1 [P2 [P1] P2] M1] M2]

I refer to this structure model as the 'semantic layer structure model'.

2.3.2 Semantic layer structure and grammatical categories

With regard to the proposed model, it should be pointed out that the grammatical categories 'voice', 'aspect', 'tense' and 'modality' are related systematically to the semantic layers mentioned above. Voice, aspect, tense and modality are basic grammatical categories that specify important facets of grammatical meaning primarily in the predicate position and these grammatical categories are linked to the semantic layers, as described below.

First, the layer of core proposition characterizes event types. The central grammatical elements of this layer are the predicate and its arguments, that is, 'argument structure' in the sense of Grimshaw (1990). Relevant to this layer is the grammatical category 'voice' (e.g. the passive voice (for example, the passive voice *yuki ni hur-areru*) and the causative voice (e.g. *yuki o hur-aseru*)),[9] which involves reorganizations of the argument structure.[10] Consider sentences such as *kono atari dewa, hagesiku yuki ni hur-areru koto wa mezurasiku-nai* ((lit.) in this area, it is not surprising that one gets affected by heavy snowfall) and *kono atari dewa, kanki ga hagesiku yuki o hur-aseru koto wa mezurasiku-nai* (in this area, it is not surprising that the cold wave causes heavy snowfall).

Second, the layer of spatio-temporal situation locates a given event in space and time. As a consequence, the grammatical categories 'aspect' and 'tense' come into play in this layer.

Finally, the layer of modality of judgement and the layer of modality of utterance express the speaker's attitude towards the proposition and the speaker's mode of utterance, respectively. As the names of these layers indicate, the grammatical category 'modality' is relevant here.

One cannot dispense with the concepts of voice, aspect, tense and modality to give adequate grammatical descriptions of the world's languages, including Japanese, and each of these concepts has its own position in the model I have presented.

2.4 Conditional constructions in Japanese

In order to argue for the proposed model of sentence structure, I will briefly demonstrate how conditional constructions in Japanese can be handled in this model.[11]

To the best of my knowledge, Japanese is one of the languages in which research into conditionals has made striking progress. A remarkable characteristic of Japanese conditionals, which has promoted in-depth analysis of the constructions, is that predicates in protasis clauses take diverse forms. To be noted in particular is the fact that the most representative conditional form, that is the *ba*-form, has diverged into three forms, that is the *(r)eba*-form, the *tara(ba)*-form and the *nara(ba)*-form.[12] The following sentences are typical examples of the (r)eba-form conditional, the tara(ba)-form conditional and the nara(ba)-form conditional:

> (7) a. *Zyuyoo ga huer-<u>eba</u>   kakaku ga   agaru.*
>   demand   increase-Cond price   go up
>   'If the demand goes up, the prices also go up.'
>
>   b. *Mukoo ni   tui-<u>tara</u>,   renraku-site   hosii.*
>   there   reach-Cond   contact   want
>   'On reaching there, please contact me.'
>
>   c. *Anata ga   happyoo-suru   <u>nara</u>,   watasi mo   happyoo-suru.*
>   you   make a presentation Cond   I   also   make a presentation
>   'If you make a presentation, I will do so, too.'

The basic characteristic of the (r)eba-form conditional is that it describes a general causal relation. In (7a), there is a general causal relation between the two given event types, that is the event of growth in demand and that of rise in price. The tara(ba)-form conditional has the characteristic of describing the notion of temporal dependency. In (7b), there is a strict temporal order between the two specific events: the event of the protasis precedes that of the apodosis. In the case of the nara(ba)-form conditional, its basic function is to express the hypotheticality of the situation described by the protasis. In (7c), the speaker takes the stance that he or she is not certain whether the hearer will make a presentation.

This differentiation, apparently arbitrary, turns out to be highly motivated in light of its relation to the proposed semantic layer structure. Each of the three variants of the ba-forms indicates a specific layer where a given condition is set.

Leaving details aside, the relations between the three ba-forms and the layers of condition-setting can be summarized as follows:

> (8) i.   The (r)eba-form indicates condition-setting in the layer of core proposition.
>   ii. The tara(ba)-form indicates condition-setting in the layer of spatio-temporal situation.
>   iii. The nara(ba)-form indicates condition-setting in the layer of modality of judgement.

It should also be noted that there is a correlation between the morphological form of the conditional predicate and the type of condition-setting: (r)eba is a basic, unmarked form, which correlates with a general causal relation, while *tara(ba)* and *nara(ba)*, which originate from the auxiliary verbs *tari* and *nari',*[13] correlate with the notion of temporality and that of speaker's judgement, respectively.

2.5 Modality of judgement

2.5.1 Two subtypes of modality of judgement

A significant point in which Japanese modality is in close contact with the Western concept of modality is what is referred to as modality of judgement in this chapter.

In this section, therefore, I will discuss modality of judgement in Japanese. Modality of judgement is divided into two categories, what I call 'modality of epistemic judgement' (*singi-handan no modariti*) and 'modality of evaluative judgement' (*kachi-handan no modariti*). These two categories remind us of 'epistemic modality' and 'deontic modality'.

Epistemic modality and deontic modality are representative modalities that have been elucidated in the general linguistic literature. Palmer (2001), for example, deals with epistemic modality under the heading 'propositional modality', and with deontic modality under the heading 'event modality'.

In Japanese, it should be noted that most of the forms that express modality of evaluative judgement are composites and are semantically transparent to some extent, for example, *hoo ga ii* (had better do), *(r)eba ii* (should do), *te wa ikenai* (should not do), *nakereba ikenai* (must do), which contain the evaluative adjective *ii* (good) or its negative counterpart *ikenai* (not good). It is because evaluative meaning is fairly explicit in these expressions that I use the term 'modality of evaluative judgement'.

I argue that there are reasons for setting up the superordinate category 'modality of judgement', which combines the modalities of epistemic judgement and evaluative judgement. This argument is an extension of the view proposed by Mikami (1963) and Teramura (1984), whose observations regarding epistemic modality I will briefly describe below.

2.5.2 Mikami's and Teramura's view

With respect to epistemic modality in Japanese, Mikami (1963) proposed the opposition called *teigen/gaigen* (assertive/probable),[14] which in his view is expressed by the unmarked form of a predicate and the marked form such as a predicate plus the auxiliary verb *daroo.*[15]

Teramura (1984), following Mikami's conceptualization, provided a detailed description of *gaigen* expressions like *daroo, kamo-sirenai* (be possible), *yooda* (seem) and *rasii* (seem).[16]

The *teigen/gaigen* opposition (or *kakugen/gaigen* opposition in Teramura's words) is reminiscent of the linguistic concept of *realis/irrealis*. This concept has attracted the attention of a number of linguists such as Chung and Timberlake (1985), Givón (1994), Mithun (1999) and Palmer (2001).

2.6 The principle of *realis/irrealis* opposition

Extending the view of Mikami and Teramura and drawing on the linguistic concept of *realis/irrealis*, I propose that the whole modality of judgement be characterized in terms of the *realis/irrealis* opposition. That is, the modality of judgement is a modal category, characterized by the contrast of the unmarked *realis* form and the marked *irrealis* form of the predicate.

More specifically, modality of epistemic judgement has the semantic opposition *kakugen/gaigen* (strong assertion/weak assertion), as exemplified below:

(9) a. [*kakugen* (strong assertion)]
    Kono keikaku wa umaku iku.
    this plan   well   go
    'This plan will succeed.'

  b. [*gaigen* (weak assertion)]
    Kono keikaku wa umaku iku   daroo.
    this plan   well   go   Weak Assertion
    'Probably, this plan will succeed.'

Similarly, modality of evaluative judgement has the semantic opposition *genzitu zoo/risoo zoo* (real situation/desirable situation); that is, a given proposition is construed as either a real situation or a non-real situation, as shown in the following:

(10) a. [*genzitu zoo* (real situation)]
    Kisoku wa mamorareru.
    rule   be observed
    'The rules are observed.'

b. [*risoo zoo* (desirable situation)]
   Kisoku   wa   zettai   mamorareru   bekida.
   rule   absolutely   be observed   should
   'The rules should be absolutely observed.'

I maintain that the oppositions *kakugen/gaigen* and *genzitu zoo/risoo zoo* are to be subsumed under the *realis/irrealis* opposition. I refer to this view as the principle of *realis/irrealis* opposition. Incidentally, the idea of uniting the *kakugen/gaigen* opposition and the *genzitu zoo/risoo zoo* opposition nicely fits languages like English, where the same modal auxiliaries such as *must* and *may* express both epistemic modality and deontic modality. The polysemy of modal auxiliaries in these languages has been discussed extensively in Traugott (1989) and others.

2.7 The *-tai* construction

A meaning-extension phenomenon observed in the *-tai* construction provides further evidence of the advantages of collapsing the *kakugen/gaigen* opposition and the *genzitu zoo/risoo zoo* opposition into the unitary concept of *realis/irrealis* opposition.[17]

The *-tai* construction is said to be a desiderative expression, as illustrated below:

(11) *Nanika   tumetai   mono   ga   nomi-tai.*
     something   cold   thing   drink-Desi
     'I want to drink something cold.'

The important characteristics of this expression are that (i) the subject of the construction is, by default, the speaker, and (ii) the expression assumes a subjective nuance.

However, it is pointed out that the *-tai* construction can express a meaning of necessity under certain contexts. This usage is fairly common in newspaper editorials, guidebooks for tourists and similar, which are abundant with personal opinions and useful advice. For instance, observe the following sentence:

(12) *Huyu wa   sekisetu   ya   tooketu e no taisaku ga   hituyoona node,   doraibaa wa*
     winter   fallen snow   and   freezing   measures   necessary since driver
     sintyoona   unten   o   kokorogake-tai.
     cautious   driving   bear in mind-Desi
     '(lit.) In winter, drivers want to drive cautiously since it is necessary to take care on snowy and icy roads.'

This example, quoted from a tourist guidebook, differs from a more typical desiderative expression (e.g. in (11)) in that (i) the subject of the construction is not the speaker but a third party, i.e. *drivers*, and (ii) it does not assume a subjective nuance, as indicated by the fact that it appears in a guidebook. (12) is close to (13) in meaning:

(13) *Huyu wa   sekisetu   ya   tooketu e no taisaku ga   hituyoona node,   doraibaa wa*
     winter   fallen snow and freezing   measures   necessary since   driver
     sintyoona   unten   o   kokorogakeru   bekida.
     cautious   driving   bear in mind   should
     'In winter, drivers should drive cautiously since it is necessary to take care on snowy
     and icy roads.'

This observation suggests that there are two types of desirability in given situations, as in the following:[18]

(i) subjective desire (desiderative)
(ii) necessity (evaluative judgement)

These two types of meaning are also observed in the *-(r)eba ii* construction. Compare the following sentences:

(14) [desiderative]
     Yume   ga   zitugensur-eba   ii   naa.
     dream   come true-Cond   good   Modal Prt
     'I wish my dream will come true.'

(15) [evaluative judgement]
     Senmonka   ni   soodansur-eba ii   to   omou   yo.
     expert   consult-Cond   good   think   Modal Prt
     'I think you should consult an expert.'

This construction can be used to mean either 'desiderative' as in (14) or 'evaluative judgement' as in (15).

It is interesting to see that both *-tai* and *-(r)eba* observe semantic extension phenomena in which the same expressions can express a (subjective) desire or an evaluative judgement of necessity – both clearly instances of (unactualized) *risoo zoo* (desirable situation) – and are therefore *irrealis* expressions. This supports the claim that the *genzitu zoo/risoo zoo* opposition should be characterized in terms of the concept of *realis/irrealis*, just as the *kakugen/gaigen* opposition is based on the concept of *realis/irrealis*.

2.8 Remaining problems

This section deals with some remaining problems surrounding the view of modality as presented in this chapter.

2.8.1 The issue of subjectivity

First, I will address what might be called 'the issue of subjectivity'. Defining modality as the expression of the speaker's attitude is likely to lead to the understanding that modality is the expression of subjectivity. The intimate relation between subjectivity and modality is suggested by Lyons, as in the following quote:

> The parallelism between parenthetical and performative verbs was noted by Benveniste (1958a), independently of both Austin and Urmson; and Benveniste emphasized their non-descriptive role as markers of subjectivity ('indicateurs de subjectivité') – i.e. as devices whereby the speaker, in making an utterance, simultaneously comments upon that utterance and expresses his attitude to what he is saying. This notion of subjectivity is of the greatest importance, as we shall see, for the understanding of both epistemic and deontic modality. (Lyons 1977: 739)

Two points are to be noted here regarding this issue. In the first instance, we need to distinguish between two types of subjectivity: what might be called 'compositional subjectivity', that is, those subjective elements that can be captured in terms of compositional structure, and 'non-compositional subjectivity', that is, those subjective elements that cannot be captured that way.[19] Only the former type of subjectivity falls under the scope of the modality concept in this chapter.

Another point is that with respect to 'compositional subjectivity', being conceptually subjective is not a sufficient condition for a given subjective element to be conceived of as a modal element, as exemplified by honorifics. Honorifics are understood to be conceptually subjective, since they express the speaker's evaluative judgement on a person involved. It is, however, necessary to take into account how honorific expressions manifest themselves in the compositional structure of the sentence. As discussed by Harada (1976), two types of honorifics should be distinguished on the basis of whether they are expressed at the propositional level or at the super-propositional level; Harada (1976) refers to these two types as 'propositional honorifics' and 'performative honorifics (polite speech)'.[20] In the present analysis, only the latter type is regarded as belonging to the modal component.

2.8.2   The relation between modality and mood

A second issue to be discussed is that of the modality/mood distinction.

A grammatical category related to the concept of modality is 'mood'. Symbolizing this relation is Palmer's (2001) title *Mood and Modality*. The concept of modality is a semantic category at the sentence level, whereas that of mood is a morphological category at the word (i.e. predicate) level.

Of particular importance for the concept 'semantic/morphological distinction' is the view of grammatical categories advanced by Bondarko (1991).[21] Distinguishing between 'morphological category' and 'functional–semantic category', Bondarko states that morphological categories like aspect, tense, mood and voice play the role of nucleus (centre) of their corresponding functional–semantic categories like 'aspectuality', 'temporality', 'modality' and 'functional–semantic voice'.

On the basis of Bondarko's statement above, I propose a semantic/morphological distinction of grammatical categories: 'semantic voice vs voice', 'aspectuality vs aspect', 'temporality vs tense' and 'modality vs mood'.[22] While semantic categories are valid cross-linguistically, morphological categories are not necessarily present in every language.

This proposal requires a revision of the description given above in section 2.3.2. There, it was pointed out that the grammatical categories of voice, aspect, tense and modality are related systematically to the semantic layer structure: voice is relevant at the layer of core proposition, aspect and tense at the layer of spatio-temporal situation, and modality at the layers of modality of judgement and modality of utterance. It is evident, however, that grammatical categories as related to the semantic layer structure are semantic categories rather than morphological categories. Accordingly, the categories of voice, aspect and tense should be replaced by 'semantic voice', 'aspectuality' and 'temporality'.

2.8.3   Types of predication

Lastly, a few words are in order regarding the relevance of what I call 'the types of predication' to the present topic.[23]

For the purpose of grammatical description, I posit two different types of predication, which are referred to as 'the event predication' and 'the property predication'.[24] The event predication is a description of an event that takes place in a certain spatio-temporal situation, as illustrated in (16):

(16) *Kodomo ga waratta.*
    child   laughed
    'A child laughed.'

The basic composition of the event predication sentence takes the form of predicate–argument structure.

The property predication, on the other hand, attributes a certain property to a given object, as exemplified in the following:

(17) *Nihon   wa   simaguni   da.*
    Japan   Topic   island-country   Copula
    'Japan is an island country.'

A characteristic of the property predication sentence is that it is basically realized as a topic–comment structure.[25] If, for instance, *Nihon* (Japan) were marked by the nominative marker *ga* instead of the topic marker *wa*, the sentence would be degraded. This is, however, not the case in the event predication sentence, as shown in (16).

The proposed model of sentence structure works well for the event predication. Sentence (3) above, on the basis of which the semantic layer structure model was explicated, is an example of the event predication sentence. Significant grammatical (semantic) categories such as semantic voice, aspectuality and temporality are associated with the event predication. It can be said that those grammatical categories characterize the event predication sentence, and they can fit nicely into one of the semantic domains: semantic voice into the domain of core proposition and aspectuality and temporality into the domain of spatio-temporal situation.

However, as for the property predication, a fairly different conceptualization of sentence structure is required. This point is important because such remarkable features of Japanese as the topic–comment relation have much to do with the property predication, as shown in (17); unlike event predication sentences, property predication sentences substantially involve a topic–comment structure. The semantic layer structure model proposed in this chapter does not assume a distinctive domain for topic or comment.

Thus, it should be pointed out that the proposed sentence structure model is restricted in its scope of applicability, namely, only for the event predication. In order to account for property predication sentences, another type of semantic layer structure model needs to be investigated independently from the one proposed here.

2.9 Concluding remarks

It has been shown that Japanese sentence grammar requires explorations into the modal domain as well as the propositional domain. In fact, for the past 20 years grammatical research in Japan has produced a vast amount of detailed analyses of modal expressions. In the field of linguistics in the Japanese tradition, modality has become one of the most popular research topics. In sharp contrast, previous general linguistic research had focused on the propositional aspects of the sentence, for example, explications of argument structure and event structure.

Thus, with regard to the study of modality, Japanese is in a favourable position for raising various issues that can be tested in other languages. In the present chapter, I mentioned only grammatical aspects of modality. The concept of modality, however, has a wider range of application because of its speaker- and context-relatedness. Issues related to communicative functions (e.g. politeness) are examples of such applicability, and previous research of Japanese modality has shed much light on such pragmatic aspects of modality too.[26]

As pointed out earlier, much of the Japanese research on this topic has been, and is still, inaccessible to non-Japanese speakers, and as a consequence has failed to get recognition outside of Japan. To promote a wider circulation of these research results is certainly in the interest of the global scholarly community.

I would like to close this chapter by saying that linguistic facts of Japanese argue strongly for the view that proposition and modality are on a par in terms of their grammatical significance. This means that Fillmore's (1968) celebrated sentence structure model can be prototypically observed in the Japanese language.

Acknowledgements

*This chapter is a revised version of my oral presentation at the conference entitled Revisiting Japanese Modality held at SOAS, University of London, on 24–25 June 2006. I would like to thank Drs Barbara Pizziconi and Mika Kizu for providing me an opportunity of giving a talk at the conference. I am grateful to conference participants for their valuable comments on my presentation. My thanks also go to Dr Donna Tatsuki,

Dr Mark Campana and Dr Prashant Pardeshi, who gave me advice on stylistic matters.

Notes

1. Moriyama et al. (2000) and Miyazaki et al. (2002) summarize the past research results on Japanese modality.
2. See Narrog (2005, this volume) for a detailed survey of the grammatical analyses of modality in the Japanese tradition.
3. A precursor of Fillmore's (1968) view of sentence structure is Bally (1932), in which it is argued that the sentence consists of 'dictum' and 'modus'.
4. It is interesting to note that Mikami's *koto* and Fillmore's 'proposition' are equivalent to the extent that *koto* and 'proposition' are characterized as consisting of a predicate and its dependent nominals.
5. See Goldberg (1995) and Levin and Rappaport Hovav (2005) for this line of research.
6. A similar conceptualization of sentence structure is proposed by Dik (1989). Dik's model, called 'layered structure', is also a four-layer structure model.
7. Due to space limitation, I will confine myself to the description of the outline of this model. See Masuoka (2007) for details.
8. A few words are necessary with respect to the linear order in Japanese. The basic linearization principle is: the semantic head ('H') is preceded by its complement ('C'), which in turn is preceded by the adjunct ('A') of the head. Thus, the elements of sentence (3) are realized, as represented below:

(i) *nee dooyara sakuya hagesiku yuki ga hut-ta yooda yo*

P1   *hagesiku yuki ga huru*

      A   C   H

P2   *sakuya [hagesiku yuki ga huru] ta*

   A   C   H

M1   *dooyara [sakuya hagesiku yuki ga hutta] yooda*

   A   C   H

M2   *nee [dooyara sakuya hagesiku yuki ga hutta yooda] yo*

   A   C   H

9. The passive suffix (*r*)*are* and the causative suffix (*s*)*ase* are attached productively to verb stems, deriving a passive form and a causative form.
10. In grammatical analyses of voice in Japanese, the idea of including the causative expression in the category of voice is fairly common. See Teramura (1982) and Sato (2005) for relevant observations.
11. See Masuoka (2006a, 2007) for a detailed analysis.

12. The fact that the *tara(ba)*-form and the *nara(ba)*-form are usually realized as the reduced forms *tara* and *nara* indicates that these are grammaticalized forms.

13. The Old Japanese auxiliary verbs *tari* and *nari* are said to express temporality and speaker's judgement. See Kobayashi (1996) for a detailed analysis of the diachronic change of the *ba*-forms in Japanese.

14. The English terms 'assertive' and 'probable' are Mikami's (1963). Mikami (1963) states that the auxiliary verb *daroo* is used when one makes a mild assertion.

15. It is interesting to note that *daroo* can be used when the speaker wants to draw the hearer's attention to some event or situation, as shown in the following:

> (i) *Hora,*   *asoko*   *ni*   *takai*   *tatemono*   *ga*   *aru*   *daroo.*
>   Look   over there   tall   building   exist
>   'Look! There is a tall building over there.'

16. Takubo (2006, this volume) argues that two classes of *gaigen* expressions should be distinguished, i.e. '*daroo*-class' and '*yooda*-class'.

17. See Masuoka (2006b, 2007) for details.

18. In this connection, see Akatsuka (1992).

19. A typical example of non-compositional subjectivity is the notion of deixis, which is expressed in lexical rather than in structural terms. The verbs *iku* (go) and *kuru* (come), for instance, express the notion of movement in relation to the speaker's location. See Iwasaki (1993) for some relevant observations.

20. Harada (1976) points out that propositional honorifics are used when the propositional part of a sentence contains an NP that refers to a person socially superior to the speaker, while performative honorifics (polite speech) are used when the hearer is a person socially superior to the speaker. Examples of the two types of honorifics from Harada (1976) follow:

> (i) [propositional honorifics]
>   *Sasaki sensei wa watasi ni koo*   *o-hanasi ni nat-ta.*
>   I   this way   Hon-speak-Past
>   'Sasaki sensei told me this way.'
> (ii) [performative honorifics(polite speech)]
>   *Ame ga*   *huri-masi-ta.*
>   rain   fall-Polite-Past
>   'It rained.'

Only propositional honorifics can appear in subordinate clauses, as illustrated below:

> (iii) *Sasaki sensei ga watasi ni koo*   *o-hanasi ni natta koto*   *wa zizitu desu.*
>   I   this way   Hon-speak-Past   Nominalizer fact   Copula
>   'It is true that Sasaki sensei told me this way.'

(iv) *Ame ga   huri-masi-ta   koto   wa   zizitu desu.
     rain   fall-Polite-Past   Nominalizer   fact   Copula
     'It is true that it rained.'

21. See Kudo (1995) for a similar view of grammatical categories.
22. Modality, for instance, is a semantic category at the sentence level, so that modal elements include modal adverbs such as *tabun* (probably) and *saiwai* (fortunately).
23. See Masuoka (1987, 2004, 2008) for the details of the concept of type of predication.
24. See Carlson and Pelletier (1995) and Kageyama (2006) for a similar distinction, i.e. 'the stage-level predication vs the individual-level predication'.
25. An example that indicates the significance of the concept of type of predication is passivization in Japanese. We need to make a distinction between the 'event-predication passive' and the 'property-predication passive'. See Masuoka (1987) and Kageyama (2006) for details.
26. See Ide (2006) in this respect.

References

Akatsuka, N. (1992). Japanese modals are conditionals. In D. Brentari et al. (eds). *The Joy of Grammar*. Amsterdam and Philadelphia: John Benjamins: 1–10.
Bally, C. (1932). *Linguistique Générale et Linguistique Française*. Berne: Francke Verlag.
Bondarko, A. V. (1991). *Functional Grammar: a Field Approach*. Amsterdam and Philadelphia: John Benjamins.
Carlson, G. N. and F. J. Pelletier (eds) (1995). *The Generic Book*. Chicago: University of Chicago Press.
Chung, S. and A. Timberlake (1985). Tense, aspect, and mood. In T. Shopen (ed.), *Language Typology and Syntactic Description*. Cambridge: Cambridge University Press: 202–58.
Dik, S. (1989). *The Theory of Functional Grammar: Part 1*. Dordrecht: Foris Publications.
Fillmore, C. J. (1968). The case for case. In E. Bach and R. Harms (eds), *Universals in Linguistic Theory*. New York: Holt, Rinehart, and Winston: 1–88.
Givón, T. (1994). Irrealis and the subjunctive. *Studies in Language* 18, 265–337.
Goldberg, A. E. (1995). *Constructions: a Construction Grammar Approach to Argument Structure*. Chicago: University of Chicago Press.
Grimshaw, J. (1990). *Argument Structure*. Cambridge, Mass.: MIT Press.
Harada, S-I. (1976). Honorifics. In M. Shibatani (ed.), *Japanese Generative Grammar*. New York: Academic Press: 499–561.
Ide, S. (2006). *Wakimae no Goyooron* [Pragmatics of 'Wakimae']. Tokyo: Taishukan Shoten.
Iwasaki, S. (1993). *Subjectivity in Grammar and Discourse*. Amsterdam and Philadelphia: John Benjamins.
Kageyama, T. (2006). Property description as a voice phenomenon. In T. Tsunoda and T. Kageyama (eds), *Voice and Grammatical Relations*. Amsterdam and Philadelphia: John Benjamins: 85–114.

Kobayashi, K. (1996). *Nihongo Zyooken-hyoogensi no Kenkyuu* [Studies on the History of Japanese Conditionals]. Tokyo: Hitsuji Shobo.

Kudo, M. (1995). *Asupekuto-tensu Taikei to Tekusuto* [Aspect–Tense System and Text]. Tokyo: Hitsuji Shobo.

Levin, B. and M. Rappaport Hovav (2005). *Argument Realization*. Cambridge: Cambridge University Press.

Lyons, J. (1968). *Introduction to Theoretical Linguistics*. Cambridge: Cambridge University Press.

Lyons, J. (1977). *Semantics 2*. Cambridge: Cambridge University Press.

Masuoka, T. (1987). *Meidai no Bunpoo* [A Grammar of Proposition]. Tokyo: Kuroshio Shuppan.

Masuoka, T. (2004). Nihongo no syudai: zyozyutu no ruikei no kanten kara [Topic constructions in Japanese: from the viewpoint of predication type]. In T. Masuoka (ed.), *Syudai no Taisyoo* [Contrastive Studies on Topic Constructions]. Tokyo: Kuroshio Shuppan: 3–17.

Masuoka, T. (2006a). Nihongo ni okeru zyooken-keisiki no bunka [On the diversification of conditional forms in Japanese). In T. Masuoka (ed.), *Zyoken-hyogen no Taisyoo* [Contrastive Studies on Conditionals]. Tokyo: Kuroshio Shuppan: 31–46.

Masuoka, T. (2006b). *Tai*-kobun ni okeru imi no kakutyoo [On the meaning extension of the *tai*-construction]. In T. Masuoka et al. (eds), *Nihongo Bunpoo no Sin-tihei 2* [New Horizons in Japanese Grammar 2]. Tokyo: Kuroshio Shuppan: 63–76.

Masuoka, T. (2007). *Nihongo Modariti Tankyuu* [Investigations of Japanese Modality]. Tokyo: Kuroshio Shuppan.

Masuoka, T. (2008). Zyozyutu-ruikeiron ni mukete [Toward a theory of types of predication]. In T. Masuoka (ed.), *Zyozyutu-ruikeiron* [A Theory of Types of Predication]. Tokyo: Kuroshio Shuppan: 3–18.

Mikami, A. (1942). Gohoo-kenkyuu e no iti-teisi [An essay on Japanese grammatical inquiry]. *Kotoba* 4, 4–24.

Mikami, A. (1963). *Nihongo no Koobun* [Japanese Constructions]. Tokyo: Kuroshio Shuppan.

Minami, F. (1974). *Gendai Nihongo no Koozoo* [The Structure of Modern Japanese]. Tokyo: Taishukan Shoten.

Minami, F. (1993) *Gendai Nihongo Bunpoo no Rinkaku* [The Outline of Modern Japanese Grammar]. Tokyo: Taishukan Shoten.

Mithun, M. (1999). *The Languages of Native North America*. Cambridge: Cambridge University Press.

Miyazaki, K. et al. (2002). *Modariti* [Modality]. Tokyo: Kuroshio Shuppan.

Moriyama, T. et al. (2000). *Modariti* [Modality]. Tokyo: Iwanami Shoten.

Narrog, H. (2005). On defining modality again. *Language Sciences* 27, 165–92.

Palmer, F. R. (2001). *Mood and Modality*. Cambridge: Cambridge University Press.

Sato, T. (2005). *Zidoosi-bun to Tadoosi-bun no Imiron* [Semantics of Intransitive and Transitive Sentences]. Tokyo: Kasama Shoin.

Takubo, Y. (2006). Nihongo Zyooken-bun to Modariti [Japanese conditionals and modality]. PhD dissertation, Kyoto University.

Teramura, H. (1982). *Nihongo no Sintakusu to Imi I* [Syntax and Semantics of Japanese I]. Tokyo: Kuroshio Shuppan.

Teramura, H. (1984) *Nihongo no Sintakusu to Imi II* [Syntax and Semantics of Japanese II]. Tokyo: Kuroshio Shuppan.

Traugott, E. C. (1989) On the rise of epistemic meanings in English: an example of subjectification in semantic change. *Language* 65, 31–55.

3
West meets East: a Kindaichian Approach to Subjective Modality

Lars Larm

Introduction

'Modality is concerned with the status of the proposition that describes the event' (Palmer 2001: 1). Consider the following examples:

(1) *Ken   ga   ik-e!*[1]
    Ken   NOM   go-IMP
    (lit.) 'Ken go!'

(2) *Ken   ga   ika-na-kute   wa   ik-e-na-i.*
    Ken   NOM   go-NEG-GER   TOP   go-POT-NEG-NPAST
    'Ken must go.'

(3) *Ken   wa   ik-u   daroo.*
    Ken   TOP   go-NPAST   CONJ
    'I guess Ken will go.'

(4) *Ken   wa   ik-u   hazu   da.*
    Ken   TOP   go-NPAST   ASSUM   COP.NPAST
    'Ken is expected to go.'

(5) *Ken   wa   ik-u   rashi-i.*
    Ken   TOP   go-NPAST   EXEV-NPAST
    'It seems that Ken is going.'

(6) *Ken   wa   ik-u   soo   da.*
    Ken   TOP   go-NPAST   QUOT   COP.NPAST
    'I hear that Ken is going.'

The final markers in these sentences qualify the content 'Ken goes' in terms of factuality. The imperative in (1) and the obligative construction in (2) are markers of 'deontic modality', which pertains to notions such as 'obligation', 'prohibition' or 'permission'. The conjectural marker in (3) and the assumptive in (4) have to do with knowledge and belief, and are thus 'epistemic'. The last two expressions, the external evidence marker *rashii* in (5), and the quotative *soo da* in (6), are 'evidentials' and say something about the source of the information.

The classification above is based on meaning, which is, of course, perfectly acceptable. However, in order to get a more complete picture of a modal expression it is necessary to consider two additional perspectives: the form of the expression and its degree of subjectivity. For example, the imperative marker in (1) is an inflectional suffix and the obligative in (2) is an analytic expression. Further, the difference in meaning between these two markers can be explained partly by saying that the former encodes subjective deontic modality and the latter objective deontic modality (see Kindaichi 1953a: 224 and Lyons 1983a: 101). That is, the imperative is always deictically anchored to the here and now of the speaker, while no such restriction applies to the obligative.

In Japan, the distinction between subjective and objective modality has been well known since the 1950s, although the terminology used is not the same as in Western frameworks. Since then the most distinctive characteristic of the indigenous theories on modality has been the emphasis upon subjectivity. This chapter attempts to contribute to this debate by arguing for a distributional approach in which the elusive distinction between subjective and objective modality is subjected to scrutiny by the employment of a battery of overt tests, which are adopted from both the Japanese and the general literature. These diagnostics are designed to ensure that the theoretical distinction rests on empirical foundations.

The theoretical foundation of the present work is built, to a large extent, on the conceptual framework developed by Haruhiko Kindaichi and subsequent Japanese grammarians taking the same theoretical approach. These scholars have highlighted the fact that the expression of subjectivity permeates linguistic coding – a theoretical insight that presents itself directly from the structural facts of Japanese. As for sources within the frame of general linguistic and semantic theory, I am particularly theoretically indebted to John Lyons.

The chapter is structured as follows. Section 3.1 provides a basic theoretical overview of various aspects of modality, including definitions and terminology. The subjective/objective dichotomy is discussed in section 3.2, with particular reference to the ideas of Kindaichi. Next, in section 3.3, the achievements of the Japanese grammarians are put into the larger context of general theoretical linguistics and the philosophy of language. This leads to section 3.4 where a battery of tests used for determining the degree of subjectivity of modal expressions is introduced, and these diagnostics are then applied in section 3.5 to the conjectural *daroo*, which displays a highly subjective character. Then, in section 3.6, a first attempt to establish a three-way taxonomy of the whole modal system is put forward. In the final section, I emphasize the importance of a structural and empirical approach in the context of analysing modals, and then conclude the chapter with an indication of how the approach can be further extended.

3.1   What is modality?[2]

Before attempting to define modality, we need to make clear the distinction between 'notional' and 'encoded' meanings. The importance of drawing this line was pointed out already in 1790 by James Gregory (quoted in Leclerc 2002: 78):

> [...] the moods of verbs may be considered in two different points of view; either *with relation to any particular human language*, or *with relation to human thought*, which must be supposed the same in all ages and nations. For the sake of distinctness, I shall call the expression of them, by inflection or otherwise in language, *grammatical moods*; and the thoughts, or combination of thoughts, though not always, or perhaps never expressed in the same way, I shall call *energies*, or *modifications*, or *moods of thought*.

Essentially the same point was made by Jespersen (1924: 313), who said that mood 'is a syntactic, not a notional category'. And later on, after having discussed different kinds of modal notions, he concluded that 'there are many "moods" if once one leaves the safe ground of verbal forms actually found in a language' (ibid.: 321).[3]

This 'notional' versus 'coded' dichotomy is, more generally, a crucial one in linguistic typology, and it can be applied to other categories as well. For instance, in his work on grammatical roles and relations, Palmer (1994: 4–6) emphasizes the importance of not confusing grammatical and notional roles. It follows naturally that an investigation of modality should be consistent with this general approach. However, there are works, within both the general and the indigenous Japanese tradition, that do not lay particular stress on this distinction, which is particularly unfortunate in an intricate and complicated field of research such as modality.

Yet a further theoretical distinction should be drawn. It is important to distinguish between 'semantic' and 'notional' categories. 'Semantics', then, is what the linguistic encoding means, that is, it presupposes that we are talking about the meaning of certain forms in a certain language. The word 'notional', on the other hand, refers to the typological, cognitive category, which is independent of any particular language. For example, the notional category underlying tense is the universal concept of 'time', which is independent of individual languages. However, when this category manifests itself linguistically in, for instance, certain tense forms of the verb, then the meaning of these forms can be discussed in terms of 'semantics'.

After these clarifications, we can now attempt a definition of the notional category underlying modality. Compared to a category such as tense, which is fairly easy to define by saying that it pertains to 'time', modality is considerably more elusive. It is even difficult to prove the existence of a unified and universal category. In Palmer's wording (1999a: 229):

> The main difficulty with establishing modality as a cross-linguistic category is that, although there are considerable similarities between what appear to be the modal systems of different languages, the semantics is often vague and diffuse, and there is no single semantic feature with which modality can be correlated in the way that a tense can be regarded as the grammatical expression or 'grammaticalization' of time.

Thus, it is hardly surprising that an array of definitions have been put forward over the years. Palmer lists the following proposals (1999a: 229):

1. attitudes and opinions of the speaker
2. speech acts
3. subjectivity
4. non-factivity
5. non-assertion
6. possibility and necessity
7. with special reference to the English modal verbs, a group of concepts that include possibility, necessity, permission, obligation, volition and ability.

Considering the vast literature on the subject, an attempt to single out the major standpoints may run the risk of overgeneralization; but, broadly speaking, we may distinguish the following two main theoretical currents. On the one hand, some scholars emphasize the notion of subjectivity. Jespersen (1924: 313), for instance, says that 'moods' express 'certain attitudes of the mind of the speaker towards the content of the sentence'. This view is also common among Japanese scholars (however, see, for example, Onoe 2001 for a dissenting position). On the other hand, there are those advocating a 'possible worlds' or 'reality' versus 'unreality' type of approach. For example, Kiefer (1999: 223) states:

> The essence of 'modality' consists in the relativization of the validity of sentence meanings to a set of possible worlds. Talk about possible worlds can thus be construed as talk about ways in which people could conceive the world to be different.

Palmer's view is akin to the latter position, especially in his later writings (1999b and 2001), where the distinction between *realis* and *irrealis* plays an important role. He explains these terms by saying that 'in terms of modal status, propositions may be regarded either as "real"/"factual" or as "unreal"/"non-factual"' (1999b: 235). Regardless of which of these two positions one adheres to, the important thing is that in adopting one or the other, one is consistent within that framework. Thus, if one takes the subjectivity approach, then it follows that expressions such as interjections and illocutionary force markers must be included in the category of modality. Some scholars within the Japanese tradition use the term 'modality' in this way, and, as long as modality in such an analysis consistently refers to performativity or illocutionary force, then this is merely a terminological point.

The view taken here is that modality and subjectivity are quite different notions. It is, however, possible to reconcile the *realis/irrealis* and the 'subjectivity' approaches by saying that modality has to do with unreality or non-factivity, but that the dimension of subjectivity also has to be taken into account in order to yield a precise semantic description of a modal marker. To illustrate this point, consider the following example:

(7) *Kare wa   kuru   daroo.*
     he   TOP   come.NPAST   CONJ
     'I think he will come.'

The conjectural particle *daroo* 'I think' displays a dual character. It encodes the epistemic modal notion of a 'conjecture', while simultaneously expressing subjectivity (for details, see section 3.5). Thus, as this example shows, both modality (i.e. 'non-factivity') and subjectivity can be encoded linguistically in the same form. And if something is encoded, then it is part of the semantics of the expression. It is important to emphasize, however, that the fact that both subjectivity and modality can be coded into the same form in examples such as (7) does not mean that they are the same thing. Some, but by no means all, modal markers co-encode modality ('non-factivity') and subjectivity.

My proposal, then, is that modal expressions can be analysed from three perspectives: their meanings, their forms and their degree of subjectivity. Later on in this chapter the particle *daroo* will be used as a test case to illustrate the details of such a three-way analysis. To anticipate the conclusion, it will be suggested that *daroo* can be characterized as follows:

Meaning:	conjectural
Form:	particle
Degree of subjectivity:	high

To provide an approximate semantic description of the marker to see where it fits in the overall modal system is not too problematic. In the case of *daroo*, for example, we can say that it has a conjectural meaning, and that as such it can be placed in the subsystem of epistemic modals. Nor do the formal properties pose any major difficulties; *daroo* does not inflect, and can accordingly be characterized as a particle.[4] But, the question of how to establish the degree of subjectivity requires careful consideration. At this stage of the analysis care must be taken, since the notion of subjectivity is an elusive one, and it is easy to get lost in the philosophical literature on this topic. The meaning of this key term must be clarified and defined, and this is the task of the following two sections.

3.2 Kindaichi

As stated earlier, the distinction between subjective and objective modality has been well known in Japan for about 50 years, although the terminology differs from that of general linguistic frameworks. Starting in the 1950s, much progress was being made as a result of the work of scholars such as Kindaichi (1953a, b), Watanabe (1953), Haga (1954),

Mikami (1972 [1953], 1972 [1959]), Minami (1993, 1997), Teramura (1984, 1992, 1993) and Sawada (1975, 1978, 1993). Through such research, the distinction between propositional (objective) and non-propositional (subjective) content was made explicit, and the indigenous term *chinjutsu*, which was originally used in the meaning of 'predication' or 'unification', started to be used in the sense of subjective modality or illocutionary force. The dichotomy of 'dictum' and 'modus' also entered the discussion and is used in a similar way, with the word 'modus' referring to the subjective part of the sentence (for details, see Narrog in this volume).

Although all the above-mentioned scholars certainly deserve due recognition, the attention here is focused on Kindaichi, whose seminal articles on what he labels *fuhenka jodooshi* 'non-inflectional auxiliaries' (1953a, b) have had a lasting influence on Japanese theories of modality and set the stage for subsequent research. The central question posed by Kindaichi is what it means to say that a certain expression is subjective. Earlier, the traditional grammarian Motoki Tokieda (1941 *et passim*) had drawn a distinction between *shi* and *ji* expressions, considering the former category of words to be objective and the latter subjective. However, Tokieda's notion of subjectivity is too broad; even case particles are treated as subjective.

This position is not shared by Kindaichi.[5] He narrows down the range of subjective expressions to the hortative suffix *-oo* (*yoo*), the negative conjectural *mai*, the conjectural particle *daroo*, and the imperative suffix *-e* (*-ro*), and he notes that in being exclusively subjective they resemble final particles and interjections.[6]

Let us take a look at the main arguments that Kindaichi puts forward to support his position. First, subjective markers are morphologically invariable; they are only found in their *shuushikei* 'predicative' form, which is a feature that they share with the subjective *kandooshi* 'interjections' and *kandoojoshi* 'final particles'. Kindaichi explains that this common characteristic of being unchangeable in form reflects a semantic similarity, namely that they all '*subjectively express the speaker's state of mind at the time of the utterance*' (1953a: 213, my translation and emphasis). On the other hand, elements that inflect, for example the evidential *rashii* and the negative suffix *-nai*, are objective expressions, and in this sense they are similar to verbs and adjectives. Since objective expressions denote a state of affairs, one can assume that this state can be talked about and that it can be negated or put in the past tense. It also follows naturally that such expressions have conditional, adverbial and *mizen* 'irrealis' forms, and that they can be placed in an adnominal position. Subjective expressions, on the other hand, cannot be modified by negation and pastness, and this is reflected in the fact that they have only one form.

Kindaichi repeatedly comes back to the point that objective expressions denote some kind of 'state'. Therefore, a seemingly subjective expression such as an evidential turns out to express objective notions such as 'is in the state of being conjectured' or 'is in the state of looking as if' or 'has the property of looking as if'.

Second, exclusively subjective elements always appear in sentence-final position, while no such restriction applies to objective expressions.[7] This can also be expressed, in present-day terminology, by saying that subjective modality takes scope over objective modality.

Next, let us take a look at some of Kindaichi's examples and detailed analyses. One of the strengths of Kindaichi's account is that he uses overt, grammatical features to substantiate his points. For instance, the subjective hortative morpheme -oo (yoo) is contrasted with the objective way of expressing the same idea using the structural noun tsumori 'intention' (1953a: 216):[8,9]

(8) Watashi   wa   Fujisan   e   nobor-oo/ * ta.
     I   TOP   Mount Fuji   to   climb-HORT
     'I shall climb Mount Fuji.' (no corresponding past form)

(9) Watashi   wa   Fujisan   e   nobor-u   tsumori
     I   TOP   Mount Fuji   to   climb-NPAST   intention
     da/datta.
     COP.NPAST/COP.PAST
     'It is/was my intention to climb Mount Fuji.'

In example (8) the hortative form of the verb is used, and in (9) we find the noun tsumori 'intention' followed by the copula. Now, as I have indicated in the examples, it would not have been possible to put (8) in the past tense, but example (9) shows no such restriction; and, therefore, of these two sentences it is only the first one that can be regarded as subjective. This amounts to saying that the past tense can take scope over objective expressions but not over subjective elements.

Another example is the evidential rashii '(it) seems', which must be analysed as objective, since it inflects. Kindaichi notes, for instance, the existence of the form rashikatta '(it) seemed' (1953a: 236). Thus, the evidential rashii is different from a subjective modal fuhenka jodooshi 'non-inflectional auxiliary' like daroo, whose essentially subjective character is formally reflected in the fact that the form is morphologically invariable.[10] Moreover, the evidentiality expressed by *rashii* does not have to originate from the speaker, and for this reason it is possible for a question marker to take scope over this form, as in (Kindaichi 1953a: 236):

(10)   *Kare* *mo* *ik-u*   *rashi-i*   *kai*
      he   also go-NPAST EXEV-NPAST QP
      'Does it seem as if he is going too?'

Here the speaker asks the addressee about what he or she thinks about something, so the origin of the evidentiality can be traced to the addressee, not to the speaker.[11]

From the discussion so far, two important points should be noted. First, Kindaichi defines and delimits the notion of subjectivity, and second, he uses overt features of the language to illustrate his points. A third feature of Kindaichi's conceptual framework, which seems to have passed unnoticed in the literature on this subject, is the clear distinction between meaning and usage. He does not, of course, use the terms semantics and pragmatics, but instead he employs the Saussurean notions of *langue* and *parole* to express the same distinction. Kindaichi explains that if we view an expression from a *parole* point of view, then there must always be an element of subjectivity. On the other hand, a sentence of the *langue* may or may not contain a subjective element (1953b: 259). It is thus clear that Kindaichi invoked the *langue–parole* dichotomy in a way that matches the distinction between semantics and pragmatics.[12]

3.3   The general relevance of the Japanese grammarians

The conceptual framework developed by Kindaichi, and subsequent Japanese grammarians of the same theoretical orientation, has given rise to an approach in which pragmatic notions are expressed in terms of grammar.[13] This way of looking at language resonates well with recent developments in linguistic theory and the philosophy of language.

Perhaps John Lyons is the general linguist who has most strongly advocated the importance of subjectivity (1977, 1981, 1982, 1983a, b, 1995). He says (1981: 240):

The inadequacy of truth-conditional semantics as a total theory, not only of utterance-meaning, but also of sentence-meaning, derives ultimately from its restriction to propositional content and its inability to handle the phenomenon of subjectivity. Self-expression cannot be reduced to the expression of propositional knowledge and beliefs.

Lyons uses the labels 'subjective modality' and 'objective modality' (1981: 237–8, *et passim*).[14] The primary question to ask, then, is exactly what is meant by the word 'subjective'. A partial answer has already been given in the previous section, but let us elaborate further on this question. There are three points to consider. First, subjective modality is anchored to the speaker, as Lyons (1995: 337) makes clear when he defines 'locutionary subjectivity' as

[. . .] the locutionary agent's (the speaker's or writer's, the utterer's) expression of himself or herself in the act of utterance: locutionary subjectivity is, quite simply, self-expression in the use of language.

Second, while objective modality is propositional and truth-conditional, subjective modality is non-propositional and non-truth-conditional. Third, as we saw in the previous section, Kindaichi observes that subjective markers '*subjectively express the speaker's state of mind at the time of the utterance*' (1953a: 213, my translation and emphasis). Thus it seems that the difference between 'objective' and 'subjective' expressions corresponds to the distinction Austin (1975) drew between 'constative' and 'performative' utterances, and the three features 'speaker-oriented', 'non-truth-conditional' and 'momentaneous' also capture the nature of performative utterances. In Austin's wording: 'There is something which is *at the moment of uttering being done by the person uttering*' (1975: 60, emphasis in original). This connection between subjectivity and performativity has been noted in the literature by, for instance, Verstraete, who claims that '[. . .] the mechanisms behind the various criteria that have been proposed can be explained in terms of one basic functional principle of *performativity*' (2001: 1506, emphasis in original).

Linguistic subjectivity has also received some attention in syntactic theories. Already in 1970 Ross put forward the hypothesis that all sentences have a performative component in their deep structure. Speech act projections also play an important role in recent works such as, for example, Cinque (1999), Tenny (2006) and Speas and Tenny (2003) (see also Kizu in this volume). In Tenny's words: '[. . .] there is a *syntax of sentience* at the outer periphery of the clause where the syntax/discourse interface is located and where natural language encodes mind' (2006: 281, emphasis in the original). Similar ideas are also found in functional grammar, although the terminology is different (see Van Valin 2005).

3.4 Testing the subjectivity

We have seen that linguistic subjectivity is an issue of high importance to linguists and philosophers. The main concern then, in the context of the present work, is how one can determine the degree of subjectivity of a given modal marker. Much of the answer to this question has already been hinted at, but we are now in a position to complete the picture. The following nine criteria, adopted from both the Japanese and the general literature on modality, can be employed to determine the degree of subjectivity:

1. Past tense cannot take scope over subjective modals (Kindaichi 1953a, Sawada 1975, Palmer 1990, Nitta 1999, Sugimura 2000).
2. Negation cannot take scope over subjective modality (Sawada 1975, Nakau 1979, Nitta 1999, Sugimura 2000) (anticipated in Kindaichi 1953a).
3. Subjective modals (in Japanese) cannot be adnominalized (Kindaichi 1953a, Sugimura 2000).
4. 'Subjective modality always has wider scope than objective modality' (Lyons 1977: 808). In Japanese this is manifested by the fact that exclusively subjective markers always appear in sentence-final position, while no such restriction applies to objective expressions (Kindaichi 1953a).
5. Subjective modality cannot be embedded in the antecedent of conditional sentences (Sawada 1975, Lyons 1977, Takayama 2002) (anticipated in Hare 1970).
6. Subjective modal markers (in Japanese) cannot precede the causal connective *node* 'because' (Kinsui, personal communication, Takayama 2002) (anticipated in Nagano 1952 and Minami 1993, 1997).
7. Subjective modality cannot be questioned (Kindaichi 1953a, Sawada 1975, Nakau 1979, Sugimura 2000).
8. Subjective modality cannot appear in complement clauses of propositional attitude verbs, e.g. *know* (Lyons 1983a).[15]
9. 'No simple utterance may contain more than a single subjective epistemic modality (though this single modality may be expressed [...] in two or more places)' (Lyons 1977: 808).

In the next section I will show how these tests can be applied. Owing to limitations of space, the analysis will be confined to the epistemic modal *daroo*, whose subjective behaviour is well known in the literature.

3.5 The case of *daroo*

This section provides a descriptive structural account of the conjectural particle *daroo*. This marker is of particular interest from the point of view of subjectivity and has received a fair amount of attention in the literature (see e.g. Akatsuka 1990, Moriyama 1992, Larm 2005). *Daroo* will be analysed with respect to meaning, form and subjectivity. Special attention will be paid to the grammatical properties relating to the degree of subjectivity, and the diagnostics identified in the previous section will be used.

3.5.1 Meaning

Daroo indicates that the speaker is making an epistemic judgement about the propositional content of the sentence. It can be translated as 'I think', 'I suppose' or 'I guess'.[16] Consider the following examples:

(11) *Ashita   wa   ame   ga   fur-u   daroo.*
     tomorrow   TOP   rain   NOM   fall-NPAST   CONJ
     'I suppose it will rain tomorrow.'

(12) *Moo   tsui-ta   daroo.*
     already   arrived-PAST   CONJ
     'I suppose (s/he) has already arrived.'

Daroo can combine with adverbs such as *tabun* 'perhaps', *osoraku* 'probably' and *sazo* 'surely':

(13) *Ken   wa   tabun   ko-na-i   daroo.*
     Ken   TOP   perhaps   come-NEG-NPAST   CONJ
     'Perhaps Ken won't come.'

(14) *Osoraku   okor-u   daroo.*
     probably   get angry-NPAST   CONJ
     '(S/he) will probably get angry.'

(15) *Sazo   onaka   ga   sui-ta   daroo.*
     surely   stomach   NOM   empty-PAST   CONJ
     'You must be hungry.'

3.5.2   Grammatical properties

Daroo is a particle with the polite form *deshoo*.[17] It follows the non-past or past form of verbs as in the examples above, and it can also come after the non-past or past form of adjectives, as in (16):

(16)   *Ken   wa   haya-i/hayakat-ta   daroo.*
      Ken   TOP   fast-NPAST/fast-PAST   CONJ
      'I suppose Ken is/was fast.'

Daroo also follows directly after the stem of nominal adjectives and after nouns, as in (17) and (18) below. We can consider this as a case where the copula is phonologically null, and accordingly represent this zero-copula with the symbol Ø:

(17)   *Kore   wa   benri   Ø   daroo.*
      this   TOP   useful   COP.NPAST   CONJ
      'I suppose this is useful.'

(18)   *Are   wa   fune   Ø   daroo.*
      that   TOP   ship   COP.NPAST   CONJ
      'I suppose that is a ship.'

However, if the event described has past time reference, then *daroo* appears after the overtly expressed past tense form of the copula, as can be seen in (19) and (20):

(19)   *Kore   wa   benri   dat-ta   daroo.*
      this   TOP   useful   COP-PAST   CONJ
      'I suppose this was useful.'

(20)   *Are   wa   fune   dat-ta   daroo.*
      that   TOP   ship   COP-PAST   CONJ
      'I suppose that was a ship.'

Other possible positions are after an adverb, after the nominalizer *no*, and also after the connective particle *kara* 'because', as is illustrated below. The situation here is reminiscent of that in (17) and (18), where the presence of an unexpressed copula was assumed:

(21)   *Pabu   ga   shimar-u   made moo   sukoshi Ø   daroo.*
      pub   NOM   close-NPAST   until   more   a little   COP.NPAST   CONJ
      'I suppose the pub will close before long.'

(22) Ken   wa   naze   itsumo   uso   o   tsuk-u   no
      Ken   TOP   why   always   lie   ACC tell-NPAST NML
      Ø   daroo.
      COP.NPAST CONJ
      'I wonder why Ken is always lying.'

(23) Okusan ga   kowa-i   kara   Ø   daroo.
      wife   NOM   scary-NPAST because COP.NPAST   CONJ
      'I suppose it is because he is afraid of his wife.'

The form can also occur on its own, as is illustrated below:

(24) a. Ken   wa   ko-na-i   to   omo-u.
          Ken   TOP   come-NEG-NPAST   COMP   think-NPAST
          'I don't think Ken will come.'
      b. Daroo   ne.
          CONJ   FP
          'I suppose (that Ken won't come).'

3.5.3 Subjectivity

Kindaichi (1953a) states that *daroo* is essentially subjective and that this characteristic is formally reflected in the fact that the form is morphologically invariable. Let us now determine the degree of subjectivity by applying the criteria from the previous section.

First, *daroo* does not have a past tense form, nor can the modal expression be propositionalized by using the past tense of the copula. This is illustrated by Kato and Fukuchi (1989: 115) in the following example, which is seriously ungrammatical:

(25) * Kanojo wa   ronbun o   kakiage-ta   daroo dat-ta.
        she   TOP   thesis ACC write up-PAST   CONJ   COP-PAST
        (Presumably intended to mean) 'It was probable that she wrote up her thesis.'

Second, negation cannot take scope over *daroo*. In other words, the modality itself cannot be negated, as we can see in the following ungrammatical example (Kato and Fukuchi 1989: 115):

(26) * Kare wa   shiken ni   toot-ta   daroo (de) na-i.
        He   TOP   exam   in   pass-PAST   CONJ   (COP).NEG-NPAST
        (Probably intended to mean something like) 'I do not suppose that he passed the exam.'

Third, *daroo* resists adnominalization. However, there are data that seem to provide counter-evidence for this view. Let us therefore consider some examples from the literature where *daroo* appears in adnominal position in relative clauses:[18]

(27) *Kare ga   kuru   daroo koto wa   kii-te   i-ru.*
     he   NOM come.NPAST CONJ fact TOP hear-GER be-NPAST
     'I have heard that he probably will come.' (Saji 1989: 155)

(28) *Kore ga   seikoo suru   daroo koto wa   utagainai.*
     this NOM success do.NPAST CONJ fact TOP no doubt
     'There is no doubt that this will probably come out well.'
     (Yamaguchi 2001: 460)

(29) *Kare ga   shoochi suru   daroo koto wa   machigainai.*
     he   NOM consent do.NPAST CONJ fact TOP no mistake
     'There is no doubt that he will probably agree.' (Tanaka 1971:
     468)

In these sentences, *daroo* is modifying the structural noun *koto*. My informant found them somewhat peculiar, but would not mark them as ungrammatical. Examples like these seem to be borderline cases; they are not completely unacceptable, but there is something strange about them.[19] Furthermore, Yamaguchi (2001: 460) presents an example where *daroo* adnominalizes to an ordinary noun:

(30) *Kare ga   saigo ni kuru   daroo hito   da.*
     he   NOM end in come.NPAST CONJ person COP.NPAST
     'He is the man who probably will be the last to come.'

However, my informant considers this sentence to be 'odd'.

Fourth, *daroo* cannot be followed by any other modal (or evidential) construction, such as the reportative *soo da* 'I hear' or *rashii* 'It seems':

(31) * *Ame ga   fur-u   daroo soo   da.*
     rain NOM fall-NPAST CONJ QUOT COP.NPAST
     (Intended to mean) 'I hear that it will probably rain.'

(32) * *Ame ga   fur-u   daroo rashi-i.*
     rain NOM rain-NPAST CONJ seem-NPAST
     (Intended to mean) 'It seems that it is probably going to rain.'

The unacceptability of the above sentences stems from the general principle that objective modality cannot take scope over subjective modality. Of course, this is not to say that *daroo* cannot co-occur with other modals. For instance, it can be placed after the assumptive predicate extension *hazu da*:

(33) *Nanika*   *at-ta*   *hazu*   Ø   *daroo.*
      something   be-PAST   ASSUM   COP.NPAST   CONJ
      'I think that something must have happened.'

The point here is that *hazu da* is an objective modal (see Larm 2006: 148–52). Thus, this example illustrates that subjective epistemic modality can take scope over objective epistemic modality.

Fifth, *daroo* cannot appear in the antecedent of a conditional sentence:

(34) * *Moshi*   *ame*   *ga*   *fur-u*   *daroo*   *nara*   *ashita*   *no*   *haikingu*   *wa*
      if   rain   NOM   fall-NPAST   CONJ   if   tomorrow   GEN   hiking   TOP

      chuushi   *da.*
      cancellation   COP.NPAST
      (Presumably intended to mean) 'If it is probable that it will rain tomorrow then the hiking will be called off.' (Takayama 2002: 42)

The sixth point relates to the two causal connectives *kara* and *node*, which both can be translated as 'because'. The difference between these connectives has been extensively debated (for example, Nagano (1952), Miyagawa and Nakamura (1991), Kanbayashi (1994) and Iwasaki (1995) are articles devoted specifically to this topic). A detailed discussion would take us too far afield from our present purposes, but the gist of the matter is that clauses preceding *kara* have subjectivity, while clauses preceding *node* do not. And, in this connection, the main point to note is that scholars such as Nagano (1952: 37), Kinsui (personal communication) and Minami (1993: 88, 97; 1997: 38) have observed that *daroo* can precede *kara* but not *node*.[20] This distributional difference is illustrated in the following example:

(35) *Haha*   *ga*   *kuru*   *daroo*   * *node/kara*   *hayaku*   *kaer-u.*
      mother   NOM   come.NPAST   CONJ   because/because   early   go home-NPAST
      'I'll leave early because I think my mother is coming (to visit me).'

Thus, in the same way as *daroo* has been used to explain the difference between *kara* and *node*, we can, conversely, use these connectives when examining the degree of subjectivity of a certain expression.

Hence, it appears that *daroo* cannot be part of the propositional content of the sentence, and that Japanese grammarians are right in regarding the form as essentially subjective. However, there are some further points that need to be considered.

First, the interrogative particle *ka* can take scope over *daroo*, as in:[21]

(36) *Eri wa kuru   daroo ka.*
     Eri TOP come.NPAST CONJ   QP
     'I wonder if Eri will come.'

In the previous section we noted that subjective modality cannot be questioned. If this is so, then it seems odd that *daroo* can be followed by an interrogative particle. This problem is also noted by Kindaichi (1953a: 236), who argues that the question in this case is directed to the addressee, but that what is being talked about is nevertheless the inference of the speaker. Therefore, the form *daroo ka* does not cause any problems, since the modality can still be said to originate from the speaker. An alternative explanation is offered by Masuoka and Takubo (1992: 135–7), who state that a question directed to an addressee, with the purpose of obtaining information, is accompanied with a rising intonation (see also Moriyama 1999). They also note that a question with *daroo ka* cannot be directed to the addressee (Masuoka and Takubo 1992: 137). Accordingly, example (36) above is unacceptable with a rising intonation. Thus, we need to revise the subjectivity test 7 from section 3.4 above, as follows:

7. In Japanese, subjective modality cannot occur in interrogative sentences *uttered with a rising intonation.*

In the case of *daroo ka*, the situation is clear since this construction is always used to express doubt, but there are also instances where the interrogative particle *ka* might be associated with either a rising or a falling intonation. In any case, however, the important point is that only interrogative sentences with a rising intonation can be used to test the subjectivity of a modal marker. This functional difference relating to the intonational pattern applies to both yes/no questions and wh-questions.

Another seemingly problematic fact is that *daroo* can be followed by the complementizer *to* and the verb *omou* 'think':

(37) *Ashita   wa   ame   ga   fur-u   daroo   to   omo-u.*
     tomorrow TOP rain NOM fall-NPAST   CONJ   COMP think-NPAST
     'I think that it will probably rain tomorrow.'

However, when the psychological predicate *omou* 'think' is in the non-past form, as in the example above, then the subject must be in the first person (cf. Nakau 1979, who points out that *to omou* is used in subjective statements). Accordingly, the function of this construction seems to be to reinforce the subjective modality.[22] That is, the meaning of the above sentence remains basically the same even if we delete *to omou*:

(38) *Ashita   wa   ame   ga   fur-u   daroo.*
     tomorrow TOP rain NOM fall-NPAST   CONJ
     'I think it will rain tomorrow.'

Thus, the *daroo to omou* construction, with the non-past form of the verb *omou* 'think', does not pose a problem for the view that *daroo* is subjective.

It must be mentioned, however, as Hara (2006: 25) observes, that 'the expressive meaning [of *daroo*] can be associated with an agent other than the actual speaker'. This point can be formally proven by the fact that *daroo* can also be followed by *omotte iru* 'be thinking', the stativized version of *omou* 'think', which marks objectivity and accordingly can be used also when the cognitive agent is the third person. Consider Hara's example (2006: 25, modified gloss and translation):

(39) *Mary wa   John ga   kuru   daroo   to   omot-te   i-ru.*
     Mary TOP John NOM come.NPAST CONJ   COMP think-GER   be-NPAST
     'Mary thinks that John will probably come.'

This can be viewed as a case of propositionalization. Furthermore, this is not a case of direct quotation, as Hara makes clear by the following example (2006: 25, modified gloss and translation):

(40) *Mary wa   John ga   watashi   ni   ai   ni*
     Mary TOP John NOM me   DAT meeting DAT

     kuru   daroo   to   omot-te   i-ru.
     come.NPAST CONJ   COMP think-GER   be-NPAST
     'Mary thinks that John will probably come to see me.'

The *watashi* of the embedded clause here refers to the speaker, which would not have been the case had it been a direct quote.[23]

Considering the data presented in this section, it can be concluded that *daroo* can be described as a particle that is used almost exclusively to express subjective epistemic modality. However, although the form is highly subjective, it is important to remember that it can be objectified (propositionalized) when appearing in the clausal complement of the psychological predicate *omotte iru* 'be thinking'.

In short, *daroo* can be described as follows:

Form: particle
Meaning: epistemic: conjectural
Degree of subjectivity: high

3.6   The modal system: a three-way taxonomy

We have seen that modal expressions can be characterized from three points of view: their meaning, their form, and their degree of subjectivity. Here, this model has only been applied on one modal expression, *daroo*, but if the description is extended to include other modal markers, we arrive at a three-way taxonomy of the whole modal system. What follows in this section is merely the report of a first attempt to set up such a taxonomy, based on my previous research. For reasons of space, the empirical data will have to be left out, and the reader is referred to Larm (2006) for details.

The forms available for the expression of modality in Japanese are:

• **Inflections**

  – Literary conjectural *-oo* (*-yoo*)
  – Imperative *-e* (*-ro*)
  – Hortative *-oo* (*-yoo*)
  – Polite imperative *-nasai*

• **Particles**

  – Conjectural *daroo*
  – Negative conjectural *mai*
  – Negative imperative *na*

• **Predicate extensions**

  – Speculative *kamoshirenai*
  – Deductive *ni chigainai*

- Assumptive *hazu da*
- Inferential *yoo da*
- Informal inferential *mitai da*
- External evidence: *rashii*
- Quotative *soo da*
- Moral obligative *beki da*

- **Derivational suffixes**

  - Sensory evidential *-soo da*

- **Analytic expressions**

  - The prohibitive *-te wa ikenai*
  - Obligative *-nakute wa ikenai*
  - Obligative *-nakereba ikenai*
  - Permissive *-te mo ii*

This map shows how modality is overtly encoded in the grammar, and it leads us to the next step, which is a map of the semantic categories expressed.

Generally, the most basic subtypes of modality, which long have been recognized, are epistemic and deontic modality. Epistemic modal markers have to do with knowledge and belief, and deontic modality pertains to notions such as 'obligation', 'prohibition' and 'permission'. However, in order to obtain a more complete picture of modality, in particular when describing the modal system of Japanese, the category of 'evidentiality' needs to be included. Evidential markers say something about the source of the information. Thus, the semantic taxonomy comprises three subsystems: epistemic, deontic and evidential modality, as illustrated below. Palmer (2001) has served as a useful general guideline and point of comparison, and some of his labels of categories have been applied here (for example, 'Speculative', 'Deductive', 'Assumptive'):

- **Epistemic modality**

  - Conjectural
  - Literary conjectural
  - Negative conjectural
  - Speculative
  - Deductive
  - Assumptive

- **Evidential modality**

  - Inferential
  - Informal inferential
  - External evidence
  - Sensory evidential
  - Quotative

- **Deontic modality**

  - Imperative
  - Negative imperative
  - Polite imperative
  - Hortative
  - Moral obligative
  - Prohibitive
  - Obligative
  - Permissive

I do not claim that these are complete descriptions of the grammatical and the semantic systems; as the research on modality develops further, these lists will have to be updated and reviewed. They are intended to be a starting point for further investigations, rather than a fixed structure.

Advancing even further, in the direction of subjectivity, we come closer to the area of pragmatics. However, the tests that have been employed to determine the degree of subjectivity are based on overt features. Therefore, the rigid structural analysis has provided us with an empirical method to say something about an intrinsically deictic and pragmatic phenomenon. The degree of subjectivity of each modal marker is outlined below:

- **Maximum**

  - Imperative -*e (-ro)*   – inflection
  - Negative imperative *na* – particle
  - Polite imperative -*nasai* – inflection

- **High**

  - Conjectural *daroo*   – particle
  - Literary conjectural -*oo (-yoo)* – inflection
  - Hortative -*oo (-yoo)*   – inflection
  - Negative conjectural *mai*   – particle

- **Intermediate**

  - Quotative *soo da* – predicate extension

- **Low**

  - Speculative *kamoshirenai*   – predicate extension
  - Deductive *ni chigainai*   – predicate extension
  - Inferential *yoo da*   – predicate extension
  - Informal inferential *mitai da* – predicate extension
  - External evidence: *rashii*   – predicate extension

- **Zero**

  - Assumptive *hazu da*   – predicate extension
  - Sensory evidential *-soo da*   – derivational suffix
  - Moral obligative *beki da*   – predicate extension
  - Prohibitive *-te wa ikenai*   – analytic expression
  - Obligative *-nakute wa ikenai* – analytic expression
  - Obligative *-nakereba ikenai*   – analytic expression
  - Permissive *-te mo ii*   – analytic expression

We can now see that there is a correspondence, albeit inexact, between the forms of the markers and their degree of subjectivity. One might show this in the form of a tree diagram (see Figure 3.1 on next page).

My conception of the structural representation of subjectivity is close to that of the Japanese linguist Sawada (1975, 1978, 1993). Furthermore, examples can be constructed to illustrate the different layers. In example (41) below, the illocutionary force takes scope over subjective deontic modality, and (42) makes clear the scopal relations between illocutionary force, subjective epistemic modality, objective epistemic modality and objective deontic modality:

(41) *Haya-ku   ik-e   yo!*
     quick-INF   go-IMP   FP
     'Go quickly!'
     (subjective deontic modality – illocutionary force)

(42) *Tabe-te   mo   ii   hazu   Ø   daroo   yo.*
     eat-GER   even   good.NPAST   ASSUM   COP.NPAST   CONJ   FP
     'I suppose it can be assumed that one may eat (it).'
     (objective deontic – objective epistemic – subjective epistemic –
     illocutionary force)

The structures of (41) and (42) can be represented as in Figure 3.2 (a, b).

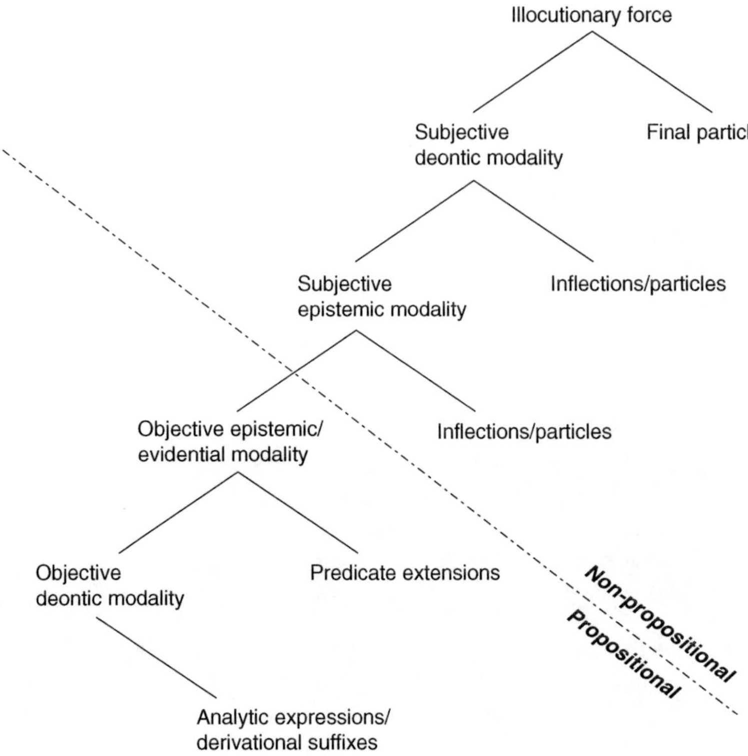

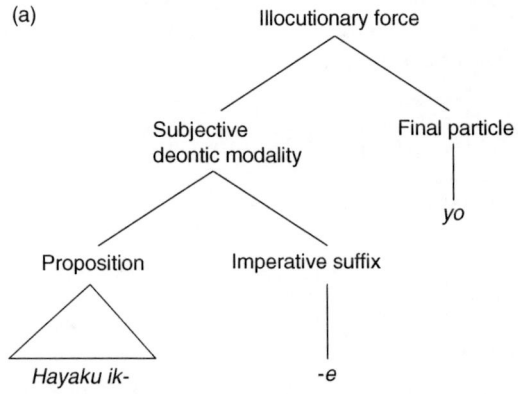

Figure 3.1 The relationship between form and degree of subjectivity

Figure 3.2 (a) Representation of example (41) (b) Representation of example (42)

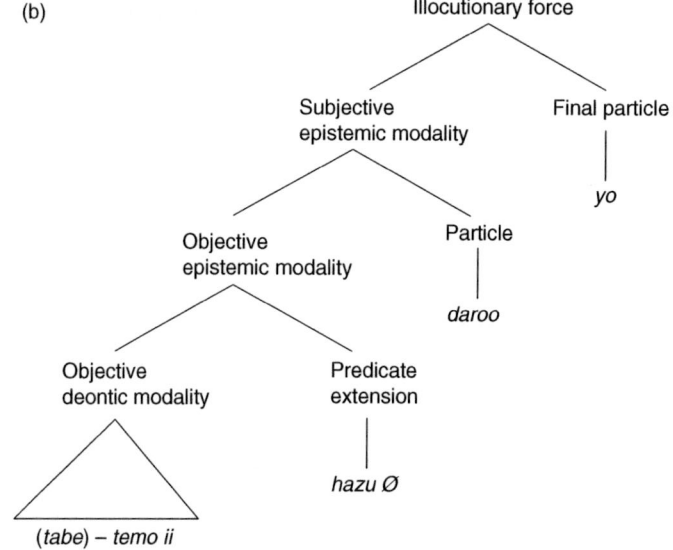

(b)

Figure 3.2   (Continued)

These last observations reconfirm what scholars such as, for example, Kindaichi (1953a, b) and Watanabe (1953) have said about subjectivity, and we thus come back to the indigenous tradition.

3.7   Conclusion and future directions

The synthesis between Western and Japanese scholarship opens up new dimensions for the study of modality, and much can be gained from a revaluation of traditional Japanese linguists, such as Kindaichi, in the light of modern linguistics. The studies conducted by these grammarians have general implications for the understanding of linguistically encoded subjectivity and illocutionary force, and it is hoped that this chapter adds to the significance of their works.

   How, then, can the results presented here be taken further? A provisional answer to this question emerges from a return to the main point of the present discussion. I have argued for the importance of a strictly distributional analysis. The advantage of this kind of approach is that, since the investigation is based on overt features, it is the language itself that guides us to the appropriate semantic description of a particular item. That is, by gradually moving from the overt to the covert we can get a firm grip on even such an elusive notion as subjectivity. The next logical step of my research is, therefore, to consider how this method of close and detailed observation and description can be extended to other notions that have not been dealt with in the present chapter. One possible direction of future research is to explore how notions of 'usage' and 'context', which are, of course, of central importance to pragmatic theory, could be reworked following the descriptive method used here, and a further development of the present work could therefore suggest ways in which pragmaticians should look at these issues. Even the very concept of 'context' itself is in principle amenable to a systematic descriptive approach.

The Japanese language has a lot to offer in this area. In view of this, it follows naturally that a future project should look further into what the Japanese scholars have said in terms of usage. From this different perspective we may extract further theoretical and descriptive insights from them.

Acknowledgements

This chapter is based on my doctoral thesis. I wish to express my sincere gratitude to David Cram and Bjarke Frellesvig, my supervisors, for their constant support and guidance throughout my research. I also owe a great deal of gratitude to Yukinori Takubo, Mary Dalrymple and Satoshi Kinsui for detailed comments and helpful suggestions on my work. Another big thank you goes to the organizers and participants of the conference 'Revisiting Japanese Modality', held at the School of Oriental and African Studies, University of London, in June 2006. In particular, I should like to thank Barbara Pizziconi and Mika Kizu for all their help.

Notes

1. The Hepburn system of romanization is used throughout this chapter, with a few modifications.
2. The literature on modality is extensive. See Palmer (2001) and Hoye (2005), and the references cited there. Hoye (2005) is a two-part review article of contemporary research.
3. A terminological clarification: the traditional label 'mood' is standardly used in the literature to refer only to inflections, such as, for example, imperative verb forms. In both Gregory's and Jespersen's terminologies, however, 'mood' seems to be an umbrella expression meaning 'encoded modality', which encompasses all types of grammaticalized markers.

4. In some works (e.g. Bloch 1946), *daroo* is treated as a form of the copula *da*. However, the distribution of *daroo* is different from that of *da*. The former but not the latter can follow finite forms of verbs and adjectives:

> *Ken   wa   kuru   *da/daroo.*
> Ken   TOP   come.NPAST   COP.NPAST/CONJ
> 'Ken will come/ I suppose Ken will come.'

A more detailed argumentation on this point is given by Okutsu (1993: 75–87).

5. Kindaichi (1953b: 254) remarks that he is in line with Mikami on this point, and also that he is inspired by psychologist William James's view of the nature of relations. However, to say that case particles are objective is a rather obvious point to make, and the problem here is rather the difficulty of understanding what Tokieda had in mind when he classified case particles as being speaker-oriented.

6. In order to make the material more readily accessible to a general linguistic audience, I have modified some details in the terminology. For instance, Kindaichi treats the hortative suffix *-oo* (*yoo*) as an auxiliary, and he does not explicitly present the imperative as the morpheme *-e* (*-ro*). Furthermore, to say that these invariable markers only have the *shuushikei* 'predicative form' may sound peculiar. Nevertheless, these points are not really relevant to his main argument.

7. Final particles can follow the *fuhenka jodooshi* 'non-inflectional auxiliaries'. This fact, which Kindaichi is well aware of, confirms his position that *fuhenka jodooshi* represent an intermediate category between objective elements and final particles. He also notes that *fuhenka jodooshi* can be followed by conjunctional particles, while this is not the case for final particles (1953a: 212).

8. The same line of argument is used for the imperative, which is also, as was mentioned above, included in the category of subjective expressions. The imperative is viewed as the subjective version of objective deontic modal expressions like *-nakereba naranai* and *beki da*. This is in line with Lyons, who also views the imperative as a marker of subjective deontic modality (Lyons 1983a: 101).

9. Structural nouns are nouns that require modification.

10. It should be pointed out that there is a polite form of this particle: *deshoo*. However, this form can be seen as belonging to a different register, rather than being an inflected form of *daroo*. This is also the position taken by Kindaichi (1953a: 238–40).

11. Note that the subjective *daroo* can also be followed by the question particle, but the reason for this combination is quite a different matter. That is, in the case of *daroo ka* it is still the case that the modality originates from the speaker. Kindaichi does not overlook this point either.

12. For details and examples, see Larm (2006: 65–7).

13. It should be emphasized that this does not entail a rejection of the competence–performance distinction. On the contrary, as was pointed out at the end of the previous section, Kindaichi clearly distinguishes between sentence meaning and utterance meaning.

14. A useful survey of the literature on subjective and objective modality can be found in Verstraete (2001).
15. More precisely, Lyons states that epistemic modals, for example the epistemic 'must', can occur in this position, but that the modality in such situations has been 'propositionalized'. In effect, this means that subjective modality cannot appear in complement clauses of propositional attitude verbs, without first being objectified (Lyons 1983a: 99–100). The same point also applies to criterion 5 (about conditional sentences).
16. A further use of *daroo* is when the speaker wants to confirm something with the listener, or, as in the following example, urge the listener to do something:

> *Ik-u   daroo?*
> go-NPAST   CONJ
> 'You will go, won't you?'

This usage can probably be regarded as an extension of the conjectural use. Sentences are often ambiguous between the two readings. For instance, the sentence

> *Ken   wa   kuru   daroo.*
> Ken   TOP   come.NPAST   CONJ
> 'I suppose Ken will come.'

could also mean 'Ken will come, won't he?', depending on the intonational contour of the utterance. I have chosen to provide only one translation for each example sentence.
17. There is also a phonologically reduced form used in past tense contexts, as in

> *Eri   wa   it-taroo.*
> Eri   TOP   go-PAST.CONJ
> 'I suppose Eri went.'

Possibly, this could be viewed as a grammaticalized past conjectural form. However, there seems to be free variation between, for example, *it-taroo* and *itta daroo* and the meaning is exactly the same.
18. There are no relative pronouns in Japanese. A relative clause is formed when the modifying constituent occurs in adnominal position. For example, the first example below is a declarative sentence, and the second a relative clause:

> *Inu   ga   hoe-ta.*
> dog   NOM   bark-PAST
> 'The dog barked.'

> *Hoe-ta   inu*
> bark-PAST   dog
> 'The dog that barked.'

19. Tanaka (1971: 468), who also states that *daroo* strongly resists adnominal-ization, points out that these kinds of examples are very rare and that they can be found in translational style. Satoshi Kinsui (personal communication) provides an alternative explanation. He explains that the historical development of *daroo* shows that it has undergone subjectification, which explains why the form can no longer be adnominalized. In fact, the change has progressed to the point where intersubjective uses are possible as well (see note 15). Thus, the development of *daroo* follows the general pattern of change described by Traugott (1995 *et passim*).

20. Minami (1993: 88, 97; 1997: 38) also observes that the negative conjectural *mai* and the hortative *-oo* (*yoo*) behave like *daroo* in this respect.

21. As is noted by Kato and Fukuchi (1989: 116), *daroo* can co-occur with the interrogative words *dare* 'who', *naze* 'why' and *nani* 'what'.

22. It is worth pointing out that a phenomenon called 'modal harmony' has been observed in the literature. Modal harmony is described by Bybee et al. (1994: 214–25) and Lyons (1977: 807–8).

23. Note also that *deshoo*, the polite form of *daroo*, cannot be placed before the psychological predicate, in accordance with the general constraint that polite forms are only allowed in direct quotes. For an illuminating article on the distinction between direct and indirect speech in Japanese, see Hirose (1995).

References

Akatsuka, N. (1990). On the meaning of *daroo*. In: Kamada, O. and Jacobsen W.M. (eds), *On Japanese and How to Teach It*. Tokyo: The Japan Times: 67–75.

Austin, J.L. (1975). *How to Do Things with Words* (2nd edn). Oxford: Clarendon Press.

Bloch, B. (1946). Studies in colloquial Japanese I: inflection. *Journal of the American Oriental Society* 66(2), 97–109.

Bybee, J.L., R.D. Perkins and W. Pagliuca (1994). *The Evolution of Grammar: Tense, Aspect, and Modality in the Languages of the World*. Chicago and London: The University of Chicago Press.

Cinque, G. (1999). *Adverbs and Functional Heads: a Cross-Linguistic Perspective* (Oxford Studies in Comparative Syntax). Oxford: Oxford University Press.

Haga, Y. (1954). Chinjutsu to wa nanimono? [What is *chinjutsu*?]. *Kokugo Kokubun* [National Language and Linguistics] 23(4). Reprinted in: Hattori, S. et al. (eds), *Nihon no Gengogaku* [Linguistics in Japan], vol. 3. Tokyo: Taishuukan: 284–303.

Hara, Y. (2006). Non-propositional modal meaning. Manuscript. [Available at http://ling.bun.kyoto-u.ac.jp/~yhara/download/darou_hara.pdf].

Hare, R.M. (1970). Meaning and speech acts. *The Philosophical Review* 79(1), 3–24.

Hirose, Y. (1995). Direct and indirect speech as quotations of public and private expression. *Lingua* 95, 223–38.

Hoye, L.F. (2005). 'You may think that; I couldn't possibly comment!' Modality studies: contemporary research and future directions (parts 1 and 2). *Journal of Pragmatics* 37(8), 1295–321; 37(9), 1481–506.

Iwasaki, T. (1995). Node to kara [*Node* and *kara*]. In: Miyajima, T. and Nitta, Y. (eds), *Nihongo Ruigi Hyoogen no Bunpoo* [The Grammar of Synonymous Expressions in Japanese], vol. 2. Tokyo: Kuroshio: 506–13.

Jespersen, O. (1924). *The Philosophy of Grammar*. London: George Allen & Unwin Ltd.

Kanbayashi, Y. (1994). Kara/node [*Kara/node*]. *Nihongogaku* [Japanese Linguistics] 13(8), 74–80.

Kato, Y. and T. Fukuchi (1989). *Tensu, Asupekuto, Muudo* [Tense, Aspect, Mood] (Gaikokujin no tame no Nihongo Reibun, Mondai Shiriizu 15) [Japanese Example Sentences and Questions for Foreigners 15]. Tokyo: Aratake Shuppan.

Kiefer, F. (1999). Modality. In: Brown, K., Miller, J. and Asher, R.E. (eds), *Concise Encyclopedia of Grammatical Categories*. Amsterdam: Elsevier: 223–9.

Kindaichi, H. (1953a). Fuhenka jodooshi no honshitsu – shukanteki hyoogen to kyakkanteki hyoogen no betsu nitsuite [The nature of non-inflectional auxiliaries: on the distinction between subjective and objective expressions]. *Kokugo Kokubun* [National Language and Linguistics] 22(2–3). Reprinted in: Hattori, S. et al. (eds), *Nihon no Gengogaku* [Linguistics in Japan], vol. 3. Tokyo: Taishuukan: 207–49.

Kindaichi, H. (1953b). Fuhenka jodooshi no honshitsu, sairon – Tokieda hakase, Mizutanishi, ryooka ni kotaete [The nature of non-inflectional auxiliaries, rediscussion: in reply to Dr Tokieda and Mr Mizutani]. *Kokugo Kokubun* [National Language and Linguistics] 22(9). Reprinted in: Hattori, S. et al. (eds), *Nihon no Gengogaku* [Linguistics in Japan], vol. 3. Tokyo: Taishuukan: 250–60.

Larm, L. (2005). On the nature of subjective modality. In: McNay, A. (ed.), *Oxford Working Papers in Linguistics, Philology and Phonetics* 10, 143–54.

Larm, L. (2006). Modality in Japanese. D.Phil. thesis, University of Oxford.

Leclerc, A. (2002). Verbal moods and sentence moods in the tradition of universal grammar. In: Vanderveken, D. and Kubo, S. (eds), *Essays in Speech Act Theory* (Pragmatics and Beyond New Series 77). Amsterdam and Philadelphia: John Benjamins Publishing Company: 63–84.

Lyons, J. (1977). *Semantics*, vol. 2. Cambridge: Cambridge University Press.

Lyons, J. (1981). *Language, Meaning and Context*. London: Fontana.

Lyons, J. (1982). Deixis and subjectivity: *loquor, ergo sum?* In: Jarvella, R.J. and Klein, W. (eds), *Speech, Place, and Action: Studies in Deixis and Related Topics*. Chichester: John Wiley & Sons, Ltd: 101–24.

Lyons, J. (1983a). Deixis and modality. *Sophia Linguistica: Working Papers in Linguistics* 12. Tokyo: Sophia University: 77–117.

Lyons, J. (1983b). Subjectivity and objectivity as reflected in language. *Sophia Linguistica: Working Papers in Linguistics* 12. Tokyo: Sophia University: 134–46.

Lyons, J. (1995). *Linguistic Semantics: an Introduction*. Cambridge: Cambridge University Press.

Masuoka, T. and Y. Takubo (1992). *Kiso Nihongo Bunpoo* [Basic Japanese Grammar], rev. edn. Tokyo: Kuroshio.

Mikami, A. (1972 [1953]). *Gendai Gohoo Josetsu: Shintakusu no Kokoromi* [An Introduction to Modern Grammar: a Syntactic Attempt]. Tokyo: Kuroshio.

Mikami, A. (1972 [1959]). *Tsuzuki: Gendai Gohoo Josetsu: Shugo Haishiron* [Sequel: an Introduction to Modern Grammar: the Abolition-of-Subject-Theory]. Tokyo: Kuroshio.

Minami, F. (1993). *Gendai Nihongo Bunpoo no Rinkaku* [An Outline of Modern Japanese Grammar]. Tokyo: Taishuukan.

Minami, F. (1997). *Gendai Nihongo Kenkyuu* [Research on Contemporary Japanese]. Tokyo: Sanseidoo.

Miyagawa, S. and M. Nakamura (1991). The logic of *kara* and *node* in Japanese. In: Georgopoulos, C. and Ishihara, R. (eds), *Interdisciplinary Approaches to Language: Essays in Honor of S.-Y. Kuroda*. Dordrecht: Kluwer Academic Publishers: 435–48.

Moriyama, T. (1992). Nihongo ni okeru 'suiryoo' o megutte [On epistemic modality in Japanese]. *Gengo Kenkyu* [Language Research] 101, 64–83.

Moriyama, T. (1999). Modaritii to intoneeshon [Modality and intonation]. *Gengo* [Language] 28(6), 74–9.

Nagano, M. (1952). 'Kara' to 'node' to wa doo chigau ka [What is the difference between *kara* and *node*?]. *Kokugo to Kokubungaku* [National Language and Literature] 29(2), 30–41.

Nakau, M. (1979). Modaritii to meidai [Modality and proposition]. In: Hayashi Eiichi Kyooju Kanreki Kinen Ronbunshuu Kankoo Iinkai (eds), *Eigo to Nihongo to: Hayashi Eiichi Kyooju Kanreki Kinen Ronbunshuu Kankoo* [English and Japanese: a Publication of Collected Papers for the 60th Birthday of Professor Eiichi Hayashi]. Tokyo: Kuroshio: 223–50.

Nitta, Y. (1999). Modaritii o motomete [In search of modality]. *Gengo* [Language] 28(6), 34–44.

Okutsu, K. (1993). *'Boku wa Unagi da' no Bunpoo* [The Grammar of *Boku wa Unagi da*], 8th edn. Tokyo: Kuroshio.

Onoe, K. (2001). *Bunpoo to Imi* [Grammar and Meaning], vol. 1. Tokyo: Kuroshio.

Palmer, F.R. (1990). *Modality and the English Modals*, 2nd edn. Longman: London and New York.

Palmer, F.R. (1994). *Grammatical Roles and Relations*. Cambridge: Cambridge University Press.

Palmer, F.R. (1999a). Mood and modality: basic principles. In: Brown, K., Miller, J. and Asher, R.E. (eds), *Concise Encyclopedia of Grammatical Categories*. Amsterdam: Elsevier: 229–35.

Palmer, F.R. (1999b). Mood and modality: further developments. In: Brown, K., Miller, J. and Asher R.E. (eds), *Concise Encyclopedia of Grammatical Categories*. Amsterdam: Elsevier: 235–9.

Palmer, F.R. (2001). *Mood and Modality*, 2nd edn. Cambridge: Cambridge University Press.

Ross, J.R. (1970). On declarative sentences. In: Jacobs, R.A. and Rosenbaum, P.S. (eds), *Readings in English Transformational Grammar*. Waltham, Mass.: Ginn: 222–72.

Saji, K. (1989). Bunpoo [Grammar]. In: Kato, A. Saji, K. and Morita Y. (eds), *Nihongo Gaisetsu* [An Outline of Japanese]. Tokyo: Oofuu: 107–85.

Sawada, H. (1975). Nichieigo shukanteki jodooshi no koobunronteki koosatsu – toku ni 'hyoogensei' o chuushin to shite [A syntactic consideration of Japanese and English subjective auxiliaries: with a special reference to their 'expressivity']. *Gengo Kenkyu* [Language Research] 68, 75–103.

Sawada, H. (1978). Nichieigo bunfukushirui no taishoo gengogakuteki kenkyuu: 'speech act' riron no shiten kara [A contrastive study of Japanese and English sentence adverbials: from the viewpoint of speech act theory]. *Gengo Kenkyu* [Language Research] 74, 1–36.

Sawada, H. (1993). *Shiten to Shukansei: Nichieigo Jodooshi no Bunseki* [Point of View and Subjectivity: an Analysis of Japanese and English Auxiliaries]. Tokyo: Hitsuji Shoboo.

Speas, P. and C. Tenny (2003). Configurational properties of point of view roles. In: Di Sciullo, A.M. (ed.), *Asymmetry in Grammar: Syntax and Semantics*, vol. 1 (Linguistik Aktuell/Linguistics Today 57). Amsterdam and Philadelphia: John Benjamins: 315–44.

Sugimura, Y. (2000). Yooda to sooda no shukansei [The subjective character of *yoo da* and *soo da*]. *Nagoya Daigaku Gengo Bunka Ronbunshuu* [Studies in Language and Culture, Nagoya University] 22(1), 85–100. [Available at http://www.lang.nagoya-u.ac.jp/~sugimura/achivement/pdf/014.pdf].

Takayama, Y. (2002). *Nihongo Modaritii no Shiteki Kenkyuu* [Historical Research on Japanese Modality]. Tokyo: Hitsuji Shoboo.

Tanaka, A. (1971). Daroo [*Daroo*]. In: Matsumura, A. (ed.), *Nihon Bunpoo Daijiten* [A Comprehensive Grammar of Japanese]. Tokyo: Meiji Shoin: 468.

Tenny, C.L. (2006). Evidentiality, experiencers, and the syntax of sentence in Japanese. *Journal of East Asian Linguistics* 15, 245–88.

Teramura, H. (1984). *Nihongo no Shintakusu to Imi* [Japanese Syntax and Meaning], vol. 2. Tokyo: Kuroshio.

Teramura, H. (1992). *Teramura Hideo Ronbunshuu 1: Nihongo Bunpoohen* [Collected Writings by Hideo Teramura 1: Japanese Grammar]. Tokyo: Kuroshio.

Teramura, H. (1993). *Teramura Hideo Ronbunshuu 2: Gengogaku-Nihongogakuhen* [Collected Writings by Hideo Teramura 2: Linguistics and Japanese Linguistics]. Tokyo: Kuroshio.

Tokieda, M. (1941). *Kokugogaku Genron* [Principles of National Linguistics]. Tokyo: Iwanami Shoten.

Traugott, E.C. (1995). Subjectification in grammaticalisation. In: Stein, D. and Wright, S. (eds), *Subjectivity and Subjectification: Linguistic Perspectives*. Cambridge: Cambridge University Press: 31–54.

Van Valin, R.D. (2005). *Exploring the Syntax–Semantics Interface*. Cambridge: Cambridge University Press.

Verstraete, J-C. (2001). Subjective and objective modality: interpersonal and ideational functions in the English modal auxiliary system. *Journal of Pragmatics* 33, 1505–28.

Watanabe, M. (1953). Jojutsu to chinjutsu – jutsugo bunsetsu no koozoo [Description and illocutionary force – the structure of the predicate phrase]. *Kokugogaku* [National Linguistics] 13–14. Reprinted in: Hattori, S. et al. (eds), *Nihon no Gengogaku* [Linguistics in Japan], vol. 3. Tokyo: Taishuukan: 261–83.

Yamaguchi, A. (2001). Daroo [*Daroo*]. In: Yamaguchi, A. and Akimoto, S. (eds), *Nihongo Bunpoo Daijiten* [A Comprehensive Grammar of Japanese]. Tokyo: Meiji Shoin: 460–1.

4
What Is and Is not Language-Specific about the Japanese Modal System? A Comparative and Historical Perspective

Tetsuharu Moriya and Kaoru Horie

4.1 Introduction

In Japanese linguistics, the definition of modality varies between different schools of scholars, particularly in relation to how key notions such as *tinzyutu* ('predication', but see Narrog in this volume for a discussion of this notion) should be treated (Masuoka 1991, Nitta 1991, Onoe 2001). Some scholars equate modality with subjective meaning (Nitta 2000), while others regard it as describing grammatical expressions outside the propositional content of a sentence (Masuoka 1991, 2000, 2007). It has also been debated how such definitions are compatible with that of modality as defined in general linguistic literature (Narrog 2005, Horie and Narrog, to appear). Although numerous studies on Japanese modality are published every year, it is indeed quite difficult to determine what is and is not language-specific about the Japanese modal system relative to other languages. The purpose of this chapter is to address this research question based on observations of the Japanese modal auxiliary system and through comparisons with English and Korean.

In this chapter, we will first show (i) that epistemic modality was predominant in Old Japanese modal auxiliaries (e.g. *mu*, *meri*, *mazi*), and (ii) that new periphrastic forms such as *kamo-sire-nai* (epistemic 'may') or *nakere-ba-naranai* (deontic 'must') began to emerge around the seventeenth century, when the distinction between deontic and epistemic modal auxiliaries became more explicit. Both of these facts lead us to conclude that (iii) a unidirectional development model from deontic to epistemic modality (Traugott 1989) is not straightforwardly applicable to Japanese, although 'subjectification' is partly involved in the development (Traugott and Dasher 2002, Onodera 2004, Horie 2007, Narrog 2007). These points suggest that analyses based on the 'unidirectionality' model are not appropriate and that grammaticalization is arguably not to be considered as a process governed by a set of unique rules, but rather as an epiphenomenon derived from several independent laws (Newmeyer 1998). Next, we compare Japanese and Korean modal auxiliaries and show (iv) that Korean, having a similar system of periphrastic modal auxiliaries, has also evolved in favour of a more explicit distinction between deontic and epistemic modalities similarly to Japanese. We will also suggest (v) that a cultural/typological factor (for example, BECOME-Language vs DO-Language; Ikegami 1991) may contribute to the observed cross-linguistic similarity. Finally, based on these arguments, we will conclude by stressing the need to examine diachronic and cross-linguistic data to investigate the nature of modal auxiliaries in Japanese.

This chapter is organized as follows: section 4.2 will first explain properties of grammaticalization in general and then compare developments of English and Japanese modal auxiliaries to show that the developmental mechanism proposed for English is simply not applicable to Japanese. Furthermore, we will argue that such differences lead us to choose a more restrictive definition of modality. Section 4.3 will compare characteristics of modal auxiliaries in Japanese and Korean to look into a possible cognitive typological factor that may have caused the parallel development in both languages. In section 4.4, we will summarize the discussion and stress the necessity and usefulness of examining diachronic and cross-linguistic data in the study of Japanese modality.

4.2   Development of modal auxiliaries in English and Japanese

In this section, we will compare the developmental pathways of modal auxiliaries in English and Japanese and show that the developmental mechanism proposed for English is not straightforwardly applicable to Japanese. We will further argue that the process of subjectification, 'a shift to a relatively abstract and subjective construal of the world in terms of language' (Hopper and Traugott 2003: 86), is observable in both English and Japanese but in different ways. Before going into the discussion, we will first review the concept of grammaticalization and its characteristics, since development of modal auxiliaries in major European languages, including English, is usually regarded as an instance of the grammaticalization process. It is therefore important to examine whether the characteristics proposed for grammaticalization help explain different developmental pathways in English and Japanese.

4.2.1 Grammaticalization

Grammaticalization (also called *grammaticization*) is a process through which a lexical item takes on a grammatical meaning. It has been studied from both diachronic and synchronic perspectives. In the former perspective, grammaticalization is a subset of linguistic changes, while in the latter, it is seen as 'primarily a syntactic, discourse pragmatic phenomenon, to be studied from the point of view of fluid patterns of language use' (Hopper and Traugott 2003: 2).

A typical example of grammaticalization in the diachronic sense is the development of an auxiliary *be going to* from a progressive form of the movement verb *go* in construction with a purposive infinitival complement. As pointed out by Hopper and Traugott (2003: 2–4), this example illustrates morphosyntactic and semantic–pragmatic consequences of grammaticalization, such as pragmatic inference, reanalysis, phonological reduction and abstraction of meaning:

(1) a. John *is going to* marry Mary.
     b. John *is going to* like Mary.
     c. John *is gonna* like Mary.

Grammaticalization begins in a very local context such as (1a), in which *go* co-occurs with a non-finite purposive complement, meaning something like *John is leaving/travelling to marry Mary*. The change in meaning is triggered by pragmatic inference: if John is leaving in order to marry, the marriage will be in the future. As this inference is conventionalized, *[John is going [to marry Mary]]* is reanalysed as *[John [is going to] marry Mary]*. This reanalysis also affects the verb following *be going to*. Consequently, the verbs that were originally incompatible with a purposive meaning have become compatible, as in (1b). As the expression *be going to* starts to be used quite often, it begins to be perceived as one word, as evidenced by its phonological reduction in (1c). Through this process, the original meaning of *go* has been mostly lost and more abstract and subjective meanings have been added.

Grammaticalization is also prevalent in the history of Japanese. For example, many of the complex postpositions such as -*ni-tuite* ('about, concerning'), *-o-megutte* ('over, about, centring around'), both of which can be translated as 'about/on', are derived from main verbs *tuku* ('touch, arrive') and *meguru* ('go around') respectively. The former forms are thus considered to have evolved through grammaticalization.

(2) a. *Nebanebasuru*   *mono-ga*   *te-ni*   <u>*tui-ta.*</u>
        sticky   object-NOM   hand-LOC   get attached-PERF
        'Sticky objects got attached to my hand.'

    b. *Watasitati-wa*   *sono mondai*   <u>*ni-tui-te*</u>   *giron-si-ta.*
        we-TOP   that issue   about   discussion-do-PERF
        'We discussed the issue.'

    c. *Taro-wa*   *futatu-no-tera-o*   <u>*megut-ta*</u>
        Taro-TOP   two-GEN-temple-ACC   go-around-PERF
        'Taro visited two temples one after another.'

    d. *Watasitati-wa*   *sono mondai*   <u>*o-megut-te*</u>   *tairitu-si-ta.*
        we-TOP   that issue   about/on   opposition-do-PERF[1]
        'We opposed each other on (lit. "centring around") that issue.'

In (2a), *tui-ta* is a complex of a main verb and a tense marker which signifies a type of physical attachment/movement of the sentential subject. In (2b), *tui-te,* the non-finite gerundive (or conjunctive) form of *tuku,* functions as a complex postposition. The same is also true of (2c) and (2d). *Megut-ta* in (2c) is a verb complex meaning 'went around', but *megut-te* in (2d) functions as a postposition meaning 'about/on'.[2]

There are several criteria by which to judge whether a particular linguistic change can be categorized as grammaticalization. Ohori (2002: 182–7) gives five such criteria:

   (i)   schematicity
   (ii) closed class
  (iii) obligatoriness
   (iv) boundness
   (v) interaction.

Schematicity (i) stands for the degree of abstractness of meaning. For example, a Japanese completive marker *-te-simau* originates in the verb *simau* meaning 'put away'. But in the former, the original meaning of putting away is lost and the grammatical meaning of completion is present (Ohori 2002: 182). The second criterion (ii) is whether a grammaticalized word is a closed-class item or not. *Te-simau* is one of the closed-class items expressing aspectuality in Japanese. A grammaticalized word is regarded as obligatory (iii) when one cannot express a specific grammatical meaning in any other way than using the word. A typical example is the French negator *pas*, which originally meant 'step' and was optionally used to strengthen the force of negation. *Pas* has thus become an obligatory negative marker in Modern French. Boundness (iv) refers to the morphosyntactic dependency of a morpheme on some other free morpheme. *Te-simau* satisfies this property. It cannot be used as a matrix verb by itself, but has to be attached to a matrix verb as in *tabe-te-simau* ('have eaten'). Interaction (v) refers to an agreement or concord relationship holding between a grammaticalized item and other element(s) in the same sentence. Ohori (2002) notes that all these five properties are manifested only in typical grammaticalization processes, but even if a particular process manifests only some of these properties, we can still regard it as a less typical instance of grammaticalization.

The development of modal auxiliaries only satisfies the properties (i) schematicity and (ii) 'closed class'-hood of grammaticalization listed above. Deontic and epistemic meanings of modal auxiliaries can be viewed as more schematic relative to meanings expressed by original lexical verbs. Modal auxiliaries obviously form a closed class. But modal auxiliaries are neither obligatory nor bound, at least in English. Furthermore, concordance or agreement is not necessary. This suggests that the development of modal auxiliaries can be subsumed under grammaticalization, although it is not one of the most typical examples.

In the functionalist literature, grammaticalization is normally regarded as a unidirectional process:

(3) What is common to most definitions of grammaticalization is, first, that it is conceived of as a process. Most frequently it has been claimed to form essentially a diachronic process... A third characteristic that is implicit in these definitions and has frequently been mentioned as an intrinsic property of the process is that grammaticalization is unidirectional, that is, that it leads from a 'less grammatical' to a 'more grammatical' unit, but not vice-versa. (Heine et al. 1991: 4)

Newmeyer (1998: 233–4) argues that the term 'process' is not used here as a mere synonym with 'phenomenon', but is rather used to mean 'a process *of a particular type*, namely, one driven by a distinct set of principles *governing the phenomenon alone*' and he refers to such a phenomenon as 'a distinct process'.

This unidirectionality is considered to be applicable to all component changes in grammaticalization. For example, body-part nouns, having undergone grammaticalization, can be employed to express points of orientation, but the reverse change from points of orientation to body parts is not likely (Heine et al. 1991: 31). As we see below, in the case of modal auxiliaries, change from deontic to epistemic meanings is considered to be a specific instantiation of unidirectionality involved in grammaticalization.

Next, we will examine characteristics of English modal auxiliaries and see how their developmental process manifests unidirectionality.

4.2.2   English

English modal auxiliaries have several distinct meanings. For example, according to the *Oxford Advanced Learner's Dictionary* (7th edition, 2005), *may* is 'used to say that something is possible', as in *He may have missed the train* or 'used to ask for or give permission', as in *May I come in*? The same is true of *must*, which is 'used to say that something is likely or logical', as in *You must be hungry after all that walking* or 'used to say that something is necessary or very important (sometimes involving a rule or a law)' as in *Cars must not park in front of the entrance*. The former usages expressing possibility or likelihood are referred to as 'epistemic', while the latter usages expressing permission or obligation are referred to as 'deontic' or 'root'. The same string of words can express both epistemic and deontic meanings (Sweetser 1990: 49):

(4) a. John *must* be home by ten; Mother won't let him stay out any later.
    b. John *must* be home already; I see his coat.

In (4a) *must* is used to express obligation ascribed to John, while *must* in (4b) expresses assessment of probability based on perceived evidence. Sweetser (1990: 49) emphasizes the universality of such ambiguity:

(5) This ambiguity is not peculiar to English; indeed, there is an evident cross-linguistic tendency for lexical items to be ambiguous between these two sets of senses. Many unrelated languages (Indo-European, Semitic, Philippine, Dravidian, Mayan, and Finno-Ugric, among others) are alike in having some set of predicates which carry both the root and epistemic modal meanings as English modal verbs do.

Some scholars argue that the two meanings are unrelated, and thus *may* and *must* are just homophonous.[3] But most functionally oriented linguists appear to accept the universality of unidirectional development from deontic to epistemic meanings. As pointed out in the literature, English modal auxiliaries are generally derived from main verbs. Also, epistemic meanings are considered to have originated from deontic meanings:

(6) There is strong historical, sociolinguistic, and psycholinguistic evidence for viewing the epistemic use of modals as an extension of a more basic root meaning, rather than viewing the root sense as an extension of the epistemic one, or both as sub-sets of some more general superordinate sense. (Sweetser 1990: 49–50)

(7) It is clear that the epistemic senses develop later than, and out of the agent-oriented senses. In fact, for the English modals, where the case is best documented, the epistemic uses do not become common until quite late. (Bybee et al. 1994: 195)

As a typical example, the modal auxiliary *must* is derived from the Old English verb *motan*, which means 'be obliged to', and its strong epistemic meaning does not appear until the seventeenth century (Traugott 1989: 42). Bybee and Pagliuca (1985: 66) claim that there is a 'unidirectional evolution of agent-oriented modalities into epistemic modalities' and that 'the opposite direction of development is not possible'.

Two explanations have been presented for this directionality. One is metaphorical extension. For example, Sweetser (1990) argues that the meaning of epistemic necessity is derived from that of sociophysical force by metaphor. The other explanation is pragmatic strengthening, through which conversational implicature becomes conventionalized (Traugott 1989: 50–1). In either case, the unidirectional change from deontic to epistemic meaning is considered very robust and is held to apply not only to English but also to many other languages.

As we see below, however, this pattern is not observable in the development of Japanese auxiliaries.

4.2.3 Japanese

Contrary to what was stated in section 4.2.2, languages like Japanese do not appear to follow the supposedly universal tendency for deontic meaning to derive epistemic meaning. As demonstrated by Horie (1997),

Table 4.1   Ambiguous modal auxiliaries in Old Japanese

	Deontic	Epistemic
-besi	Obligation, intention	Certainty
-mu	Intention	Probability
-masi	Wish	Counterfactual conjecture

it cannot be confirmed that Japanese modal auxiliaries evolved in a similar manner, in spite of the cross-linguistic generalization presented in Bybee and Pagliuca (1985) and Bybee et al. (1994). In Old Japanese, there were indeed several auxiliaries that encoded both epistemic and deontic meanings as shown in Table 4.1.

Although this situation is superficially similar to the one manifested in Modern English, it is very difficult to decide whether the epistemic meaning was derived from the deontic meaning or vice versa; both deontic and epistemic senses had already been present by the time the oldest extant documents were written (Horie 1997: 441). In fact, the epistemic meanings seem to have been fairly dominant in the overall system of Old Japanese, as explicated by scholars of Old Japanese (Takayama 2002: 11, Kurotaki 2005: 128). Based on these facts, it is quite difficult to argue that Japanese modal auxiliaries first developed deontic meanings, and then later epistemic meanings were derived.[4]

Indeed, modal auxiliaries in Modern Japanese are quite different from those in Old Japanese. We can point out two main characteristics of their diachronic development. First, only a few Old Japanese auxiliaries survived in Modern Japanese. For example, *meri* and *nari*, which primarily expressed 'evidential' meanings in Old Japanese, have not survived in Modern Japanese. Those that survived, such as *beki-da* (<-*besi*), underwent semantic narrowing (Kondo 2000: 479). In Modern Japanese, *beki-da* is used mostly as a deontic modal expression, and more often *beki* is used as a nominal modifier rather than as a sentential predicate (for example, *suru-beki-koto* (DO-beki-THING), which means 'something to do'). As another example, *-yoo* and *-daroo* (<-*mu*) mostly function as sentence-final predicates and are rarely used to modify nouns (Kondo 2000: 249).

The second characteristic is the emergence of periphrastic modal auxiliaries. From around the seventeenth century, new periphrastic modal auxiliaries began to appear as if to complement decreasing Old Japanese modal auxiliaries. Although English also has periphrastic modal auxiliaries such as *have to* and *be going to*, the number is quite small and they are usually ambiguous similar to non-periphrastic auxiliaries. The following list, based on Kitahara et al. (2000), shows the earliest dates of attestation of periphrastic modal auxiliaries:

(8) *kamo-sire-nai* (probability): around the end of the sixteenth century
    nakere-ba-nara-nai (obligation): 1638
    ni-tigai-nai (certainty): 1734
    temo-ii (permission): 1833

Consequently, in Modern Japanese, there are few instances of modal auxiliaries exhibiting deontic–epistemic ambiguity, unlike the case in English.[5] Furthermore, in contrast to non-periphrastic auxiliaries in English, deontic and epistemic periphrastic auxiliaries in Japanese can co-occur in the same clause:

(9) *Kare-wa asu   gakko-ni   ika-**nakere-ba naranai***
    he- Top tomorrow   school-to   go- must
    ka mo sirenai.
    may
    'He may have to go to school tomorrow.'

Absence of a clear indication of unidirectional development from deontic to epistemic modality in Japanese, along with the seemingly predominant nature of epistemic modality in Old Japanese, casts doubts on the validity of the hypothesis of unidirectional semantic change from deontic to epistemic meanings. Furthermore, the emergence of periphrastic modal auxiliaries has made deontic and epistemic modal auxiliaries virtually distinct. Thus, the absence of systematic ambiguity in modal meaning in Modern Japanese also presents a contrast with the patterns observed in English and other languages.

4.2.4 Implications for the definition of modality

As seen in section 4.2.3, the change from deontic to epistemic meanings is not observable in Japanese modal auxiliaries. Rather, both deontic and epistemic meanings apparently coexisted in Old Japanese auxiliaries and later became distinct in the course of development, partly owing to the emergence of periphrastic modal expressions.

It is important to explain why Japanese modal auxiliaries do not show the 'unidirectional' development observed in English and many other languages since this unidirectionality is considered to be almost exceptionless by some scholars (see (6) and (7) above). We assume that the unidirectionality in this sense is just a result of some separate developmental factors and not an independent principle of linguistic change. Japanese and English are thus governed by different laws of development owing in part to cross-linguistic differences such as source syntactic categories of modal auxiliaries. In line with this observation, we argue that Japanese modal auxiliaries conform to their own laws of development, which are different from those of English and many other languages.

The unidirectional shift from deontic to epistemic meanings is in some cases characterized by force dynamics. Based on Talmy (1988), Sweetser (1990: 50) proposes that deontic meanings are extended to epistemic meanings through a metaphorical process whereby the logic of the external (sociophysical) world is applied to that of the internal mental world:

(10) Thus, we view our reasoning processes as being subject to compulsions, obligations, and other modalities, just as our real-world actions are subject to modalities of the same sort.

To be more specific, the deontic *may* encodes 'an absent potential barrier in the sociophysical world' while the meaning of epistemic *may* would be that 'there is no barrier to the speaker's process of reasoning from the available premises to the conclusion expressed in the sentence qualified by *may*' (Sweetser 1990: 59). The fact that *may* and *must* are potentially ambiguous leads to another possibility that the modal auxiliaries have some core meaning, from which deontic and epistemic meanings are derived.[6] However, Sweetser (1990) does not endorse the view that English modal auxiliaries have a single 'core' meaning, which is interpreted deontically or epistemically according to a specific pragmatic context, because the metaphorical mapping seems fairly conventional.

On the other hand, as pointed out by Onoe (2001: 459), force dynamics as proposed by Talmy (1988) and Sweetser (1990) is most likely not to be involved in the development of Japanese modal auxiliaries because modal auxiliaries in Modern Japanese, such as -*u* and -*yoo*, did not derive from matrix verbs. In fact, they derived from Old Japanese -*mu*, which was an uninflected modal auxiliary/suffix itself. -*U* was derived from -*mu* through the dropping of a consonant, and -*yoo* was then derived from -*u* by vowel change. Therefore, it is difficult to consider that force dynamic metaphorical mapping is involved in the development of Japanese modal auxiliaries. Why, then, did some of the Old Japanese modal auxiliaries show ambiguity?

To answer this question, we have to return to the problems involved in the definition of modality. We must point out that the deontic-to-epistemic shift is not the only logical possibility to explain the deontic–epistemic ambiguity in the modal auxiliary system. The alternative possibility is to postulate a schematic meaning covering both deontic and epistemic meanings. One piece of evidence that supports this view is the semantic property of Old Japanese *-mu*. *-Mu* had a wide variety of meanings such as epistemic conjecture, volition, order, request and hypothesis. If *-mu* had a schematic meaning of *irrealis*, it is natural that the word had a set of meanings related to unrealized events (Onoe 2001: 457).[7] If our view is on the right track, then it can lend support to the view of modality as expression of the *realis/irrealis* (or factuality) distinction adopted in Narrog (2005) (see also Palmer 2001). Narrog (2005: 168) points out that linguistic modality has been defined in three different ways:

(11) the expression of the attitude of the speaker or the expression of subjectivity and the speaker's opinions and emotions (for example, Lyons 1968, 1977, Palmer 1986, Bybee et al. 1994, Nitta 2000 for Japanese);

(12) something including all linguistic expression outside the proposition (for example, Fillmore 1968);

(13) the expression of *realis* vs *irrealis* or factuality distinctions (for example, Givón 1995, Palmer 1998, 2001, Dietrich 1992 for German, Narrog 2002, Nomura 2003 for Japanese).

The definitions (11) and (12), including the synthesis of these two, are quite dominant among Japanese linguists, as described in Narrog (2005, this volume). This is partly due to the Japanese linguistic notion *tinzyutu* (what makes a sentence function as a sentence). These definitions led Japanese linguists to deal with a wide variety of forms and functions under the label of modality, such as negation, tense and topic–focus distinction. Furthermore, although meanings expressed by modal auxiliaries and sentence-final particles are different in kind, both of them are subsumed under the rubric of modality. Thus, in spite of the abundance of studies on modality in Japanese linguistics, it is quite difficult to compare their research findings directly with the observations on modality in other languages. This divergence prompts us to reconsider the definition of modality that has been employed in Japanese linguistics from the viewpoint of cross-linguistic compatibility.

As seen in section 4.2.3, some modal auxiliaries in Old Japanese were ambiguous between deontic and epistemic meanings similar to those in English, but no diachronic development from deontic to epistemic meanings has apparently been observed in the former. Furthermore, in the Old Japanese modal auxiliary system, epistemic meanings were arguably predominant. We can explain this situation by hypothesizing that modal auxiliaries themselves first had a schematic meaning which signified *irrealis*, and it took on epistemic or deontic meaning depending on a given linguistic context. This view accords with modality as defined in (13). Although the developmental patterns in English and Japanese are different, this difference can be interpreted as different manifestations of the development of schematic *irrealis* meaning in each language. In English, the force dynamic property of main verbs has caused deontic meanings to be primary and epistemic meanings to be derived. In Japanese, in contrast, both deontic and epistemic meanings were equidistant from the *irrealis* meaning owing to the absence of force dynamic property because Japanese modal auxiliaries have been a part of verbal inflection and do not express 'force' as defined by Talmy (1988) or Sweetser (1990).

Unlike Japanese, it appears to be less obvious whether English developmental facts support the idea of the schematic *irrealis* meaning; however, in fact, the developmental pathway of the English modal auxiliary system shows that the *realis/irrealis* distinction was also relevant in English. As pointed out in Harsh (1968), a subjunctive mood in English has become less frequently used and has been replaced by modal auxiliary verbs. The core meaning of the subjunctive mood in English was *irrealis*, just like that of Old Japanese *-mu*:

(14) Like the term imperative, the term subjunctive refers to a particular verb form. In Old English, special verb forms existed to communicate non-facts, e.g., wants, hopes, and hypothetical situations. The subjunctive is somewhat weak in Modern English, but there are speakers who use it routinely. (Berk 1999: 149–50)

In Japanese, *-mu* was replaced by *-u* and *-yoo*, which are also a part of verbal inflection and thus can be regarded as mood markers, while in English, the subjunctive mood weakened and was mostly replaced by auxiliary verbs, which were derived from main verbs and carried with them force dynamic properties.

To summarize, one of the main differences between English and Japanese modal auxiliaries is the difference in terms of source categories. English modal auxiliaries derived from main verbs, while Japanese modal auxiliaries have been a part of verbal inflections. That is why force dynamic metaphorical extension is observable in English but not in Japanese. The Japanese modal auxiliary system is thus an exception in relation to the unidirectional deontic-to-epistemic development. Unless force dynamic extension is involved, no clear development from deontic to epistemic meanings in modal auxiliaries can be observed. Furthermore, the differential developmental pathways lend support to the view of modality as the expression of factuality distinction. If we interpret modality this way, we can regard both Japanese and English modal auxiliary systems as different manifestations of the *realis/irrealis* distinction, and it will not be necessary to regard the English system as the norm and the Japanese system as an exception. Developmental pathways of respective languages also show that this hypothesis is on the right track.

Although we cannot observe the development from deontic to epistemic meanings, we can observe manifestations of subjectification in some parts of the Japanese modal auxiliary system, although it is manifested in a different way from that in English. Next, we will examine how subjectification manifests itself in the Japanese modal auxiliary system.

4.2.5 Subjectification in the Japanese modal auxiliary system

Subjectification is a term whose definition varies between researchers. In cognitive grammar, for example, subjectification is defined as 'a process whereby some feature of a designated situation gradually drifts from the profile and comes to occupy the ground' (Taylor 2002: 408):

(15) a. I *can* solve this problem.
     b. This problem *can* be solved.

In (15a), the ability meaning encoded by *can* is ostensibly ascribed to the first person subject. However, in (15b), the locus of ability cannot be ascribed to the subject, even though the sentence can be interpreted to express some property concerning the subject *the problem*. Therefore, the locus of ability is backgrounded and is ascribed to the implicit agent.

In this chapter, we adopt the view that subjectification is 'a shift to a relatively abstract and subjective construal of the world in terms of language' (Hopper and Traugott 2003: 86). One example of subjectification given by Hopper and Traugott (2003) is the semantic shift of *while*. *While* originally encoded simultaneity ('at the same time that') in Old English (OE) as in the OE example (16a). Conversational inferences brought about the semantic shift from simultaneity (of two situations) to cause/reason for a situation as in the Middle English (ME) example (16b). In other words, *while* acquired the sense of reason or cause for a situation expressed in the main clause. Later on, a surprise reading was ascribed to *while* by a different inferential process as in the Modern English (ModE) example (16c), which ultimately led to its concessive meaning:

(16) a. &   wicode pær pa   *hwile*   pe man pa burg   worhte   &   getimbrode.
      and lived   there that:DAT time:DAT that one that fortress worked-on and built
      'And camped there at the time that/while the fortress was worked on and built.'
   b. Thar mycht succeed na female,
      Quhill foundyn mycht be ony male.
      'No female was able to succeed while any male could be found.'
   c. *Whill* others aime at greatnes boght with blod,
      Not to bee great thou strves, bot to bee good.
      'While others aim at greatness that is bought with blood, you strive to be not great but good.'

Hopper and Traugott (2003: 90–1)

Through this whole process, the meaning of *while* has become abstract and subjective in that it has come to signify the speaker's assessment of the situation. Subjectification in this sense is undoubtedly suitable to describe the deontic-to-epistemic semantic shift in English modal auxiliaries as discussed by Sweetser (1990). We will argue below that even though the developmental pathway of Japanese modal auxiliaries is different from that in English, it nevertheless manifests some features of subjectification.

As seen in section 4.2.3, it is obvious that periphrastic modal auxiliaries contributed to the disambiguation of the modal auxiliary system in Japanese. However, they served not only to disambiguate the system, but also to restructure the semantic organization of the modal auxiliaries, such that the Modern Japanese auxiliary *-u/-yoo*, deriving from the Old Japanese modal auxiliary *mu*, for instance, was assigned an ostensibly speaker-oriented 'subjective' meaning. To illustrate this, we will now examine how morphosyntactic environments, which enabled modal auxiliaries to occur, changed from Old Japanese to Modern Japanese.

Table 4.2 shows that in Old Japanese *besi* can occur in 'yes-no' questions, in the scope of negation, and in adverbial clauses expressing time, hypothetical situations, reason and antithesis, while *mu* can occur only in yes-no questions and in an adverbial clause expressing antithesis. This contrast indicates that the modal meaning of *besi* is more objective than

Table 4.2 Co-occurrence restrictions of Old Japanese modal auxiliaries

| | Question | Negation | Adverbial clause | | | |
			Time	If	Reason	Antithesis
besi	○	○	○	○	○	○
mu	○	×	×	×	×	○

Source: Based on Takayama (2002: 50).

that of *mu* because it can be questioned or negated, and be used in various kinds of adverbial clauses, including non-assertive ones, while the modality of *mu* cannot be negated or expressed in non-assertive contexts.

We will now compare the co-occurrence restrictions of Old Japanese modal auxiliaries with those of Modern Japanese (see Table 4.3).

Several remarkable differences emerge out of this comparison. First, *yoo*, which is the deontic descendant of Old Japanese *mu*, has become more subjective in the sense that it cannot occur in any non-assertive context. But the status of the epistemic modal descendant of *mu*, namely, *daroo*, is not clear because it can occur in a certain type of reason clause. Takayama (2002) points out that *daroo* cannot be regarded as a pure descendant of *mu*. Second, periphrastic forms such as *ka-mo-sire-nai* and *ni-tigai-nai* are less subjective than *yoo* or *daroo* because they can be used in reason clauses. We can interpret the fact in the following way. While *mu* has become more subjective, in accordance with the general tendency pointed out by Traugott (1989), the newly

Table 4.3 Co-occurrence restrictions of Modern Japanese modal auxiliaries

| | Q | Neg. | Adverbial clause | | | | | |
| | | | Time | If | Reason | | | Adversative |
					-node	-kara	
beki (obligation) (<*besi*)	○	○	×	○	○	○	○
te-mo-ii (permission)	○	○	×	○	○	○	○
ka-mo-sire-nai (possibility)	×	×	×	×	○	○	○
ni-tigai-nai (certainty)	×	×	×	×	○	○	○
daroo (prediction) (<*mu*)	×	×	×	×	×	○	○
yoo (volition) (<*mu*)	×	×	×	×	×	×	×

Source: Based on Takayama (2002: 49).

emerging periphrastic auxiliaries served to restructure the semantic organization of modal auxiliaries as noted earlier, in addition to serving to disambiguate the system as a whole.

As we have seen above, Japanese modal auxiliaries differ from English ones in that the unidirectional deontic-to-epistemic shift is not observable in their development. However, some (if not all) Japanese modal auxiliaries manifest subjectification. This indicates that grammaticalization is not a process governed by coherent laws of development, but is an epiphenomenon caused by an interaction of independent factors. Subjectification is one of these factors. This view accords with that advocated in Newmeyer (1998: 237):

> (17) Grammaticalization, as I will argue, is nothing more than a label for the conjunction of certain types of independently occurring linguistic changes.

In this section, we first observed that the developmental pathways of modal auxiliaries differ in English and Japanese. We then argued that it is therefore not appropriate to apply the model of unidirectional semantic shift to Japanese modal auxiliaries, although the model has successfully explained the semantic change of modal auxiliaries in English and many other languages. Rather, if we interpret modality as encoding the *realis* vs *irrealis* distinction, we can take the Old Japanese modal auxiliary system to inherently instantiate *irrealis* meaning. We also argued that the process of subjectification was involved in the development of Japanese modal auxiliaries.

In the next section, we will compare the Japanese modal auxiliary system with that of Korean and then examine what factors have contributed to the disambiguation process in the Japanese modal auxiliary system.

4.3 Factors contributing to the parallel development of modal auxiliaries in Japanese and Korean

In this section, we will first point out that Korean modal auxiliaries are similar to their Japanese counterparts in important respects. We will then examine a cultural/typological factor contributing to the similarity.

4.3.1 Parallelism of modal auxiliary systems

Korean shows remarkable similarity to Japanese in the coding of modality. Horie (2003) points out two major similarities between the two languages: (i) auxiliaries encoding epistemic modality are formally distinguishable from those encoding deontic modality, and (ii) the majority of modal auxiliaries are periphrastic constructions. The inventory of Korean modal auxiliaries on the basis of which Horie (2003) proposes these generalizations is illustrated in Table 4.4.

Table 4.4 The inventory of Japanese and Korean modal auxiliaries

(a) Epistemic modality

[Japanese]

Form	Meaning
-ka mo sirenai	Possibility (weak)
-ni tigai nai	Possibility (strong)
-hazu da	Probability
-daroo	Probability

[Korean]

-nun/n/l ci moluta	Possibility (weak)
-nun/n/l kes kathta	Possibility (strong)
-nun/n/l tus hata	Possibility (strong)
-nun/n/l kes-ita	Probability

(b) Deontic modality

[Japanese]

-(r)eru, -koto ga dekiru	Ability
-nakereba nara nai	Obligation
-beki da	Obligation
-te mo ii	Permission
-(r)enai, koto ga dekinai	Negation of ability
-te wa ikenai / naranai	Negation of permission
-tai	Desire

[Korean]

-l swu issta	Ability
-to toyta / cohta	Permission
-ya hata / toyta	Obligation
-ci anh-umyen an toyta	Obligation
-l swu epsta, mo + verb	Negation of ability
-myen an toyta	Negation of permission
	Negation of obligation
-ko siphta	Desire

Source: Partially adapted from Horie (2003: 208).

Concerning the first point, that is, (i) auxiliaries encoding epistemic modality are formally distinct from those encoding deontic modality, Wymann (1996: 116) argues that Korean does have modal auxiliaries showing deontic–epistemic ambiguity as in (18), but that they are rather exceptional:

(18) *te*   *hwullyungha-n*   *tayhanminkwuk-i*
     more   be:excellent-ADN:PRES   Republic of Korea-NOM

     toy-e   *seykye-e pichna-ke*
     become-CSfx   world-LOC be:outstanding-ADV

     toyl   **kes-ip-ni-ta**
     become-ADN:FUT thing-UFS-IND-SCSfx
     'An even more excellent Republic of Korea *will* arise and shine forth in the world.' (epistemic)
      'An even more excellent ROK *must* arise and shine forth in the world.' (deontic)

In fact, our informants rejected the deontic reading of (18), which supports the claim that such ambiguity is quite rare, if it exists at all.

Fujii (2000: 59) also argues that such ambiguity in modal meaning exists in Japanese:

(19) *Go-kai*   *no*   *ano heya-ni*   *akari-ga*   *tuite-ire-ba*
     fifth-floor GEN   that room-LOC   light-NOM   turn-on-exist-if

     moo   *kaet-te*   **i-nakereba-naranai**
     already   return-PERF:CONJ   exist-must
     'If the light of (the room on) the fifth floor is turned on, (he/she) *must* be already back.'

Fujii (2000) notes that the modal auxiliary *nakereba-naranai* in (19), which is normally interpreted as deontic, can be interpreted as epistemic, since the first half of the sentence specifies the evidence for epistemic judgement. But even if some native speakers of Japanese agree with this observation, such cases are surely much less frequent than in English or other European languages.

Concerning the second point, that is, (ii) the majority of modal auxiliaries are periphrastic constructions, there are some cases, both in Japanese and Korean, where a less periphrastic modal expression coexists with a more periphrastic one expressing the same kind of modality. But even in such cases a slight semantic difference exists between these expressions, as illustrated by pairs of 'synthetic' deontic auxiliaries of obligation in Japanese (20a) and Korean (21a) and their more periphrastic counterparts (20b and 21b, respectively):

(20) a. *Kono*   *tegami-o*   *yomu-beki-da*
      this   letter-OBJ   read-must-DECL
   b. *Kono*   *tegami-o*   *yoma-nakereba-naranai*
      this   letter-OBJ   read-must-DECL
      '(He) must read this letter.'
(21) a. *i-phyenci-lul*   *ilk-e-ya-ha-pnita*
      this letter-OBJ   read-must-POL:DECL
   b. *i-phyenci-lul*   *ilk-ci-anh-umyon an toy-pnita*
      this letter-OBJ   read-CONJ-must-DECL:POL
      '(He) must read this letter.'

(20a) typically expresses a more subjective attitude than (20b). For example, if a speaker wants to urge someone to read the letter, she or he will use (20a) (Niwa 1991). On the other hand, if some external factor compels someone to read the letter, and the speaker merely reports the situation, she or he will use (20b). Thus, (20a) conveys more subjective deontic modal meaning than (20b).[8] The same is also true for (21). According to Wymann (1996: 108–9), *ci-anh-umyon an toy-ta* is far less frequent and judged to 'encode a lesser degree of stringency of obligation' than *e-ya-ha-ta*. Our informants' judgements on (21) also accord with Wymann's observation. The correctness of this observation is confirmed by (22a, b), where one is appropriate, while the other is not:

(22) a. ??*Nihon-de-wa*   *kuruma-wa*   *hidari-gawa-o*   *tooru-bekida*
      Japan-LOC-TOP   car-TOP   left-side-ACC   go-*must*
   b. *Nihon-de-wa*   *kuruma-wa*   *hidari-gawa-o*   *toora-nakereba-naranai*
      Japan-LOC-TOP   car-TOP   left-side-ACC   go-*have to*
      'In Japan, cars have to use the left lane.'

(22a) sounds odd because traffic regulations are usually not something a person has control over, while (22b) sounds natural because traffic regulations are naturally regarded as factors external to the speaker or the immediate speech situation. Korean sentences corresponding to (22a) and (22b) show the same contrast, although the difference is not as clear as in Japanese.

As stated in section 4.2.3, Japanese periphrastic modal auxiliaries such as *nakereba-naranai* are historically newer than their less periphrastic counterparts such as *beki-da*. The differing degrees of grammaticalization between the two groups of auxiliaries is reflected in their differential degrees of formal reduction and the accompanying semantic differences, in line with principles of grammaticalization proposed by Bybee et al. (1994). Since similar contrasts exist in Korean, as illustrated in (21), it is not unreasonable to assume that more periphrastic modal auxiliaries in Korean such as *ci-anh-umyon an toy-ta* are historically newer than less periphrastic modal auxiliaries such as *e-ya-ha-ta*.[9]

Thus, the fact that Korean and Japanese share periphrastic modal auxiliaries such as (20b) and (21b) is very interesting for the following reasons. First, although the development of the Korean language is not as well documented as that of Japanese, given the similar inventories of modal expressions in both languages, it is not unreasonable to assume that modal auxiliaries in both languages underwent similar developmental pathways. If that is the case, the Korean and Japanese data can be used to show (i) that the developmental pathway of modal expressions is more variable than has been envisaged by previous typological work on grammaticalization such as Bybee et al. (1994), and (ii) that it is therefore necessary to re-examine the universalist claim of unidirectional semantic change in the development of modal auxiliaries. Second, the remarkable similarities in the inventory of the periphrastic modal expressions could be attributed to some common cultural/typological factor(s) between the two linguistic communities.

One possible venue of the commonality is the influence exerted by Classical Chinese on the lexico-grammatical structures of Japanese and Korean. As pointed out by Yamada (1935), numerous expressions in Japanese, such as *sude-ni* ('already'), *iwa-yuru* ('so-called') and *ie-domo* ('although'), are known to have evolved from Classical Chinese through translation. Old Korean is known to have developed a similar way of translating from Classical Chinese, as evidenced by the excavation of Old Korean historical relics (Sohn 1999: 124–8). It is thus quite probable that the similar ways of translating Classical Chinese led to parallel developments of periphrastic modal expressions in both Korean and Japanese. If this conjecture is proven to be correct, it can help shed light on such issues as how sociocultural factors can influence and constrain the way grammaticalization proceeds in a linguistic community, and why Japanese and Korean have a lot of periphrastic modal expressions in common.[10]

But we have yet to address precisely why Japanese and Korean elected to develop periphrastic expressions to disambiguate older synthetic/polysemous modal expressions, rather than supplementing new modal expressions or extending the use of old synthetic/polysemous modal expressions. We will address this question from a cultural/typological perspective in the following subsection.

4.3.2 Cultural/typological factors

In this subsection, we will argue that periphrastic modal expressions in Japanese and Korean are closely related to the cultural and typological characteristics of these languages.

4.3.2.1 *'DO-language' vs 'BECOME'-language*

Ikegami (1991: 290) points out that there is a contrast between 'a language which focuses on the human being (especially, one acting as agent)' and 'a language which tends to suppress the notion of the human being (especially, one acting as agent)'. He notes that English belongs to the former type, while Japanese belongs to the latter. Manifestations of this contrast are observable in various aspects of the languages, including two types of semantic contrasts, that is, the HAVE/BE contrast and the DO/BECOME contrast.

English is known as a HAVE-language, in which possession is expressed using a special verb HAVE. In contrast, Japanese is a BE-language, in which possession can be expressed using a locative expression with a copulative verb (Ikegami 1991: 299):

(23) a. John has two children.
    b. *John   ni   wa   kodomo   ga   hutari   iru*
        John   LOC   TOP   child   NOM   two   be
        'John has two children.'

According to Ikegami (1991), in languages which preferentially encode human agency in the grammatical structure (for example, subject), possession is naturally expressed by focusing on the possessor, which in most cases is a human being. But in languages which tend to suppress linguistic coding of agency, possession is naturally expressed by asserting the existence of the thing possessed. We must point out here that Korean also belongs to the BE-languages:

(24) *Na-   ege-   nun   ai-ga   tumyong   issta*
      I   LOC   topic   child-NOM   two   be:DECL
      'I have two children.'

In both Japanese and Korean, a possessing agent is expressed with a locative marker, thus indicating its defocused status.

Another characteristic of human-focusing languages is that they favour structures for higher transitivity, with the most typical one being the transitive construction, while human-defocusing languages favour grammatical structures encoding lower transitivity, with the most typical one being the intransitive construction. Thus English favours a scheme of representation 'someone DOing something' while Japanese favours a representation in terms of 'BECOMing' (Ikegami 1991: 319). Such a difference manifests itself in the following example (Ikegami 1991: 316):

(25) *Watakusitati   wa   konotabi   kekkonsuru   koto*
     we   topic   now   marry   NOML
     ni   nari   masita.
     to   become   polite-past
     '(It) has become (that is, come to pass) that we are now getting married.'

The use of *naru* ('become') implies that 'the event in question is a natural (and almost inevitable) consequence beyond the control of the two persons involved' (Ikegami 1991: 317). In this respect, Korean also favours 'BECOMing' expression as exemplified below:

(26) *Uli   yuwol-e   kyolhonha-ge   toe-oss-sumnida*
     we   June-LOC   marry to   become-past DECL:POL
     '(It) has become that we are getting married in June.'

We will see that this tendency to defocus human agency has arguably given rise to a wealth of periphrastic modal auxiliaries.[11,12]

4.3.2.2 *Periphrastic modal expressions in BECOME-languages*

We can see the same kind of contrast as seen above in the area of modal expressions. Namely, while English has basically modal expressions based on 'DOing' expressions, Korean and Japanese tend to have modal expressions based on 'BECOMing' expressions and this causes these languages to have developed periphrastic modal auxiliaries.

As pointed out in Ikegami (1991: 302), the structure of English and Japanese epistemic modal expressions typically differs, with the former as in (27a) and the latter as in (27b):

(27) a. John *may/must* be ill in bed.
     b. It is *possible/certain* that John is ill in bed.

Ikegami (1991) maintains that this is a reflection of person-orientation in English and event-orientation in Japanese. Notice here that the construction in (27b) corresponds to periphrastic modal expressions in

Japanese and Korean. These languages express epistemic modality by defocusing the agent and focusing the event as a whole.

As for deontic modal expressions, Araki (1985) and Ando (1986) note that deontic modal expressions in Japanese have the characteristic of 'BECOMing' expressions (Ando 1986: 260):

(28) *Kimi wa   ima   ika-nakutewa   nara-nai.*
     you TOP   now   go-NEG-if   become-not
     'If you do not go, (it) will not become.'

(28) shows a typical way of expressing deontic modality in Japanese. This is a roundabout expression (or circumlocution), as is clear in the literal English translation. Deontic modality is expressed with negation using *naru* (become), thus asserting that your not going can lead to an unfavourable result. The same is also true of the deontic modal expression *chi-anumyon-an-doe-da* in Korean.

In this connection, Akatsuka (1998), based on Akatsuka and Clancy (1993) and Clancy et al. (1997), points out that Japanese and Korean children acquire conditional clauses earlier than American children because conditional clauses in Japanese and Korean are more frequent as an expression of deontic modality.

Thus it is clear that modal expressions in Japanese and Korean reflect the overall tendency in these languages to favour human-defocusing and 'BECOMing' expressions. While the modal system was developing in the direction of disambiguation, this overall tendency arguably affected the manner in which newer modal systems were constructed.

Typological/cultural explanations set out in this section need further refinement and substantial experiential evidence. But at least they suggest a possible account for the factors behind the attested differences in terms of developmental pathways between both Japanese and Korean, and English and many other languages.

4.4 Conclusion

In this chapter, we compared the developmental pathways of English and Japanese modal auxiliaries, and went on to show that the developmental mechanism proposed for English cannot be applied to Japanese since a semantic shift from deontic to epistemic modalities is not observable in Japanese. Rather, viewing modality as the expression of the *realis* vs *irrealis* distinction, as was evident in Old Japanese modal auxiliaries like -*mu* and in the English subjunctive mood, the developmental pathway of Japanese modal auxiliaries is characterized as one instantiation of how the schematic *irrealis* meaning develops more substantial deontic and epistemic meanings, while the developmental pathway of English modal auxiliaries is just another instantiation. Furthermore, we have argued that the similarity between modal auxiliaries in Japanese and Korean may have been caused by common cultural/typological factors.

Through our cross-linguistic and diachronic analyses, it has become clear that the Japanese modal auxiliary system shares some common features with English, while consistently exhibiting overall similarity with Korean. Research findings gained in this study caution against blindly applying the account of 'unidirectional' development from deontic to epistemic modalities and underscore the importance of cross-linguistic and diachronic perspectives in evaluating the semantic properties of modal auxiliaries synchronically.

Acknowledgements

Thanks are due to two anonymous reviewers and Andrew Barke for constructive criticism, and particularly to Barbara Pizziconi and Mika Kizu for careful editorial guidance and advice. The usual disclaimer applies.

Notes

1. The following abbreviations are used in this chapter: ACC = accusative, ADV = adverb, ADN = adnominal, COMP = complementizer, CSfx = connective suffix, DAT = dative, FUT = future, GEN = genitive, IND = indicative mood, LOC = locative, NEG = negation, NOM = nominative, NOML = nominalizer, PERF = perfective, PRES = present, SCSfx = sentence concluding suffix, TOP = topic, UFS = upward formal speech level.
2. For a detailed discussion on semantic change in the grammaticalization of verbs into postpositions, see Matsumoto (1998).
3. See Lakoff (1972) and Lyons (1977: 791).
4. Kurotaki (2005) argues that even in Modern Japanese epistemic meanings are basic and deontic meanings are derived from them.
5. *Beki-da*, which derived from the potentially ambiguous *besi* in Old Japanese, preserves its ambiguity in some contexts. For example, *kuru beki hito* either means 'a person who (morally) should come' or 'a person who is (epistemically) supposed to come'. But we cannot find periphrastic modal auxiliaries which show such ambiguity.
6. Chung and Timberlake (1985) entertain this view with respect to English.
7. Based on synchronic data, Masuoka (2007) also claims that the *realis/irrealis* contrast is important in characterizing Japanese epistemic and deontic modality.

8. Kuno (1983) points out that a similar difference exists between *-(r)enai* and *-koto ga dekinai*, which both express negation of ability:

    (i) *Sibafu-ni-wa*   *hai-renai*
        lawn-to-TOP   enter-not:able
    (ii) *Sibafu-ni-wa*   *hairu-koto-ga-dekinai*
        lawn-to-TOP   enter-COMP-NOM-not:able
    'You cannot enter the lawn.'

Kuno (1983: 151) notes that (ii) is more natural as a notice sign because it implies that the prohibition is imposed by some external authority, while (i) indicates lack of ability of someone who might try to enter the lawn.

9. Similar contrasts also exist in English. For example, *must* and *have to* have different meanings in sentences (i) and (ii):

    (i)   My daughter *must* come back by ten.
    (ii)   My daughter *has to* come back by ten.

In (i), the source of obligation is most likely the speaker. On the other hand, (ii) implies that some external factors, such as dormitory regulations, oblige the daughter to come back by that time. In this case, too, the periphrastic auxiliary *have to* is objective while *must* is subjective.

10. Yong-key Kim-Renaud (personal communication) suggests that politeness strategies common in Japanese and Korean may be a factor influencing the prevalence of periphrastic modal expressions in both languages. Furthermore, she adds that this factor may also explain why the two languages generally have a lot of periphrastic verbal expressions. This is an interesting research topic that needs further investigation.

11. We must point out that there is another important factor responsible for the emergence of periphrastic auxiliaries: the Japanese language as a whole underwent a morphosyntactic change characterizable as that from synthesis to periphrasis in the modern period (Tanaka 2001: 585–8). For example, *-mai*, which is potentially ambiguous between the sense of negative probability and that of negative intention, has become rarely used and is replaced by *-nai-daroo* or *-nai-rasii* (negative probability) and *-nai-tumori-da* or *-wa-yosoo* (negative intention) (Tanaka 2001: 587). Investigation into the interplay of various linguistic and non-linguistic factors inducing this change will need to await future study.

12. We must note that the tendency to supplement the 'synthetic' modal auxiliary system with periphrastic ones is manifested also in English and its related languages. For example, *be supposed to* in Modern English encodes the meaning which was previously encoded by *should* or *can*. But the number of periphrastic modal auxiliaries relative to that of synthetic modal auxiliaries is much greater in Japanese and Korean compared to English, suggesting that the commonly observed tendency is attributable to some commonality in cultural/typological profiles between the former group of languages.

References

Akatsuka, N. (1998). Zyooken bun to desirability no kasetu [Conditional clauses and the desirability hypothesis]. In: Akatsuka, N. and Tubomoto, A, *Modarity to Hatuwa Kooi* [Modality and Speech Act]. Tokyo: Kenkyusha: 1–97.

Akatsuka, N., and P. Clancy (1993). Affect and conditionals: evidence from Japanese and Korean acquisition. In: Clancy, P. (ed.), *Japanese/Korean Linguistics* 2. Stanford: CSLI: 176–92.

Ando, S. (1986). *Eigo no Ronri, Nihongo no Ronri* [Logic in English and Logic in Japanese]. Tokyo: Taishukan.

Araki, H. (1985). *Yamato Kotoba no Jinruigaku* [Anthropology of Japanese Language]. Tokyo: Asahi Shinbun.

Berk, L.M. (1999). *English Syntax: From Word to Discourse*. New York: Oxford University Press.

Bybee, J. and W. Pagliuca (1985). Cross-Linguistic Comparison and the Development of Grammatical Meaning. In: Fisiak, J. (ed.), *Historical Semantics and Historical Word-Formation*. Berlin: Mouton: 60–83.

Bybee, J., R. Perkins, and W. Pagliuca (1994). *The Evolution of Grammar: Tense, Aspect, and Modality in the Languages of the World*. Chicago: The University of Chicago Press.

Chung, S. and A. Timberlake (1985). Tense, Aspect and Mood. In Shopen, T. (ed.), *Language Typology and Syntactic Description III*. Cambridge: Cambridge University Press: 202–58.

Clancy, P., N. Akatuska, and S.G. Strauss (1997). Deontic modality and conditionality in discourse: a cross-linguistic study of adult speech to young children. In: Kamio, A. (ed.), *Directions in Functional Linguistics*. Amsterdam: John Benjamins: 19–57.

Dietrich, R. (1992). *Modalität im Deutschen*. Opladen: Westdeutscher Verlag.

Fillmore, Ch. (1968). The case for case. In: Bach, E. and Harms, R.T. (eds), *Universals in Linguistic Theory*. New York: Holt, Rinehart and Winston Inc: 1–88.

Fujii, S. (2000). Ninsiki-teki modariti to sono syuuhen tono kanren - bunpooka, tagisei no kanten kara [Epistemic modality and related phenomena: exploring their relations in view of grammaticalization and polysemy]. In: Kokuritu Kokugo Kenkyusho [The National Institute for Japanese Language] (ed.), *Ninsiki no Modariti to Sono Syuuhen – Nihongo, Eigo, Tyuugokugo no Baai* [Epistemic Modality and Related Phenomena: the Cases of Japanese, English and Chinese]. Tokyo: Bonjinsya: 52–71.

Givón, T. (1995). *Functionalism and Grammar*. Amsterdam: John Benjamins.

Harsh, W. (1968). *The Subjunctive in English*. Tuscaloosa, Ala.: University of Alabama Press.

Heine, B., U. Claudi, and F. Hünnemeyr (1991). *Grammaticalization: a Conceptual Framework*. Chicago: The University of Chicago Press.

Hopper, P. and E.C. Traugott (2003). *Grammaticalization*, 2nd edn. Cambridge: Cambridge University Press.

Horie, K. (1997). Form–meaning interaction in diachrony: a case study from Japanese. *English Linguistics* 14, 428–49.

Horie, K. (2003). Differential manifestations of 'modality' between Japanese and Korean: a typological perspective. In: Chiba, S. et al. (eds), *Empirical and*

Theoretical Investigations into Language: a Festschrift for Masaru Kajita. Tokyo: Kaitakusha: 205–16.

Horie, K. (2007). Subjectification and intersubjectification in Japanese: a comparative-typological perspective. *Journal of Historical Pragmatics* 8, 311–23.

Horie, K. and H. Narrog (to appear). What typology reveals about modality in Japanese: a cross-linguistic perspective. In: Ono, T. and Kabata, K. (eds), *Functional Approaches to Japanese Grammar*. Stanford: CSLI.

Ikegami, Y. (1991). 'DO-language' and 'BECOME-language': two contrasting types of linguistic representation. In: Ikegami, Y. (ed.), *The Empire of Signs: Semiotic Essays on Japanese Culture*. Amsterdam: John Benjamins: 285–326.

Kitahara, Y. et al. (eds) (2000). *Nihon Kokugo Daiziten, Dai 2 Han* [Comprehensive Japanese Language Dictionary, 2nd edn]. Tokyo: Shogakukan.

Kondo, Y. (2000). *Nihongo Kizyutu Bunpoo-no Riron* [The Theory of Japanese Descriptive Grammar]. Tokyo: Hituzi Syobo.

Kuno, S. (1983). *Sin Nihon Bunpoo Kenkyuu* [A New Study of Japanese Grammar]. Tokyo: Taishukan.

Kurotaki, M. (2005). *Deontic-kara Epistemic-eno Huhensei to Sootaisei: Modariti-no Niti-ei Taishoo Kenkyuu* [Universality and Relativity of Change from Deontic to Epistemic: a Contrastive Study on Modality in Japanese and English]. Tokyo: Kurosio.

Lakoff, R. (1972). The pragmatics of modality. In: Peranteau, P.M., Levi, J.N., and Phares, G.C. (eds), *Papers from the Eighth Regional Meeting, Chicago Linguistic Society*, Chicago: Chicago Linguistic Society: 229–46.

Lyons, J. (1968). *Introduction to Theoretical Linguistics*. Cambridge: Cambridge University Press.

Lyons, J. (1977). *Semantics*, vol. 2. Cambridge: Cambridge University Press.

Masuoka, T. (1991). *Modariti no Bunpoo* [The Grammar of Modality]. Tokyo: Kurosio.

Masuoka, T. (2000). Meidai to odariti no kyokai o motomete [Seeking the boundary between proposition and modality]. In: Masuoka T. (ed.), *Nihongo Bunpoo no Syosoo* [Aspects of Japanese Grammar]. Tokyo: Kurosio: 87–98.

Masuoka, T. (2007). *Nihongo Modariti Tankyuu* [Exploration in Japanese Modality]. Tokyo: Kurosio.

Matsumoto, Y. (1998). Semantic change in the grammaticalization of verbs into postpositions in Japanese. In Ohori, T. (ed.), *Studies in Japanese Grammaticalization: Cognitive and Discourse Perspcetive*. Tokyo: Kurosio: 25–60.

Narrog, H. (2002). Imironteki kategorii to siteno modariti [Modality as a semantic category]. In: Ohori, T. (ed.), *Ninti gengogaku II: Kategoriika* [Cognitive Linguistics II: Categorization]. Tokyo: Tokyo University Press: 217–51.

Narrog, H. (2005). On defining modality again. *Language Sciences* 27, 165–92.

Narrog, H. (2007). Modality and grammaticalization in Japanese. *Journal of Historical Pragmatics* 8, 269–94.

Newmeyer, F. (1998). *Language Form and Language Function*. Cambridge, Mass.: MIT Press.

Nitta, Y. (1991). *Nihongo no modariti to ninsyoo* [Japanese modality and person]. Tokyo: Hituji Shobo.

Nitta, Y. (2000). Ninsiki no modariti to sono syuuhen [Epistemic modality and its periphery]. In: Moriyama, T., Nitta, Y. and Kudo, H. (eds), *Modariti* [Modality]. Tokyo: Iwanami.

Niwa, T. (1991). 'Bekida' to 'nakereba-naranai' [The modals of obligation in present-day Japanese: 'bekida' and 'nakereba-naranai']. *Osaka Gakuin Daigaku Jinbun Sizen Ronso* [The Bulletin of the Cultural and Natural Sciences in Osaka Gakuin University]: 53–72.

Nomura, T. (2003). Modariti keisiki no bunrui [On the classification of Japanese modal forms]. *Kokugogaku* 54 (1), 17–31.

Ohori, T. (2002). *Ninti Gengogaku* [Cognitive Linguistics]. Tokyo: University of Tokyo Press.

Onodera, N. (2004). *Japanese Discourse Markers: Synchronic and Diachronic Discourse Analysis*. Amsterdam: John Benjamins.

Onoe, K. (2001). *Bunpoo to Imi* vol.1 [Grammar and Meaning, vol. 1]. Tokyo: Kurosio.

Palmer, F.R. (1986). *Mood and Modality*. Cambridge: Cambridge University Press.

Palmer, F.R. (1998). Mood and modality: basic principles. In: Brown, K. and Miller, J. (eds), *Concise Encyclopedia of Grammatical Categories*. Oxford: Elsevier: 229–35.

Palmer, F.R. (2001). *Mood and Modality*, 2nd edn. Cambridge: Cambridge University Press.

Sohn, H-M. (1999). *The Korean Language*. Cambridge: Cambridge University Press.

Sweetser, E. (1990). *From Etymology to Pragmatics: Metaphorical and Cultural Aspects of Semantic Structure*. Cambridge: Cambridge University Press.

Takayama, Y. (2002). *Nihongo Modality no Shiteki Kenkyu* [A Historical Study on Japanese Modality]. Tokyo: Hituzi Shobo.

Talmy, L. (1988). Force dynamics in language and cognition. *Cognitive Science 2*, 49–100.

Tanaka, A. (2001). *Kindai Nihon no Bunpoo to Hyoogen* [Grammar and Expressions in Modern Japanese]. Tokyo: Meiji Syoin.

Taylor, J.R. (2002). *Cognitive Grammar*. Oxford: Oxford University Press.

Traugott, E.C.(1989). On the rise of epistemic meanings in English: an example of subjectification in semantic change. *Language* 65, 31–55.

Traugott, E. and R. Dasher (2002). *Regularity in Semantic Change*. Cambridge: Cambridge University Press.

Wymann, A. T. (1996). The expression of modality in Korean. PhD dissertation, University of Berne (http://www.wymann.info/Korean/atw_diss.pdf).

Yamada, Y. (1935). *Kanbun kundoku-tai ni yori-te tutae-rare-taru gohoo* [Usage derived from the Japanese way of reading classical Chinese]. Tokyo: Hobunkan.

Part II

Japanese Modality from Semantic and Syntactic Perspectives

5
Tense and Settledness in Japanese Conditionals[1]

Setsuko Arita

5.1 Introduction

The purpose of this chapter is to discuss the non-factuality encoded by conditional constructions through some phenomena regarding temporal and modal dimensions in Japanese. We will show that, unlike English, Japanese has grammatical markers of epistemic conditionals.[2] Epistemic conditionals are one of three types of conditionals discussed in this chapter, along with predictive and counterfactual ones. Under the framework developed in this study, we argue that the antecedent in epistemic conditionals is settled, but the speaker does not know its truth value. What we mean by 'settled' is that the truth value of a proposition is already determined at the time of utterance. We demonstrate the existence of grammatical markers of epistemic conditionals in Japanese to argue that either the semantic notion of settledness or the fact that the speaker does not know the truth, or both of them, play an essential role in the grammar of conditionals in Japanese. In the following section, we point out that the aspect marker, -*tei*-, when occurring in the antecedent clause of Japanese epistemic conditionals, plays the role of settledness marker.

As we mentioned above, the fact that the speaker does not know the truth is crucial for the analysis of epistemic conditionals. We will demonstrate that the conditional marker *n(o)nara*[3] indicates that the speaker does not know the truth value of the antecedent proposition. We will also show that speaker's ignorance of the proposition's truth is encoded by *no(da)* particularly often.

As is well known, in English and many other Indo-European languages, counterfactuality or low probability is grammatically marked by either verbal inflection (such as backshifted tense) or subjunctive mood. In Japanese, in contrast, no special marker of counterfactuality or low probability appears in the antecedent clause. Settledness of the antecedent proposition and speaker's ignorance of the truth are rather marked by certain grammatical forms used for marking tense, aspect and modality.

In what follows, we first discuss two types of open conditionals and claim that they are distinct from each other in terms of the uncertainty of the antecedent. Second, to deal with this uncertainty, we introduce the semantic feature of settledness, and then discuss its crucial role both in the selection of conditional forms in Japanese and in the distribution of the aspect marker *-tei-*.[4] Finally, we show the strong connection between speaker's knowledge state and some modal expressions in Japanese. In particular, we will look into the epistemic functions of the aforesaid modal auxiliary *n(o)da* and its conditional form *n(o)nara*.

Japanese conditional clauses can be tensed or non-tensed. Therefore, examining the distinct temporal features of conditional clauses is crucial for looking into the non-factuality expressed in subordinate clauses as discussed by Arita (2004, 2007). We assume that conditionals explicitly indicate inference based on an uncertain state of knowledge, whereas the uncertainty is concerned with both settledness of an antecedent proposition and the speaker's ignorance of the truth of the antecedent proposition.

In this study, we consider modality as a notional category, following Kratzer (1981). It is not seen as a grammatical feature of verbs, but rather a property of sentences (Roberts 1989). Non-factuality is expressed by a variety of conventional means, including subjunctive mood, modal auxiliaries like *would* or *could*, or adverbials like *probably* or *supposedly*. Since conditional constructions should be considered as explicit indicators of non-factuality, which is typically expressed by modals, they fall within the scope of the study of modality.

5.2 Preliminaries

5.2.1 Scope of the study

Our investigation focuses mainly on 'direct conditionals', where 'the truth of the proposition in the matrix clause is a consequence of the fulfilment of the condition in the conditional clause' (Quirk et al. 1985: 1088), as in examples (1) and (2) (ibid.: 1088–9):

(1) If you put the baby down, she'll scream.

(2) If you don't put the baby down, she won't scream.

On the other hand, 'indirect conditionals' where the condition is not related to the content described in the matrix clause (Quirk et al. 1985: 1089) are excluded from our study. These expressions, illustrated by the following examples, are sometimes called 'speech-act conditionals' (Sweetser 1990, Dancygier 1998, among others):

(3) She's far too considerate, if I may say so.

(4) She and I are just good friends, if you understand me.

In Quirk et al. (1985), direct conditional clauses are categorized as 'adjuncts', while indirect conditional clauses are called 'disjuncts'. Even though we admit that the latter type of conditionals appears quite frequently in both spoken and written contexts (Ono and Jones 2005, Dancygier and Sweetser 2005) and that it is strongly related to the former type, our current concern is limited to the core, that is, direct uses of conditionals.

5.2.2 Two types of open conditionals

The dichotomy between 'open' and 'hypothetical' conditionals is frequently assumed in the literature. Quirk et al. (1985: 1091) define open and hypothetical conditionals as follows:

> Open conditionals are neutral: they leave unresolved the question of the fulfilment or nonfulfilment of the condition [...] A hypothetical condition, on the other hand, conveys the speaker's belief that the condition will not be fulfilled (for future conditions), is not fulfilled (for present conditions), or was not fulfilled (for past conditions) [...]

Sentences (5) and (6) exemplify these two types of conditionals (Quirk et al. 1985: 1091):

(5) If Collins is in London, he is undoubtedly staying at the Hilton. (open)

(6) If he changed his opinion, he'd be a more likeable person. (hypothetical)

Some recent work on conditionals, however, states that the class of open conditionals exemplified in (7) and (8) is not homogeneous, as the common label would suggest (Funk 1985, Kaufmann 2005). Consider the following sentences:

(7) I will be happy if we find a solution.

(8) (I hope Bolton won their home match yesterday.) If they did, they still have a chance of winning the championship.

Funk (1985: 375–6) classifies the open conditionals into two types, according to the uncertainty of the antecedent:

> In the case of [(7)], the uncertainty is largely due to the fact that the state-of-affairs described and predicated of does not yet exist, i.e., is still subject to manifestation (so that it cannot be affirmed or denied – it is unverifiable) at the moment of the sentence being uttered. In [(8)], however, the state-of-affairs does exist at the time of speaking (either in the positive or negative sense, it is 'manifested' and could thus be verified), but the speaker has not got enough information (or is otherwise not disposed) to be sure about it and hence to affirm or deny it. Accordingly, the meaning of the conditioning frame can be said to vary from 'if it happens that...' to 'if it is true that...'.

According to Funk, in the case of example (7), whether we find a solution in the future or not is uncertain for everyone at the time of speaking. However, in (8), whether Bolton won their home match yesterday or not is already established at the time of speaking, although the speaker does not have enough information to affirm or deny it.

The next section is devoted to introducing the notion of 'settledness' in relation to conditionals.

5.3   Uncertainty relative to settledness and to speaker's knowledge

5.3.1   Settledness

In this section, we will introduce the notion of 'settledness' based on discussion in Arita (2004, 2007) to capture the different types of uncertainty pointed out by Funk (1985). The idea of an issue being settled at a given time corresponds to the notion of necessity with respect to *historical alternatives* or *historical necessity* (Thomason 1984, Condoravdi 2002, among others). A sentence is historically necessary at time t if it is true at t, regardless of what the future is like (Condoravdi 2002). Historical necessity depends on the asymmetry between the past and the future. The former is determined while the latter is undetermined. To capture the idea of settledness, we follow Thomason's (1984) world–time model assuming T×W frames, and elaborated by Condoravdi (2002), Kaufmann (2005) and Kaufmann et al. (2006). We take a set W of possible worlds, each with the same fixed time axis T. We represent a world–time pair as $<w, t>$. There is an earlier-than relation $<$ on the set T of moments in time. We will refer to the times in world–time pairs as $t_1, t_2, \ldots$ etc. and indicate the relations between times as '$t_1 \leq t_2$' for '$t_1 < t_2$ or '$t_1 = t_2$'. Propositions are represented as p, q, r. We assume that each proposition describes a situation such that at a certain interval i a given state of affairs holds. We will call i 'an interval specified in a proposition' and we represent the proposition as p_i, where necessary to specify its interval.

The truth value of a proposition p ($[\![p]\!]$) is determined relative to each world–time pair ($<w, t>$) and it is defined as follows:

(9) The truth value of a proposition p in $<w, t>$
 a. $[\![p]\!]_{<w,\ t>} = 1$ iff p holds in $< w, t >$
 b. $[\![p]\!]_{<w,\ t>} = 0$ iff $\neg p$ holds in $< w, t >$
 c. $[\![p]\!]_{<w,\ t>} = *$ iff neither a nor b holds

In (9), we assume the third value, $*$, possessed by propositions that are neither true nor false in a given world w at a given time t. We assume that a proposition p_i is assigned $*$ in any possible world temporally located prior to i. In other words, the evaluation of a proposition p_i is 1 or 0 in any possible world occurring later than i, as stated in (10):

(10) $\forall w \forall t [(i \leq t) \rightarrow ([\![p_i]\!]_{<w,\ t>} = 1 \vee [\![p_i]\!]_{<w,\ t>} = 0)]$

Subsequently, we will introduce '$\Phi < w, t >$' to denote the set of propositions which are given truth values 1 or 0 in a certain world at a certain time:

(11) $\Phi < w, t > = \{p | [\![p]\!]_{<w,\ t>} = 1 \vee [\![p]\!]_{<w,\ t>} = 0\}$

Then, the following formula is provable, given (10) and (11) as a theorem:

(12) Theorem: In any world–time pair, $< w, t >$, and $t' > t$, the following formula holds:

$$\forall w \forall t [\Phi < w, t' > \supseteq \Phi < w, t >]$$

Based on the above definitions, we can introduce the notion of settledness. Settledness is a semantic notion regarding propositions, as defined in (13):

(13) Settled propositions:
A proposition *p* is settled iff $p \in \Phi < w, t_s >$, where 't_s' designates the time of speaking.

The definition in (13) states that a proposition's truth value is determined at the time of speaking. Propositions which do not fall under the above definition are unsettled.

In what follows, we assume that all sentences that do not refer to the future are settled:

(14) Bolton won their home match (yesterday).

(15) Nakata is in the locker room (now).

In example (14), whether or not Bolton won their home match at a certain time in the past is determined and cannot be changed. The propositions denoted by simple past sentences are considered settled. In (15), whether Nakata is in the locker room or not is verifiable at the time of speaking. The propositions denoted by simple present sentences like (15) are also considered as settled.

Not all simple present sentences describe a present situation. In English, the simple present tense of non-stative predicates can describe not the present, but a future situation:

(16) The sun sets at 8:39 tomorrow.

(17) The plane leaves for Ankara at 8 o'clock tonight.

(18) It rains tomorrow.

The above examples raise the following question: Is every sentence that refers to the future unsettled in English? Quirk et al. state that 'in main clauses, simple present referring to the future occurs with time-position adverbials to suggest that the event is unalterably fixed in advance, and is as certain as it would be, were it taking place in the present' (Quirk et al. 1985: 182).

Sentences such as (16) can be treated as settled when their truth can be deduced from past and present facts together with natural laws that are considered deterministic ('presumption of decidedness', Kaufmann

2005: 240). Sentences like (17) can be considered settled when they have a 'scheduling reading' (Kaufmann 2005: 234). Finally, sentences like (18) are usually odd, but can be acceptable to some extent, for example, when used by 'the Almighty' (Edgington 1997: 101; Kaufmann 2005: 253). In other words, the truth value of the propositions in (16)–(18) can be determined at the time of speaking based on some settled propositions that entail that they will hold in the near future. We will collectively call the propositions that are denoted by these sentences 'settled propositions in a broad sense', defined as follows:

(19) Settled propositions in a broad sense:
We use 'w_R' to refer to the real world, 't_s' to the time of speaking and '$\Psi < w_R, t_s >$' to a set of propositions that is a subset of $\Phi < w_R, t_s >$.
A proposition p is settled in $< w_R, t_s >$ in a broad sense iff $\Psi < w_R, t_s >$ entails the truth of p.

5.3.2 Speaker's knowledge

In this section, we will introduce another essential notion, 'speaker's knowledge (K)', discussed by Arita (2004, 2007). Settledness, whether in a narrow or broad sense, is defined independently of what the speaker knows. The truth values of settled propositions are determined at the time of speaking, but the speaker might not know all of them. If we use '$K < w, t_s >$' to refer to speaker's knowledge, it is obvious that the following formula holds:

(20) $K < w, t_s > \subseteq \Phi < w, t_s >$

Now, let us define settledness relative to $K < w, t_s >$ in the following way:

(21) Settledness in $K < w, t_s >$:
a. A proposition p is settled in $K < w, t_s >$ iff $p \in K < w, t_s >$
b. A proposition p is not settled iff $p \notin K < w, t_s >$

Definition (21a) states that a proposition is settled for the speaker iff s/he knows its truth value. Let us look at some examples:

(22) Lewis came to the office yesterday.

(23) Lewis must have come to the office yesterday.

(24) Lewis may have come to the office yesterday.

(25) Lewis comes to the office tomorrow (according to the schedule).

(26) Lewis must come to the office tomorrow.

(27) Lewis may come to the office tomorrow.

The truth value of the proposition in (22), 'Lewis came to the office yesterday', is determined at the time of speaking, thus the proposition is settled. English sentences with modal auxiliaries like (23) and (24) say explicitly that the speaker does not know the truth value of the settled proposition. The truth value of the proposition 'Lewis comes to the office tomorrow' is determined if and only if the speaker knows some information that entails the truth or falsity of the proposition. English sentences with modal auxiliaries like (26) and (27) convey explicitly that the speaker does not have enough information to infer the truth value of the proposition.

Simple past/present sentences like (22) and (25), on the other hand, can be treated as conveying that the speaker knows the truth value of the proposition, as in (22), or has enough information to presume the truth value of the proposition, as in (25).

Let us differentiate the class of open conditionals departing from the notion of uncertainty of the antecedent introduced by Funk (1985):

(28) I will be happy if we find a solution.

(29) (I hope Bolton won their home match yesterday.) If they did, they still have a chance of winning the championship.

One type of open conditional like (28) is characterized by an unsettled antecedent, whose truth value is uncertain to everybody. On the other hand, the other type, as in (29), is characterized by a settled antecedent, whose truth value is objectively determined but is unknown to the speaker. We will call the former type of conditionals 'predictive conditionals' and the latter type 'epistemic conditionals'.

In addition to the above class, there is one more type of conditionals whose antecedent is settled. They differ from the epistemic conditionals in that their antecedent is settled for the speaker. In epistemic conditionals like (29), the antecedent proposition is not settled for the speaker. On the other hand, the other type of settled antecedents is one whose falsity is certain to the speaker, that is, settled for the speaker. We call

Table 5.1 Conditionals and settledness

	Settledness in antecedent	Settledness for speaker in antecedent
Predictive conditionals	Unsettled	Unsettled
Epistemic conditionals	Settled	Unsettled
Counterfactual conditionals	Settled	Settled

this type of conditionals 'counterfactual conditionals'. Below are some English examples from Quirk et al. (1985: 1091):

(30) If he changed his opinions, he'd be a more likeable person.

(31) They would be here with us if they had the time.

(32) If you had listened to me, you wouldn't have made so many mistakes.

They are termed 'hypothetical conditionals' in Quirk et al. and they are treated as conveying the following implications:[5]

(33) He very probably won't change his opinions. ((30))

(34) They presumably don't have the time. ((31))

(35) You certainly didn't listen to me. ((32))

Table 5.1 summarizes the settledness conditions in the three types of conditionals.

The next section will analyse Japanese conditionals from the viewpoint of the factors contained in Table 5.1.

5.4   Japanese and settledness

5.4.1   Settledness and Japanese tenses

The morphemes *-(r)u* (a general form for the infinitive form of predicates) and *-ta* (past) have been studied as tense forms in Japanese linguistic literature. It is generally considered that Japanese has no overt present-tense morpheme, nor does it have a future-tense morpheme suffixed to the predicates. Also, Japanese has no future auxiliaries equivalent to *will* in English. Instead, future-oriented interpretations are usually expressed by the bare *-(r)u* sentences. Explicit reference to future events, if necessary, is made in terms of future-oriented nouns like *tumori* ('intention') and *yotei* ('plan') or through one of the epistemic auxiliaries like *daroo* ('prediction') (Ogihara 1999).

Regarding sentences with the past-tense morpheme *-ta*, they are considered as describing a settled proposition in a narrow sense because the propositions in both (36) and (37) specify a certain interval that is earlier than the time of speaking:

(36) *Kinoo*   *Boruton-ga*   *hoomu-de*   *kat-ta.*
     yesterday   Bolton-NOM home-in   win-PAST
     'Bolton won the home match yesterday.'

(37) *Nakata-wa*   *tyoosi-ga*   *warukat-ta.*
     Nakata-TOP   condition-NOM bad-PAST
     'Nakata was in a bad condition/Nakata did not feel well.'

There is no difference with regard to settledness between non-stative predicates like *katu* ('win') in (36) and stative predicates like *warui* ('bad') in (37).

Sentences with the infinitive morpheme *-(r)u*, on the other hand, can denote present or future states of affairs. A present-tense reading generally occurs with stative predicates as in (38), while future-tense readings are expressed by both stative ((41)) and non-stative predicates ((39) and (40)):

(38) *Nakata-wa*   *rokkaaruumu-ni* *i-ru.*
     Nakata-TOP   locker.room-in   be-NPAST
     'Nakata is in the locker room.'

(39) *Asita*   *taiyoo-wa* *8zi39hun-ni* *sizum-u.*
     tomorrow   sun-TOP   8:39-at   set-NPAST
     'The sun sets at 8:39 tomorrow.'

(40) *Ankara-iki-no*   *hikooki-wa* *konya 8.zi-ni*   *syuppatu.su-ru.*
     Ankara-for-GEN plane-TOP   tonight 8.o'clock-at leave-NPAST
     'The plane leaves for Ankara at 8 o'clock tonight.'

(41) *Asita-wa*   *undookai-ga*   *ar-u.*
     tomorrow-TOP sports-meeting-NOM   be-NPAST
     'A sports meeting will be held tomorrow.'

The *-(r)u* sentence referring to the present in (38) is considered as describing a settled proposition in a narrow sense because the proposition specifies a certain interval identical to the time of speaking. The *-(r)u* sentences referring to the future like those in (39)–(41) can be treated as involving settled propositions in a broad sense.

Interestingly, bare present sentences in Japanese sometimes describe speaker's prediction, as shown in (42) and (43):

(42) *Tabun*   *Nakata-wa*   *ima*   *rokkaaruumu-ni*   *i-ru.*
     perhaps   Nakata-TOP   now   locker.room-in   be-NPAST
     'Perhaps Nakata *will* be in the locker room now.'

(43) *Ankara.iki-no*   *hikooki-wa*   *kitto*   *konya*   *8zi-ni*   *syuppatu.su-ru.*
     Ankara.for-GEN plane-TOP   certainly tonight   8.o'clock-at   leave-NPAST
     'The plane for Ankara *will* certainly leave at 8 o'clock tonight.'

Tabun ('perhaps') and *kitto* ('certainly') are adverbials that describe the speaker's epistemic state. In Japanese, they can occur not only with an epistemic modal auxiliary like *daroo* ('prediction'), but also with the bare present tense (Morimoto 1994). In contrast, English adverbials like *perhaps* and *certainly* hardly occur in bare-present-tense sentences that describe a future state of affairs.[6] They usually appear with a certain epistemic auxiliary like *will*.

Bare present sentences with epistemic adverbials in Japanese can be considered to convey that the speaker does not know the truth value of the proposition. This suggests that the bare present tense in Japanese is more widely distributed than in English, not only in sentences describing settled propositions in K$< w, t_s >$, but also in those described as propositions unsettled in K$< w, t_s >$. In contrast, the bare present tense in English appears only in sentences describing propositions settled in K$< w, t_s >$.

Let us now turn to Japanese conditionals. Japanese has at least four basic conditional forms:[7] *-eba, -tara, -nara* and *-n(o)nara.* The first two markers, *-eba* and *-tara,* are inflectional endings of predicates.[8] In (44), *-eba* comes after the stem form *hur-* ('to rain') and in (45) *-tara* follows *hut-,* an allomorph of *hur-*:

(44) *Asita*   *ame-ga*   *hur-eba,*   *siai-wa*   *tyuusis-arer-u-daroo.*
     tomorrow   rain-NOM   fall-*eba*[9]   match-TOP   cancel-PASS-NPAST-will
     'If it rains tomorrow, the match will be cancelled.'

(45) *Asita*   *ame-ga*   *hut-tara,*   *siai-wa*   *tyuusis-arer-u-daroo.*
     tomorrow   rain-NOM   fall-*tara*   match-TOP   cancel-PASS-NPAST-will
     'If it rains tomorrow, the match will be cancelled.'

In contrast, -*nara* and -*n(o)nara* are connectives[10] that select tensed clauses, as exemplified below in (46)–(49). In (46) and (47), -*nara* and -*n(o)nara* follow the present-tense morpheme -*(r)u*. In (48) and (49), -*nara* and -*n(o)nara* come after the past-tense morpheme -*da* (an allomorph of -*ta*):

(46) *Asita   Tookyoo-iki-no   hikooki-ga   tob-u-**nara**,   kyoo-no*
tomorrow Tokyo-for-GEN   plane-NOM leave-NPAST-*nara*, today-GEN
yotei-wa   kae-nai-tumori-da.
plan-TOP   change-NEG-intention-be
'If the plane for Tokyo {will leave/leaves} tomorrow, I will not change my plans for today.'

(47) *Asita   Tookyoo-iki-no hikooki-ga   tob-u-**n(o)nara**,   kyoo-no*
tomorrow Tokyo-for-GEN plane-NOM   fly-NPAST-n(o)nara   today-GEN
yotei-wa   kae-nai-tumori-da.
plan-TOP   change-NEG-intention-be
'If the plane for Tokyo will leave tomorrow, I will not change my plans for today.'

(48) *Kinoo   Tookyoo-iki-no   hikooki-ga   ton-da-**nara**,   yotei doori*
yesterday Tokyo-for-GEN   plane-NOM fly-PAST-*nara*   plan according.to
konban   kuukoo-ni mukae-ni-ik-oo.
tonight   airport-at pick.up-to-go-intention
'If the plane for Tokyo left yesterday, I am going to pick him/her up at the airport according to the plan.'

(49) *Kinoo   Tookyoo-iki-no   hikooki-ga   ton-da-**n(o)-nara***
yesterday Tokyo-for-GEN   plane-NOM   fly-PAST-n(o)nara
yotei doori   konban   kuukoo-ni mukae-ni-ik-oo.
plan according.to tonight   airport-at pick.up-to-go-intention
'If the plane for Tokyo left yesterday, I am going to pick him/her up at the airport according to the plan.'

As observed so far, Japanese conditional clauses followed by the four basic conditional forms can be classified into two groups: non-tensed conditional clauses and tensed conditional clauses. Our first claim is that the distributional characteristics of these two clause types can be explained by settledness in the antecedent clause. Much has been said in the literature about the distributional differences among them. Most authors try to ascribe the differences to the types of causal relations.[11] Little attention, however, has been given to the point we will argue for. Let us examine this in detail in the next subsection. (See more detailed discussion about distributional characteristics of the two types of conditional clauses in Arita 2004, 2007.)

5.4.2 Unsettled antecedent in Japanese

We start this section with a discussion of predictive conditionals in Japanese. Predictive conditionals, as stated above, are characterized as having a proposition in the antecedent that is not settled, as exemplified in (50) and (51) for English:

(50) I will be happy if we find a solution.

(51) If oil prices keep rising, the Japanese economy will collapse.

Confirming what we have already seen in (7) and (28), example (50) conveys that the speaker predicts that the fulfilment of the consequent proposition 'I am happy' depends on the fulfilment of the antecedent proposition 'we find a solution' at a time later than the time of speaking. Similarly, example (51) conveys that the speaker predicts that the collapse of the Japanese economy depends on the rise of oil prices.

In Japanese these readings are conveyed by non-tensed conditional clauses, *-eba* and *-tara*-clauses:

(52) *Mosi   kaiketusaku-ga   {mitukar-eba/mitukat-tara} uresii-des-u.*
    if[12]   solution-NOM   {be.found-*eba*/be.found-*tara*} happy-be-NPAST
    'I will be happy if a solution is found.' ('I will be happy if we find a solution.')

(53) *Genyu kakaku-ga   {agari.tuzuker-eba/agari.tuzuke-tara}*
    oil   price-NOM   {keep.rising-*eba*/keep.rising-*tara*}
    nihonkeizai-wa   hatan.sur-u-daroo.
    Japanese.economy-TOP   collapse-do-NPAST-will
    'If oil prices keep rising, the Japanese economy will collapse.'

What about tensed conditional clauses? One of them, a *-n(o)nara*-clause, is not interchangeable with (52) and (53). *-N(o)nara* cannot be used to express an unsettled antecedent:

(54) #*Mosi   kaiketusaku-ga   mitsukar-u-n(o)nara,   uresii-des-u.*
    if   solution-NOM   be.found-NPAST-n(o)nara,   happy-be-NPAST
    'I will be happy if a solution is found.' ('I will be happy if we find a solution.')

(55) #*Genyu   kakaku-ga   agari.tuzuker-u-n(o)nara*
    oil   price-NOM   keep.rising-NPAST-n(o)nara
    nihonkeizai-wa   hatan.sur-u-daroo.
    Japanese.economy-TOP   collapse-do-NPAST-will
    'If oil prices keep rising, the Japanese economy will collapse.'

(54) and (55) could be grammatical if the *-n(o)nara*-clauses are construed as meaning 'if it is certain that we will find a solution (in the future)' and 'if it is certain that oil prices will keep rising (in the future)'. In other words, *-n(o)nara*-clauses do not merely convey an unsettled proposition, but also indicate the uncertainty of future fulfilment of this (unsettled) proposition at the time of speaking. For example, (54) not only says that the proposition 'solution is found' is unsettled, but also conveys that, at the time of speaking, we do not know for sure whether a solution would be found in the future. Therefore, *-n(o)nara*-clauses cannot be treated as describing unsettled propositions.

The same applies in the case of *-nara*-clauses, another tensed conditional clause in Japanese:

(56) #*Mosi kaiketusaku-ga   mitukar-u-**nara**,   uresii-des-u.*
     if   solution-NOM   be.found-NPAST-*nara*,   happy-be-NPAST
     'I will be happy if a solution is found.' ('I will be happy if we find a solution.')

(57) #*Genyu kakaku-ga   agari.tuzuker-u-**nara***
     oil   price-NOM   keep.rising-NPAST-*nara*
     nihonkeizai-wa   hatan.sur-u-daroo.
     Japanese.economy-TOP   collapse-do-NPAST-will
     'If oil prices keep rising, the Japanese economy will collapse.'

(56) and (57) are also grammatical when the *-nara*-clauses are interpreted as 'if it is certain that...'. Therefore, *-nara*-clauses cannot be treated as describing unsettled propositions either.

Interestingly, some speakers of Japanese accept that *-ta*(PAST)-*nara*-clauses can describe an unsettled antecedent:

(58) *Mosi   kaiketusaku-ga   mitukat-ta-**nara**,   uresii-des-u.*
     if   solution-NOM   be.found-PAST-*nara*,   happy-be-NPAST
     'I will be happy if a solution is found.' ('I will be happy if we find a solution.')

(59) *Genyu kakaku-ga   agari.tuzuke-ta-**nara***
     oil   price-NOM   keep.rising-PAST-*nara*
     nihonkeizai-wa   hatan.sur-u-daroo.
     Japanese.economy-TOP   collapse-do-NPAST-will
     'If oil prices keep rising, the Japanese economy will collapse.'

Note that the past tense form *-ta* in the *-nara*-clause does not denote the past but the future in (58)–(59). How can we account for this seeming anomaly?

Ogihara (1996) concludes that -*ta* in Japanese is a 'relative tense' morpheme. This means 'every embedded occurrence of the morpheme -*ta* indicates anteriority over the time indicated by the tense in the higher clause' (Ogihara 1999: 333). For example, -*ta* in the antecedent clause in (58) can be analysed as indicating anteriority over the time indicated by the tense in the matrix clause *uresii-des-u* ('I will be happy'), thus a -*ta-nara*-clause can describe an unsettled proposition. In the present chapter, we apply Ogihara's hypothesis to -*ta* in *nara*-clauses that describe unsettled propositions.

In contrast, a -*ta-n(o)nara*-clause cannot describe an unsettled antecedent. -*Ta* in a *n(o)nara*-clause cannot be treated as a relative past morpheme, as demonstrated in (60) and (61):

(60) #*Mosi kaiketusaku-ga mituka-ta-n(o)nara,*   *uresii-des-u.*
     if   solution-NOM   be.found-PAST-n(o)*nara,*   happy-be-NPAST.
     'I will be happy if a solution is found.' ('I will be happy if we find a solution.')

(61) #*Genyu kakaku-ga*   *agari.tuzuke-ta-n(o)nara*
     oil   price-NOM   keep.rising-PAST-n(o)*nara*
     nihonkeizai-wa   *hatan.sur-u-daroo.*
     Japanese.economy-TOP   collapse-do-NPAST-will
     'If oil prices keep rising, the Japanese economy will collapse.'

The *ta-n(o)nara*-clauses in both (60) and (61) refer to a state of affairs located at a certain time in the past, interpreted as 'If (it is certain that) a solution was found, I am happy' and 'If (it is certain that) oil prices keep rising, the Japanese economy will collapse'. They are always presumed decided, thus they cannot be the antecedent of predictive conditionals.

In this section, we have discussed predictive conditionals in Japanese. We have established that non-tensed conditional clauses, -*eba* and -*tara*-clauses, describe unsettled propositions; thus, they can be the antecedent of predictive conditionals. On the other hand, tensed conditional clauses, *nara* and *n(o)nara*-clauses, do not denote unsettled propositions, except for -*ta-nara*-clauses.

5.4.3   Settled antecedents in Japanese

Let us turn to settled antecedents in Japanese. We will start with the settled antecedent of epistemic conditionals. Counterfactual conditionals will be discussed in section 5.5.

As discussed in the previous section, Japanese tensed conditional clauses (except *-ta-nara*-clauses) do not denote unsettled propositions. They always convey settled propositions. Therefore, they can be appropriately expressed as English settled protases as in (62) and (63):

(62) (I hope Bolton won their home match yesterday.) If they did, they still have a chance of winning the championship.

(63) If Collins is in London, he is undoubtedly staying at the Hilton.

(64) (I hope Bolton won their home match yesterday.)
Mosi (kinoo)   *kat-ta {**nara/n(o)nara**}*   *yuusyoo.sur-u*
if   (yesterday) win-PAST {*nara/n(o)nara*} championship.do-NPAST
tyansu-ga   *aru.*
chance-NOM exist-NPAST
'If they won, they have a chance of winning the championship.'

(65) *Mosi*   *Korinzu-ga*   *Rondon-ni*   *ir-u-{**nara/n(o)nara**}*,
if   Collins-NOM   London-in   be-NPAST-{*nara/n(o)nara*}
matigai-naku   *Hiruton-ni*   *syukuhaku-si-tei-ru.*
wrong-NEG   Hilton-in   stay-do-ing-NPAST.
'If Collins is in London, he is undoubtedly staying at the Hilton.'

Sentences (62) and (64) are uttered in a situation in which the speaker does not know whether Bolton won the previous day or not. *Nara* and *n(o)nara* following the past morpheme *-ta* are appropriate for such settled antecedents. Sentences (63) and (65) are uttered in a situation in which the speaker does not know whether Collins is in London or not at the time of speaking. In Japanese, *nara* and *n(o)nara* following the infinitive *-(r)u* are appropriate in the antecedents of the above sentences.

Can non-tensed conditional clauses denote settled antecedents in Japanese? As the following sentences illustrate, *-eba* and *-tara* are also used for settled antecedents like (62) and (64), provided that they follow the aspect morpheme *-tei-*, the continuative/resultative/habitual aspect morpheme, as in (66):

(66) (I hope Bolton won their home match yesterday.)
a. *Mosi*   *(kinoo)*   *kat-teir-**eba***   *yuusyoo.sur-u*
if   (yesterdaty) win-ASP[13]-*eba*   championship.do-NPAST
tyansu-ga   *ar-u.*
chance-NOM   exist-NPAST
'If they won, they have a chance of winning the championship.'

b. *Mosi*   *(kinoo)*   *kat-tei-tara* *yuusyoo.sur-u*   *tyansu-ga*
    if   (yesterday)   win-ASP-*tara* championship.do-NPAST   chance-NOM
    ar-u.
    exist-NPAST
    'If they won, they have a chance of winning the championship.'

Without *-tei-*, neither *-eba* or *-tara* can denote such settled antecedents as in (67a) and (67b):

(67) (I hope Bolton won their home match yesterday.)

    a. #*Mosi*   *(kinoo)*   *kat-eba*   *yuusyoo.su-ru*   *tyansu-ga*
       if   (yesterday)   win-*eba*   championship.do-NPAST   chance-NOM
       ar-u.
       exist-NPAST
       'If they won, they have a chance of winning the championship.'

    b. #*Mosi*   *(kinoo)*   *kat-tara*   *yuusyoo.su-ru*   *tyansu-ga*
       if   (yesterday)   win-*tara*   championship.do-NPAST   chance-NOM
       ar-u.
       exist-NPAST
       'If they won, they have a chance of winning the championship.'

Note that (67a) and (67b) are grammatical as predictive conditionals. Their antecedents cannot be treated as settled propositions, and they are not acceptable as antecedents of epistemic conditionals.

Non-tensed conditional clauses in Japanese can be used for settled protases like (68a) and (68b), where the speaker's uncertainty about the present situation is expressed:

(68) a. *Mosi*   *Korinzu-ga*   *Rondon-ni*   *ir-eba,*   *matigai-naku*
      if   Collins-NOM   London-in   be-*eba,*   wrong-NEG
      Hiruton-ni   *syukuhaku-si-teir-u.*
      Hilton-in   stay-do-ing-NPAST.
      'If Collins is in London, he is undoubtedly staying at the Hilton.'

    b. *Mosi*   *Korinzu-ga*   *Rondon-ni*   *i-tara,*   *matigai-naku*
      if   Collins-NOM   London-in   be-*tara,*   wrong-NEG
      Hiruton-ni   *syukuhaku-si-teir-u.*
      Hilton-in   stay-do-ing-NPAST.
      'If Collins is in London, he is undoubtedly staying at the Hilton.'

If the function of *-tei-* is to change non-stative predicates into stative predicates, Japanese non-tensed conditional forms can appear in settled protases only when they follow stative predicates. We will return to this issue in detail in section 5.4.3.

Let us take a look at the settled propositions in a broad sense conveyed by antecedent clauses. In the previous section, we defined a settled proposition in a broad sense as a proposition whose truth value can be determined at the time of speaking based on some settled propositions that entail that it holds in the near future. An antecedent clause which describes a settled proposition must have a reading like 'if it is certain now that the fulfilment of the proposition will happen in the future...'.

These properties remind us of some examples discussed in section 5.4.2, like the following:

(69) *Mosi   kaiketusaku-ga   mitukar-u-**n(o)nara**,   uresii-des-u.*
     if   solution-NOM   be.found-NPAST-*n(o)nara*   happy-be-NPAST
     'I am happy if it is certain now that a solution will be found.' ('I am happy if it is certain now that we will find a solution.')

(70) *Genyu kakaku-ga   agari.tuzuker-u-**n(o)nara***
     oil   price-NOM   keep.rising-NPAST-*n(o)nara*
     nihonkeizai-wa   hatan.sur-u-daroo.
     Japanese.economy-TOP   collapse-do-NPAST-will
     'If it is certain now that oil prices will keep rising, the Japanese economy will collapse.'

(71) *Mosi kaiketusaku-ga   mitukar-u-**nara**,   uresii-des-u.*
     if   solution-NOM   be.found-NPAST-*nara*,   happy-be-NPAST
     'I am happy if it is certain now that a solution will be found.' ('I am happy if it is certain now that we will find a solution.')

(72) *Genyu kakaku-ga   agari.tuzuker-u-**nara***
     oil   price-NOM   keep.rising-NPAST-*nara*
     nihonkeizai-wa   hatan.sur-u-daroo.
     Japanese.economy-TOP   collapse-do-NPAST-will
     'If it is certain now that oil prices will keep rising, the Japanese economy will collapse.'

In the antecedents of Japanese conditional clauses, the certainty to the speaker at the time of speaking is explicitly conveyed only by tensed conditional clauses. Non-tensed conditional clauses cannot indicate such involvement in the antecedent but can express unsettledness of the proposition as shown in section 5.4.2.

English exhibits different properties as far as the relation of tense and certainty of a proposition is concerned. As we discussed in section 5.3.2,

English simple present sentences should be seen as conveying that the speaker has enough information to presume the truth value of the proposition, while in Japanese they can describe the speaker's prediction about the truth value of the proposition. Our claim is that the difference between the two languages reflects the role of tense and modality in settled propositions in a broad sense described by the antecedent of epistemic conditionals, as defined in (19). Consider the following examples:

(73) If you will be alone on Christmas Day, let us know now.
(Dancygier 1998: 118)

(74) If he won't arrive before 9, there is no point in ordering for him.
(Dancygier 1998: 62)

In (73), the addressee's plan for Christmas Day at the time of speaking is taken up. The sentence can be paraphrased as 'If it is certain that you will be alone on Christmas Day, let us know now.' Example (74) can be paraphrased as 'If it is certain that he won't arrive before 9, there is no point in ordering for him (now).' Without *will* in the antecedent, the implication 'if it is certain that' is not involved.

In contrast, in Japanese, it is the simple present tense in the antecedent that carries the implication of certainty, as can be seen in (75) and (76):

(75) *Mosi* *Kurisumasu-no-hi-ni* *hitori-de i-ru-{nara/n(o)nara},* *ima*
     if   Christmas-GEN-day-on   alone-by be-NPAST-{nara/n(o)nara}, now
     osiete.
     let.know
     'If you will be alone on Christmas Day, let us know now.'

(76) *Mosi* *9.zi-mae-ni* *kare-ga* *ko-na-i-{nara/n(o)nara},*
     if   9.o'clock-before-at he-NOM come-NEG-NPAST-{nara/n(o)nara}
     kare-no-tame-ni *tyuumonsur-u* *imi-ga* *na-i.*
     he-GEN-for-to   order-NPAST   point-NOM not.exist-NPAST
     'If he won't arrive before nine, there is no point in ordering for him.'

The antecedent in example (75) conveys that 'if it is certain that you will be alone on Christmas Day...' and that of (76) implies that 'if it is certain that he won't arrive before 9...'. Unsettled conditional clauses do not convey such implication in the settled conditional clause, because they do not include the present-tense form.

We conclude this subsection with a brief discussion of a subtype of epistemic conditionals illustrated in (77a) and (77b):

(77) a. Speaker A: Ken says he lived in France for seven years.
       Speaker B: I didn't know that! If he lived in France that long, his French must be pretty good.
   (Akatsuka 1983: 10)

   b. Speaker A: I'm going to the Winter LSA this year.
       Speaker B: I didn't know that. Well, if you're going, I'm going too.
   (Akatsuka 1983: 11)

These examples have two notable properties:

(78) a. The source of information indicated in the antecedent of speaker B's utterance is the speaker of A.

   b. Speaker B regards the information as certain.

However, note the contrast with regard to (78b) in (79) and (80). In (79), the proposition that 'Ken lived in France for seven years' is not treated as certain by speaker B. In (80), whether or not speaker A is going to the Winter LSA is not certain to speaker B:

(79) Speaker A: Ken says he lived in France for seven years.
    Speaker B: Well, if he lived in France that long, why can't he speak French at all?
   (Akatsuka 1983:10)

(80) Speaker A: I'm thinking of going to the Winter LSA this year.
    Speaker B: I didn't know that, if you go, I'll go too.
   (Akatsuka 1983: 11)

A distributional contrast between non-tensed and tensed conditional clauses in Japanese is found with regard to (78b). That is to say, tensed conditional clauses can convey that speaker B regards the information given by speaker A as certain, as in (81) and (83), while non-tensed conditional clauses cannot have this implication, as in (82) and (84):

(81) Speaker A: *Ken-wa*   *huransu-ni*   *7-nen-kan*   *sun-dei-ta-tte*
Ken-TOP   France-in   seven-year-for   live-ASP-PAST-that
it-teir-u-yo.
say-ASP-NPAST-PARTICLE
'Ken says he lived in France for seven years.'

Speaker B: *Sore-wa*   *sira-na-katta!*   *Huransu-ni*   *sonnani nagaku*
that-TOP   know-NEG-PAST   France-in   that   long
sun-dei-ta-{n(o)nara/nara},   *huransugo-ga*
live-ASP-PAST-{*n(o)nara/nara*}, French-NOM
totemo-zyoozu-nitigainai.
pretty-well-must
'I didn't know that! If he lived in France that long, his French must be pretty good.'

(82) Speaker B: *Sore-wa*   *sira-na-katta!*   *Huransu-ni*   *sonnani nagaku*
that-TOP   know-NEG-PAST   France-in   that   long
sun-{deir-#eba/dei-#tara},   *huransugo-ga*
live-{ASP-*eba*/ASP-*tara*},   French-NOM
totemo-zyoozu-nitigainai.
pretty-well-must
'I didn't know that! If he lived in France that long, his French must be pretty good.'

(83) Speaker A: *Kotosi-no*   *huyu-no*   *LSA-ni*
this.year-GEN   winter-GEN   LSA-*to*
iku-kotonisi-ta-yo.
go-decide-PAST-PARTICLE
'I'm going to the Winter LSA this year.'

Speaker B: *Sore-wa*   *sira-na-katta.*   *Anata-ga*
that-TOP   know-NEG-PAST   you-NOM
ik-u-{n(o)nara/nara}   *watasi-mo iko-o.*
go-NPAST-{*n(o)nara/nara*}   I-also   go-will
'I didn't know that, if you're going, I'm going too.'

(84) Speaker B: *Sore-wa*   *sira-na-katta.*   *Anata-ga*   {*ik-#eba/it-#tara*}
that-TOP know-NEG-PAST   you-NOM   {go-*eba*/go-*tara*}
watasi-mo   *ik-oo.*
I-also   go-will
'I didn't know that. If you're going, I'm going too.'

As shown in (81) and (83), the tensed conditional clauses with -*n(o)nara*- and -*nara* convey that the speaker regards the information as certain. In contrast, non-tensed -*eba*- and -*tara*-clauses do not allow this interpretation, as shown in (82) and (84).

When the speaker does not regard the information as certain, *-tara* can appear in the antecedent. As the distribution of *-eba* is more limited than that of *-tara*, we will take up *-tara* for simplicity of argument. (See details in Arita 1999.) Since examples (85) and (86) are translations of (79), they convey that the speaker B doubts that Ken lived in France for seven years. As can be seen in (85)–(86), not only tensed conditional clauses with *-nara* or *-n(o)nara*, but also non-tensed *-tara*-clauses can appear in a context where the speaker B regards the information given by the speaker A as uncertain:

(85) Speaker A: *Ken-wa   huransu-ni   7-nen-kan   sun-dei-ta-tte*
Ken-TOP   France-in   7-year-for   live-ASP-PAST-that
it-teir-u-yo
say-ASP-NPAST-PARTICLE
'Ken says he lived in France for 7 years.'

Speaker B: *Hee,   huransu-ni   sonnani   nagaku   sun-dei-ta*
***{n(o)nara/nara}**,*
well   France-in   that   long   live-ASP-PAST
{n(o)nara/nara}
naze mattaku huransugo-ga   hanas-e-na-i-no?
why not.at.all French-NOM speak-able-NEG-NPAST-PARTICLE
'Well, if he lived in France that long, why can't he speak French at all?'

(86) Speaker B: *Hee,   huransu-ni   sonnani   nagaku   sun-dei-**tara***
well   France-in   that   long   live-ASP-*tara*
naze mattaku huransugo-ga hanas-e-na-i-no?
why not.at.all French-NOM speak-able-NEG-PRES-PARTICLE
'Well, if he lived in France that long, why can't he speak French at all?'

The same contrast can be seen between (87) and (88). Since example (87) is a translation of (80), it communicates that the speaker is not certain about going to the next LSA at the utterance time as can be seen from using *omot-teiru* ('be thinking'). Not only the tensed conditional markers *-nara/-n(o)nara*, but also the non-tensed conditional marker *-tara* can appear in such a context as in (88):

(87) Speaker A: *Kotosi-no-huyu-no   LSA-ni   ik-oo-ka-to*
this.year-GEN-winter-GEN   LSA-to   go-will-PART-that
omot-teir-u-n(o)da.
think-ASP-NPAST-MOD
'I'm thinking of going to the Winter LSA this year.'

Speaker B: *Sore-wa   sira-na-katta.   Anata-ga*
that-TOP   know-NEG-PAST you-NOM
ik-u{n(o)nara/nara}   watasi-mo-ik-oo.
go-NPAST-{n(o)nara/nara} I-also-go-will
'I didn't know that, if you go, I'll go, too.'

(88) Speaker B: *Sore-wa   sira-na-katta.   Anata-ga it-**tara***
that-TOP   know-NEG-PAST you-NOM go-*tara*
watasi-mo-ik-oo.
I-also-go-will
'I didn't know that, if you go, I'll go, too.'

Therefore, both the source of information and the speaker's belief in the truth of this information have an impact on the distribution of non-tensed conditional clauses. While the tensed conditional clauses marked by *-nara/-n(o)nara* can convey the information newly given by the addressee at the current discourse whether the information is treated as certain to the speaker or not, the non-tensed ones marked by *-tara/-eba* can solely communicate that the information is regarded as uncertain by the speaker.

Thus far, we have focused on open conditionals, attributing their properties to the differences in settledness of the antecedents. To complete the picture of the properties exhibited by the conditional forms in Japanese, the next subsection delves into the properties of the aspectual morpheme necessary for non-tensed conditionals to have a settled reading.

5.4.4 *-Tei-* in non-tensed conditional clauses

Let us now look at the properties of settled *-eba/-tara*-clauses. Most works on *-tei-* in the literature divide its semantics into three different interpretations: 'ongoing process reading' (similar to *-ing* in English), 'resultant state reading' and 'experiential state reading'. Examples (89)–(91) illustrate the respective meanings:

(89) *Taro-ga   kooen-o   hasit-**teir**-u.*   (ongoing process/durative verb)
Taro-NOM park-ACC   run-ASP-NPAST
'Taro is running in the park.'

(90) *Asoko-ni   hito-ga   taore-**teir**-u.*   (result state / instantaneous verb)
there-in   man-NOM   fall-ASP-NPAST
'A man fell down there.'

(91) a. *Taro-wa   zyukken-mo ie-o   tate-**teir**-u.* (experience/durative verb)
Taro-TOP 10-also   house-ACC build-ASP-NPAST
'Taro has the experience of having built as many as ten houses.'

b. *Taro-wa konomae-no reesu-de taore-teir-u.*
(experience/instantaneous verb)
Taro-TOP last-GEN race-in mfall-ASP-NPAST
'Taro has the experience of falling down in the last game.'

The ongoing process reading in (89) and the resultant state reading in (90) both reflect the interaction of the aspectual characteristics of the verbs with *-tei-*. That is, the ongoing process interpretation is associated with verbs of durative aspect, while the result state interpretation comes with instantaneous verbs. The durative and instantaneous dichotomy was proposed by Kindaichi (1950) and is roughly defined as follows: durative verbs refer to dynamic actions that last for an unspecified length of time (for example 'run', 'dance, 'study', 'sing' and so on), while instantaneous verbs denote actions that take place instantaneously (for example, 'fall', 'die' or 'break') (Ogihara 1998).

Notice that both durative and instantaneous verbs can refer to the experiential states. *Tate-* ('build') in (91a) is durative, while *taore-* ('fall') in (91b) is an instantaneous verb. Thus, the experiential reading is not sensitive to the aspect of the verb. In this regard, Ogihara (1998) proposes that the morpheme *-te-* of *-tei-* has a bivalent perfectivity feature: [±perfect]. When *-te-* has the feature [–perfect], the predicate followed by *-tei-* receives ongoing process or result state readings as in (89) and (90). Since *-te-* [–perfect] does not add a temporal meaning to the predicate, the interpretation reflects the aspectual meaning of the verb. On the other hand, when *-te-* has the feature [+perfect], it adds a certain temporal meaning to the predicate, and the predicate receives the 'experience' interpretation, which can be modified by past adverbials as in (92) and (93):

(92) *Taro-wa* **kyonen** *zyukken-mo ie-o* **tate-teir-u.**
Taro-TOP last.year ten-as-many-as house-ACC build-ASP-NPAST
(experience)
'Taro has the experience of having built as many as ten houses last year.'

(93) *Taro-wa* **kyonen-no** **reesu-de** *taore-teir-u.* (experience)
Taro-TOP last.year-GEN race-in fall-ASP-NPAST
'Taro has the experience of having fallen down in the race last year.'

What about the *-i(r)* of *-tei(r)-*? *-I(r)* is commonly treated as an aspectual auxiliary. In Takubo (1993), X-*te-i-ru* is analysed as expressing that the property denoted by X-*te* belongs to the current situation. Based on Takubo's claim, when *-te-* is [+perfect], X-*te-i-ru* says that X already exists in the present situation, that is, in our terms, it is settled. Thus, we may conclude that the perfect *-te-* + *i(r)* contributes to settledness in *-eba/-tara*-clauses that have no tense.

The next section discusses the properties of *-tei-* in counterfactual conditionals in Japanese. The purpose of the next section is to show that the feature of settledness can also be used to account for the properties of counterfactual conditionals. The distribution of *-tei-* in *-eba/-tara* conditional clauses in Japanese supports this claim.

5.5 Counterfactual conditionals and settledness for speaker

5.5.1 *-Tei-* and counterfactuality

It has often been pointed out that the *-tei-* form tends to appear in counterfactual usage of Japanese conditional clauses (Takahashi 1987, Takubo 1993, Jacobsen 1990, 2002). This means that (94) is preferred to (95) as expressing a counterfactual antecedent:

(94) *Motto   benkyoo-si-{teir-eba/tei-tara} siken-ni   ukat-tei-ta-daroo-ni.*
     more   study-do-{ASP-*eba*/ASP-*tara*} exam-DAT   pass-ASP-PAST-*ni*
     'If he had studied more, he would probably have passed the exam.'

(95) *Motto benkyoo-{sur-eba/si-tara}   siken-ni   ukat-tei-ta daroo-ni.*
     more study-{do-*eba*/do-*tara*},   exam-DAT   pass-ASP-PAST-*ni*
     'If he had studied more, he would probably have passed the exam.'

-Ni, which appears in sentence-final position in (94) and (95), is a sentence-final particle that conveys that the proposition described in the sentence followed by *-ni* is not fulfilled.

Jacobsen (2002) regards *-tei-* as a device for 'heightening' the counterfactual meaning in Japanese conditionals. He attributes the hypotheticality or counterfactuality of a sentence to the stativity of the verb. Stativity, according to Jacobsen, is a property of non-uniqueness. By this he means that states implicitly refer to multiple points in time and, by extension, multiple worlds which may include, but are not limited to, the world of the speaker. In other words, Jacobsen claims that stativity itself bears hypotheticality or counterfactuality. In this study, we argue against this claim. First, stative predicates are not necessarily related to either hypotheticality or counterfactuality in Japanese. Stative predicates in matrix sentences like (96) do not indicate either a counterfactual or a hypothetical situation:

(96) *Tanaka-ga   paatii-ni   syusseki-si-tei-nai.*
     Tanaka-NOM   party-in   participation-do-ASP-NEG
     'Tanaka has not participated in the party.'

Second, -*tei-tara*-clauses sometimes express a factual state of affairs, as in (97):

(97) *Sinsaibasi-o   arui-tei-tara,   Tanaka-ni   deat-ta.*
Sinsaibashi-ACC   walk-ASP-*tara*   Tanaka-DAT   meet-PAST
'When I was walking in Sinsaibashi Avenue, I met Tanaka.'

Thirdly, when counterfactuality is marked explicitly in the apodosis – for example, by the conditional *mosi*, with (*no*)*ni* in sentence-final position indicating that the state of affairs was not fulfilled – -*eba* and -*tara*-clauses do not necessarily include -*tei*-:

(98) *Mosi Taro-ga   {kur-eba/ki-teir-eba},   Hanako-ga*
if   Taro-NOM   {come-*eba*/come-ASP-*eba*}   Hanako-NOM
yorokon-da-noni
happy-PAST-*noni*
'If Taro had come, Hanako would have been happy.'

(99) *Mosi Taro-ga   {ki-tara/ki-tei-tara},   Hanako-ga*
if   Taro-NOM   {come-*tara*/come-ASP-*tara*}   Hanako-NOM
yorokon-da-noni.
happy-PAST-noni
'If Taro had come, Hanako would have been happy.'

Thus, the view proposed by Jacobsen that -*tei*- is a device for strengthening hypotheticality or counterfactuality cannot explain the distribution of -*tei*- in counterfactual clauses. More seriously, it cannot explain the fact that -*tei*- is followed by -*eba* and -*tara* to describe a settled proposition, as discussed in the previous section.

In section 5.4.3, we claimed that -*tei*- in non-tensed clauses indicates settledness, in lieu of past-tense marking. Also, we have shown that the function of -*tei*- changes in counterfactual contexts, as demonstrated in examples (98) and (99) involving (*no*)*ni*.

5.5.2   *N(o)nara* as an epistemic indicator

In this section, we will look into one more important phenomenon related to Japanese counterfactual conditionals. Of the tensed conditional forms, -*n(o)nara* does not appear in 'true' counterfactual protases. What we mean by a 'true' counterfactual antecedent is an antecedent that presupposes counterfactuality. -*N(o)nara* cannot be used in such contexts while -*nara*, -*eba* and -*tara* are grammatical, as illustrated in (100):

(100) (Unfortunately, Bolton lost their home match yesterday.)
  Mosi {*kat-tei-ta-**nara**/*kat-tei-ta-**n(o)nara**/kat-teir-**eba**/kat-tei-**tara**}*,
  if   {win-ASP-PAST-*nara*/*win-ASP-PAST-*n(o)nara*/win-ASP-*eba*/win-ASP-*tara*}
  yuusyoo.su-ru   *tyansu-ga*   *at-ta-noni.*
  championship.do-PRES   chance-NOM   exist-PAST-*noni*
  'If they had won, they would have had a chance of winning the championship.'

Why does *n(o)nara* not denote a counterfactual antecedent, whereas *nara* does? What causes the difference between *nara* and *n(o)nara*? An obvious answer is to ascribe the difference to the epistemic status of *no(da)*, a modal auxiliary, of which *n(o)nara* is the conditional form.

Let us briefly take up some characteristics of *n(o)da* relevant for the current discussion. First, when *n(o)da* follows the past-tense morpheme *-ta*, it conveys that the given state of affairs existed in the past, as in (101):

(101) *Kinoo-wa   Boruton-ga   hoomu-de   kat-ta-n(o)da.*
     Yesterday-TOP   Bolton-NOM   home-at   win-PAST-*n(o)da*
     'Bolton won their home match yesterday.'

Second, when *n(o)da* follows infinitival *-(r)u*, it implies that the speaker has some reason for the assertion he or she is making. For example, in (102) the speaker makes the assertion perhaps because he or she heard it on the news:

(102) *Asita-wa   ame-ga   hur-(u)-n(o)da.*
     tomorrow-TOP   rain-NOM   fall-N.PAST-*n(o)da*
     '(The fact is that) It rains tomorrow.'

Are there then any differences in certainty between the simple tensed sentences and *n(o)da* marked sentences? For example, is there any difference between (102) with *n(o)da* or without *n(o)da*?

It is sometimes pointed out in Japanese linguistic literature that the *n(o)da*-marked sentences behave quite differently depending on whether they are uttered to an addressee or to the speaker himself or herself (Noda 1997). For example, when (102) is uttered to the addressee, it means that the speaker already has some evidence to assert that it would rain the next day and he or she conveys the information to the addressee. In this situation, the speaker assumes that the addressee does not know this information. In contrast, when (102) is uttered to the speaker himself or herself, it means that the speaker has just noticed that it is certain or highly probable that it will rain the next day – for example by watching the weather on TV. In other words, in the latter context, *n(o)da* implies that the speaker has just learned of some evidence to assert the truth at the time of utterance. The difference between the former and the latter usage is whether or not the addressee's knowledge state is taken into consideration. This distinction is relevant only in the case of the major, not the subordinate, clauses. Since our current concern is the conditional form of *n(o)da*, we will focus on the *n(o)da* sentences uttered to the speaker himself or herself.

Let us observe some more examples of the *n(o)da*-marked sentences that the speaker utters to himself or herself:

> (103) *Dooro-ga*   *nure-teir-u.*   *Ame-ga*   *hut-ta-n(o)da.*
> road-NOM   wet-ASP-NPAST   rain-NOM   fall-PAST-*n(o)da*
> 'The road is wet. It must have rained.'

In (103), the *n(o)da*-marked sentence asserts that the situation 'the road is wet' is caused by the fact that 'it rained'. In addition, example (103) implies that having learned that 'the road is wet', the speaker infers the event 'it rained'. Without *n(o)da*, 'it rained' cannot be interpreted as the 'cause' as in (104):

> (104) *Dooro-ga*   *nure-teir-u.*   *#Ame-ga*   *hut-ta.*
> Road-NOM   wet-ASP-NPAST   rain-NOM   fall-PAST
> 'The road is wet. It must have rained.'

(104) is acceptable if the second sentence denotes an event that followed.

Given the data, we may assume that *n(o)da* acts as a marker of abductive inference (Takubo 2006). In (103), for example, the speaker first notices 'the wet road' and then infers the cause: 'it rained'.

This assumption leads us to speculate that *n(o)da* conveys that the speaker does not strictly know the truth of the proposition, because it is inferred from another proposition. Rather we should say that it is postulated to be true. In our framework, a *n(o)da*-marked proposition is not settled for the speaker.

Again, why is it impossible for a *n(o)nara*-marked antecedent to be counterfactual? The speaker infers the truth value of P-*noda* from the broad-sense settledness of other propositions. The truth of P is not presupposed. Therefore, it follows that 'not P *n(o)nara*', the conditional form of *n(o)da*, cannot presuppose the falsity of the proposition either.

Interestingly, a *n(o)nara*-marked clause is often used to lead to a conclusion that is false in the real world, as in (105):

(105) *Ame-ga*   *hut-tei-ta-n(o)nara,*   *dooro-ga*   *nure-teir-u-hazuda.*
      rain-NOM   fall-ASP-PAST-*n(o)nara,*   road-NOM   wet-ASP-NPAST-must
      Sikasi,   *mattaku*   *nure-tei-na-i.*
      but   at.all   wet-tei-NEG-NPAST
      'If it had rained, the road would be wet. But, it is not wet at all.'

In this example, the speaker conveys implicitly the falsity of the antecedent by showing that the apodosis is counterfactual. Strictly speaking, the antecedent is not counterfactual because it does not presuppose the falsity of the proposition.

We have shown so far that a *n(o)nara*-clause does not express a counterfactual antecedent. Recall that only *n(o)nara* cannot be the antecedent in predictive conditionals discussed in section 5.4.2. This means that *n(o)nara* is a conditional form restricted to epistemic antecedents.

Considering that the epistemic antecedent is defined as its truth value is objectively determined, but is unknown to the speaker, as shown in section 5.3.2, we can state that what the speaker knows (or does not know) is explicitly marked in Japanese conditionals, rather than counterfactuality or low probability.

5.6 Concluding remarks – settledness and hypotheticality

In this chapter, we have discussed non-factuality as a modal concept encoded by conditional constructions. We have shown that the distributional differences between tensed and non-tensed conditional clauses in Japanese are best explained by referring to the settledness of the antecedent. One of the main claims of the chapter is that settledness of the antecedent of Japanese conditionals is marked by tense forms or the aspect form, *-tei-*. We rejected earlier claims that *-teir* in the antecedent clause indicates counterfactuality or hypotheticality. *-Tei-* does not necessarily appear in a counterfactual antecedent if counterfactuality is represented explicitly in the consequent clause. On the other hand, in antecedents of epistemic conditionals, either *-tei-* or tense form should appear to indicate settledness of the antecedent. This contrasts strikingly with English conditionals, where counterfactuality or a high degree of hypotheticality is indicated by a backshifted tense.

One important point that we have discussed throughout this chapter is that *-n(o)nara*, one of the tensed conditional forms, describes exclusively an epistemic antecedent. An epistemic antecedent is defined as one that is settled objectively but unsettled for the speaker. Therefore, not only settledness but also unsettledness from the speaker's viewpoint is explicitly marked in Japanese. This leads us to elucidate modality in subordinate clauses in Japanese.

In particular, the latter claim reminds us of other phenomena of Japanese grammar, for example, Takubo's work on one of the topic markers, *-tte*, or on discourse referential usages of one of the demonstrative expressions, *so* (Takubo 1991). These forms are treated as noun-phrase-level modality markers in that they refer to entities that cannot be directly accessible for the speaker. The phenomena concerning *n(o)nara* conditional clauses could be due to the same property that governs the use of the constructions analysed by Takubo. Further research is needed to establish whether the property of settledness could be considered the common denominator to all the phenomena discussed above.

Notes

1. This project is partly supported by a grant-in-aid from the Japan Society for the Promotion of Science (JSPS). I gratefully acknowledge the hospitality of Professor Stefan Kaufmann and the Northwestern Institute on Complex Systems (NICO) during my term as a Visiting Researcher at Northwestern University, where much of this work was carried out.
2. 'Epistemic' as a class of conditionals was introduced by Sweetser (1990). She assumes three types of cognitive domains: content-level, epistemic-level and speech-act-level. According to her, an if–then construction in the epistemic-level domain 'expresses the idea that knowledge of the truth of the hypothetical premise expressed in the antecedent would be a sufficient condition for concluding the truth of the proposition expressed in the apodosis' (Sweetser 1990: 116). In our treatment of epistemic conditionals we adopt her assumption that epistemic conditionals describe the dependency relation between what the speaker knows and what s/he concludes. See more details in Arita (2004, 2007).
3. Morphologically *n(o)nara* consists of a modal auxiliary *no(da)* and conditional form *nara*.
4. *-Tei-* can be analysed into *-te* and *-i(ru)-*, but for the sake of simplicity we consider it one morpheme. See section 5.4.3.
5. Strictly speaking, the hypothetical conditionals in Quirk et al. could have a non-counterfactual interpretation such as the probability of their antecedent being considered to be low for the speaker. As we will claim in section 5.5.2, in Japanese, there is a non-trivial difference between low probability and counterfactuality of the antecedent clause.

6. Both *perhaps* and *certainly* can occur in bare-present-tense sentences that describe a present situation as below:

    He's **certainly** there by now.
    Perhaps she is there.　　　　　(Lewis Gebhardt, p.c.)

7. *-To* is often included in basic conditional forms. Its conditional uses are, however, much more limited than those of the other four forms. See details in Arita (1999) and Hasunuma et al. (2001).
8. There are good reasons for distinguishing *-ta* being part of *-tara* from the past form *-ta*, which can appear in *-nara* conditional clauses. Temporal interpretation of a *-tara*-clause depends on that of the main clause, while a *-ta-nara*-clause can have a temporal interpretation independent from that of the main clause as shown below:

    a. *Hanako-no　ie-ni　　it-tara,　Ziroo-ni a-e-ru-daroo.*
    Hanako-GEN house-to go-*tara* Jiroo-to see-can-N.PAST-will
    'If you go to Hanako's house, you will be able to see Jiro there.'
    b. *Hanako-no　ie-ni　　it-tara, Ziroo-ga　ki-tei-ta.*
    Hanako-GEN house-to go-*tara* Jiroo-NOM come-ASP-PAST
    'When I went to Hanako's house, (I found that) Jiroo was there.'
    c. *(Kinoo)　　Hanako-no　ie-ni　　it-ta-nara,　kyoo-wa　　ik-anai-hoogaii.*
    (yesterday) Hanako-GEN house-to go-PAST-*nara* today-TOP go-NEG-had.better
    'If you went to Hanako's house (yesterday), you had better not go there today.'
    d. *(Kinoo)　　Hanako-no　ie-ni　　it-ta-nara,　Ziroo-ni aw-anak-atta?*
    (yesterday) Hanako-GEN house-to go-PAST-*nara* Jiroo-to see-NEG-PAST
    'If you went to Hanako's house (yesterday), didn't you see Jiro there?'

In example (a), the *-tara*-clause has only a future interpretation, while example (b) carries only a past interpretation. By contrast, the *-ta-nara*-clause bears a past interpretation whether the temporal interpretation of the main clause can be past or not. The independent temporal interpretation expressed by the *-ta-nara*-clause is encoded by *-ta* as a past-tense form. Therefore, we cannot consider the *-ta* in the *-tara*-clause as past tense, but as an inflectional form of the verb that expresses the perfective aspect.

9. *-Eba, -tara, nara* and *n(o)nara,* as basic conditional forms of Japanese, will not be glossed in the examples.
10. *-Nara* is analysed as an inflectional form of copula, *da* ('be') and *n(o)nara* as an inflectional form of auxiliary, *n(o)da*. The meaning of *n(o)da* will be discussed in section 5.5.2.
11. An overview of research on Japanese conditionals is given in Arita (1993).
12. *Mosi* is treated as one of *tinzyutu hukusi* ('declarative adverbs'). Its occurrence is limited only to conditional antecedents to indicate that the given proposition is treated hypothetically by the speaker. English 'if' is not appropriate as a gloss of *mosi* because the latter is optional in Japanese conditional constructions, while the former is obligatory in English, but we use 'if' as its counterpart for the sake of simplicity of argument.
13. Since the *-tei-* form has a variety of aspectual meanings, as discussed in section 5.4.2, we tentatively use 'ASP' as its English gloss.

References

Akatsuka, Noriko (1983). Conditionals. *Papers in Japanese Linguistics* 9, 1–33.

Arita, Setsuko (1993). Nihongo zyookenbunkenkyuu no hensen [History of studies on Japanese conditionals]. In: Masuoka, Takashi (ed.), *Nihongo no zyookenhyoogen* [Japanese conditional expressions]. Tokyo: Kuroshio Publishers: 225–78.

Arita, Setsuko (1999). Purototaipu kara mita nihongo no zyookenbun [Japanese conditionals and prototypical conditionality]. *Gengo Kenkyu* 115, 77–108.

Arita, Setsuko (2004). (Hu)kanzenziseisetu to nihongozyookenbun [(In)complete tensedness and Japanese conditionals]. PhD thesis, Kyoto University.

Arita, Setsuko (2007). *Nihongo zyookensetu to ziseisetusei* [Japanese conditionals and tensedness]. Tokyo: Kuroshio Publishers.

Condoravdi, Cleo (2002). Temporal interpretation of modals: modals for the present and for the past. In: Beaver, David I. et al. (eds), *The Construction of Meaning*. Stanford: CSLI: 59–87.

Dancygier, Barbara (1998). *Conditionals and Prediction: Time, Knowledge, and Causation in Conditional Constructions*. Cambridge: Cambridge University Press.

Dancygier, Barbara and Eve Sweetser (2005). *Mental Spaces in Grammar: Conditional Constructions*. Cambridge: Cambridge University Press.

Funk, Wolf-Peter (1985). On a semantic typology of conditional sentences. *Folia Linguistica* 19(3/4), 365–414.

Edgington, Dorothy (1997). Commentary. In: Woods, Michael (ed.), *Conditionals*. Oxford: Clarendon Press: 97–137.

Hasunuma, Akiko, Setsuko Arita and Naoko Maeda (2001). *Zyookenhyoogen* [Conditional Expressions]. Tokyo: Kuroshio Publishers.

Jacobsen, Wesley (1990). Zyookenbun ni okeru 'Kanrensei' nituite [On 'relevance' in conditional sentences. *Nihongogaku* 9(4), 93–108.

Jacobsen, Wesley (2002). On the interaction of temporal and modal meaning in Japanese conditionals. In: Akatsuka, Noriko and Strauss, Susan (eds), *Japanese Korean Linguistics*, 10. Stanford: CSLI: 3–17.

Kaufmann, Stefan (2005). Conditional truth and future reference. *Journal of Semantics* 22(3), 231–80.

Kaufmann, Stefan, Cleo Condoravdi and Valentina Harizanov (2006). Formal approaches to modality. In: Frawley, William (ed.), *The Expression of Modality*. Berlin: Mouton de Gruyter: 71–106.

Kindaichi, Haruhiko (1950). Kokugo dooshi no itibunrui [A classification of Japanese verbs]. In: Kindaichi, Haruhiko (ed.), (1976). *Nihongo doosi no asupekuto* [Aspect of Japanese verbs]. Tokyo: Mugishobo: 5–26.

Kratzer, Angerika (1981). The notional category of modality. In: Eikmeyer, Hans-Jürgen and Rieser, Hannes (eds), *Words, Worlds, and Contexts*. Berlin: Walter de Gruyter: 38–74.

Morimoto, Junko (1994). *Hanasite no syukan o arawasu hukusi ni tuite* [On some adverbs describing the speaker's subjective attitudes]. Tokyo: Kuroshio Publishers.

Noda, Harumi (1997). *'Noda' no kinoo* [The function of *noda*]. Tokyo: Kuroshio Publishers.

Ogihara, Toshiyuki (1996). *Tense, Attitudes, and Scope*. Dordrecht: Kluwer Academic Publishers.

Ogihara, Toshiyuki (1998). The ambiguity of the -*te iru* form in Japanese. *Journal of East Asian Linguistics* 7, 87–120.

Ogihara, Toshiyuki (1999). Tense and aspect. In: Tsujimura, Natsuko Tsujimura (ed.), *The Handbook of Japanese Linguistics*. Malden: Blackwell: 326–48.

Ono, Tsuyoshi and Kimberly Jones (2005). Bunpoo-kisoku no siyoo to keisiki no sentaku no zissai: kaiwa ni okeru 'zyookensetu' no kansatu kara [Use of grammatical rules and selection of grammatical forms: behaviour of 'conditional clauses' in conversation]. In: Minami, Masahiko (ed.), *Gengogaku to nihongokyooiku 4* [Linguistics and Japanese teaching]. Tokyo: Kuroshio Publishers: 73–85.

Quirk, Randolph et al. (1985). *A Comprehensive Grammar of the English Language*. Edinburgh: Pearson Education Limited.

Roberts, Craige (1989). Modal subordination and pronominal anaphora in discourse. *Linguistics and Philosophy* 12, 683–721.

Sweetser, Eve (1990). *From Etymology to Pragmatics: Metaphorical and Cultural Aspects of Semantic Structure*. Cambridge: Cambridge University Press.

Takahashi, Taro (1987). Doosi sono 3 [Verb, Part 3]. In: Takahashi, Taro (ed.) (2003), *Doosi 9-syoo* [Nine chapters on verbs]. Tokyo: Hitsuji Shobo: 221–57.

Takubo, Yukinori (1991). Meisiku no modariti [Modality in noun phrases]. In: Masuoka, Takashi (ed.), *Nihongo no modariti* [Japanese modality]. Tokyo: Kuroshio Publishers: 211–33.

Takubo, Yukinori (1993). Danwa kanri riron ni yoru nihongo no hanzizitu zyookenbun [On Japanese counterfactual conditionals and discourse management theory]. In: Masuoka, Takashi (ed.), *Nihongo no zyookenhyoogen* [Japanese conditional expressions]. Tokyo: Kuroshio Publishers: 169–83.

Takubo, Yukinori (2006). Zyookenbun to modariti [Conditionals and modality]. PhD thesis, Kyoto University.

Thomason, Richmond H. (1984). Combinations of tense and modality. In: Gabby, Dov and Guenthner, Franz (eds), *Handbook of Philosophical Logic: Extensions of Classical Logic*. Dordrecht: Reidel: 135–65.

6
Conditional Modality: Two Types of Modal Auxiliaries in Japanese[1]

Yukinori Takubo

6.1 Introduction

In this chapter, I will discuss propositional modality[2] in Japanese in the context of conditional reasoning.[3] Propositional modality is sometimes divided into epistemic and evidential modality. Modal auxiliaries in Japanese that express propositional modality have traditionally been classified into two subclasses: epistemic modals that include *daroo* ('will probably'[4]), *hazuda* ('should'), *nitigainai* ('must'), *kamosirenai* ('it is possible'), henceforth the *daroo*-class modals, and evidential modals that include *yooda* ('it appears'), *rasii* ('it seems'), and possibly, *sooda*1 ('I hear') and *sooda*2 ('looks like'), henceforth the *yooda*-class.[5] The distinction is based on the existence of overt evidence on which to base the inference for the *yooda*-class, as opposed to its absence for the *daroo*-class (Teramura 1984, Aoki 1986, Morimoto 1994, Miyake 1995, Oosika 1995, Takubo 2001).

I propose in this chapter that these two types of modality in Japanese can be differentiated by the types of inference involved, which are manifested in their scope properties. I will show that *daroo*-class modals take only the consequent of the conditionals in their scope, the premise being outside it, whereas with *yooda*-class modals the premise of conditional sentences must also be included in their scope. The scope differences in the two types of modals can be accounted for by the generalization made in Takubo (1987) that wide-scope conditional adjuncts do and must modify epistemic modals, but narrow-scope conditional adjuncts cannot. I will then show that the scope properties follow from the nature of inference involved and the informational structure associated with the linguistic manifestation of the inference: *daroo*-class modals generally involve deduction, most typically, in the form of

150

modus ponens, with the minor premise as a presupposition and the conclusion as an assertion, whereas *yooda*-class modals involve either abduction, i.e. the inverse of deduction, or induction. The scope facts, therefore, serve to differentiate the epistemic modals from evidential modals, thereby suggesting that the latter do not involve epistemic judgement, of the type associated with modals of the former.

I will relate the differences in the type of inference to the nature of the complement that modals take and what the entire sentence, with the modal as head, denotes. I will argue that the direction of inference is tied up with the nature of knowledge on which the inference is based and the conclusion that is drawn.

In the tradition of Japanese linguistics, modals or modal auxiliaries are characterized as expressions of subjectivity. It has generally been agreed that the notion of subjectivity is related to the cognitive act involved in the use of modals, although what is meant by subjectivity has not always been so clear. Not all predicates that are generally classified as modals belong to this category. In his pioneering work, Kindaichi (1953) argued that modals which only have conclusive use (or finite forms) and do not inflect, such as *yoo* ('volitional'), *mai* ('will not'), and *daroo* ('probably'), are subjective, by which he seems to suggest that they involve a cognitive act of epistemic judgement. The subjectivity with which he characterizes these uninflecting modals can be interpreted as involving the act of epistemic judgement, such as making a decision or drawing a conclusion from a set of premises. I depart from Kindaichi, however, in including other *daroo*-class modals as lexically coding the cognitive act of epistemic judgement, when they are used as finite. In Takubo (2006), I suggested that the 'subjective' force is latent in those modals and becomes activated by the addition of a zero morpheme that behaves like *daroo*,[6] thereby arguing that *daroo*-class modals in Japanese can be 'decomposed' into two components, that which indicates the information source and that which indicates that the information is a new addition to the knowledge base. The decompositional approach is in a way along the lines of traditional Japanese grammar, which distinguishes between true modality and pseudo-modality.[7] It can give a unified account of the similarities and the differences between evidential and epistemic modal expressions in Japanese, and the behaviours of *daroo*-class modals in non-root and root sentences.

This chapter is organized as follows. In section 6.2, I will first define what counts as propositional modal predicates in Japanese, and on the basis of that discuss how the two classes of propositional modals are to be characterized in terms of the scope and inferential properties. In section 6.3, I will show that the differences in the two modal classes can be accounted for if we assume that *daroo*-class modals are epistemic and those of the *yooda*-class are direct evidential, and do not necessarily involve epistemic judgement. Section 6.4 is the conclusion.

6.2   The two classes of modals

6.2.1   Modal class of predicates in Japanese

Before we go into the discussion of modality in Japanese, we must first decide what to include in the modal auxiliaries. In English, auxiliaries can be identified by the syntactic properties that they exhibit, i.e. by what Huddleston (1976) calls 'NICE' properties, an acronym taken from the initial letters of the phenomena listed below.

(1)   Negation: *Not* comes after the auxiliaries.
      John **will** not come.
      *John come not.

(2)   Inversion: Auxiliaries are fronted to form a question.
      Will John come to the party?
      *Comes John to the party?

(3)   Code: Auxiliaries remain after verb phrases are elided.[8]
      John **will** [come the party] and so **will** Mary.

(4)   Emphasis: Auxiliaries carry emphatic stress:
      John **will** come to the party?

Modals in English all show these properties and can thus be syntactically identifiable as auxiliaries. In Japanese, no such criteria can be given. The category of modal 'auxiliaries', therefore, is not syntactically definable in Japanese. The lexical items that have traditionally been classified as 'modal auxiliaries' include various morphological classes, both in terms of the verbal forms they are attached to and the classes of inflection that they belong to.[9] We cannot come up with linguistic tests that identify all these forms as one morphological, syntactic or semantic category. For the purpose of the present chapter, therefore, I will follow the principles in Takubo (1982a, b) and define modal predicates by their subcategorization properties: that they take a clause as their complement and that they do not assign a theta-role to their subject position.[10]

The first criterion is more or less obvious. The second distinguishes propositional modals from deontic or root modals, which usually assign a theta-role to the subject, and thus have a selectional restriction with the subject, in a way similar to control predicates, such as *tumori-da* ('intend'), *-tai* ('want'), *te hosii* ('want'), which impose selectional restrictions on their subjects and assign a theta-role, e.g. experiencer, to them.[11] In contrast, the class of predicates that are characterizable as propositional modals are similar to so-called subject-raising verbs in English, e.g. *seem, is likely, appear*, etc., in that they do not impose selectional restrictions on the subject position.[12] Deontic modals thus have the structure as follows with a theta-role assigned to the subject position as in (5):

(5) $[_{IP}$ NP $[_I$ modal $[_{VP}$ PRO V']]]

May in the deontic interpretation, for example, cannot take an inanimate or pleonastic element as its subject. In (6a), the subject 'Kate' receives a theta-role, i.e. the recipient of permission, from the deontic modal *may*, while in (6b), that interpretation is not possible because 'it' cannot be the recipient of permission:

(6) a. Kate may come in now = Kate has permission to come in.
    b. It may be raining≠ *It has permission to rain.

May in the epistemic interpretation, on the other hand, has the raising structure as in (7):

(7) $[_{IP}\Delta$ $[_I$ modal $[_{VP}$NP V']]]

Therefore, it does not have animacy restriction in the subject position and allows any subject if it satisfies the selection of the verb following the modal, with which it is related, as can be seen in (8):

(8) a. Kate may be at home now = It is possible that Kate is at home now.
    b. It may be raining outside = It is possible that it is raining outside.

The difference in theta-role assignment properties between propositional modals and deontic modals in Japanese is the same as that in English:

(9) a. *Tanaka-ga*   *kuru*   *hazu-da.*
      Tanaka-NOM come should.
      'Tanaka must come.'
  b. *Ame-ga*   *huru*   *hazu-da.*
      rain-NOM   fall   should
      'It must rain.'

The structures of (9 a, b) are as in (10 a, b) respectively, with the subject position empty:

(10) a. [$_{IP}$ Δ [$_{I'}$ [$_{VP}$ *ame-ga huru*] *hazu-da*]]
      b. [$_{IP}$ Δ [$_{I'}$ [$_{VP}$ *Tanaka-ga kuru*] *hazu-da*]]

With deontic modals like *beki-da* ('should') or control predicates like *tumori-da* ('intend'), the subject position must be animate because it is assigned a theta-role:

(11) a. *Tanaka-ga*   *kuru*   *beki-da.*
      Tanaka-NOM come should
      'Tanaka should come.'
    b. ??*Ame-ga*   *huru*   *beki-da*
      rain-NOM   fall   should
      'It should rain.'

(12) a. *Tanaka-ga*   *kuru*   *tumori-da.*
      Tanaka-NOM come intend
      'Tanaka intends to come.'
    b. *Ame-ga*   *huru*   *tumori-da*
      rain-NOM   fall   intend
      'The rain intends to fall.'

The structure of (11) and (12), therefore, is like those in (13) and (14):

(13) a. [$_{IP}$ *Tanaka-ga* [$_{I'}$ [$_{VP}$ PRO *kuru*] *beki-da*]]
      b. ?? [$_{IP}$ *Ame-ga* [$_{I'}$ [$_{VP}$ PRO *huru*] *beki-da*]]

(14) a. [$_{IP}$ *Tanaka-ga* [$_{I'}$ [$_{VP}$ PRO *kuru*] *tumori-da*]]
      b. *[$_{IP}$ *Ame-ga* [$_{I'}$ [$_{VP}$ PRO *huru*] *tumori-da*]]

The deontic modals can thus be seen to behave like control predicates, and will be treated as a separate class from the propositional modals. I will, therefore, not include them in our description of propositional modals in Japanese.

6.2.2 Scope properties

In this subsection we will examine the scope properties of the two classes of propositional modality. *Daroo*-class modals do not include the conditional premise in *-reba* forms in their scope.[13] In (15), only the consequent may be asserted.[14]

(15) *Kootei buai-ga*   *sagar-eba, keiki-ga*   *yokunaru*   ***daroo.***
Official-discount-NOM   fall-if,   economy-NOM   become-good   will.
'If the official discount rate is lowered, the economy will probably improve.'

Yooda-class modals cannot take a conditional premise as an adjunct which modifies modals, and so they have to include a conditional premise within their scope and thus can only serve as an assertion of a general conditional statement rather than a conditional inference (see (16)):

(16) *Kootei buai-ga*   *sagar-eba, keiki-ga*   *yokunaru*   ***yooda.***
Official-discount-NOM   fall-if,   economy-NOM   become-good   will.
'It appears (to be the case) that if the official discount rate is lowered, the economy will improve (accordingly).'

That the two subclasses differ in their scope properties is based on the following facts.

With *daroo*-class modals, the antecedent and the consequent in the conditional statement (15) can each be expressed by different speakers, as in (17):

(17) A: *Kootei buai-ga*   *sagatta-yo.*
      Official-discount-NOM   fell-SFP
      'The official discount rate has been lowered.'
    B: *Zya,*   *keiki-ga*   *yokunaru*   ***daroo.***
      then   economy-NOM   become-good   will
      'Then, the economy will probably improve.'

In (17), speaker B accepts the statement made by A as a hypothetical premise and concludes on the basis of deductive inference that the economy will improve.

Speaker B can repeat the information presented by A as a conditional premise as in (18), indicating that the premise is a presupposition and not the part asserted in the sentence:

(18) A: *Kootei buai-ga*   *sagatta-yo.*
Official-discount-NOM fell-SFP
'The official discount rate has been lowered.'

  B: *Kootei buai-ga*   *sagar-eba, keiki-ga*   *yokunaru*   [*daroo/hazu-da*].
Official discount-NOM fall-if,   economy-NOM become-good {will, should}.
'If the official discount rate is lowered, the economy will/should improve.'

Thus with *daroo*-class modals, conditional premises such as *-reba*-clause or *-tara*-clause need not be included in the assertion of the sentence.[15]

With the *yooda*-class, the assertion involves the conditional relation between the antecedent and the consequent, i.e. the conditionals denote a generic conditional statement. So the consequent cannot be uttered independently of the antecedent. If they are separately asserted by different speakers, as in (19), the result is unacceptable:

(19) A: *Kootei buai-ga*   *sagatta-yo.*
Official-discount-NOM   fell-SFP
'The official discount rate has been lowered.'

  B: ??*Zya, keiki-ga*   *yokunaru*   [*yooda/rasii*].
then   economy-NOM   become-good   {appear/seem}
'Then, the economy appears to improve.'

Speaker B cannot repeat the statement by A as a premise. B in (20) does not sound like a cooperative response to A's statement, because the premise is not treated as information provided by A:

(20) A: *Kootei buai-ga*   *sagatta-yo.*
Official-discount-rateNOM   fell-SFP
'The official discount rate has been lowered.'

  B: # *Kootei buai-ga*   *sagar-eba, keiki-ga*   *yokunaru*   **yooda**.
Official-discount-rate-NOM fall-if,   economy-NOM become-good appear.
'If the official discount rate is lowered, the economy appears to improve.'

The distributional facts observed above can be accounted for if we assume that with *daroo*-class modals, the conditional premise in the *-reba* form is outside the scope of the modal and that with the *yooda*-class, the conditional premise is within its scope. Thus the structure of sentence (15) will be like (21) and that of (16) like (22), respectively:

(21) [*Kootei buai-ga sagar-eba* [[*keiki-ga yokunaru*] **daroo**]].
'If the official discount rate is lowered, the economy will probably improve.'

(22) [[*Kootei buai-ga sagar-eba keiki-ga yoku naru*] **yooda**].
'It appears (to be the case) that if the official discount rate is lowered, the economy will improve (accordingly).'

The contrast becomes more salient when the conditional ending -*nara* is used in the premise. *Nara* is used to mark the premise as newly acquired information, which is most typically provided by the conversation partner:

(23) A: *Kootei buai-ga*   *sagatta-yo.*
Official-discount-NOM   fell-SFP
'The official discount rate has been lowered.'

B1: *Kootei buai-ga*   *sagat-ta-**nara**,*   *keiki-ga*   *yokunaru*   ***daroo**.
Official-discount-rate-NOM   fall-if,   economy-NOM   become-good   will.

B2: ??*Kootei buai-ga*   *sagat-ta-**nara**,*   *keiki-ga*   *yokunaru*   ***yooda**.
Official-discount-rate-NOM   fall-if,   economy-NOM   become-good   appear.
'If the official discount rate goes down, the economy seems to look up.'

The low acceptability of (23B2) can be accounted for if we assume that, unlike -*reba* or -*tara* conditional clauses, which optionally take narrow scope as shown in (22), the conditional premise with -*nara* must always have a wide scope and functions as an adjunct for epistemic modal phrases.[16]

The assumption that -*nara* always takes wide scope with respect to the propositional modals can be shown to be well founded by the following facts. Conditional clauses headed by -*nara* cannot contain wh-words,[17] a fact which shows that the -*nara* clause has a wide scope and is an epistemic adjunct, modifying an epistemic predicate, as suggested by Takubo (1987) and argued for more explicitly in Arita (2007).[18]

(24) a. **Nani-ga**   *sagar-eba* *keiki-ga*   *yokunaru*   *no.*
What-NOM   fall-if   economy-NOM   become-good   Q
(lit.) 'If what has been lowered, will the economy improve?'
'The lowering of what will lead to the improvement of the economy?'

b. *?**Nani-ga**   *sagat-ta-**nara** keiki-ga*   *yokunaru*   *no.*[19]
What-NOM   fell-if,   economy-NOM   become-good   Q
(lit.) 'If what has been lowered, will the economy improve?'
'The lowering of what will lead to the improvement of the economy?'

The reason why wh-words cannot appear in -*nara* clauses has to do with the impossibility of focus placement in wide-scope, non-restrictive adjuncts. As discussed in Takubo (1987), it is generally the case that wide-scope, non-restrictive adjuncts are presuppositions and constitute old information, and thus cannot contain a focused element such as wh-words. Subordinate conjunctives such as -*keredo* ('but') or -*ga* ('but/and'), for example, are wide-scope, non-restrictive adjuncts, or disjuncts in the sense of Greenbaum (1969), only providing background information and thus cannot contain new information, such as wh-words, within the clause they are attached to.

A conditional premise with -*nara*, thus, cannot be in the scope of *yooda*-class modals or modify *yooda*-class modals, ruling out both (25a) and (25b), accounting for the unacceptability of (23B):

(25) a. *[[*Kootei buai-ga sagat-ta-**nara**, keiki-ga yoku naru*] **yooda**].
  'It appears (to be the case) that if the official discount rate goes down, the economy will improve (accordingly).'
  b. *[*Kootei buai-ga sagat-ta-**nara** [[keiki-ga yoku naru*] **yooda**]].

Another phenomenon that shows the differences in the scope properties of the *daroo* and *yooda*-classes is their scope relation with a reason clause. In (26), the proposition expressed in the reason clause is known to the speaker. (27), on the other hand, cannot be interpreted in the same way, i.e. the proposition expressed in the reason clause cannot be interpreted as 'known' to the speaker:

(26) *Kootei buai-ga   sagatta-**kara**, keiki-ga   yokunaru   **daroo**.*
  Official discount-NOM fell-because, economy-NOM become-good will.
  'Since the official discount rate has been lowered, the economy will probably improve.'

(27) *Kootei buai-ga   sagatta-**kara**, keiki-ga   yoku naru   **yooda**.*
  Official discount-NOM fell-because, economy-NOM become-good appear.
  'It appears (to be the case) that because the official discount rate goes down, the economy will improve (accordingly).'

The interpretive differences observed above can also be described by the scope properties of each class. For *daroo*-class predicates, the truth of the reason clause is presupposed, because it is an adjunct clause outside the scope of epistemic modals. In contrast, for *yooda*-class predicates, the reason clause is to be interpreted as falling within the scope of the modal, thereby making 'the official discount rate' interpretable as being undecided as to the truth value.[20]

The scope difference of the two classes is more salient when the predicate in the reason clause has -*masi*, the continuative form of the addressee honorific form -*masu*, as in (29), which forces a wide-scope and thus epistemic interpretation of a reason clause:

(28) *Kootei buai-ga*   *sagari-masi-ta-kara*   *keiki-ga*   *yokunaru*   **desyoo.**
Official discount -NOM fall-HON-PAST-because, economy-NOM become-good will-HON
'Since the official discount rate has been lowered, the economy will improve.'

(29) * *Kootei* buai-ga   *sagari-masi-ta-kara,*   *keiki-ga*   *yoku naru*   **yoodesu.**
Official discount-NOM fall-HON-PAST-because, economy-NOM become-good appearHON
'It appears (to be the case) that because the official discount rate goes down, the economy will improve (accordingly).'

Takubo (1987) shows that reason clauses with a wide-scope reading are to be interpreted as epistemic adjuncts, i.e. they are to be interpreted as modifying the epistemic judgement expressed by the predicates, and those with narrow-scope reading are to be interpreted as restrictive adjuncts, i.e. they modify propositional content.[21] The wide-scope reading of the reason clause is presupposed and cannot be focused; the reason clause cannot include a wh-word within it or be in the focus part of pseudo-cleft sentence.[22] *Kara*-clauses can be ambiguous between epistemic and restrictive adjuncts but the addition of *-masu* disambiguates the interpretation of the clause, making it interpretable only as an epistemic adjunct, as observed by Takubo (1987). *Masu-kara*-clauses, thus, do not allow wh-elements inside, as in (30b), and can never be focused in the pseudo-cleft, as in (31b):

(30) a. **Nani-**ga   *sagat-ta-kara*   *keiki-ga*   *yokunat-ta*   **(no) daroo.**
What-NOM fall-PAST-because, economy-NOM became-good will.
(lit.) 'Because what has been lowered, the economy could have been improved.'
'The lowering of what could have caused the improvement of the economy.'

    b. *****Nani-**ga   *sagari-**masi**-ta-kara,*   *keiki-ga*   *yokunat-ta*   **(no) desyoo.**
What-NOM fall-HON-PAST-because, economy-NOM become-good will-HON
'The lowering of what could have caused the improvement of the economy.'

(31) a. *Keiki-ga*   *yokunat-ta*   *no-wa*   *kooteibuai-ga*
economy-NOM became-good COMP-TOP, official-discount-rate-NOM
sagat-ta-kara-da.
fall-PAST-because-COP
'It is because the official discount rate was lowered that the economy improved.'

    b. **Keiki-ga*   *yokunatta*   *no-wa*   *kooteibuai-ga*
economy-NOM became-good COMP-TOP, official-discount-rate-NOM
*sagari-**masi**-ta kara-desu.*
fall-PAST-because-COP
'It is because the official discount rate was lowered that the economy improved.'

The hierarchical structure of (28) and (29) will be like (32) and (33), respectively:

(32) [*Kootei buai-ga sagari-masi-ta-kara,* [[*keiki-ga yoku naru*] **desyoo**]].
'Since the official discount rate has been lowered, the economy will improve.'

(33) * [*Kootei buai-ga sagari-masi-ta-kara*, [[*keiki-ga yoku naru*] **yoodesu**]].
'It appears (to be the case) that if the official discount rate has been lowered, the economy will improve (accordingly).'

The acceptability status of (28) and (29) can be accounted for if we assume that *daroo*-class modals are epistemic and *yooda*-class modals are not, and that the reason clause as an epistemic adjunct, with its wide-scope property, can modify a predicate phrase with *desyoo*, a honorific form of *daroo*, whereas it cannot modify the one with *yoodesu*, a honorific form of *yooda* because it can only take a narrow-scope adjunct, which necessarily is not epistemic.

6.2.3 Inferential properties

In this subsection I will show that the scope properties of the two classes of modals can be attributed to the type of inference involved. The inference involved in the *daroo*-class is deductive, i.e. sentences headed by *daroo*-class modals are interpreted as the conclusion of the modus ponens deduced by the speaker, with the conditional and reason clause serving as a minor premise. In the case of example (15), the major premise is the knowledge on the part of the speaker of the relation between interest rates and economy.

(34) Major premise: If the official discount rate is lowered, the economy improves.
Minor premise: The official discount rate has been lowered.

Conclusion: The economy improves.

Daroo-class modals are attached to the conclusion inferred, given the major premise and the minor premise.[23] The major premise is some general knowledge presupposed in the discourse. The minor premise is some newly acquired information that triggers inference. It may be given anew by the conversational partner, in which case conditional forms, *-reba* or *-nara*, are used, or they may be some new knowledge that the speaker has acquired, in which case *-kara* forms are used. Given the nature of deductive inference, the major and minor premise are presupposed at the time of the utterance, and constitute old information, while the conclusion is asserted and constitutes new information. In terms of the informational structure, the conditional sentences with *daroo*-class auxiliaries can be represented as follows:

(35) [*Kootei buai-ga sagar-eba,* [[*keiki-ga yokunaru*] **daroo**]].

Old	New

'If the official discount rate has been lowered, the economy
will improve.'

The informational structure we posit for *daroo*-class modals follows
from our assumption that the conclusion is added anew to the knowledge base of the speaker by deductive inference. The scopal properties
of *daroo*-class modals follow from the informational structures posited.

The relation of scope properties and inferential direction proposed for
daroo-class modals can be demonstrated by facts concerning the expression *imagoro*. *Imagoro* denotes a counterpart of the utterance time on
some timescale, as in *asita no imagoro* ('tomorrow at about this time').
It can be used in referring to the utterance time itself when it identifies
the time of an event displaced from the deictic location as in (36):

(36) *John-wa*   ***imagoro***   *Nagasaki-ni*   *tuiteiru*   **daroo**.
     John-TOP   about-now   Nagasaki-LOC   has-arrived   will
     'John will have arrived in Nagasaki about this time.'

Imagoro in (36) refers to the utterance time but the event associated
with it occurs at some displaced location, the truth value of which may
only be inferred on the basis of one's knowledge. In such a case *imagoro*
may be used instead of *ima* (now) to indicate that the event in question is not within one's deictic space. John's arrival in Nagasaki is the
conclusion of the speaker based on some knowledge, e.g. his itinerary.
The inference involved can also be expressed as a generalized form of
modus ponens. An itinerary can be expressed as a function $f(t) = e$, i.e.
a function from a set of time points to a set of events.[24] Thus given
the knowledge of an itinerary and a time point t_i, one can infer that
e_j occurred at t_i. The itinerary function $f(t) = e$ is the major premise,
t_i is the minor premise and e_j is the conclusion. Here the time point
is given but the occurrence of the event is the conclusion reached by
modus ponens. The information structure can be accounted for if we
assume a structure in which *imagoro* is outside the scope of *daroo*-class
modals. The syntactic structure that we posit for (36) is supported by
the intonation contour that it takes. Modals in Japanese can associate
a focus with a constituent in their scope, i.e. the constituents in their
c-command domain. The focused constituent receives a phonological
salience and begins a new phonological phrase. In (36), the expression

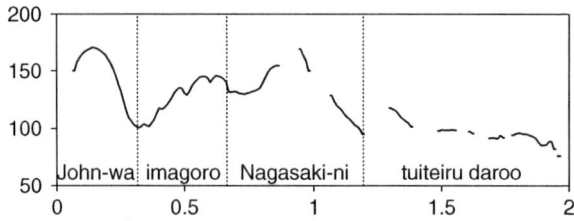

Figure 6.1 Pitch contour in (38)

for an event *e* receives a phonological salience. There must, therefore, be an intonational break between *imagoro* and *Nagasaki-ni* in (36) and *imagoro* never receives phonological salience. The salience falls instead either on *Nagasaki-ni* or *tuiteiru*, suggesting that *imagoro* is not in the scope of *daroo*. The phonological phrasing may be represented as in (37), with the syntactic structure as in (38):

(37) {*John-wa*} {*imagoro*} {*Nagasaki-ni tuiteiru **daroo***}.

(38) [*John-wa* [*imagoro* [[*Nagasaki-ni tuiteiru*] ***daroo***]]].

As can be seen in Figure 6.1, the initial lowering in *Nagasaki* is the reflection of a phonological phrase boundary between *imagoro* and *Nagasaki*.[25]

In contrast, with *yooda*-class modals, *imagoro* must be focused, with obligatory phonological emphasis on it as in (39):

(39) *John-wa   IMAGORO   Nagasaki-ni   tuita   **yooda**.*
John-TOP about now Nagasaki-LOC arrived appear
'John appears to have reached Nagasaki at this (late) hour.'

The intonational pattern shows that *IMAGORO Nagasaki-ni tuita yooda* forms one phonological phrase, with the peak on *IMAGORO*, and gradually falling towards the end of the sentence including the modal, suggesting that *IMAGORO* is within the scope of *yooda* to receive focus. The fact that there is no phonological phrase boundary between *IMAGORO* and *Nagasaki* is reflected in the absence (or weakening) of initial lowering in *Nagasaki* as can be seen in Figure 6.2. The phonological fact can be accounted for if *yooda*-class modals utilize the inverse function, making it necessary to place focus on time. *Imagoro* used in *daroo*-class modals involves identification of

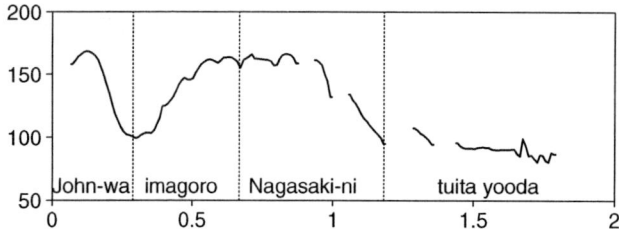

Figure 6.2 Pitch contour in (40)

an event e_j, given some general knowledge $f(t) = e$, and time t_i. We propose, therefore, that with *yooda*-class modals, the inverse function $f^{-1}(e) = t$ is involved, which gives time given f and e. The new information, thus, is the time point; with an event and the general knowledge being presupposed, giving an informational structure similar to a pseudo-cleft, i.e. 'the time that John arrived in Nagasaki is this time (and not the time expected)'. The informational structure and the intonational pattern can be accounted for if we assume the syntactic structure (40), with *IMAGORO* within the scope of *yooda*-class modals, which can be mapped to the phonological phrasing represented in (41):

(40) [*John-wa* [[*IMAGORO Nagasaki-ni tuita*] **yooda**]]

(41) {*John-wa*} {*IMAGORO Nagasaki-ni tuita* **yooda**}

Thus the inference involved in the *yooda*-class is abductive, in the sense that it identifies the minor premise, given a major premise and a conclusion. More generally, it involves the inverse f^{-1} of $f(x) = y$, and identifies x, given y. In some cases, x may not be uniquely determined given y, then the inference only provides a most plausible candidate for explaining y in the context of utterance and is defeasible, in which case, the mapping f^{-1} is not a function in the strict sense, because we cannot determine the value of x given y.

Look at the situation in (42):

(42) Situation: Taroo looks at the newly published alumni newsletter and finds that one of his classmates has changed her surname.

a. *Kanozyo-wa kekkon-sita* **yooda**.
she-TOP   married   appear
'It appears that she has got married.'

b. #*Kanozyo-wa kekkon-sita* **daroo**.
she-TOP   married   will
'She will have got married.'

The knowledge used in the inference is the general practice in Japan of women changing names after marriage. So the inference can be stated as in (43):

(43) Major premise: If a woman gets married, she changes her name.
Minor premise: She changed her name.
- -
Conclusion: She has got married.

The inference involved apparently is not modus ponens. In fact, *daroo*-class modals cannot be used here, as shown by the inappropriateness of (42b). The inference involved is abduction as represented in (44), which is not a logically valid inference, but a form of hypothesis formation:

(44) Major premise: $p \supset q$
Minor premise: q
- -
Conclusion: p

Thus in (42), the speaker abductively concludes the friend's marriage as a possible cause of her name change. For the speaker to deductively conclude 'she has got married', given her name change, the major premise must be something like (45), which is quite strange:[26]

(45) Major premise: If a woman changes her name, she gets married.
Minor premise: She changed her name.
- -
Conclusion: She has got married.

The scope facts about conditionals can be accounted for in the same way. The whole conditional 'if p then q' must be in the scope of *yooda*-class modals as in (46):

(46) [[if p then q] **yooda**].

Unlike *imagoro*, which requires obligatory focus, the focus can be placed on any constituent within the scope. Given the abductive nature of *yooda*-class modals, 'if p then q' can be interpreted as providing an explanation for observed facts, say p followed by q. 'If p, then q-*yooda*' can also be understood as providing a major premise, or some general knowledge which serves to account for observed facts, the minor premise and the conclusion. (46), for example, may be taken to express inductive inference.

6.2.4 Abduction in *daroo*-class: *no* as a scope expansion marker

In the preceding subsection, we have seen that *daroo*-class modals and *yooda*-class modals differ in the direction of inference involved; deduction in the former and abduction and induction in the latter. There is, however, a set of facts that seem to run counter to the generalization we have just made. If we add *no*, a complementizer, to *daroo*-class modals, abductive interpretation becomes possible as in (47). In fact, *no* followed by a copula *da* can be interpreted as involving abductive inference:

(47) Situation: Taroo looks at the newly published alumni newsletter and finds that one of his classmates has changed her surname.
    a. *Kanozyo-wa kekkon-sita **no-daroo**.*
       she-TOP   married   no-will
       'It will be case that she has got married.'
    b. *Kanozyo-wa kekkon-sita **no kamosirenai**.*
       she-TOP   married   no-may
       'She must have got married.'
    c. *Kanozyo-wa kekkon-sita **no-da**.*
       she-TOP   married   no-copula
       'It must be case that she has got married.'

Conditionals can also be in the scope of these modals, suggesting that they allow induction interpretation:

(48) [[*Kootei buai-ga sagar-eba, keiki-ga yokunaru*] **no-daroo**].
    'It must be the case that if the official discount rate goes down, the economy will improve (accordingly).'

Morphologically, *no-daroo* can be analysed as a combination of *no*, a complementizer, and *daroo*. *No* places the preceding sentence in the scope of modals, thereby serving as a scope expansion marker. *Nitigainai* is more or less in free variation with *no nitigainai*, so it can be treated in the same way as *no-daroo* with regard to its scope properties. *Kamosirenai* generally must be preceded by *no* to allow scope expansion. We will call those *daroo*-class modals that allow abductive interpretation *daroo*-class b (i.e. the *no-daroo* class) and those that do not, *daroo*-class a, for ease of reference.

One may conclude from these observations that the differences between the two classes of propositional modals lie in their scope properties: *yooda*-class modals have wider scope than *daroo*-class modals, with the scope of the latter being expandable by *no*. One may further like to reduce the difference in the directionality in inference to the scopal properties, by saying that narrow-scope modals induce deduction and wide-scope modals induce abduction or induction.

In the next section, we will show that the differences in the two types of modals cannot be reduced to their scope properties and that *daroo*-class b has properties distinct from the *yooda*-class. We will also show that the two classes differ in their reference to the knowledge base and the type of conclusion to be reached.

6.2.5 The nature of abductive inference in *yooda*-class modals

Firstly, the nature of the minor premise is different in *yooda*-class and *daroo*-class b. For *daroo*-class b, as in *daroo*-class a, the speaker need not know the information conveyed in the minor premise beforehand and this can be provided by the conversation partner. The speaker, therefore, may not be committed to the truth of the premise. *Zya* ('then') is a discourse connective used to indicate that the conclusion is based upon the premise that the conversational partner has just provided, indicating that the information was unknown to the speaker prior to the discourse session:

(49) A: *Keiki-ga   yokunatta-yo.*
economy-NOM became-good-SFP
'The economy has been improving.'

B: *Zya, kooteibuai-ga   sagatta{no-daroo /??daroo}*
then official-discount-rate-NOM fell {no-will/ will}
'Then, the official discount rate must have been cut down.'

(50) A: *Keiki-ga   yokunatta-yo.*
economy-NOM became-good-SFP
'The economy has been improving.'

B: *keiki-ga   yokunatta   no nara, kooteibuai-ga*
economy-NOM become-good comp-if official-discount-rate-NOM
sagatta {no-daroo /??daroo}.[27]
fell {no-will/ will}
'If the economy has been improving, the official discount rate must have been cut down.'

The inference the speaker B makes can be illustrated as in (51). The abduction is based on the major premise and the newly acquired information provided by A:

(51) Major premise (general knowledge):
　　　 If the official discount rate goes down, economy improves.
　　 Minor premise: provided by the hearer
　　　 Economy improves
_____

　　　 Conclusion by abduction:
　　　 Official discount rate has been cut down.

In contrast, *yooda*-class modals cannot be used with a sentence beginning with *zya*, indicating that the minor premise may not be provided by the conversational partner:[28]

(52) A: *Keiki-ga*　　　　*yokunatta-yo.*
　　　　 economy-NOM　became-good-SFP
　　　　 'The economy has been improving.'
　　 B: *Zya, kooteibuai-ga*　　　*sagatta* {??*yooda*, ??*rasii*}.
　　　　 Official-discount-NOM　fell {appear, seem}
　　　　 '?Then, the official discount rate seems to have been cut down.'

The abductive judgement associated with *yooda*-class modals cannot be based upon the minor premise provided by the conversational partner. Note that the minor premise provided by A in (53) can never be expressed in any of the conditional forms: (*no*) *nara* cannot be in the scope of *yooda*-class modals because of scope reasons, and cannot modify them either, so *yooda* cannot co-occur with (*no*) *nara*. -*Reba* or -*tara* forms cannot express information about which B has learned from A:[29]

(53) A: *Keiki-ga*　　　　　*yokunatta-yo.*
　　　　 economy-NOM　became-good-SFP
　　　　 'The economy has been improving.'
　　 B: *keiki-ga*　　　　　{*yokunat-ta* (*no*) *nara, yokunat-te ir-eba*}
　　　　 economy-NOM　become-good COMP if
　　　　 kooteibuai-ga　　　　　　*sagatta* {??*yooda*, ??*rasii*}.
　　　　 official-discount-rate-NOM　　fell {appear, seem}
　　　　 '?Then, the official discount rate seems to have been lowered.'

Both the minor premise and the conclusion of the abductive inference must be provided by one speaker for *yooda*-class modals to be used:

(54) B: *Kooteibuai-ga*   *sagatta* {*yooda, rasii*}.
       Official-discount-NOM   fell {appear, seem}
       'The official discount rate seems have been cut down.'
    A: *Doosite.*
       why
       'What are your grounds for saying that?'
    B: *Keiki-ga*   *yokunatta.*
       economy-NOM become-good
       'The economy has been improving.'

In (54), B's utterance *Kootei buai-ga sagatta yooda* is the conclusion abductively drawn from B's observation: The economy has been improving. The premise from which the conclusion is drawn must be B's own observation and cannot be provided by the conversational partner.[30]

The abductive inference for *daroo*-class b and the *yooda*-class, thus, have different constraints. The abductive inference involved in *daroo*-class b can still be characterized as inference based on some general knowledge and some newly acquired knowledge, and the conclusion is drawn by the addition of the newly acquired knowledge. According to Palmer (2001: 8), 'with epistemic modality speakers express their judgements about the factual status of the proposition'. In the domain of conditional reasoning, the content of the speaker's judgements about the factual status of the proposition can best be characterized in terms of the 'epistemic conditionals' in the sense of Sweetser (1990: 116): 'In the epistemic domain, *if–then* conjunction expresses the idea that knowledge of the truth of the hypothetical premise expressed in the protasis is a sufficient condition for concluding the truth of the proposition expressed in the apodosis.' In this sense, abductive inference in *daroo*-class b can still be characterized as epistemic. In contrast *yooda*-class modals cannot be epistemic and the inferential force may come from other sources.

In the next section, we will show how the constraints on inference in the two classes of modals can be explained.

6.3   Proposal: evidential nature of *yooda*-class and epistemic nature of *daroo*-class modals

In this section we will show that all the characteristics of *yooda*-class modals can be derived if we assume that sentences with *yooda*-class modals, i.e. p-*yooda*, p-*rasii* and possibly p-*sooda*1 and p-*sooda*2, describe the ongoing situations which are perceptible to the speaker, i.e. that part of the speaker's reality in which the speaker knows the truth of all the propositions.[31]

We say that a proposition is 'settled' when its truth has already been objectively determined by the actual situation at hand (although the speaker may not know it).[32] When the speaker knows a proposition to be true by past experience or deictically by perception, i.e. without any inference, we say that s/he 'd-knows' it, and the propositions that are d-known to the speaker will be called a 'd-proposition'. D-propositions are all settled by definition. We argue that unlike *daroo*-class modals, *yooda*-class modals express d-propositions and are not really modals that involve quantification over possible worlds, and that the inferential force comes from somewhere else.[33]

6.3.1 Evidential nature of *yooda*-class modals

We propose A below as the definitional characteristics of *yooda*-class modals. In what follows we use YOODA as a cover term for an instance of *yooda*-class modals for ease of reference.

A. The proposition expressed by 'p-YOODA' must be a d-proposition.

Saito (2006) proposes that the following constraints hold between the complement of *yooda* and *rasii* and the whole sentences including the modals:

B: Lexical constraints on *yooda* and *rasii*:
$$p \rightarrow p\text{-}yooda\text{: } \{w: p = 1 \text{ in } w\} \subset \{w: p\text{-}yooda' = 1 \text{ in } w\}$$
$$p\text{-}rasii \rightarrow p\text{: } \{w: p\text{-}rasii' = 1 \text{ in } w\} \subset \{w: p = 1 \text{ in } w\}$$

The proposition p-*yooda*, expressed by attaching *yooda* to a sentence expressing a proposition p, thus, is interpreted as constituting a necessary condition for p. For p-*rasii*, it is to be interpreted as a sufficient condition for p. Saito's (2006) constraint can follow naturally by positing the lexical properties for *yooda* and *rasii* as suggested by Takubo (2006) as follows:

(55) p-*yooda*: *look as if* p   p → *look as if* p
     p-*rasii*: *typical sub-cases of* p   *typical sub-cases of* p → p

Cases in which p is true subsume cases in which p-*yooda* is true, where the situation expressed by p-*yooda* obviously has the property such that it looks as if p, since when p is true, it trivially follows that p looks as if p. In contrast, when p-*rasii* is true, it does not follow that p is true, because there are always non-typical cases of p.

We will show that A and B will account for the evidential nature of *yooda*-class modals and why they invariably induce abductive (or inductive) reasoning.

From the lexical characterizations for *yooda* and *rasii* in B and the assumption A, the following corollaries can be derived:

C1: *Hikyoo* (simile) use is possible only for *yooda* and not for *rasii*.

Hikyoo usage of *yooda* is to be found in cases where the speaker knows that p is false and p-*yooda* is true, i.e. where the speaker d-knows both ¬p and p-*yooda* as in (56). The adverbial *marude* ('in such a way as if') indicates that the proposition *taihuu-ga kita* ('The typhoon came') is false, and that the speaker knows it:

(56) *kono heya-wa   marude taihuu-ga   kita   yooda.*
     this room-TOP as-if   typhoon-NOM came appear
     'This room looks as if a typhoon had come.'

With *yooda*, this value assignment is possible because [p → p *yooda*] can be true even if p is false. *Rasii*, on the other hand, cannot have this usage. P-*rasii*, being a d-proposition, must always be true, so p cannot be false without making [p-*rasii* → p] false. In fact, *rasii* cannot be used with *marude* as in (57):

(57) **kono heya-wa   marude taihuu-ga   kita   rasii.*
     this room-TOP as-if   typhoon-NOM came appear
     'This room looks as if a typhoon had come.'

C2: P in p-*yooda* and p-*rasii* must be settled.

For p-*yooda* it is obvious that p must be settled. Given that p is the sufficient condition for p-*yooda*, if p-*yooda* is a d-proposition, and is thus settled, then p must be settled because {w: p = 1 in w}⊂{w: p-*yooda* = 1 in w}. For p-*rasii*, since {w: p-*rasii* = 1 in w}⊂{w: p = 1 in w}, just from the inclusion relation alone we cannot say that p is settled. However, since the speaker asserts p-*rasii* to be true when s/he says it, s/he is committed to the truth of the p-*rasii*. Then the cases where the premise p-*rasii* is false are excluded from consideration. Since p is the necessary condition for p-*rasii* to hold, in all the possible worlds where p-*rasii* is true, p must also be true, although the speaker may not be sure of it. P, therefore, must be settled, when p-*rasii* is a d-proposition. The difference between *yooda* and *rasii* is that with *yooda*, the consequent of a conditional 'if p then p-*yooda*' is asserted, whereas with *rasii*, the premise of conditional 'if p-*rasii*, then p' is asserted.

C3: P in p-*yooda* and p-*rasii* cannot be a d-proposition.

In the case of p-*yooda*, it is more informative to say p than p-*yooda*, if the speaker knows p as his/her own knowledge prior to the utterance.[34] The speaker, therefore, cannot assert p-*yooda* if s/he d-knows that p holds, without violating the Gricean maxim of quantity.[35] In the case of p-*rasii*, on the other hand, it is redundant to say p-*rasii* when the speaker d-knows p. Since [p-*rasii* → p] is always true if p is true, asserting p-*rasii* fails to contribute new information.[36] Therefore, the complement of *yooda* and *rasii* cannot be a d-proposition, if s/he is engaged in an informative exchange.

From C1, C2 and C3, it follows that for non-simile use of p-*yooda* and p-*rasii*, propositions expressed by p must be settled but not known to the speaker, and those expressed by p-*yooda* and p-*rasii* must be known to the speaker either by past experience or deictically by perception, prior to the utterance. If the speaker does not know whether p is true or not, s/he can abductively infer p, given the knowledge p → p-*yooda* or p-*rasii* → p and the minor premise given by p-*yooda*, or p-*rasii*, which is a d-proposition. Let me illustrate this with example (42a) repeated here as (58a) and with (58b), where *yooda* is changed to *rasii*:

(58) Situation: Taroo looks at the newly published alumni newsletter and finds that one of his classmates has changed her surname.
   a. *Kanozyo-wa kekkon-sita* **yooda**.
      she-TOP   married   appear
      'It appears that she has got married.'
   b. *Kanozyo-wa kekkon-sita* **rasii**.
      she-TOP   married   seem
      'It appears that she has got married.'

(58 a, b) mean almost the same and are mutually indistinguishable. For both a and b, the name change is the newly perceived fact that needs to be explained, and corresponds to the proposition expressed by p-*yooda* and p-*rasii*. In the case of p-*yooda*, the speaker relates the newly perceived knowledge expressed by p-*yooda* to what follows if a woman gets

married, e.g. she wears a wedding ring, she walks with her husband, and she changes her name, etc. So from the newly acquired knowledge that she has changed her name, Taro can abductively infer quite plausibly that she may have got married, causing her to change her name. Since p is only a necessary condition and not a sufficient condition, the speaker can assert p-*yooda*, and deny p as in (59):

(59) *Kanozyo-wa ikken*　　*kekkon-siteiru* **yooda**-*ga,*　*hontoo-wa kekkonsiteinai.*
　　　she-TOP　　apparently is-married　　appear-but in-reality　married-not
　　　'She looks as if she is married but in fact she is not.'

In the case of p-*rasii*, on the other hand, the speaker relates the newly perceived knowledge to one of the sufficient conditions. Thus one cannot assert p-*rasii* and at the same time deny p:

(60) **Kanozyo-wa kekkon-siteiru* **rasii**-*ga,*　　*hontoo-wa kekkonsiteinai.*
　　　she-TOP　　is- married　appear-but in-reality　married-not
　　　'She seems to be married but in fact she is not.'

At first blush, the characterization of *rasii* given above may not immediately account for the abductive nature of the inference involved in *rasii*. Drawing the conclusion p from the major premise 'if p-*rasii*, then p' and the minor premise 'p-*rasii*' by modus ponens is, of course, deductive. Then how can the abductive nature of *rasii* and the characterization given above be explained? The answer lies in the partition of the worlds involved. The lexical constraint B requires p-*rasii* to be a sufficient condition for p. The set of possible worlds, thus, is partitioned into the following:

$W_{\neg p}$: {w | ¬p and ¬(p-*rasii*) in w}
W_p　: {w | (p and p-*rasii* in w) or (p and ¬ p-*rasii* in w)}

The lexical constraint A requires p-*rasii* to be a d-proposition, i.e. a proposition true by direct experience. P-*rasii* serves to relate a set of observed facts to the proposition p, e.g. 'A changed her name' 'A has a ring on her ring finger' etc. to 'A got married.' The selection of the form p-*rasii* leads the speaker to conclude that the current world s/he is in is the one in W_p rather than $W_{\neg p}$: the proposition expressed in p-*rasii* is true if s/he is in a world in which p is true. The inference, thus, is a form of abduction in that p serves as the explanation for the state of affairs as stated in p-*rasii*.

The nature of abductive inference is very different from that involved in *daroo*-class modals, where abduction is the inverse function, but still epistemic in the sense of Sweetser (1990). In the case of *yooda*-class modals, the abductive character stems from the constraint in inference. The direction of inference in *yooda*-class modals necessarily involves d-propositions to propositions the truth of which are settled but still unknown. The inference, therefore, must always go from knowledge based upon what is already known to what is settled but not known, the reverse of the causation chain.[37]

6.3.2 Epistemic nature of *daroo*-class modals

Daroo-class modals are always attached to the conclusion of the inference, which can either be deductive, abductive or inductive, depending on the scope of the modals. The lexical characterization of *daroo*-class modals dictates that its complement must not be known to the speaker prior to the utterance and thus, is added anew to the knowledge base by inference, i.e. the complement of *daroo*-class modals must not be a d-proposition. Premises can either be known to or new to the speaker; the speaker can make an inference based on his knowledge or experience, or on some new information provided by the conversational partner. For *daroo*-class b, the premise can be some evidence newly acquired by personal experience, e.g. perception, and may be classified as evidential as in (61):

(61) *Kinko-ga*   *akerare-te-iru.*   *Zimusyo-ni*   *doroboo-ga*   *haitta*   **nitigainai.**
     safe-NOM   be-opened   office-LOC   burglar-NOM   entered   must
     'The safe has been opened. There must have been a burglary at our office.'

In (61), the premise *kinko-ga ake-rare teiru* ('the safe has been opened') is knowledge obtained by perception, from which the conclusion *doroboo-ga haitta* ('there was a burglary') has been drawn by abduction. *Yooda*-class modals can be used in the same situation:

(62) *Kinko-ga*   *akerare-te-iru.*   *Zimusyo-ni*   *doroboo-ga*   *haitta*   **yooda.**
     safe-NOM   be-opened   office-LOC   burglar-NOM   entered   appear
     'The safe has been opened. There appears to have been a burglary.'

Yooda-class modals relate the perceived situation described or implicitly assumed in the premise with the current but non-perceived situation, basically by means of causality chain. So *yooda*-class modals are descriptions of current state. The inferential force is not coded in the modals themselves but derives from the geometry of knowledge space where the pair of information sources that they relate are located. In contrast, *daroo*-class modals lexically code online inference made to draw a conclusion on the basis of the perception, together with other knowledge. That the cognitive act of inference is involved in *daroo*-class modals but not in *yooda*-class can be seen in the type of performative verbs used in the quote. The verb *omou* ('think') in present basic form (*kihonkei*) expresses an indirect quote and indicated that the sentence quoted involves the cognitive act of epistemic judgement.[38] *Omou* can quote (61) as in (63) but not (62) as in (64):[39]

> (63) *Kinko-ga   akerare-te-iru. Zimusyo-ni doroboo-ga   haitta   **nitigainai** to   omou.*
>   safe-NOM be-opened   office-LOC burglar-NOM entered must   quote think
>   'The safe has been opened. There must have been a burglary at our office.'

> (64) *Kinko-ga   akerare-te-iru. ??Zimusyo-ni doroboo-ga   haitta   **yooda** to   omou.*
>   safe-NOM be-opened   office-LOC burglar-NOM entered appear quote think
>   'The safe has been opened. There appears to have been a burglary.'

In fact, those uninflecting modals Kindaichi (1953) gives as involving subjective, such as *yoo* ('volitional'), *mai* ('will not'), *daroo* ('will') as subjective all allow quote by *omou*. If we assume the decompositional approach that *daroo*-class modals other than *daroo* have a zero morpheme corresponding to *daroo* attached, we can account for the fact that they allow quote by *omou*.

6.4   Concluding remarks

In this chapter, we have shown the following. *Daroo*-class modals are epistemic in that they are attached to the conclusion of epistemic inference. Thus, the complement of *daroo*-class modals must not be a d-proposition. We have argued that P-YOODA is a d-proposition. *Yooda*-class modals are direct evidentials which serve to relate the perceptible part of the current situation expressed by the predicate p-YOODA and the situation outside the perceptible part expressed by p, its complement, on the other. The inferential force comes from the lexical properties of each lexical item and where the information expressed in p is located.[40] The inferential force of YOODA can be operative only if the complement p is settled but is not a d-proposition. The inferential force of YOODA cannot, therefore, be deductive, but is abductive or inductive.

Notes

1. This chapter is a revised and extended version of the paper read at the
15th Japanese and Korean Linguistics Conference held at the University
of Wisconsin-Madison, and at the Revisiting Japanese Modality conference
held at SOAS, London in June 2006. Takubo (2007), a shorter version of
the paper, appeared in McGloin et al. (2007). I would like to thank CSLI
Publications for permitting me to use the content of the paper for this version. I also thank the organizers of the SOAS workshop, Barbara Pizziconi
and Mika Kizu, for inviting me to the workshop. I thank Shigeru Sakahara,
Hiroshi Mito, Tomohide Kinuhata and Matt Berends for pointing out various problems and improving the style in earlier versions of this chapter
and an anonymous reviewer for insightful comments. Thanks are also due
to Toshio Matsuura for important advice on phonological interpretation of
the scope facts. I also thank Sanae Tamura and Maggie Camp for reading
the manuscript of this chapter, and giving me useful comments on both the
style and the content. All the remaining errors are my own. This work is
supported in part by JSPS Research Grants, Basic Research (B) No. 16320053,
Basic Research (A) No. 15202009 and Basic Research (A) No. 17202010.
2. See Palmer (2001) for the notion 'propositional modality'.
3. I will not deal with deontic or root modality for the reasons given in
section 6.2.
4. The modal force of *daroo* is not lexically specified, so the exact translation cannot be given out of context. It can be glossed as 'will probably'
or 'will without doubt' depending on the modal adverb it co-occurs with.
With this caveat, I will gloss it as 'will' and translate it as 'will probably' for
convenience. See Hara (2006) for discussion.
5. I use the term 'modal auxiliary' following the tradition of Japanese linguistics, although Japanese modals do not exhibit the kind of properties
discussed in section 6.2.1, separating them from other predicates. I also use
the terms 'modal predicates' or simply 'modals'.
6. The zero form can combine with bare conclusive forms, forms without
modals attached, accounting for the epistemic modal interpretation of these
forms, as in (i), which ends in a form without an overt modal attached:

(i) *Kootei buai-ga sagari-**masi-ta-kara** kitto keiki-ga*
Official discount-NOM fall-HON-PAST-because, surely economy-NOM
yoku-nari-masu.
become-good-HON
'Since the official discount rate has been lowered, the economy is sure to improve.'

7. See Nitta (1989) and Noda (1989).
8. Some give 'Contraction' for C, as in Bender et al. (2003).
9. *Sooda2* ('look like') is attached to the continuative form (*ren'yookei*) and
inflects like a nominal adjective (*keiyoo doosi*), *rasii* ('seem') is attached to the
stem of nominal adjectives and to the adnominal/conclusive form of verbs
and adjectives, and inflects like an adjective. *Sooda1*('I hear') is attached to
a conclusive form (*syuusikei*), and inflects like a nominal adjective. *Yooda*

is attached to the adnominal form (*rentaikei*) and inflects like a nominal adjective. *Kamosirenai* and *nitigainai* begin with *ka* and *ni*, respectively, both functioning as complementizers, and end with the negative *nai*.

10. The description of modals in Masuoka and Takubo (1992: Part 2 Chapter 5 and Part 3 Chapter 6) includes deontic modals in the auxiliaries.

11. Although modals in English can be ambiguous between the deontic and epistemic use, modern Japanese must systematically use distinct forms for the deontic meaning and the epistemic meaning:

  a. *John-wa*   *syoosin-no*   *tame-ni eigo-no siken-ni gookaku-si* **nakereba naranai**.
     John-TOP promotion-GEN for   English test-LOC   pass   must
     'John must pass the English proficiency test to be promoted.' [deontic]

  b. *soto-wa*   *ame-ga*   *hutteiru nitigainai*.
     outside-TOP rain-NOM falling   must
     'It must be raining outside.' [epistemic]

12. It is still controversial whether deontic modals invariably have a control structure. It is possible to say (i), which apparently has a raising structure, with a deontic interpretation. See Brennan (1993) and Wurmbrand (1999) for discussion.

   (i) There should be a flower vase here.

13. In Japanese, basic means of changing a clause into a conditional premise is to add suffixes such as -*to*, -*reba*, -*tara* and -*nara* to a predicate. Of these four only -*nara* can be attached to a tensed predicate and always has wide scope over propositional modals. -*Reba* and -*tara* are basic conditional forms, which can either be taken to be conjugation forms of predicates or suffixes added to one of the stem forms of predicates. -*To* expresses temporal sequence of two events, only some of which can be interpreted as a conditional dependence between events. Since the conditional interpretation of -*to* rarely interacts with propositional modals, I do not include it in this discussion.

14. *Daroo* has a non-epistemic usage, which allows a wh-word or a focused constituent in the premise, as in (i):

   (i) A: *Kono natu **nani-o**   ur-eba ii   **daroo**.*
            this summer-ACC   sell-if good   will
            'What do you think we should sell this summer?'
        B: ***Eakon-o***   *ur-eba ii   **daroo**.*
            air-conditioner-ACC sell   good   will
            'I think we should sell air conditioners.'

This usage is not possible with the other modals in the *daroo*-class.

15. The behaviour of -*reba* and -*tara* is the same for the phenomena discussed in this chapter, so we only use -*reba* in the examples.

16. Since *-daroo* cannot include a conditional premise, we cannot tell whether a *-nara*-clause can take a narrow scope or not by looking at (23B1), which must always be analysed as (ii) and not as (i):

    (i) *[[*Kootei buai-ga sagat-ta-nara keiki-ga yokunaru*] *daroo*].
       'If the official discount rate goes down, the economy will improve.'
    (ii) [*Kootei buai-ga sagat-ta-nara* [[*keiki-ga yokunaru*] *daroo*]].

We can tell the scopal properties of *-nara* by adding a complemetizer *no* to the complement of *-daroo*. As we will see in section 6.2.4, *no* functions as a scope expansion marker. Thus, the narrow-scope interpretation of the *-reba* clause with *no daroo* becomes possible as in (iii), with the focus on the conditional sentence, in addition to a wide-scope interpretation in (iv):

    (iii) [[*Kootei buai-ga sagar-eba keiki-ga yokunaru*] *no daroo*].
       'It may be that if the official discount rate goes down, the economy will look up.'
    (iv) [*Kootei buai-ga sagar-eba* [[*keiki-ga yokunaru*] *no daroo*]].

A narrow-scope interpretation of a *-nara*-clause remains impossible even if *no* is added. It must be the case, therefore, that *nara* always has wide scope:

    (v) *[[*Kootei buai-ga sagat-ta-nara keiki-ga yokunaru*] *no daroo*].
    (vi) [*Kootei buai-ga sagat-ta-nara* [[*keiki-ga yokunaru*] *no daroo*]].

17. See note 18 for the explanation as to the possibility of a wh-question out of adjuncts in Japanese.
18. The point for *no-nara* is argued for more explicitly in Arita (2007), which she argues must be used as an epistemic adjunct, based on semantic evidence. With *no-nara*, wh-questions become completely unacceptable.
19. As pointed out by one of the reviewers, this sentence can be acceptable as an echo question.
20. This interpretation is not entirely natural, unless a special information focus is placed on the reason clause, e.g. with an emphatic stress on *-kara*.
21. The relevant distinction has to do with that between B- and C-class predicates in the sense of Minami (1974, 1993). C-class predicates are epistemic modals and are hierarchically higher in position than the B-class predicates, which comprise tensed predicates without modals. B-class predicates correspond roughly to content-level predicates and C level to epistemic level of Sweetser (1990). See also Masuoka in this volume.
22. Notice that in Japanese a wh-question is generally possible out of an adjunct clause, because surface movement is not involved. The wh-movement at LF, which is needed to arrive at wh-semantics, apparently violates subjacency. Huang (1982) argues that subjacency is not operative at LF, while Nishigauchi (1986) argues that there are subjacency effects at LF, and

explains the apparent subjacency violation cases by positing a massive pied-piping. In our wh-adjunct cases, the wh-phrase moves to the COMP position of the adjunct clause, and then the whole adjunct moves to the higher COMP position, without violating subjacency. For our purposes, it suffices to note that a wh-question out of an adjunct clause is possible in Japanese.

23. Kindaichi (1953) seems to have been aware of the deductive nature of *daroo* but Oosika (1995) is probably the first who first explicitly described *daroo* as involving a modus ponens. Miyake (1995) also refers to the deductive nature of *daroo*, albeit not so explicitly as Oosika (1995).

24. Itinerary belongs to the more general schedule function which takes the form of $f(t) = e$.

25. The preparation of Figures 6.1 and 6.2 and the interpretation of the pitch pattern are due to Toshio Matsuura.

26. The inference can be rephrased as a form of deduction if a conditional involves statives or the perfect, as in (i). Unlike the major premise in (43), which expresses the causal relation between the premise and the consequent, the conditional in (i) is epistemic in the sense of Sweetser (1990), and we can insert 'we can infer that' in the consequent:

> (i) *Onna-no hito-ga   namae-o   kae-te i-reba,   kanozyo-wa kekkon-site-i-ru.*
> female   person-NOM name-ACC have-changed-if she-TOP   be-married
> 'If a woman's name has been changed, (we can infer that) she is married.'

We can use *daroo* in the conclusion *kanozyo-wa kekkon-siteiru **daroo*** ('she is married-would'), as the result of the deductive inference, given (i) and the minor premise that she has changed her name. The premise and the consequent in (i) are two states of affairs that are true in a set of worlds in which a woman's marriage is necessarily followed by her name change. In such a world, the two states of affairs always coincide with each other and we can infer from the existence of one the existence of the other. *Daroo*, however, cannot be used in a sentence that expresses an abductive inference, that is, a sentence expressing a hypothesis for the cause of the situation just perceived.

27. The conditional forms *-reba* or *-tara* are not appropriate for cases like this, because in order to make abductive judgement, the truth of the conditional premise must already be decided, or 'settled' (see note 29) for obvious reasons: one can only provide a causal explanation for a situation in question when the situation has already occurred. *No-nara* is the conditional form in Japanese that indicates that the premise is settled and provided by the conversational partner. *Te- i reba* or *te-i tara*, the perfective forms of verbs with *-reba* and *-tara* conditionals, can be interpreted as settled but cannot be interpreted as indicating that the premise is provided by the conversational partner.

28. The major premise cannot be provided by the conversational participant as a form of induction either.

29. This is true even if they are in perfective forms *te i-reba* or *te- itara*. See note 24.

30. Interestingly, the conditional forms in -*to* may be used to express the abductive judgement based on the observation one has made when verbs of observation are used:

    (i) *keiki-ga*   *yoku-natta*   *no o*   *miruto,*   *kooteibuai ga*
    economy-NOM became-good COMP see-when official-discount-rate-NOM
    sagatta rasii.
    fell   seem
    'Now that (we observe) the economy has become better, it seems that the
    official discount rate has been lowered.'

31. Miyake (1995) claims that *yooda*-class modals, within which he includes *yooda, rasii, mitaida, sooda* and *toyuu*, express what he calls *zissyooteki handan* ('empirical judgement'), that is, judgement based upon what the speaker experienced, and tries to relate the directionalities inference in evidential modals in Japanese to the type of judgement involved. Oosika (1995) makes similar observations.
32. Cf. Kaufmann (2005) for more formal and precise definition of this notion.
33. *Daroo*-class can co-occur with adverbs of quantification such as *tabun* ('probably'), *kitto* ('certainly'), *osoraku* ('perhaps'), which cannot modify *yooda*-class modals. If sentences with *yooda*-class modals are d-propositions, it is natural that they cannot be modified by these adverbs, because as d-propositions they are constants.
34. See Saito (2006) for details.
35. When the speaker knows that saying p violates the territoriality of the hearer and thus has to behave as if s/he does not know the truth of p, it becomes possible to use p-*yooda* in place of p to respect the territoriality of the hearer (cf. Kamio 1990). Our characterization of *yooda* accounts for the fact that among the *yooda*-class modals, only *yooda* (or *mitaida*, the synonym of *yooda* in colloquial speech), can be used for this usage.
36. *Rasii* can be used as a suffix taking a nominal to express prototypes, e.g. *otoko-**rasii*** ('manly'), '*Tanaka-**rasii*** ('typical of Tanaka'). In the nominal taking cases of *rasii*, however, C3 does not hold; *otoko-rasii otoko* ('manly man') is perfect, due to the difference in syntactic position.
37. See Aksu-Koç and Slobin (1986) and DeLancey (1986) for relevant discussion. The distinction has to do with D-domain and I-domain in the sense of discourse management theory (Takubo and Kinsui 1997). D-domain is a domain of constants, names and d-propositions. I-domain as originally conceived only housed variables. With the introduction of 'settledness', the discourse domain now is divided into R-domain, which houses constants, and I-domain, which houses variables. R-domain can further be subdivided into D-domain and R-D domain, which is the complement of D-domain. D-domain consists of d-propositions, or direct knowledge on the part of the cognitive agent, and R-D domain consists of settled propositions, or propositions that have already been decided and verifiable in principle. See Takubo (2006) for details.

38. More generally, there are classes of verbs of saying, thinking, etc. in Japanese that are subcategorized for performatives and interpreted as quoting performative utterances. *Omou* quotes the epistemic judgement, i.e. the act of judgement based on inference. See Takubo (1988) for discussion. *Hazuda* does not seem to allow the quote by *omou*, the reason for which is not clear.

39. Although the *yooda* itself does not lexically code online judgement, the cognitive act of epistemic judgement is involved in uttering (62). One can respond to (62) by saying (i). *Soo-da* in (i) can be taken to stand for the cognitive act of epistemic judgement:

> (i) *boku-mo soo-da to omou*
> I-also   so   think
> 'I think so, too.'

40. *Sooda1* ('I hear') does not involve inference because of its lexical properties. *Sooda2* ('looks like') allows its complement not to be a settled proposition, allowing deductive inference. Both p-*sooda1* and p-*sooda2*, however, must be a d-proposition.

References

Aksu-Koç, Ayhan A. and Dan I. Slobin (1986). A psychological account of the development and use of evidentials in Turkish. In: Chafe, Wallace and Nichols, Johanna (eds), *Evidentiality: the Linguistic Coding of Epistemology*. Norwood, New Jersey: Ablex: 159–67.

Aoki, H. (1986). Evidentials in Japanese. In: Chafe, Wallace and Nichols, Johanna (eds), *Evidentiality: the Linguistic Coding of Epistemology*. Norwood, New Jersey: Ablex: 223–38.

Arita, S. (2007). *Nihongo Zyookenbun to Ziseisetusei* [Japanese Conditionals and Tensedness]. Tokyo: Kurosio.

Bender, E. et al. (2003). *Syntactic Theory: a Formal Introduction* (CSLI Lecture Notes, No. 152). Stanford: CSLI Publications.

Brennan, V. M. (1993). Root and epistemic modal auxiliary verbs. PhD thesis, University of Massachusetts.

DeLancey, S. (1986). Evidentiality and volitionality in Tibetan. In: Chafe, Wallace and Nichols, Johanna (eds), *Evidentiality: the Linguistic Coding of Epistemology*. Norwood, New Jersey: Ablex: 203–13.

Greenbaum, S. (1969). *Studies in English Adverbial Usage*. London: Longman.

Hara, Y. (2006). Japanese discourse items at interfaces. PhD thesis, University of Delaware.

Huang, J. (1982). Logical relations in Chinese and the theory of grammar. PhD thesis, MIT.

Huddleston, R. (1976). Some theoretical issues in the description of the English verb. *Lingua* 40, 331–83.

Kamio, A. (1990). *Zyoohoo no nawabari riron* [The theory of territory of information]. Tokyo: Taisyuukan.

Kaufmann, S. (2005). Conditional predictions: a probabilistic account. *Linguistics and Philosophy* 1, 45–77.

Kindaichi, H. (1953). 'Huhenkazyodoosi no Honsitu [The True Nature of Noninflecting Auxiliaries]. *Kokugo kokubun*, 22 (2–3), [Kyoto University Kokubungakkai]. Reprinted in Hattori, S. et al. (eds) (1978) *Nihon no Gengogaku* [Linguistics in Japan], vol. 3. Tokyo: Taishukan: 207–49.

McGloin, N. et al. (eds) (2007). *The Proceedings of JK Linguistic Conference 15.* Stanford: CSLI Publications.

Masuoka, T. and Y. Takubo (1992). *Kiso Nihongo Bunpoo* [Basic Grammar of Japanese]. Tokyo: Kurosio.

Minami, H. (1974). *Gendai Nihongo no Koozoo.* [The Structure of Modern Japanese]. Tokyo: Taishukan.

Minami, H. (1993). *Gendai Nihongobunpoo no Rinkaku.* [The Outline of Japanese Grammar]. Tokyo: Taishukan.

Miyake, T. (1995). Suiryoo ni tuite [On conjecture]. *Kokugogaku*, No. 183, 86–75.

Morimoto, J. (1994). *Hanasite no Shyukan-o Arawasu Hukusi-ni tuite* [On Adverbs Expressing Speaker's Subjectivity]. Tokyo: Kurosio.

Nishigauchi, T. (1986). Quantification in syntax. PhD thesis, University of Massachusetts.

Nitta, Y. (1989) Gendainihongobun no Modaritii no Taikei to Kozoo [The System and Structures of Modality in Modern Japanese Sentences]. In: Nitta, Y. and Masuoka, T. (eds), *Nihongo no Modairitii* [Modality in Japanese]. Tokyo: Kurosio: 1–56.

Noda, H. (1989). Sinsei Modaitii o Motanai Bun [Sentence without True Modality]. In: Nitta, Y. and Masuoka, T. (eds), *Nihongo no Modaritii* [Modality in Japanese]. Tokyo: Kurosio: 131–57.

Oosika T. (1995). Hontaihaaku- *rasii* no setu [Theory of *rasii* as 'capturing main body']. In: *Professors Miyazi Hirosi and Miyazi Atuko Sensei Koki Kinen Ronsyuu* [Festschrift for Professors Miyazi Hirosi and Miyazi Atuko's 70th birthday]. Tokyo: Meizi Syoin: 527–48.

Palmer, F.R. (2001). *Mood and Modality*, 2nd edn. Cambridge: Cambridge University Press.

Saito, M. (2006). Sizengengo no syooko suiryoo hyoogen to tisikikanri [Information management and evidentials]. PhD thesis, Kyushu University.

Sweetser, E. (1990). *From Etymology to Pragmatics.* Cambridge: Cambridge University Press.

Takubo, Y. (1982a). On the derivation of Japanese modal construction. *Kansai Linguistic Society 3*, Proceedings of the 7th Annual Meeting of Kansai Linguistic Society, 63–72.

Takubo, Y. (1982b). Nihongo hukugoo zyutugo no koozoo to hasei no syomondai [Problems in the structures and the derivations of Japanese complex predicates]. In: *Ilpon-hakji*. 2. Ilpon-Munwha Yengkwuso [Institute of Japanese Culture]. Taygwu: Keymyung University: 15–27.

Takubo, Y. (1987). Toogo koozoo to bunmyaku zyoohoo [On the relationship between syntactic structures and discourse information]. *Nihongogaku* [Study of Japanese], 6.5. Tokyo: Meizi-Syoin: 37–48.

Takubo, Y. (1988). Goyooron [Pragmatics]. In: Hayashi, E. et al. (eds), *Gengogaku no tyooryuu* [Trends in linguistics]. Tokyo: Keisoo-Syoboo: 169–89.

Takubo, Y. (2001). Gendai nihongo-ni okeru nisyu no moodaru zyodoosirui-ni tuite [Two modal auxiliaries in Modern Japanese]. In: *Festschrift for Professor Umeda's 70th Birthday.* Seoul: Thayhaksa: 1003–25.

Takubo, Y. (2006). Nihongo zyookenbun to modaritii [Japanese conditionals and modality]. Doctoral dissertation, Kyoto University.

Takubo, Y. (2007). Two types of modal auxiliaries in Japanese: two directionalities in inference. In: McGloin, N. et al. (eds), *Japanese/Korean Linguistics 15.* Stanford: CSLI Publications: 440–51.

Takubo, Y. and S. Kinsui (1997). Discourse management in terms of mental spaces. *Journal of Pragmatics* 28 (6), 741–58.

Teramura, H. (1984). *Nihongo-no Sintakusu-to Imi 2* [Syntax and Semantics of Japanese, vol. 2]. Tokyo: Kurosio.

Wurmbrand, Susi. (1999). Modal verbs must be raising verbs. In: Bird, S. et al. (eds), *Proceedings of WCCFL 18.* Somerville: Cascadilla Press: 599–612.

7
Japanese Modals at the Syntax–Pragmatics Interface

Mika Kizu

7.1 Introduction

This chapter narrows down the scope of modality studies in Japanese and focuses on how Japanese modal predicates are syntactically represented within the framework of generative grammar. While various modal expressions in Japanese are discussed throughout the volume, how such linguistic items should be analysed in syntactic structures is not taken up as a main topic in any other chapter. In order to fill in this gap, this chapter presents some of the recently proposed syntactic analyses concerning Japanese modal predicates and discusses where in the syntax Japanese modality can be represented. In particular, we look at so-called 'person restrictions' on the subjects of modal (and modal-related) predicates in Japanese, which will lead us to discuss further theoretical implications in the spirit of the minimalist program (Chomsky 1995, 2001 and others).

The aim of this chapter is twofold: (1) to introduce syntactic structures that represent Japanese modal predicates; and (2) to explore to what extent syntax can deal with Japanese modality by looking at person restriction phenomena. As will be shown in subsequent sections, the present chapter owes much to the insights of previous studies such as Tenny (2006), Inoue (2007), Hasegawa (2007a, b) and, especially, Ueda (2007, 2008). Ueda proposes that two types of modals, epistemic and utterance modals, are syntactically manifested in different positions above TP (tense phrase), adopting the idea of left peripheral structures proposed by Rizzi (1997). Following Ueda's analysis, the phrase structure we will propose in this chapter is schematically illustrated as in (1):[1]

(1) [$_{U-ModP}$ ... U(tterance)-Mod(al) [$_{E-ModP}$ ... E(pistemic)-Mod(al) [$_{TP}$ ...]]]

The idea of having modality of utterance above epistemic modality (which is also known as modality of judgement or propositional modality) coincides with the previous analyses such as Masuoka (this volume, among others) and Nitta (1989, 1991). We will look at concrete examples of epistemic and utterance modal sentences concerned here and will argue for the structure in (1) in section 7.2.

Ueda's (2007, 2008) analysis in (1) is based mainly on the facts of person restrictions on the subjects of modal predicates, which have been investigated widely in Japanese traditional linguistics. Ueda argues that utterance modals, but not epistemic modals, are responsible for restricting person on the subjects. We will observe some basic examples of person restrictions in section 7.2, and will argue in section 7.3 that the person restriction phenomena do not fall into the common type of syntactic agreement system; although the person information might be represented in the syntax in these phenomena, the conditions on which person is required are rather semantic/pragmatic and are not directly encoded in the syntax.

The structure of the present chapter is as follows. Section 7.2 presents a descriptive overview of Japanese modals and other related facts, and argues for the phrase structure in (1). In section 7.3, focusing on person restrictions on the subjects of modal predicates, we discuss theoretical implications for the issue of the syntax–pragmatics interface from a cross-linguistic view. Section 7.4 is a summary and some final remarks for this chapter.

7.2 Structures beyond T(ense) P(hrase) in Japanese

7.2.1 Basic facts

Let us first observe basic facts relevant to the following sections. First, as we can find in other chapters, it has been agreed in the previous literature that Japanese modal predicates are mainly divided into two types: those which exhibit modality of judgement (including epistemic modality) and those which exhibit modality of utterance (see Masuoka in this volume and the references therein). Roughly speaking, the former express the speaker's 'attitude' towards the proposition (cf. Lyons 1968: 303), whereas the latter express the speaker's mode of utterance. Some of the instances for these two types are shown in (2) and (3), respectively:

(2) a. *Moosugu   yuki ga   huru   **daroo/kamosirenai/hazu-da**.*
      soon   snow NOM   fall   probably-will/may/should
      'It will probably/may/should snow soon.'

Mika Kizu 185

b. *Moosugu   yuki ga   huru   **rasii/sooda/yooda.***
   soon   snow NOM   fall   seem/hear/look-like
   'It seems to snow soon./I heard it would snow soon./It
   looks like it will snow soon.'

(3) a. *Issyoni   tabe-**ro/-yoo/-mai.***
       together eat-IMP/-INV/-NEG.INT
       'Eat together./Let's eat together./(I) won't eat together.'
    b. *Heya ga   kurai   **ne/yo.***
       room NOM   be-dark   SFP
       'It is dark in the room, isn't it?/I tell you.'

The modal predicates in (2) are instances of modality of judgement
or epistemic modality; those in (2a) express suppositional modality and
those in (2b) evidential modality.[2] As can be seen in the translations
in (2), these items indicate the speaker's judgement on the propositional contents. The modal predicates in (3), on the other hand, show
how the speaker expresses the utterance and conveys the information
rather than how she or he judges the content of the proposition. In this
chapter, following Ueda (2007, 2008), we specifically look at suppositional modals (henceforth, E-modals) such as those in (2a) and utterance
modals (henceforth, U-modals) such as those in (3a), excluding (2b) and
(3b) for the purpose of our discussion.[3]

Second, considering modals in predicate position morphologically
and/or syntactically, E-modals are further categorized into two types,
sinsei ('genuine') and *gizi* ('quasi') modals (Nitta 1991). Genuine modal
predicates do not inflect for tense or negation, and thus, they always
show the speaker's psychological attitude at the time of speech in
the sense of Nakau (1979) among others. This is, however, not the
case for quasi-modals; they can change the forms with tense and/or
negation. Examples to illustrate the distinction between genuine and
quasi-modals are shown in (4) and (5):

(4) a. *Yuki ga   huru   **daroo*-ta/*-nai.***
       snow NOM   fall   probably-will-PAST/-NEG
       'It probably snowed./It did not probably snow.'
    b. *Yuki wa   huru   **mai*-ta/*-nai.***
       snow TOP   fall   probably-will-not-PAST/-NEG
       'Probably it didn't snow./Probably it was not the case that
       it didn't snow.'

(5) a. *Yuki ga   huru   **kamosirenak-atta.***
   snow NOM   fall   may-PAST
   'It may have been the case that it would snow.'

   b. *Yuki ga   huru   **hazu-dat-ta/-zyanai/zyanak-atta.***
   snow NOM   fall   should-PAST/-NEG/-NEG-PAST
   'It was/is not/was not supposed to snow.'

Daroo ('probably will') and *mai* ('probably will not') in (4) are analysed as genuine modals because they cannot be conjugated by past tense or negation.[4] *Kamosirenai* ('may') in (5a) does not go with another negative form but can inflect for past tense. *Hazuda* ('should, be supposed to') can be both past-tensed and negated, as shown in (5b). Thus, the E-modals in (5) are categorized as quasi-modals.

Unlike E-modal predicates, which can be categorized as either genuine or quasi-modals, those expressing modality of utterance or U-modals are all considered as genuine modals. They do not involve any inflections; no forms such as **tabe-ro-ta* (eat-Imperative-Past) or *-*tabe-yoo-nai* (eat-Invitation-Neg) exist in the language. This chapter mainly concerns itself with genuine modals, leaving quasi-modals aside.

Third, as is well known, there are some kinds of Japanese sentences that restrict the subjects to a certain type of person. The following are examples involving genuine modals:

(6) a. *Watasi/*anata/kare   wa   iku   daroo.*
   I   you   he   TOP   go   will
   'I/you/he will probably go.'

   b. *Watasi/*anata/kare   wa   iku   mai.*
   I   you   he   TOP   go   will-not
   'I/you/he won't probably go.'

(7) a. **Watasi/anata/*kare   wa   tabe-ro.*
   I   you   he   TOP   eat-IMP
   'You eat (it).'

   b. *Watasi/*anata/*kare   ga   tabe-yoo.*
   I   you   he   NOM   eat-INT
   'I will eat (it).'

The sentences in (6) contain the E-modals, *-daroo* and *-mai*, and those in (7) the U-modals, *-ro* (imperative) and *-yoo* (invitation). The E-modal sentences in (6) must take either the first or third person pronouns in their subject position; otherwise, the sentences would be ungrammatical. The U-modal in (7a) allows only the second person pronoun, and the one in (7b) the first person pronoun.[5]

Previous research has discussed examples such as (6) and (7) extensively. These facts are commonly explained by saying either that internal feeling can only be detected by the speaker him/herself and not by somebody else (Nitta 1991: 86), or that in Japanese, it is not appropriate for speakers to 'intrude' on somebody else's personal domain (Masuoka 1997: 4–5). In other words, the analyses proposed in the literature endeavour to explain the person restriction phenomena in (6) and (7) either epistemologically or pragmatically. However, we will rather look at person restrictions from a syntactic perspective, and will discuss this in detail in section 7.3.

7.2.2 Structures for E-modals and U-modals

Some of the recent works have devoted considerable attention to the syntactic structure for Japanese modals. Inoue (2007) and Ueda (2007, 2008) propose two distinct positions for E- and U-modals above TP in Japanese, based on Rizzi's (1997) theory of left periphery. While details in Inoue's and Ueda's analyses differ, they equally argue that (A) there is a U-modal phrase above an E-modal phrase projected in the domain of CP (complementizer phrase) within which the syntax–pragmatics interface is manifested. They also claim that (B) each utterance must contain one phonologically realized genuine modal and each utterance can contain one (and not more than one) U-modal.

Considering (A) first, Nitta (1989) and also Masuoka in this volume (and his other works cited herein) have already proposed under the traditional Japanese linguistics approach that E-modals are semantically (and possibly, structurally) nested in U-modals. A similar proposal was made by Inoue (1976: 5–26) in the generative tradition. From a cross-linguistics point of view, Cinque (1999) discusses structural hierarchies of adverbs and functional categories and makes a similar proposal. Thus, these previous studies support the idea of representing U-modal phrases above E-modal phrases.

Here, we cannot apply a test to show the word order for genuine E- and U-modals since they cannot co-occur as stated in (B) above. However, as Ueda (2007, 2008) pointed out, based on Nitta (1991), E- and U-modals behave differently within the following embedded clauses marked by *ga* ('but'), shown in (8) and (9):

(8) a. *Moosugu   yuki ga   huru   daroo   ga,   dekakeru   tumorida.*
      soon   snow NOM   fall   probably-will   but   go-out   intend
      'It will probably snow soon, but (I) intend to go out.'

   b. *Yuki wa   huru   mai   ga,   samuku-naru   daroo.*
      snow NOM   fall   will-probably-not   but   be-cold-become   probably-will
      'It will probably not snow, but it will be cold.'

(9) a. **Sakana   o   tabe-ro   ga,   tabe-rare-nai.*
      fish   ACC   eat-IMP   but   eat-POT-NEG
      (lit.) 'Eat fish, but (one) cannot eat it.'

   b. **Paatii e ik-oo   ga,   ik-e-nai.*
      party to go-INV   but   go-POT-NEG
      (lit.) 'Let's go to the party, but (one) cannot go.'

E-modals, but not U-modals, can appear in the *ga*-clauses, as shown in (8) and (9) above. Assuming that an embedded clause has less phrase structure (that is, no more than E-ModP) than the matrix clause (containing both E-ModP and U-ModP), this fact indirectly supports the idea that U-modals are projected in a higher phrase structure. Although this is not very conclusive because one might say that *ga*-clauses simply select an E-ModP but not a U-ModP, let us assume that the structure in (1), repeated here in (10), is correct at this point and come back to this issue in section 7.3:

(10) [$_{\text{U-ModP}}$ ... U(tterance)-Mod(al) [$_{\text{E-ModP}}$ ... E(pistemic)-Mod(al) [$_{\text{TP}}$ ...]]]

The claim in (B), that is, 'only one genuine modal is phonologically realized in an utterance in Japanese', is empirically correct; as briefly mentioned above, any combination of a genuine E-modal and a genuine U-modal is not allowed in one sentence. Thus, no items such as *... daroo-ro* (will probably-IMP) and *... mai-yoo* (will probably not-INV) exist in the language. The latter part of the claim in (B), that is, that an utterance can contain only one U-modal, seems to be reasonable as well from a semantic or pragmatic viewpoint, because an utterance should not contain more than one type of speaker's attitude to convey a propositional content. Thus, there are no apparent counter-examples or arguments, and so we assume (B) as it is.

According to Ueda (2007, 2008), a genuine E-modal sentence such as (11a) should be depicted as in (11b):

(11) a. *Yuki ga   huru   daroo.*
      snow NOM   fall   probably-will
      'It will probably snow.'

b.

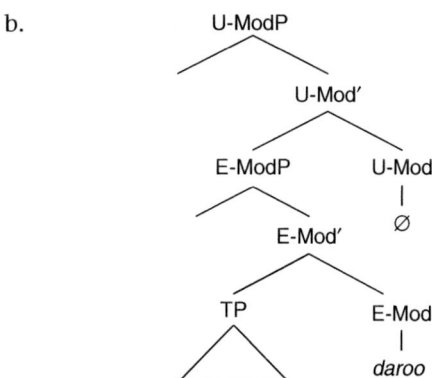

As shown in (11b), the E-modal, *daroo*, is projected within E-ModP. Although no overt U-modal is observed in the sentence in (11a), a null U-modal is assumed in the main clause by hypothesis (B).

When, on the contrary, an overt U-modal instead of an E-modal appears in sentences such as (12a), it is represented as shown in (12b), based on Ueda (2007, 2008):[6]

(12) a. *Sakana o   tabe-yoo.*
      fish ACC   eat-INV
      'Let's eat fish.'

b.

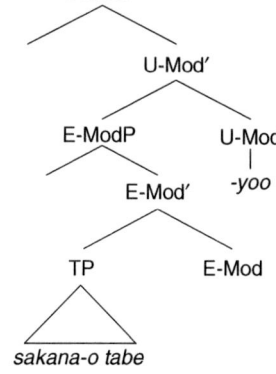

Here, unlike (11b), the U-Mod position is filled in with the overt U-modal, *yoo* in (12b).

We have seen above, as repeated below in (13a), that E-modals can appear within *ga*-clauses. Along with Ueda (2007, 2008), we can assume that the embedded clauses do not project U-ModP. The embedded clause bracketed in (13a) is illustrated in (13b):

(13) a. [*Moosugu yuki ga   huru daroo*]   *ga, dekakeru tumorida.*
     soon   snow NOM fall   probably-will but go-out   intend
     'It will probably snow soon, but (I) intend to go out.'

   b.

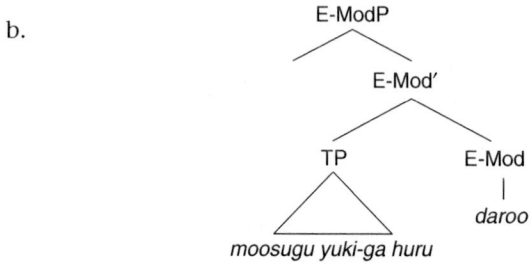

The structure in (13b) can account for why U-modals are not allowed in *ga*-clauses; only main clauses but not embedded clauses can project U-ModP, and therefore, U-modal expressions in the embedded clauses render the sentences ungrammatical.

Apparently, however, there are cases where a sentence does not contain any overt genuine modal in Japanese, as shown in (14a). Inoue (2007: 255) assumes that there exists a null genuine U-modal in such instances, and proposes the structure in (14b) for the sentence in (14a):[7]

(14) a. *Syatyoo   ga   kuru   hazu-no   yoodat-ta.*
     president   NOM   come   should   seem-PAST
     'It seemed that the president should have come.'

   b.

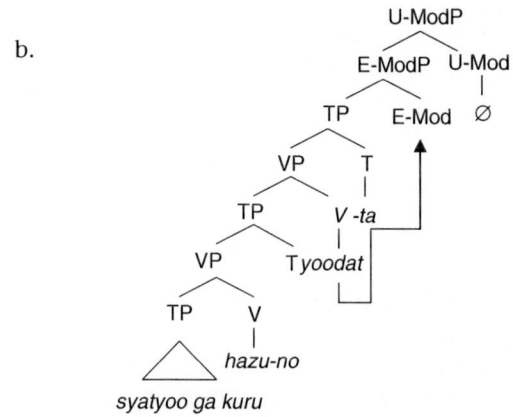

In the structure of (14b), the quasi-epistemic modals, *hazu* ('must/should') and *yoo-da* ('appears'), are first merged into the V head below TP, and then the verb closer to E-Mod, *yoo-da*, moves to the head of E-ModP via T. Although there is no overt U-modal in this sentence, it is still assumed that there exists a null E-modal in the sentence by assumption (A).

To summarize so far, we have seen that Japanese sentence structures involve two types of overt and covert modality elements in the CP structure or C system: E-modals and U-modals. The current linguistic theory enables us to pursue this line of analysis, and the Japanese language presents intriguing challenges for the theories of extended CP structure mainly developed on the basis of European languages.[8] In the next section, we will examine person restrictions on the subjects of modal predicates and discuss to what extent the syntax can deal with Japanese modality.

7.3 Person restrictions on the subjects

Bearing in mind the theory of a fine-grained C system in Japanese proposed above, this section explores what this theory can yield to explain Japanese modal and modal-related sentences. Obviously, we cannot go through every instance of syntactic phenomena concerning Japanese modality in this chapter. Rather, we focus on the issue of person restrictions on the subjects and examine how the C system, in which Japanese modal predicates are represented, can account for the facts. In the following subsections, we review Ueda's (2007, 2008) analysis on person restrictions on the subjects of genuine modals and discuss how it sheds light on the syntax–pragmatics interface.

7.3.1 Person restrictions on genuine modals

Ueda (2007, 2008) examines person restrictions on the subjects of genuine modal sentences, assuming that there are two independent phrasal categories – E-modal and U-modal phrases – within the C system in Japanese. Ueda also assumes, along with Inoue (2007), that '[o]ne utterance must contain at least one, but not more than one U-modal' (Ueda 2008: 130), as discussed in section 7.2.

Let us observe again the following examples of person restrictions on the subject of genuine modal sentences in the last section, repeated here as in (15) and (16):

(15) a. *Watasi/*anata/kare wa   iku   daroo.*
         I   you he   TOP go   probably-will
         'I/you/he will probably go.'

    b. *Watasi/*anata/kare wa iku mai.*
      I   you he TOP go will-probably-not
      'I/you/he will probably not go.'

(16) a. **Watasi/anata/*kare wa   tabe-ro.*
         I   you he   TOP eat-IMP
         'You eat (it).'
     b. *Watasi/*anata/*kare ga   tabe-yoo.*
       I   you   he   NOM eat-INT
       'I will eat (it).'

The sentences in (15) contain the suppositional E-modals, *-daroo* ('will probably') and *-mai* ('will probably not'), and those in (16) U-modals, *-ro* (imperative) and *-yoo* (invitation). The E-modal sentences in (15) require either the first or third person pronouns in their subject position, and so they have a property of [−second person]. While *-ro* in (16a) allows only the second person pronoun, *-yoo* in (16b) should take the first person pronoun. Thus, the imperative U-modal, *-ro*, has a property of [+second person] and the U-modal of intention, *-yoo*, has a [+first person] property.

One might say that both E-modals and U-modals in (15) and (16) restrict person for subjects; however, Ueda argues that it is U-modals that cause the person restrictions. This is not, of course, obvious in (15) since there is no overt U-modal involved in the sentences. However, in the previous section, we assumed that there should be a covert U-modal by hypothesis (B); each utterance must contain one and only one U-modal. In the following, we will see why U-modals are responsible for person restrictions and whether it is indeed the case that a covert or overt U-modal should exist in the main clause.

There is empirical evidence to indicate that U-modals, but not E-modals, condition person restriction phenomena. Considering the facts involving *ga*-clauses, which we reviewed in the last section, subject person restrictions are not observed in the embedded clauses, in which U-modals cannot appear. This is shown in (17):

(17) a. *Anata   wa   suru   daroo   ga,   watasi wa   s-inai.*
         you   TOP do   will   but I   TOP do-not
         'You will probably do (it), but I won't.'
     b. *Anata   wa   suru   mai   ga,   watasi wa   suru.*
         you   TOP do   won't but I   TOP do
         'You will never do (it), but I will.'

Contrary to what we have seen in (15), the second person subject is allowed in the *ga*-clauses in (17). Based on the fact that U-modals cannot occur within such *ga*-clauses, we can say that a U-modal phrase is not projected within the *ga*-clause, which is related to non-existence of person restrictions. Thus, Ueda (2007, 2008) claims that subject person restrictions are actually induced by U-modals.

If this is on the right track, then a null U-modal should be attached to the predicates in the matrix clauses even though there is no overt U-modal, as illustrated in (15)':

(15)' a. *Watasi/*anata/kare wa iku daroo-Ø.*
       I   you   he   TOP go   will-probably-UMod
       'I/you/he will probably go.'
    b. *Watasi/*anata/kare wa iku mai-Ø.*
       I   you   he   TOP go   will-probably-not-UMod
       'I/you/he will probably not go.'

In (15)', the null U-modals are responsible for the person restrictions whereas in (17), no U-modal phrases are projected within the embedded clauses.

In fact, this line of analysis has already been implied in Nitta (1991), as Ueda (2007, 2008) notes. Ueda also observes that subject person restrictions disappear within nominalized clauses headed by the formal noun *koto* ('thing'), and under the same syntactic environment, U-modals are not allowed to occur. Let us look at E- and U-modal clauses within *koto*-clauses. The examples in (18)–(21) are our own and not from Ueda; however, the same point can be made as shown below:

(18) a. ??*Watasi/anata/kare ga iku daroo koto wa*
        I   you   he   NOM go will-probably the-fact TOP
        minna   sitteiru.
        everyone know
        'Everybody knows that I/you/he will probably go.'
     b. ??*Watasi/anata/kare ga iku mai koto wa*
        I   you   he   NOM go will-not the-fact TOP
        minna   sitteiru.
        everyone know
        'Everybody knows that I/you/he will never go.'

(19) a. **Anata   ga   tabe-ro   koto   wa   minna   sitteiru.*
      you   NOM   eat-IMP   the-fact   TOP   everyone   know
      (lit.) 'Everybody knows you eat (it).'
  b. **Watasi   ga   tabe-yoo koto   wa   minna   sitteiru.*
      I   NOM   eat-INT   the-fact   TOP   everyone   know
      (lit.) 'Everybody knows I will eat (it).'

The sentences in (18) do not sound perfect, and their degree of grammaticality may depend on native speakers of Japanese. Although we find that those in (18) sound like translations from languages other than Japanese, compared to the clear ungrammaticality in the U-modal sentences in (19), arguably E-modals are marginally possible within *koto*-clauses.[9] Notice that the person restrictions observed in the matrix clauses disappear in the *koto*-clauses in (18). Person restrictions in other types of predicates, shown in (20), exhibit facts similar to those in (21):

(20) a. *Watasi/*anata/*John   wa   samui.*
      I/   you/   TOP   be-cold
      'I am cold./*You are cold./*John is cold.'
  b. *Watasi/*anata/*John   wa   kokyoo   ga   koisii.*
      I/   you/   TOP   hometown   NOM   miss
      'I am sick for my hometown./*You are sick for your hometown./
      *John is sick for his hometown.'

(21) a. *Watasi/anata/John ga   samui   koto   wa   minna   sitteiru.*
      I/   you/   NOM   be-cold   the-fact   TOP   everyone   know
      'Everybody knows that I am/you are/John is cold.'
  b. *Watasi/anata/John ga   kokyoo   ga   koisii koto   wa*
      I/   you/   NOM   hometown   NOM   miss   the-fact   TOP
      minna   sitteiru.
      everyone   know
      'Everybody knows that I am/you are/John is sick for his hometown.'

It is well known that direct experience predicates such as *samui* ('be cold') and *koisii* ('miss') impose person restrictions on the subjects. As shown in (20), they require first person in declarative sentences; however, when they occur within *koto*-clauses as in (21), such restrictions are lifted. Tenny (2006) accounts for person restrictions for direct experience predicates in Japanese and also argues that U-modal phrases (or to use her term, 'speech act phrases') are responsible for person restrictions. Since *koto*-clauses do not project U-modal phrases, no person restriction phenomena are observed. In short, subject person restrictions are not observed in the environment where U-modals are not observed; E-modals 'exhibit' the restrictions only in matrix clauses, and it is reasonable to assume a null U-modal in the matrix clause.

Ueda's (2007, 2008) analysis seems to be straightforward concerning person restrictions; U-modals, whether they are overt or covert, have properties that reflect person restrictions. The relevant person properties observed in Ueda are summarized in Table 7.1.

As Table 7.1 shows, both overt genuine E- and U-modals cannot appear with another overt E- or U-modal in the same clause. While person features vary for U-modals, those for E-modals are uniform: [–second person]. We will discuss this issue from a theoretical perspective in the next subsection.[10]

7.3.2 The nature of the phenomenon of person restrictions

In the last subsection, we provided an overview for the basic line of analysis in Ueda (2007, 2008) concerning person restrictions on the subjects of modal predicates. This subsection discusses the nature of the person restriction phenomena: whether or not these phenomena can be dealt with in syntax, and if so, to what extent syntax can explain the facts. Specifically, the question we address here is whether person restrictions are syntactic agreement of the kind usually observed in so-called inflectional languages.[11]

Looking at person restriction phenomena for direct experience predicates, Tenny (2006) argues that some stylistic or discoursal distinctions

Table 7.1 Relevant person properties observed in Ueda (2008)

E-modal form	U-modal form	Person specification
Ø	-ro, -mae (imperative)	[+second person]
Ø	-na (prohibition)	[+second person]
Ø	-masyoo (invitation)	[+first/second person]
Ø	-ro, mae (desire)	[–second person]
Ø	-yoo (intention)	[+first person]
Ø	-mai (intention)	[+first person]
-daroo (surmise)	Ø	[–second person]
-mai (negative surmise)	Ø	[–second person]
-syoo (surmise)	Ø	[–second person]
- Ø (affirmation)	Ø	[–second person]

Source: Adopted and modified from Ueda (2008: 138).

in Japanese have a syntactic basis. She clearly states that direct experience predicates bear the feature [discourse participant]; the specification of [+discourse participant] ensures that a sentence has either a first or second person pronoun in subject position, and the specification [−discourse participant] deactivates the restriction and a third person noun phrase appears instead. Tenny proposes that the feature specified as [+discourse participant] undergoes movement to the spec of the U-ModP (or speech act phrase) for checking.[12] Although Ueda (2007, 2008) uses the term 'features' for [first person] and [second person] with +/− specifications, how these features technically operate within the phrase structure proposed is not clearly stated. Let us examine here whether such features are similar to those commonly observed in the agreement phenomena in agreement-prominent languages.

It has been controversial, in previous studies, whether Japanese exhibits agreement configurations like English and other Indo-European languages, because Japanese does not have familiar types of morphologically and syntactically manifested agreement relations, for instance, between a subject and a verb in terms of person, number and/or gender.[13] However, person restrictions between a U-modal and its subject that we have seen in this chapter might be considered a type of agreement configuration. This issue is important since it is related to the question of whether person restrictions in Japanese should be explained in syntax or in another area such as pragmatics. In other words, if we find evidence that the person restrictions discussed so far are considered as syntactic agreement, it supports the idea that Japanese modality can be dealt within syntax to a larger extent than so far recognized.

In fact, the person restrictions observed in this chapter are distinct from a usual kind of syntactic agreement in the following respects. First, person restrictions are affected by different styles; they are observed only in a so-called reportive style but the restrictions disappear in a narrative style (see note 5, as well as Tenny 2006: 248, which refers to Kuroda 1973). Stylistic differences do not normally influence syntactic agreement in agreement-prominent languages.

Second, to our knowledge, a verb with an agreement feature usually requires only one type of person feature specification such as [+first person] or [+second person]. However, genuine E-modals, such as *daroo* ('will probably'), are specified as [−second person], which means that they 'agree' with either first person or third person. This is not commonly observed in syntactic agreement systems across languages; first and second person elements differ from third person elements in that first and second person elements are subject to a local binding condition, whereas third person elements are not, and therefore, only first and second person features are involved in an agreement system (Baker 2008: 123).

Third, we should note that the type of person feature specified in each modal item is not predicted solely by the modal itself. For some cases, an adverbial phrase affects person restrictions on subjects. According to Ueda (2007, 2008), an assertive *-ru* (non-past) or *-ta* (past) form accompanies a null U-modal just like other genuine E-modals. The feature for this null morpheme is specified as [−second person] as shown in Table 7.1, which means that first and third person noun phrases are allowed in subject position. However, looking at the sentences containing an assertive form of a verb and a modal adverbial such as *zehi* ('at all costs') or *dekireba* ('if possible'), it seems that the feature needs to be specified as [+first person]. This is pointed out, as shown in (22):

(22) a. *Watasi wa   zehi   /dekireba   iku.*
　　　　 I   TOP at-all-costs/if-possible go
　　　　 'I will go at all costs/if possible.'
　　 b. **Anata wa   zehi   /dekireba   iku.*
　　　　 you   TOP at-all-costs/if-possible go
　　　　 'You will go at all costs/if possible.'
　　 c. **John   wa   zehi   /dekireba   iku.*
　　　　 I   TOP at-all-costs/if-possible go
　　　　 'I will go at all costs/if possible.'

The verb *iku* ('go') in the sentences in (22) shows the intention of the subject. One possible analysis to account for the facts in (22) is that the feature of a null U-modal is not uniformly [−second person], but there is another type of null utterance modal specified as [+first person] for such sentences involving the speaker's intention. However, inventing different kinds of null elements seems to be ad hoc. Since usual syntactic agreement relations are not affected by an adverb, but they involve only major lexical categories (such as a verb, an adjective and a noun) and functional categories, the person restrictions do not seem to fall into general types of syntactic agreement.

It might be possible to think that agreement involving a U-ModP is different from usual types of agreement relations. However, at least based on current evidence, we cannot find striking similarities between person restrictions in Japanese and the common agreement phenomena. Therefore, we would like to propose here that although the syntax in Japanese has projections for modal expressions, including U-modals, their person feature specifications are dependent on something outside of syntax (i.e. semantics and pragmatics), and syntax does not seem to encode this information.

Despite the fact that person feature specifications in U-modals are not really syntactic, the phrase structures for such elements can explain other syntactic phenomena that do not appear to be related to modality. Interestingly, Ueda (2007, 2008) accounts for co-occurrence with -*wa* as a thematic topic marker. As is well known, Japanese topic marker -*wa* can be interpreted either as a thematic topic or as a contrastive topic (Kuno 1973: 38). Ueda points out that a thematic topic cannot occur with an overt U-modal. Let us consider the following contrast:

(23) a. *Asita   wa   hareru   daroo.*   [E-modal]
       tomorrow   TOP   be-fine   will
       'Speaking of tomorrow, it will be fine.'

   b. *Anata wa   hayaku si-ro.*   [U-modal]
       you   TOP quickly do-IMP
       '*Speaking of you, do (it) quickly./You, but not others, do (it) quickly.'

In (23a), the topic phrase *asita-wa* ('tomorrow-TOP') can be interpreted as a thematic topic; however, the one in (23b), *anata-wa* ('you-TOP'), does not indicate a theme but is interpreted as a contrastive topic as the translation shows. The same is true for the other U-modals discussed in Ueda (2007, 2008).

The reason Ueda offers to explain the facts in (23) is based on the assumption that a U-modal phrase lies within the CP domain, in which topicalization is involved, whereas an E-modal phrase resides within the TP domain. In fact, Rizzi (1997: 283) states:

> We can think of the complementizer system as the interface between a propositional content (expressed by the IP) and the superordinate structure (a higher clause or, possibly, the articulation of discourse, if we consider a root clause). As such, we expect the C system to express at least two kinds of information, one facing the outside and the other facing the inside.

Following this, we can consider that E-ModP is facing inside (i.e. the propositional content or TP) and U-ModP is facing outside (i.e. pragmatics).

The co-occurrence restrictions between a thematic topic -*wa* and a U-modal is linked to how Japanese satisfies the EPP (extended projection principle) feature (which ensures that each clause must have 'a subject'). Alexiadou and Anagnostopoulou (1998) propose that in null subject languages such as Greek and Catalan, it is parametrized as to whether the EPP-feature in T(ense) can be satisfied with a head X^0. Ueda claims that the EPP feature is satisfied in C rather than in T in Japanese, and a thematic topic appears in the spec of U-ModP. So when a U-modal phonologically appears in the head of U-ModP, the EPP is already satisfied, hence a thematic topic cannot co-occur. When a thematic topic appears in the spec of U-ModP, the head of UModP should be null, since the EPP is satisfied by the topic. Since an E-modal is not within the CP domain but in the TP domain in Ueda's account, a thematic topic can appear with an overt E-modal; the E-ModP is not relevant to the EPP feature in Japanese.

In previous research, it has been controversial whether or not Japanese has the EPP feature, because the EPP phenomenon has been tightly linked to nominative case checking at least until the early minimalist approach (Chomsky 1995). Languages such as Japanese do not exhibit obvious connection between the nominative case marking and the spec of TP filled in by a subject. But within the more recent minimalist account (Chomsky 2001), the feature that needs to be checked and the feature that triggers movement can be considered as separate entities. Travis (2008: 28–31) supports this idea by examining cross-linguistically intriguing empirical evidence from an Icelandic quirky case and Tagalog case agreement phenomena. For instance, regarding Tagalog case agreement phenomena, Travis states '... the EPP feature and the case-related feature are split across two different heads – Voice and T, respectively' (2008: 29). If this is one of the possibilities, it is not surprising to see that the EPP feature resides somewhere in the C system in Japanese; languages may vary depending on where the EPP feature is checked. This view conforms to Ueda's claim that Japanese is a language that satisfies the EPP in the U-modal projection rather than the TP domain like English.

To conclude, we have found that although person specifications on utterance modals and selections of person in subject position may not fall into usual syntactic phenomena, the fine-grained phrase structures within the C system explain the existence or non-existence of the person restrictions and provide opportunities to examine language variations in an interesting way.

7.4 Summary and final remarks

This chapter has presented the extended CP structures to represent Japanese modal predicates, as proposed by Inoue (2007) and Ueda (2007, 2008). There are two distinct phrases: E-ModP and U-ModP, in the C system in Japanese. Considering the person phenomena discussed in Ueda (2007, 2008), we have shown that while the person information might be represented in the syntax, the conditions on which person should appear on the subject are pragmatic. Since the person restrictions are imposed on the head of U-ModP, the U-ModP is considered to be within the domain at the syntax–pragmatics interface.

The linguistic facts discussed in this chapter have mostly been pointed out by traditional Japanese linguistics, which has devoted itself to describe a number of facts concerning Japanese modality and to determine what should or should not be inside the scope of modality in the language. Compared with such traditional approaches, how Japanese modals are syntactically represented has not been so widely explored within the generative syntax until recently. However, as shown in this chapter, Japanese presents interesting facts to pursue the theories of fine-grained CP structure. Hasegawa (2007a), in fact, points out that in Japanese, even an overall picture of very basic syntactic issues, such as 'case' and subject position, would be observed more appropriately if one does not limit the scope of one's investigation to the propositional content alone, but expands it to the entire utterance, including the modality domain. This is not always the case in many European languages, in which a proposition contains most of the intrinsic syntactic phenomena of the languages and more or less suffices for investigating the nature of languages (Hasegawa 2007a: 4). Prior to the minimalist program (Chomsky 1995), it was considered that LF (Logical Form), where logical meaning of a sentence is represented, is the final point in the system; however, the minimalist approach provides an opportunity to take more than logical meaning into consideration: 'Force' in Chomsky's (1995) terms, which is linked to some utterance meaning or pragmatic function. Analyses such as Tenny (2006), Inoue (2007), Ueda (2007, 2008) and Hasegawa (2007b), clearly reaped the benefits of traditional Japanese linguistics in their accounts, based on recently advanced syntactic theory. Possible relations between modality and other syntactic phenomena, including anaphor binding (Tenny 2006) and null arguments (Hasegawa 2007b), have also been pointed out. In future research, investigations of the syntactic structure in the expanded CP domain might provide insight into constructions in Japanese that have not yet been fully accounted for, especially those sensitive to properties of context or discourse.

Acknowledgements

I would like to thank Peter Sells and Barbara Pizziconi for their valuable suggestions and constructive comments. All remaining errors are my own.

Notes

1. In this chapter, we use conventional notations of phrase structures for our expository purpose here under the theory of the pre-minimalist program. This does not necessarily mean to emphasize the X′-theory, however.
2. The idea that epistemic modal expressions in Japanese are divided into two types, suppositional and evidential, is adopted from Johnson (2003). However, we do not take deontic/root modals discussed in Johnson into consideration in this chapter. See also Chapter 6 (Takubo), section 6.2, in this volume.
3. Sentence-final particles in Japanese have been used as typical examples of modality of utterance; however, they behave differently from the other types of utterance modals. As we will observe in subsection 7.2.2, while usual types of utterance modals cannot occur with another utterance modal in the same sentence, sentence-final particles can appear with an utterance modal, such as *tabe-ro-yo* ('Eat (it), I'm telling you') or *tabe-yoo-ne* ('Let's eat together, shall we?'). Inoue (2007), for instance, assumes that sentence-final particles occupy under C ([+Force]), which is projected above a U-modal phrase.
4. According to Ueda (2007, 2008), whose observation is based on Nitta (1991), other such instances are -*syoo* (supposition) and Ø (assertion with no overt modal marker).
5. There are other types of predicates that restrict persons to the subjects. For example, direct experience predicates such as *uresii* ('to be happy') or *itai* ('to feel pain') require first person in their subject position in declarative sentences. The person restrictions for these types of predicates are discussed in Tenny (2006) within the framework of the syntax of the left (or right) periphery, or what she calls 'syntax of sentience'. This will be briefly discussed in section 7.3. The same kind of restriction is also found for desideratives such as *tabe-tai* ('eat-want') and *hanasi-tai* ('speak-want').

   Note that these predicates can lift such person restrictions when they are past-tense forms. Here, we should bring our attention to different styles in Japanese: the 'narrative' and 'reportive' styles, and how they interact with modality in Japanese. Kinsui (1989) notes distinct linguistic behaviours between the two styles and argues that when a sentence with past tense raises a person restriction on the subject of a modal-related sentence, it is not because of the past-tense form but because the sentence is interpreted as one in a narrative style. The narrative style is something we can see, for instance, in body texts in novels to describe situations or background with no apparent premise of specific discourse participants. The reportive style is, on the contrary, one that involves specific discourse participants, the speaker and the hearer. We should note that it is essential to consider in which style sentences are uttered when analysing person restrictions in Japanese.

6. Concerning the structure in (12b), whether or not a null E-Mod element exists and E-ModP is projected in such sentences is not entirely clear. Actually, Inoue (2007) does not assume E-modal projections for sentences such as (12b), and Ueda (2007) also considers this possibility.

7. The structure in (14b) is a slightly modified version of the one proposed in Inoue (2007: 225). This is simply due to consistency for our discussion in this chapter. She assumes that the top of the structure is C [+force], which can be occupied by a sentence-final particle. This implies that sentence-final particles in Japanese should not be considered as utterance modals, along with our analysis in note 3.

   Inoue (2007) also argues that genuine modals (including E- and U-modals) are similar to inflectional affixes, whereas quasi-modals behave like verbs. It may sound contradictory that genuine modals do not inflect but are regarded as inflectional affixes. However, genuine modals do not induce further inflection and do not double the same type of modal within the same clause, and these properties are reminiscent of those for inflectional affixes. In contrast, quasi-modals can inflect and appear recursively in the same clause, which is similar to what we observe for verbs.

8. For example in English, it can be said that previous syntactic research concerning English modality has centred on examining modal auxiliaries, such as *must, may, can*, etc. Since Ross (1969), one of the central issues concerning English modal auxiliaries has been the interpretations of epistemic and root/deontic modals (see examples in Palmer 2001) and their syntactic and/or semantic representations. See Butler (2003) and the references cited therein as an overview of previous literature and more recent analyses on this issue.

9. The reason why the E-modals are not perfect within *koto*-clauses is that *koto* normally selects a proposition expressed in TP rather than E-ModP. It is possible to think that 'translatese' E-modals could be analysed as verbs and merged within VP, and thus, such items may occur within *koto*-clauses.

10. Ueda (2007) observes person restrictions of other types such as *-te kureru* ('someone does something for me'), *-te oku* ('someone does something for preparation'), and *-te miru* ('try to do ...'). In relation to this topic, Hasegawa (2007b) also proposes an interesting analysis on how modal elements are involved in licensing null arguments in Japanese. Owing to lack of space, we will not discuss these in this chapter.

11. The term 'agreement' is used descriptively in this chapter and does not presuppose any specific configurations in terms of locality and mechanisms. Thus, it simply indicates the relation between the element that provides the feature and the target whose agreement is spelled out.

12. See Tenny (2006) for details. Further critical review for her theory (based on Speas and Tenny 2003) is presented by Gärtner and Steinbach (2006).

13. One of the exceptions could be 'honorification' in Japanese, for which various works have explored a possibility to propose the familiar type of agreement even in the Japanese language. Among the recently proposed

analyses, Boeckx and Niimura (2004) propose that Japanese honorification is an instance of agreement that obeys syntactic principles. This analysis is, however, shown to be untenable by Bobaljik and Yatsushiro (2006).

References

Alexiadou, Artemmis and Elena Anagnostopoulou (1998). Parameterizing AGR: word order, V-movement, and EPP-checking. *Natural Language and Linguistic Theory* 16, 491–539.

Baker, C. Mark (2008). *The Syntax of Agreement and Concord.* Cambridge: Cambridge University Press.

Bobaljik, Jonathan David and Kazuko Yatsushiro (2006). Problems with honorification-as-agreement in Japanese: a reply to Boeckx & Niimura. *Natural Language and Linguistic Theory* 24, 355–84.

Boeckx, Cedric and Fumikazu Niimura (2004). Conditions on agreement in Japanese. *Natural Language and Linguistic Theory* 22, 453–80.

Butler, Jonny (2003). A minimalist treatment of modality. *Lingua* 113, 967–96.

Chomsky, Noam (1995). *The Minimalist Program.* Cambridge, Mass.: MIT Press.

Chomsky, Noam (2001). Derivation by phase. In: Kenstowicz, Michael (ed.), *Ken Hale: a Life in Language.* Cambridge, Mass.: MIT Press: 1–52.

Cinque, Guglielmo (1999). *Adverbs and Functional Heads: a Cross-Linguistic Perspective.* New York: Oxford University Press.

Gärtner, Hans-Martin and Markus Steinbach (2006). A skeptical note on the syntax of speech acts and point of view. In: Brandt, Patrick and Fuß, Eric (eds), *Form, Structure, and Grammar: a Festschrift Presented to Günther Grewendorf on Occasion of his 60th Birthday.* Studia Grammatica 63. Berlin: Akademie Verlag.

Hasegawa, Nobuko (2007a). Jo: Nihongo no shubun-genshoo kara mita toogoron [Preface: Syntax from a perspective of main clause phenomena in Japanese]. In: Hasegawa, N. (ed.), *Nihongo no shubun-genshoo: toogo-koozoo to modariti* [Linguistic phenomena in Japanese main clauses: their syntactic structures and modality]. Tokyo: Hitsuji Shoboo: 1–21.

Hasegawa, Nobuko (2007b). Ichininshoo no shooryaku: modariti to *kureru* [Ellipsis of first person pronouns: modality and *kureru* (a donatory verb)]. In: Hasegawa, N. (ed.), *Nihongo no shubun-genshoo: toogo-koozoo to modariti* [Linguistic phenomena in Japanese main clauses: their syntactic structures and modality]. Tokyo: Hitsuji Shoboo: 331–69.

Inoue, Kazuko (1976). *Henkei-bunpoo to Nihongo: Joo* [Transformal Grammar and Japanese: Volume 1]. Tokyo: Taishukan.

Inoue, Kazuko (2007). Nihongo no moodaru no tokuchoo saikoo [Revisiting the properties of Japanese modals]. In: Hasegawa, N. (ed.), *Nihongo no shubun-genshoo: toogo-koozoo to modariti* [Linguistic phenomena in Japanese main clauses: their syntactic structures and modality]. Tokyo: Hitsuji Shoboo: 227–60.

Johnson, Yuki (2003). *Modality and the Japanese Language.* Ann Arbor, Mich.: Center for Japanese Studies, University of Michigan.

Kinsui, Satoshi (1989). Hookoku ni tsuite no oboegaki [A note on the reportive style]. In: Nitta, Y. and Masuoka, T. (eds), *Nihongo no Modariti* [Japanese Modality]. Tokyo: Kuroshio: 121–9.

Kuno, Susumu (1973). *The Structure of the Japanese Language*. Cambridge: Mass.: MIT Press.

Kuroda, Shige-Yuki (1973). Where epistemology, style, and grammar meet: a case study from Japanese. In: Anderson, S. and Kiparsky, P. (eds), *A Festschrift for Morris Halle*. New York: Holt, Rinehart and Winston: 377–91.

Lyons, John (1968). *Introduction to Theoretical Linguistics*. Cambridge: Cambridge University Press.

Masuoka, Takashi (1997). Hyoogen no shukansei [Subjectivity of expressions]. In: Takubo, Y. (ed.), *Shiten to Gengokoodoo* [View Points and Linguistic Behaviours]. Tokyo: Kuroshio: 1–11.

Nakau, Minoru (1979). Modariti to meidai [Modality and proposition]. In: Hayashi Eiichi Kyooju Kanreki Kinen Ronbunshuu Kankoo Iinkai (ed.), *Eigo to Nihongo to* [English and Japanese]. Tokyo: Kuroshio: 223–50.

Nitta, Yoshio (1989). Gendai nihongo-bun no modariti no taikei to koozoo. [The system and structure of modality in modern Japanese sentences]. In: Nitta, Y. and Masuoka, T. (eds), *Nihongo no Modariti* [Japanese Modality]. Tokyo: Kuroshio: 1–56.

Nitta, Yoshio (1991). *Nihongo no Modariti to Ninshoo* [Japanese modality and the persons]. Tokyo: Hitsuji shoboo.

Palmer, Frank Robert (2001). *Mood and Modality*, 2nd edn. Cambridge: Cambridge University Press.

Rizzi, Luigi (1997). The fine structure of the left periphery. In: Haegeman, L. (ed.), *Elements of Grammar: Handbook of Generative Syntax*. Dordrecht: Kluwer: 281–337.

Ross, John Robert (1969). Auxiliaries as main verbs. In: Todd, W. (ed.), *Studies in Philosophical Linguistics Series I*. Evanston: Great Expectations Press: 77–102.

Speas, Peggy and Carol Tenny (2003). Configurational properties of point of view roles. In: Di Scullo, A.M. (ed.), *Asymmetry in Grammar*, vol. 1 *Syntax and Semantics*. Amsterdam: John Benjamins: 315–44.

Tenny, Carol (2006). Evidentiality, experiencers, and the syntax of sentience in Japanese. *Journal of East Asian Linguistics* 15, 245–88.

Travis, Lisa deMena (2008). The role of features in syntactic theory and language variation. In: Liceras, Juana M., Zobl, Helmut and Goodluck, Helen (eds), *The Role of Formal Features in Second Language Acquisition*. New York: Lawrence Erlbaum Associates, Taylor & Francis Group: 23–47.

Ueda, Yukiko (2007). Nihongo no modariti no toogo-koozoo to ninshoo-seigen [Syntactic structures for Japanese modality and person restrictions]. In: Hasegawa, N. (ed.), *Nihongo no shubun-genshoo: toogo-koozoo to modariti* [Linguistic phenomena in Japanese main clauses: their syntactic structures and modality]. Tokyo: Hitsuji shoboo: 261–94.

Ueda, Yukiko (2008). Person restriction and syntactic structure of Japanese modals. *Scientific Approaches to Language* No. 7. Center for Language Sciences, Kanda University of International Studies: 123–50.

Part III
Japanese Modality in Discourse

8
On the Modality of Noun Phrases as Minor Sentences in Japanese

Teruko Shin'ya

8.1 Introduction

This chapter concerns itself with the modality of noun phrases, or sentences without a predicate that are nevertheless self-sufficient functional units. These will be labelled 'minor sentences', in contrast with full/complete sentences including a predicate. Japanese minor sentences include holophrase/one-word sentences like *Ara!* ('Oh!'), elliptical sentences like *Sore-wa chotto...* ('That's a little bit...') and sentences ending with a noun like *Ii tenki!* ('Nice weather!'). None of these has a subject, predicate, copula or sentence-final particles. Among these minor sentences, I will concentrate in particular on those ending with nouns, which I will call 'noun phrase sentences' (NP sentences) hereafter.

A number of linguists have discussed the concept of modality from different perspectives, but their interest has focused on unmarked full sentences, especially on predicates. Considering that verb inflection or auxiliaries are the most grammaticalized markers of modality, it is only natural that linguists should have focused their interest on unmarked full sentences. Minor sentences have not been targeted in research on modality owing to the lack of a predicate. However, if modality is defined as the expression of the speaker's attitude at the point of speech (for example: Nakau 1979, 1994, Nitta 1991, Masuoka 1991), sentence formation, whether a full sentence or a minor one, can be said to realize modality, for the speaker's choice between an unmarked and a marked form is nothing but the expression of the speaker's attitude.

Maynard (1993) proposes to study modality from the viewpoint of 'discourse' and defines this particular angle of linguistic enquiry as follows: 'Discourse modality conveys the subjective emotional, mental or psychological attitude of the speaker toward message content, to the speech act itself or toward his or her communication partner' (Maynard, 1993: 6). In this chapter, I adopt Maynard's framework of discourse modality, and consider the discoursal function of NP sentences. Maynard refers to devices to realize discourse modality as 'D(iscourse) M(odality) indicators'. These are 'non-referential linguistic signs whose primary functions are to directly express personal attitude and feelings' (Maynard, 1993: 47). They include paralinguistic devices (e.g. intonation or tonal effects), syntactic devices (e.g. active or passive constructions or word order), independent devices (e.g. exclamatory interjections or interjectional particles), complex devices (e.g. auxiliary verbs and auxiliary adjectives) and multi-phrase devices (*da* and *desu/masu* alternation, quotative: *to yuu*). I would submit that as an elliptic construction, NP sentences too can be said to belong to syntactic DM indicators. This is because I postulate that the marked nature of NP sentences conveys an additional expressive meaning, which can be accounted for in terms of the speaker's subjective attitude and feelings towards an event.

In general, as NP sentences are only fragments of a complete propositional construction, their propositional meaning is highly context-dependent. However, even NP sentences can be full-fledged functional units. In this chapter, the modality of NP sentences will be observed from two points of view: a typology of NP sentences and their modal nature, and the expressive effects achieved by their use. The structure of the chapter is as follows. In section 8.2, I will discuss the essential expressivity of NP sentences. In section 8.3, I will classify the NP sentences that can be understood to be equivalent to full sentences in their meanings, and describe modal features of each pattern. In section 8.4, I will show cases of single noun NP sentences, while in section 8.5, I will explore the background of various patterns of NP sentences with fixed meanings. Lastly, in the final section, I will offer concluding remarks.

In this study I used two sources for the data. Both are written texts, planned by the authors to achieve certain expressive effects. The two sources are: *Asahi Sinbun* (Asahi Newspaper) 1998.4–2007.1 and *Kantoo Zuihitu* (The Leading Essay in *Bungeishunju*, a literary magazine) 1999.4–2003.8. The codes (asahi) and (zuihitu) will be used as the abbreviation of each source. Example sentences to be analysed are underlined by the author.

8.2 Essential expressivity of NP sentences

The choice of unmarked or marked sentence patterns is part of speakers' expressive repertoires and can convey the speaker's own personal attitude and feelings toward an event. In what sense can we say that an NP sentence expresses a modal meaning? To begin, compare (1) with (1').

(1) *Irete*   *mo*   *kure-nai*   *nante, hidoi.*   *Sekkaku*   *Tookyoo kara*
let me in-GER ADD BEN-NEG TOP terrible with considerable trouble Tokyo ABL
kita   *noni.*   *Zekkyoosuru*   *otto.* (zuihitu)
come-PAST ADV shout   husband
'It's terrible that he doesn't even let us in in spite of the fact that we came all the way from Tokyo. <u>My husband who shouts (My shouting husband)</u>.'

(1') *Otto*   *ga*   *zekkyoosita.*
husband NOM shout-PAST
<u>'My husband shouted.'</u>

(1') is a declarative sentence with a predicate, while (1) is an NP sentence. The syntactic structure of (1) ending with a noun is a marked pattern of description compared to the unmarked pattern of (1'). Although (1) and (1') can be said to have the same referential meaning, they differ with regard to expressivity. In (1') the event is depicted objectively with a past tense, whereas the formal manipulation of (1) conveys emotional expressivity without tense. In (1), the NP sentence is used in order to express the speaker's mental state of not being able to stay calm. Below are some other examples:

(2) *Sonna*   *kisekiteki*   *CD* *no*   *hitotu ga,*   *kono nigatu*   *ni*   *bikutaa kara*
like that miraculous CD GEN one NOM this February TEM Victor ABL
ririisu *sareta. [...] Intorodakusyon ni* *tadayou tadanaranu* *nekki.*   <u>*Kirameku oto.*</u>
release-PASS-PAST Introduction DAT float extraordinary enthusiasm dazzle sound
(zuihitu)
'One of those miraculous CDs was released by Victor last February. <u>Extraordinary enthusiasm that we can sense in the introduction. Sound that dazzles (Dazzling sound)</u>.'

(2') *Tadanaranu*   *nekki*   *ga*   *intorodakusyon ni* *tadayotte-iru. Oto*   *ga*   *kirameite-iru.*
extraordinary enthusiasm NOM introduction DAT float-PROG Sound NOM dazzle-PROG
'The air of extraordinary enthusiasm is floating from the introduction. <u>The sound is dazzling</u>.'

(3) *Daremo*   *ga*   *yuu yooni Setogawa-san wa*   *hakusiki-datta.*   <u>*Misuterii no*</u>
everyone NOM say MAN Setogawa-Mr TOP knowledgeable-COP-PAST mystery GEN
koto, *eiga*   *no*   *koto, huruhon*   *no*   *koto.* (zuihitu)
thing movie GEN thing used book GEN thing
'As many people pointed out, Mr Setogawa was knowledgeable. <u>About the mystery, about the movies, and about used books</u>.'

(3′) *Daremo   ga   yuu yooni Setogawa-san wa   misuterii no   koto   ya   eiga   no*
    everyone NOM say MAN Setogawa-Mr TOP mystery GEN thing ADD movie GEN
    koto   ya   huruhon   no   koto   ni   hakusiki-datta.
    thing ADD used book GEN thing DAT knowledgeable-COP-PAST
    'As many people pointed out, Mr Setogawa was knowledgeable about the mystery,
    movies, used books, and so on.'

In (2) the objects of sensation (the sounds) in the climax of the text are emotionally focused, whereas the corresponding sentences in (2′) describe objectively how the sounds are in the situation. In (3) the three noun phrases separated from the preceding sentence have a stronger psychological impact on the referents than those in (3′), where the nouns are merged into the preceding sentence. Thus the basic expressivity of NP sentences comes from the concentration of propositional meaning on the final noun phrases. All these examples indicate that NP sentences are markers of 'information status' of 'information qualification' (Maynard 1993: 52), which is a device to foreground a specific piece of information.

It has generally been accepted that NP sentences convey some kind of 'exclamatory expressivity' (Maynard 2000, Kawabata 2004). They foreground the speaker's feelings, emotions or yearnings and connote them with a sense of surprise, admiration or exclamation. Adachi (2002: 201) states that: 'The feature of exclamatory sentences is to end with a noun, or to be nominalized by the formal nouns *"no"* or *"koto"*. The fundamental nature of an exclamation is the expression of a feeling of surprise triggered by the quality (of some event or object), by *means of a focus on the relevant noun*' (translation by the author). The adnominal clauses in the marked sentences of (1) and (2) modify the sentence-final nouns non-restrictively; consequently, their referential meaning does not change even though the word order is switched, compared to the corresponding (1′) where the sentence is formed with the head noun of (1) as a subject and the relative clause as a predicate. This means that the adnominal clause is a logical predicate for the head noun. The word order of NP sentences, i.e. logical predicate followed by logical subject, has the effect of foregrounding the head noun. (Similar views are in Tsubomoto 1998, Masuoka 1995, Kawabata 2004, Yumoto 2004.) In addition, the phenomenon that tense and aspect are abstracted from the relative clauses of (1) and (2) also reflects the speaker's subjectivity, since it indicates that the speaker's intent is not to describe the process of event accurately or objectively, but to provide a subjective qualification of the referent. In sum, the essential expressivity of NP sentences derives from the abstraction of the predicate.

8.3 Subordinate syntactic structures and expressive functions of NP sentences

Many NP sentences are perfectly self-sufficient communicative units. However, we need to clarify how they achieve this self-sufficiency and what qualities these sentences have. This section will provide a classification of NP sentences based on their structural features and a discussion of how they compare with the arguably corresponding full sentences. In addition, I will also provide a characterization of the expressive effect resulting from the choice of an NP sentence over a full sentence.

Before focusing on the main subject, it might be beneficial to review NP sentences in general. Although there are many NP sentences whose meaning is close to full sentences, NP sentences are in general semantically incomplete by themselves, and derive complete propositional meaning specification from the verbal or non-verbal context. Note the examples below. These work as 'openings', in which a certain topic is qualified and introduced, but which is not fully explicated.

(4) <u>Sonna yakekusotekina saisinkan</u>   *ga*   *syuppansareta*   *aruhi* *no* *koto.* (zuihitu)
such desperate   current version NOM publish-PASS-PAST one day GEN matter
'(This is the story of that) one day when such a desperate new book was published.'

(5) *Napori no* *wakamono mo*   *oozei, benkyoo ni*   *kite-ita.*
Naples GEN youth   ADD   many study   DAT come-STAT-PAST

<u>*Yookide hitonatukoi*</u>   <u>*karera no*   *koto.*</u>
cheerful friendly   them GEN matter
Suguni sitasiku natte   *ie*   *ni*
soon   close   become-GER house DIR

yobareru   *koto*   *mo*   *atta.* (zuihitu)
invite-PASS matter ADD happen-PAST
'Many young men from Naples were also there to study. (Because of) those cheerful and friendly people. We became close soon, and I was invited to their houses at times.'

(4) is an expression patterned with 'time + *no* + *koto*', indicating that a certain incident has taken place at that time, but apart from the qualification of the event provided by the relative clause, we depend on the following context for a fleshed-out explanation of the events of that day to find out what has taken place. (5) is also an expression style patterned with 'characteristic expression + a personal noun + *no* + *koto*'. Again, apart from the qualification of the referents provided by the relative clause, we need further context to learn what

happened to the two referents. Therefore, both (4) and (5) are essentially mere components that form a part of an ideal proposition, depending on additional context for a fully fleshed-out propositional meaning.

However, there are also many NP sentences whose propositional meanings can be inferred independently from any additional context. (1) and (2) above are such examples. They are as substantial as full sentences. As shown there, some NP sentences are semantically independent, although they are minor sentences and can be classified into several types according to syntactic and semantic structure. 'Semantically independent' here refers to their having a meaning and function equivalent to a full sentence even without recourse to additional context.

There are various patterns of NP sentences, from those with a simple structure, composed with a single noun, to those with a complex one, including multiple phrases. Although some of them are substantially the same as full sentences, the semantic independence of NP sentences does not mean that they have the same expressive quality of the corresponding full sentences, as can be seen in the following examples:

(6) *Daga soko   wa tatiiri-kinsi-kuiki to no koto.* *Zannennagara naka e   wa*
but   that place TOP off limits area   QUOT matter regretfully   inside DIR TOP

haire-nakatta. (asahi)
enter-POT-NEG-PAST
'But (I was told) that the area was off limits. So, unfortunately I couldn't enter.'

(6′) ?*Daga soko   wa tatiiri-kinsi-kuiki to no   koto da.* *Zannennagara naka e   wa*
but   that place TOP off limits area   QUOT matter COP regretfully   inside DIR TOP

haire-nakatta.
enter-POT-NEG-PAST
'But it is that the area is off limits. So, unfortunately I couldn't enter.'

(6″) *Daga soko   wa tatiiri-kinsi-kuiki to no koto da.* *Zannennagara naka e   wa*
but   that place TOP off limits area   QUOT matter COP regretfully   inside DIR TOP

hair-e-nai   .
enter-POT-NEG
'But it is that the area is off limits. So, unfortunately I can't enter.'

The first sentence in (6) is an NP sentence, while those in (6′) and (6″) are unmarked complete sentences. Although the forms of (6), (6′) and (6″) are almost the same except for copula *da* and the tense of the second sentence, they cannot be said to be equivalent. The connections between the two sentences in (6) and those in (6″) are very smooth, but (6′) sounds rather unnatural because of the tense mismatch between the first and second sentence.[1] Unlike unmarked sentences, NP sentences are free from some tense constraints due to the lack of the predicate, which allows a smooth transition to the following, tensed, sentence.

Masuoka (1991) presented the 'modality of expressive type' (*hyoogen-ruikei no modariti*) as a category of Japanese modality, which characterizes sentences by expressive or communicative functions.[2] Within it, five subcategories were identified: 'declarative type' (*enjyutu-gata*), which offers the speaker's knowledge, 'emotive type' (*jyooihyoosyutu-gata*), which expresses the speaker's feeling, emotion or volition, 'appealing type' (*uttae-gata*), which requires the listener's action, 'interrogative type' (*gimon-gata*), which requires information from the listener or shows the speaker's uncertainty, and 'exclamatory type' (*kantan-gata*), which expresses the speaker's impression or surprise at things. Although Masuoka's classification of the 'modality of expressive type' refers to full sentences, we can observe most of these subcategories in semantically independent NP sentences as well, that is, 'emotive type', 'declarative type', 'appealing type' and 'exclamatory type'. There is no 'interrogative type' among semantically independent NP sentences, because the exclamatory expressivity that stands on the speaker's firm recognition of the situation is incompatible with the feelings such as uncertainty or doubt. All NP sentences of 'interrogative type' are not semantically independent.

Since in the case of NP sentences the lack of predicates makes the difference between 'emotive type' and 'exclamatory type' unclear, I will classify them into three types, that is, 'emotive type', 'declarative type' and 'appealing type', although, as stated in section 8.2, all NP sentences have exclamatory expressivity in common as an essential attribute. In the following section I will explore how semantically independent NP sentences are subclassified according to syntactic and semantic structure, what kind of expressivity they convey and which modality markers they contain.

8.3.1 NP sentences of emotive type

NP sentences of emotive type are the sentences that routinely express emotive nuance like admiration, impression, surprise, anger or intention. What kind of patterns do they have?

8.3.1.1 Co-occurrence of modal adverbs

Some NP sentences include modality markers in the form of modal adverbs, such as *nanto*, *nante*, *nantomo* or an adjective *nantoyuu* used to express the speaker's strong feeling such as surprise, admiration, sorrow, excitement and anger towards something.

(7) *Tomo ga   'Hontooni hukkurasita   wa   ne.   Siawase-butori*
     friend NOM really   put on weight-PAST PART PART happy-plumpness

   ne' to   itta.   Nanto yawarakai gokan. (asahi)
   PART QUOT say-PAST how soft   nuance
   'My friend said, "You really have put on weight. It's a sign that you are happy, isn't it?" How comfortable to hear the sound of the word!'

(8) *Nantomo sigekitekina midasi.* (asahi)
     How   sensational headline
     'What a sensational headline!'

(7) and (8) are NP sentences whose pattern is 'modal adverb + adjectival phrase + noun'. *Nanto* in (7) and *nantomo* in (8) provide sufficient expressivity to sentences to make them semantically independent.

The adverb *yoku* which means 'often' or 'a lot' also has a similar function when used in a structure such as '*yoku* + verbal phrase + noun'. Compare (9) with (9′) and (10) with (10′) respectively:

(9) *Yoku saboru   yatu!*
     often cut a class fellow
     'How often the guy cuts classes!'

(9′) ? *Hinpanni saboru   yatu!*
        frequently cut a class fellow
        ?' How frequently the guy cuts classes!'

(10) *Yoku taberu ko!*
      a lot eat   child
      'You eat a lot indeed, kid!'

(10′) ? *Ippai taberu ko!*
         fully eat   child
         ? 'You eat fully indeed, kid!'

(9) and (10) are exclamatory sentences that express the speaker's surprise or amazement. However, since NP sentences including other adverbs, even semantically close equivalents of the adverb *yoku* – such as *hinpanni* in (9′) and *ippai* in (10′) – sound rather unnatural as independent exclamatory sentences, we could say that *yoku* has a modal value which

is consistent with or even adds to that of the NP sentence and can be thought of as a DM indicator.

When *yoku* or *yokumo* are used in a structure such as '*yoku/yokumo* + verb + *koto*', the resulting NP sentences express surprise or amazement that something has been realized, as can be seen in the paraphrase in (11'):

(11) *Sonna ranboona atukaikata o   site   yoku koware-nakatta   koto!*
such rough   treatment ACC do-GER how break-NEG-PAST matter
'(I'm amazed) that it didn't break in spite of your rough treatment!'

(12) *Yokumo sonna zuuzuusii koto ga   ieta   koto!*
how   such impudent thing NOM say-POT-PAST matter
' How dare you say such impudent words to me?'

(11') *Sonna ranboona atukaikata o   site   koware-nakatta   koto   ni   odoroku!*
such rough   treatment ACC do-GER break-NEG-PAST matter DAT be amazed
'I'm amazed that it didn't break in spite of your rough treatment!'

This section focused on NP sentences with modal adverbs used as modality markers. Masuoka (1991) discusses the hierarchical or 'nesting' semantic structure of Japanese sentences, and in this structure correlation between a modal adverb and a predicate can be found between the beginning and the end of the sentence if the sentence is analysed linearly. In the cases of (11) and (12), the head noun *koto* is changed in its semantic quality to a modal sentence-final factor that correlates with the adverb in the beginning of the sentence.

8.3.1.2 *Attributive [clause/phrase] + noun expressing feeling or evaluation*

In this section, it will be shown that abstract nouns of feelings or perception make the whole sentence emotional when they are modified by phrases expressing the object or event that gives rise to the feeling or evaluation:

(13) *Musume-tati ni   atatakai asa-gohan o   tabesaseru siawase.* (zuihitu)
daughter-PL DAT warm   breakfast ACC eat-CAUS happiness
'The happiness (I feel) when I make a warm breakfast for my daughters.'

(14) *Biiru no   nantomo ienu umasa.* (asahi)
beer GEN indescribable good taste
'Oh, the ineffable deliciousness of beer!'

Kudoo (1989) called sentences like (13) and (14) 'pseudo exclamatory sentences' (*giji kantai* :擬似喚体) or 'pseudo independent minor sentences' (*giji dokuritugobun* :擬似独立語文). Kudoo remarks that they are extremely similar to predicate sentences in content and that they are the 'condensed' expression of predicate sentences (Kudoo 1989: 21). As shown in (14), final nouns are often modified directly by such phrases as *nantomoienai/nantomoienu* ('indescribable') or *nantoyuu* ('what to say') to emphasize the degree of the speaker's feeling. The example below is a particularly 'condensed' version of such sentences, composed merely of *nantoyuu* and a noun:

(15) *Surasuratto kotaeta   yokozuna ni   kotira   ga   azento   natta.*
smoothly   answer-PAST yokozuna DAT this side NOM dumbfounded become-PAST

Nantoyuu   kioku-ryoku. (asahi)
what to say   memory
'We were rather dumbfounded to hear the Yokozuna answer without a moment's hesitation. What a memory!'

In (15) the situation that caused the feeling is expressed in the preceding sentences.

The semantic independence of (13)–(15) is guaranteed by the syntactic and semantic structure, that is, the combination of attributive [clause/phrase] and noun that expresses feeling or evaluation. When the final noun does not express feeling or evaluation as (13') below,

(13') *Musume-tati ni   atatakai asa-gohan o   tabesaseru Hanako.*
daughter-PL DAT warm   breakfast ACC   eat-CAUS Hanako
?'Hanako who makes a warm breakfast for her daughters.'

the whole NP sentence cannot achieve the same level of expressivity. What gives independence in meaning and emotive expressivity in a sentence is a semantic structure in which the last noun is an adjectival or evaluative noun, as we have seen in (13)–(15). The importance of the semantic structure as modality marker as shown in this section is also true of NP sentences in the following sections.

8.3.1.3   [Noun + no / sono] + adjectival phrase + koto

The pattern '[noun + *no / sono*] + adjectival phrase + *koto*' exemplifies another kind of exclamatory sentence:

(16) *Gaku   no   naka   no   kao   no   nanto wakawakasii koto!* (asahi)
picture frame GEN inside GEN face   GEN how   youthful   matter
'How youthful the face in the frame is!'

(17) *Waga zinsei no   gen-huukei   no   nanto tiisana koto.......* (zuihitu)
my   life   GEN original-scenery GEN how small   matter
'How small the original scenery of my life is …'

(18) *Koko to   omoeba   mata atira de,   sono memagurusii koto.* (zuihitu)
     here QUOT think-COND again there COP its   bewildering matter
     'It bustled here and there, how bewildering!'

(19) *Sono oisii koto!* (asahi)
     its   tasty matter
     'How tasty it was!'

The subject in the adjectival phrase does not takes the nominative case *ga*, but the genitive case *no* as *kao no* in (16) and *gen-huukei no* in (17). The genitive *no* contributes in attributing the subject nouns to the final noun *koto*, effecting unification of the whole sentence as a noun phrase. This pattern can be turned into a full sentence structure by adding a predicate as shown in (16'):

(16') *Gaku   no   naka   no   kao no   wakawakasii koto   ni   odoroita.*
      picture frame GEN inside GEN face GEN youthful   matter DAT be surprised-PAST
      'I was surprised that the face in the frame was so youthful.'

It seems that constant omission of the predicate has strengthened the semantic independence of the *koto* phrase. Consequently, it could be argued that NP sentences like (16)–(19) came into being accompanied by the co-occurrence of modal adverbs like *nanto* (in (16) and (17)), and this caused a 'modalization' of the head noun *koto* in (16)–(19). Finally, consider (20) and (21):

(20) *Igirisu   no   hune   o   i-sseki   marugoto katta   n   desu   yo.*
     England GEN vessel ACC one-NUM whole   buy-PAST COMP COP-POL PART

     to yuu koto   da.   Nanto gookaida   koto! (asahi)
     QUAT matter COP how   extravagant (predicative form) matter
     'I heard that the owner bought a whole vessel with all its furniture. How extravagant!'

(21) *Maa, tanosi-soodesu   koto.*
     oh   happy-MAN-POL matter
     'Oh, you look very happy.'

While *tiisana* in (17) is an attributive form, the *i*-adjectives *wakawakasii* in (16), *memagurusii* in (18) and *oisii* in (19) are all ambiguous as to whether they are in attributive or predicative form. However, interestingly, in (20) and (21), instead of the attributive forms *gookaina* or *tanosisoona*, the predicative forms *gookaida* and *tanosisoodesu* precede *koto*, respectively. The fact that *koto* admits to be preceded by a predicative form, suggests the completion of the grammatical and semantic change of *koto*, from a noun to a complete modal word as a sentence-final particle. At the same time it also means that sentences like (20) and (21) can no longer be considered NP sentences. *Koto* therefore provides a conspicuous illustration of the phenomenon of 'subjectification' whereby meanings become increasingly based on the speaker's subjective belief-state/attitude towards the proposition (as discussed by Traugott 1995). While the functions and meanings of minor sentences with *koto* originally entirely depended on the context/discourse, they have developed into exclamatory expressions, as shown in this section as well as in the following sections.

8.3.1.4   *Repetition of a volitional verbal noun*

In this section it will be shown that repetition of a verbal noun that has a meaning of volitional action becomes a modality marker.

> (22) <u>*Kirameki-raito to   soohuu   de rihuressyusitara, saa saa sigoto sigoto!*</u> (asahi)
>   glittering-light ADD sending air INS refresh-COND now   work work
>   'We have become refreshed with the bright sunshine and fresh air, so (let's) work now!'

> (23) <u>*Doyoo   no   asa   ni   wa   tentoo ni   narabete 'Syoobai syoobai'.*</u> (asahi)
>   Saturday GEN morning TEM TOP store LOC put-GER business business
>   'On Saturday morning they display goods in the store and shout, "Business, business".'

(22) and (23) can be used as self-addressed calls of encouragement or, when addressed to the listener, to urge him/her to do something demanding. *Sigoto* ('work/business') in (22) and *syoobai* ('business') in (23) are verbal nouns, so when the light verb *suru* ('do') is attached to them, they become complete verbs, *sigotosuru* and *syoobaisuru* respectively. (22') is the unmarked full sentence corresponding to (22), but it lacks the expressive sense of bustling urgency of the NP sentence:

> (22') <u>*Kirameki-raito to   soohuu   de rihuressyusitara, saa   sigotosiyoo!*</u>
>   glittering-light ADD sending air INS refresh-COND now work-VOL
>   'We have become refreshed with the bright sunshine and fresh air, so let's get to work!'

On the other hand, (24) is an NP sentence whose final noun is verbal but not volitional, and this generates an inappropriate sentence:

> (24) <u>**moosugu kaihuku   kaihuku!*</u>
>   soon   recovery recovery (from illness)
>   '(I will have) recovery soon.'

This shows that a necessary condition for the patterns introduced in this section, is that the final, repeated noun is also volitional.

8.3.2 NP sentences of declarative type

NP sentences of declarative type are those sentences whereby the speaker's knowledge is offered. Just as sentences in which the speaker intends neither to influence the listener's mind nor to express his or her emotions and opinions but make some objective statement about some state of affairs, we can identify a sort of declarative type in NP sentences as well, although with an accompanying deep emotion and concern. NP sentences of declarative type are close to full sentences in their semantic meaning, but they have developed their own expressivity in discourse.

8.3.2.1 NP sentences with a noun of duration at the final position

NP sentences in this section end with nouns of duration. The three patterns, i.e. 'V_{dic} + *koto* + noun of duration', 'V_{-te} + noun of duration' and '[V_{-te} / V_{-te} + *kara* / noun + *kara*] + noun of duration', all express hardship through the passing of time. These patterns are used only in written language.

(25) and (26) have the pattern of 'V_{dic} + *koto* + noun of duration':

(25) *Keiba   ga   roiyaru-supootu dearu koto wa yoku sirarete-iru   ga,*
horse racing NOM royal sport   COP matter TOP well know-PASS-STAT ADV

kootaigoo   no   aityakuburi wa syumi no iki o   koete-iru   to
Her Imperial Majesty GEN attachment TOP hobby GEN level ACC exceed-STAT QUOT

itte   ii.   <u>Kore ni   bottoosuru koto   karekore 50-nen.</u> (zuihitu)
say-GER good this DAT be absorbed matter almost 50-year
'It is widely known that horse racing is a royal sport, but it is safe to say that Her Imperial Majesty's attachment to it is more than a hobby. <u>It has been fifty years or so since she started to be absorbed in it.</u>'

(26) *Kanreki   mo   sugita   to yuu noni senzitu   mo   sukottorando no*
61st birthday ADD pass-PAST QUOT ADV the other day ADD Scotland   GEN

<u>kakokuna rinkusu o   tebiki-kaato de aruku koto   renzoku   22-niti-kan.</u> (zuihitu)
harsh   links   ACC hand trolley INS walk matter continuation 22-day-duration
'I am already over 60 years old, but it was for 22 straight days that <u>I walked on the harsh golf course in Scotland pulling a golf cart.</u>'

In these sentences, action verbs precede *koto* and time adverbials are at the end of the sentence. Compare (25) and (26) with the corresponding unmarked sentences (25′) and (26′) respectively, in which the verbs preceding *koto* in (25) and (26) appear as tensed main predicates, and words expressing duration appear as adverbial phrases:

(25′) *<u>Karekore 50-nen kore ni   bottoosita.</u>*
almost   50-year this DAT be absorbed-PAST
'She has been absorbed in this for fifty years or so.'

(26′) *Sukottorando no   kakokuna rinkusu o   tebiki-kaato de renzoku   22-niti-kan*
Scotland   GEN harsh   links   ACC hand trolley INS continuation 22-day-duration
aruita.
walk-PAST
'I walked on the harsh golf course in Scotland pulling a golf cart for 22 straight days.'

In contrast to (25′) and (26′) in which the whole incident is described rather 'flatly' with an unmarked word order, (25) and (26), which are marked NP sentences, by juxtaposing the 'V_{dic} + *koto*' and the 'noun of duration', foreground the duration of the event as well as its unusualness. The use of the verbs such as *bottoosuru* and *aruku* in infinite form expressively conveys the difficulty of the action by abstracting the tense and highlighting the meaning of the verbs. Similar effects can be observed in (27) and (28) with the pattern 'V_{-te} + noun of duration':

(27) *Oooka Etizennokami Tadasuke   o   enzite   30-nen.* (zuihitu)
Oooka Etizennokami Tadasuke (proper noun) ACC perform-GER 30-year
'He has played the part of Oooka Etizennokami Tadasuke for 30 years.'

(28) *Hikooki wa ekonomii-kurasu de,   kyuukutuna zaseki ni   zitto suwatte 12-zikan.* (zuihitu)
airplane TOP economy class COP narrow   seat   LOC still sit-GER 12-hour
'I sat quietly in a narrow seat in economy class for 12 hours.'

The verbs in *te*-form preceding nouns of duration are also action verbs. In this pattern the *te*-form indicates continuation of action, and the sentences express deep emotion for the fact that someone has kept on doing some action for a long period of time.

(29)–(31) are of the third pattern of '[V_{-te} / V_{-te} + *kara* / noun + *kara*] + noun of duration':

(29) *Titi   dearu 19-sei sooke   to yuu, ookina kasa   ga   nakunatte 5-nen.* (zuihitu)
father COP 19th head of a school QUOT big   umbrella NOM be lost-GER 5-year
'(It has been) five years since my father, the 19th head of school, passed away.'

(30) *Sin-Oosaka-eki   de 'Itteki-masu'   to   haha ni te   o*
Sin-Oosaka-station LOC go and come back-POL QUOT mother DAT hand ACC
hutte   kara 6-nen. (zuihitu)
wave-GER ABL 6-year
'(It has been) six years since I waved to my mother saying "I'll be back" at Sin-Oosaka Station.'

(31) *Sekigunha   no   9-nin   ga   Haneda-hatu   Hukuoka-iki   no   Nikkoo-ki*
the Red Army GEN 9-person NOM Heneda-departure Fukuoka-going GEN Nikko plane
'Yodogoo' o   nottotta,   waga-kuni hatu no   haizyakku-ziken kara 32-nen. (zuihitu)
the 'Yodo' ACC hijack-PAST our-country first GEN hijack-case   ABL 32-year
'Thirty-two years (have passed) since the first hijack case in our country in which nine people from the Red Army took over the JAL jet "Yodo", heading from Haneda to Fukuoka.'

Sentences of this pattern have a rather different meaning of duration than the above two patterns, i.e. 'V$_{dic}$ + *koto* + noun of duration' and 'V$_{-te}$ + noun of duration'. The *te*-form indicates sequence, which means that the duration expressed by these sentences is the period from the time when some situation ended to the time of the utterance. *Te*-form verbs or nouns preceding *kara* express the situations. Although the form of 'V$_{-te}$ + noun of duration' is the same as that of the previous pattern, the aspectual classification of the verbs is different. Those of the previous pattern are action verbs, while those in this pattern are change-of-state verbs (*henka doosi*) such as *nakunaru* ('die/pass away') in (29). On the other hand in case of 'V$_{-te}$ + *kara* + noun of duration', either action verbs or change-of-state verbs are available, for the ablative particle *kara* guarantees the meaning. The last pattern focusing on the time after the completion of a certain situation has acquired expressivity to show the speaker's emotion for the length of time elapsed.

All of the three patterns above express some feelings aroused by the length of the period, and the last two patterns especially express deep emotion like reminiscence. In each pattern nouns in final position provide a focal point of convergence for the sentence's expressivity.

8.3.2.2 NP sentences with quotation

NP sentences in this section have a syntactic structure in which direct or indirect quotations are followed by sentence-final nouns with connectives such as *to*, *to yuu* and *to no* between them. All these sentences are related to the reporting of information. There are three variations in this pattern, that is, '-*to no* + informative noun', '-*to* + person noun' and '-*to no koto* / -*to no yosi* / -*yosi*'. These patterns are also used in written language.

(32) and (33) with verbal nouns in the final position express communication acts:

(32) [...] *Zyuntyooni tuduki   sukkari   ansinsite-ita   no   da   ga,*
     smoothly continue completely be relieved-STAT-PAST COMP COP ADV
     aru toki totuzen   tyotto kite-kudasai   yo   to no   o-yobi. (zuihitu)
     one time suddenly a little come-BEN-IMP PART QUOT HON-call
     'I was totally relaxed since all was proceeding smoothly, but <u>one day suddenly (there
     was) a call to me to come (to him) for a moment.</u>'

(33) *Purodyuusaa kara wa   'Ironna hito   kara denwa ga   kakattekuru. Risuku ga   takai*
     producer   ABL TOP various person ABL phone NOM come   risk   NOM high
     node kanarazu, opereetaa o   toosite   kara nama-hoosoo   ni   tunagu yooni.'
     REA surely   operator ACC pass-GER ABL live-broadcasting DAT connect IMP

to no   sizi. (asahi)
QUOT direction
'A direction (came) from the producer to connect a telephone call to live broadcasting only through the operator, because there were calls from various people that might be risky.'

Oyobi in (32) is a honorific verbal noun derived from a verb *yobu* ('call'), and *sizi* in (33) is also a verbal noun corresponding to a verb *sizisuru* ('direct'). In spite of the close similarity between these verbal nouns and the corresponding predicates, the subtraction of predication as well as tense and aspect allows these forms to assume brevity and strength, which reflects the speaker's impression of the events.

(34) and (35) have a pattern '-*to* + person noun':

(34) '*Nihon wa   hoppoo-yontoo   ni   kodawatte-orare-masu   ga,   waga-kuni   ni*
Japan TOP Northern-four-islands DAT stick-PROG-HON-POL ADV our-country LOC

wa   ariamaru   toti   ga   ari-masu.   Nannara   muryoode teikyoosi-masu yo'
TOP abundant land NOM exist-POL if you like free   offer-POL   PART

to,   daitooryoo. (zuihitu)
QUOT president
'"You insist with the Northern-Four-Islands, but there is abundant land in my country. We can offer you some land free of charge, if you like" (said) the President.'

(35) '*Demo ahuganisutan kara tegami o   dasu   no   wa   muzukasii kara,*
but   Afghanistan ABL letter   ACC let out COMP TOP difficult   REA

kokugai   ni   deru hito   ni   takusite   kossori tookansite-morau
outside the country LOC leave person DAT entrust-GER secretly post-GER-BEN

yoo-desu.'   to   Ratisu-san. (zuihitu)
MAN-POL QUOT Lattice-Mr
'"But it seems that people entrust a person who goes out of the country to post letters secretly, because it is difficult to do it from Afghanistan" (said) Mr Lattice.'

Sentences of this pattern express reported speech and only the utterer of the quoted utterance can appear in the head noun position. Compare (36) with (36') and (36"):

(36) '*Moo   ii   kai?' to   Taroo ga   daidokoro de   itta.*
already OK Q   QUOT Taroo NOM kitchen   LOC say-PAST
' "OK now?" said Taroo in the kitchen.'

(36') '*Moo   ii   kai?' to   Taroo.*
already OK Q   QUOT Taroo
'"OK now?" (said) Taroo.'

(36") *'*Moo   ii   kai?' to   daidokoro.*
already OK Q   QUOT kitchen
*'"OK now?" (from the) kitchen.'

(36′) can be derived from (36), but (36″), whose final noun is not a person noun, cannot and is unacceptable. '-*To* + person noun' is a pattern that foregrounds the utterer of the quoted proposition that attracted the speaker's attention, in the scene shared by both. This is used in more or less plain text.

The third pattern in this section has a formal noun *koto* or *yosi* in the final position:

(37) *Syomotu o   yomu hito   ga   hetta   to no   koto.* (zuihitu)
book   ACC read   person NOM decrease-PAST QUOT matter
'(I hear) that the number of those who read books has decreased.'

(38) *Sensei-gata kara wa   hanataba o   itadaki,   koomon   o   deru toki wa*
teacher-PL ABL TOP bouquet   ACC be given-HUM school gate ACC leave time TOP

'Banzai' to   minade   miokutte-kudasatta   yosi. (asahi)
'Banzai' QUOT all together see off-GER-BEN-HON-PAST report

'(I hear) that he was given a bouquet from his teachers and sent off with "Banzai" by all of them when he left the school gate.'

Sentences of this pattern express hearsay. They lack the reportive predicates such as *kiku* ('hear') or *hoozi-rare-ru* ('be reported') that might be used in full sentences, but function as hearsay expressions by their final form *to no koto* or *yosi* which have already become grammaticalized as final forms indicating that the sentences are hearsay.

The ellipsis of verbs of communicative action in the three types of NP sentences above could have been facilitated by the evocative presence of the quotative particle *to*.

8.3.2.3   Conditional clause + noun

(39)–(40) are combinations of a conditional clause and a noun:

(39) *Tadasi, gaikokuzin wa   ikanaru koto   ga   arootomo   deiri-kinsi   dearu.*
but   foreigner   TOP what   matter NOM there is-CONC no admittance COP

'Wazuka hakusen   ippon   na   n   da'   to   sono kameraman wa   itta.
merely   white line one-NUM COP COMP COP QUOT that cameraman TOP say-PAST
Dooro ni   hikareta   hakusen   o   koereba   Ahugan. (zuihitu)
road   LOC draw-PASS-PAST white line ACC cross-COND Afghanistan

'However, foreigners are prohibited from entry for whatever reason. "Only one white line makes a difference," the photographer said. Once you crossed the white line drawn on the road, (that was) Afghanistan.'

(40) *Gotoku ni   me ga   tomatta   no   wa   go-nen   mae.* [...]
tripod   LOC eye NOM stay-PAST COMP TOP five-year before [...]
Te   ni   toruto,   omoku hin'yarisita syokkan. (zuihitu)
hand LOC take-COND, heavy chilly   sense of touch

'It was five years ago when the tripod caught my eyes. [...]
(I felt) a heavy and chilly feeling when I took it in my hand.'

(41) *Huru-hon   nara   Kanda.* (zuihitu)
    used-book COND Kanda (place name)
    'If you talk about used books, Kanda (is the best.)'

Conditionals in the antecedent clause produce some expectations regarding developments in time, space or logic, which allow the missing elements to be recovered based on experiential or encyclopaedic background. For instance, because the conditional clause in (39) indicates physical movement, we can expect something like a final destination to appear in the following clause. In (40), because the conditional clause indicates the touch of an object to the body, we expect some sort of sensory expression to follow as a result. A similar expectation of an uncontroversial, universally acceptable truth generates the idiomaticity of phrases such as (41). Since the type of event that follows can be said to be predictable on the basis of previous knowledge, ending the utterance on the noun that qualifies that event further dramatizes its role. (39)–(41) show the speaker's vivid feeling that could not be conveyed by the unmarked sentences, that is, the aspiration to be in Afghanistan in (39), the strong tactile impression in (40) and the confident belief about the best place to find second-hand books in (41).

8.3.3 NP sentences of appealing type

NP sentences of appealing type are the sentences in which the listener's action is required. The sentences given below have already had their structural patterns settled as appealing type. (42) and (43), which display the pattern: [V$_{dic}$ + *koto*], are conventionally interpreted as imperative sentences:

(42) *9-zi   ni   taiikukan   ni   atumaru   koto.* (asahi)
    9-hour TEM gymnasium LOC come together matter
    'Come together to the gymnasium at 9.'

(43) (fortune telling)
    Hito   no   aida   ni   haitte   no   kuroo   ga   ooi.   Tokuni   kinsen-men
    people GEN among LOC enter-GER GEN trouble NOM many especially money-aspect

    ni   wa   yoo-tyuui!   Yoku kangaeru koto! (asahi)
    DAT TOP be careful well think matter
    'You shall have a hard time with people. Be very careful with money especially! Think twice about everything!'

In these NP sentences, naturally there is no explicit marker of command such as a verb in the imperative form. However, these patterns have come to convey a sense of forceful instruction by mere reference to the action requested. They are used in formal and businesslike contexts. The final *koto* has been grammaticalized as a form to express command, with the speaker holding an unyielding stance.

As seen in the previous three sections, some NP sentences seem to pattern in a way that corresponds to the subclassification of unmarked full sentences: exclamatory, declarative and imperative. However, NP sentences and unmarked complete sentences vary greatly in expressivity. The foregrounding of remarkable things obtained by displaying the nouns in final position and the removal of redundant information in the predicate are the strategies used to bring out the speaker's special feelings towards certain events. This entails that the NP sentence pattern itself works as a kind of modality marker.

8.4 Nouns that express the speaker's attitude

In the previous sections, it was noted that there are NP sentences that have some fixed syntactic and semantic patterns established as independent sentences of some expressive type. Given that NP sentences are capable of conveying some modality meaning by themselves, it is even more likely that nouns whose meaning is to define the speaker's attitude can achieve full semantic independence. In this section, it will be shown that there are some verbal nouns that express the speaker's attitude for themselves as illustrated below:

(44) <u>*Situmon*.</u> / *Sansei*. /   *Hantai*. /   *Kyakka*. /   <u>*Onegai*.</u> / <u>*Koosan*.</u>
Question / agreement / objection / rejection / request / surrender
'I ask you a question. / I agree with you. / I don't agree with you. /
<u>I reject the demand. / I implore you to do. / I give up.</u>'

(45) <u>*Kiritu*.</u> /   *Tyakuseki*. / *Okanzyoo*.
standing up / seating /   calculation
'Stand up. / <u>Sit down.</u> / <u>Bill, please!</u>'

(46) <u>*Omatase*.</u> /   *Siturei*.
making someone wait / impoliteness
'<u>Sorry to have kept you waiting.</u> / <u>Excuse me</u>.'

Each word in (44) functions as a performative sentence. Moreover, the three examples in (45) function as imperatives and requests, and the two in (46) as apologies. But there are not many nouns that possess this performative capacity. For instance, *situmon* can be an independent utterance, but *otazune* ('question') and *oukagai* ('question') simply remain fragmental, although their meanings are similar. The nouns in (47) are other such examples. *Owabi*, for instance, cannot have the meaning of 'I apologize', and therefore it remains a meaningless expression:

(47) **Owabi*. / **Kaitoo*. / **Inori*. / **Yookyuu*. / **Syazai*. / **Tyuukoku*. / **Syoodaku*. /
  Apology / answer / prayer / demand / apology / advice /   approval /
  *Yakusoku.
  Promise

8.5   What makes an NP sentence a full-fledged utterance?

Noda (1989) defines sentences in which modal forms do not actually express the speaker's subjective attitude at the point of speech as 'false modality' (*kyosei modariti*), while those expressing a speaker's subjective attitude at the point of speech as 'true modality' (*sinsei modariti*).[3] Since NP sentences are originally mere fragments, they generally depend on the context for their sentential functions. Therefore they should be considered sentences without true modality. However, as exemplified in sections 8.3 and 8.4, it is also true that there are many NP sentences that display a referential meaning very similar to sentences containing a predicate. If a predicate is a fundamental factor in the construction of a sentence, then how can a noun phrase be considered a sentence, instead of a mere utterance?

As the biggest factor that brought semantic independence to NP sentences, we can think of the progressive conventionalization of NP sentences that must have started with omission and simplification through pragmatic strengthening. Linguistic factors such as co-occurrence of modal adverbs, frequent use of a formal noun *koto* or the nature of verbal nouns support this interpretation. This provides further evidence to the notion that context shapes grammar, and that as long as the speaker's attitude is recoverable from contextual (linguistic and extra-linguistic) elements, grammatical completeness is not a necessary requirement. NP sentences are not suitable to describe the process of an incident objectively for the lack of predicates. However, as long as the information is predictable to the reader, the recoverable elements can and are omitted. By virtue of such omissions, the placement of nouns in final position gives them prominence and conveys the speaker's focus on the information expressed by them. This also gives discourse a dramatic rhythm: NP sentences break the monotony of full sentences and create an expressive style. The formation of NP sentences is an effective means to express events not objectively, but subjectively and emotionally from the speaker's perspective, and therefore this pattern can be considered a kind of DM indicator.[4]

8.6 Concluding remarks

In this study I investigated how modality is found in NP sentences and argued the following:

(a) Sentence formation is a kind of modality and NP sentences can be considered as DM indicators.
(b) NP sentences can express emotion as well as intention, and provide the utterance with the expressive connotation of an exclamation.
(c) Among Japanese NP sentences that are syntactically fragments, quite a few have sufficient expressivity to behave as communicative units with complete referential meanings independent from the context. They differentiate into some substructures corresponding to expressive types, that is, emotive, declarative and appealing type.
(d) The factors hypothesized to have supported the semantic independence of NP sentences in the process of conventionalization would be the co-occurrence of modal phrases, formal noun *koto* and verbal nouns.
(e) Some of the verbal nouns get conventionalized in their usage and function independently as performative, imperative and apology sentences.

Masuoka's (1991, 2007) study of full sentences argues that a sentence's expressive function is a kind of modality. I have argued that minor sentences too are capable of conveying this kind of modality and should be a target of research on modality. Marked sentence formation is an important DM indicator for linguistic devices in order to transmit the speaker's emotional attitude vis-à-vis referential contents. In fact, NP sentences are rich in expressivity. More colourful and semantically independent NP sentences are not deviant but well formed in themselves, representing full-fledged utterances.

Grammatical abbreviations

ABL: ablative case (*kara*), ACC: accusative case (*o*), ADD: addition particle (*mo, tari, si, to, ya*), ADV: adversative particle (*ga, noni*), BEN: bene-
factive, CAUS: causative affix (*-(s)ase*), COMP: complementizer (*n, no*),
CONC: concessive affix (*-tomo*), COND: conditional affix (*to, -tara, -eba,
nara*), COP: copula (*da, de, dearu, desyoo, desu, no*), DAT: dative case (*ni*),
DES: desiderative affix (*-tai*), DIR: directional case (*e, ni*), GEN: genitive
case (*no*), GER: gerund affix (*-te*), HON: honorific affix (*o-, -(r)are*), HUM:
humble form, IMP: imperative, INS: instrumental case (*de*), LOC: locative case (*ni, de*), MAN: manner affix (*soo, yoo*), NEG: negative affix (*-nai*),
NOM: nominative case (*ga*), NUM: numerative, PART: sentential particle
(*ne, wa, ya, yo*), PASS: passive affix (*-(r)are*), PAST: past affix (*-ta*), PL: plu-
ral affix, POL: polite affix (*-desu, -masu*), POT: potential affix (*-e*), PROG:
progressive affix (*-iru*), Q: question particle (*kai*), QUOT: quotative particle (*to, to no, toyuu*), REA: reason particle (*kara, node*), STAT: stative affix
(*-iru*), TEM: temporal particle (*ni*), TOP: topic marker (*wa, nante*), VOL:
volitional.

Notes

1. If *da* is replaced with *datta*, the addition of tense to the copula makes (6′) more
   acceptable. However, the sequence of the sentences still sounds rather odd, for
   the sentence with *to no koto datta* usually follows the sentence describing the
   event, that is, *Zannennagara naka e wa hairenakatta. Soko wa tatiiri-kinsi-kuiki to
   no koto datta* is quite natural.
2. The classification and naming of the categories of modality are partly changed
   in Masuoka (2007) where *Hyoogen-ruikei no modariti* is called *Hatuwa-ruikei no
   modariti* ('modality of utterance type'). All translations of Japanese terminology are by the author.
3. Nitta's (1991) *Gizi modariti* ('quasi-modality') occurs when the predicates indicating modality are in the past tense, in the negative form, or in the case of
   expressing subjectivity except for the first person's. Noda's *Kyosei modariti* is
   a broader concept, including modal forms within subordinate clauses and,
   albeit structurally independent, sentences whose modal characters depend
   on their preceding or following sentences. Moreover, Noda's *Sinsei modariti* is
   「真性」modality, while Nitta's is 「真正」modality; different *kanzi* are used. 「真性」
   means 'true' or 'genuine', while 「真正」means 'authentic'.
4. NP sentences are not used in the sentences for all the genres. 'Repetition
   of volitional verbal noun' and 'NP sentence of appealing type' are conversational, but other patterns are fundamentally exclusive to written language.
   Yet, they cannot be used in scientific domains such as academic papers, nor do
   they appear in written-language-like spoken media such as the news. We can
   make the best use of the special quality of NP sentences in more narrative,

creative type of texts such as essays. This is because essays, unlike scientific papers that are required to make accurate remarks, make allowance for subjective, expressive effects. Moreover, it is interesting to see how NP sentences are placed in discourse. NP sentences cannot appear everywhere in discourse, but are generally placed somewhere between unmarked complete sentences, thereby highlighting the expressive effects of the text without compromising reference.

References

Adachi, T. (2002). Situmon to Utagai [Question and Doubt]. In: Miyazaki, K. et al. (eds), *Sin Nihongo Bunpoo Sensyo 4: Modariti* [New Selection of Japanese Grammar 4: Modality]. Tokyo: Kurosio.

Kawabata, Y. (2004). Bunpoo to Imi [Grammar and Meaning]. In: Onoe, K. (ed.), *Asakura Nihongo Kooza 6 Bunpoo* [Asakura Japanese Language Grammar]. Tokyo: Asakura Shoten.

Kudoo, H. (1989). Gendai Nihongo no Bun no Zyohoosei: Zyosyoo [A Study on Sentence Modality System in Modern Japanese: Introduction]. In: *Tokyo Gaikokugo Daigaku Ronsyuu* [Area and Culture Studies] 39. Tokyo: Tokyo University of Foreign Studies.

Masuoka, T. (1991). *Modariti no Bunpoo* [Grammar of Modality]. Tokyo: Kurosio.

Masuoka, T. (1995). Rentaisetu no Hyoogen to Syumeisi no Syudaisei [Expression of Adnominal Clauses and Thematicity of Head Nouns]. In: Masuoka, T. et al. (eds), *Nihongo no Syudai to Toritate* [Theme and Focus in Japanese]. Tokyo: Kuroshio.

Masuoka, T. (2007). *Nihongo Modariti Tankyuu* [Exploration of Japanese Modality]. Tokyo: Kuroshio.

Maynard, S. K. (1993). *Discourse Modality: Subjectivity, Emotion and Voice in the Japanese Language*. Amsterdam: Benjamins.

Maynard, S. K. (2000). *Zyooi no Gengogaku* [Linguistics of Emotion]. Tokyo: Kuroshio.

Nakau, M. (1979). Modariti to Meidai [Modality and Proposition]. In: Hayashi Eiichi Kyoozyu Kanreki Kinen Ronbunsyuu Hensyuu-iinkai (eds), *Eigo to Nihongo to: Hayashi Eiichi Kyoozyu Kanreki Kinen Ronbunsyuu* [English and Japanese: In Honor of Prof. Eiichi Hayashi on the Occasion of His 60th Birthday]. Tokyo: Kuroshio Publishers.

Nakau, M. (1994). *Ninti Imiron no Genri* [Principle of Cognitive Semantics]. Tokyo: Taishuukan Shoten.

Nitta, Y. (1991). *Nihongo no Modariti to Ninsyoo* [Modality and Person in Japanese]. Tokyo: Hituzi Syobo.

Noda, H. (1989). Sinsei Modariti o Motanai Bun [Sentences without True Modality]. In: Nitta, Y. and Masuoka, T. (eds), *Nihongo no Modariti* [Modality in Japanese]. Tokyo: Kurosio.

Traugott, E. C. (1995). Subjectification in Grammaticalization. In: Stein, D. and Wright, S. (eds), *Subjectivity and Subjectivisation: Linguistic Perspectives*. Cambridge: Cambridge University Press.

Tsubomoto, A. (1998). Bun Renketu no Katati to Imi to Goyooron [Form and Meaning and Pragmatics of Sentence Concatenation]. In: Akatsuka, N. and Tsubomoto, A. (eds), *Modariti to Hatuwa Kooi* [Modality and Speech Act]. Tokyo: Kenkyusha.

Yumoto, K. (2004). *Nitieigo Ninti Modaritiron: Renzokusei no siza* [Cognitive Theory of Modality in Japanese and English: Viewpoint of Continuity]. Tokyo: Kurosio.

9
The Acquisition of Japanese Modality during Study Abroad

Suwako Watanabe and Noriko Iwasaki

9.1 Introduction[1]

This chapter approaches modality from a developmental perspective in the context of second language acquisition. Specifically, it reports the results of a study that examined the development of modal expressions among five students who studied in Japan for one academic year. The study compared the students' use of modal expressions in oral interviews before and after their study-abroad experience. The recent advancement of foreign/second language pragmatics research sheds some light on how second language learners acquire pragmatic competence, that is, the knowledge/ability necessary for using a target language appropriately (Kasper and Blum-Kulka 1993, Barron 2003). Many of these studies employ a method that elicits the performance of speech acts such as request and apology in constructed role-play situations. However, since the main focus of these studies is on general pragmatic competence, only a peripheral attention is paid to modality.

The current study adopts a broad scope of modality that encompasses discourse-level as well as sentential-level elements that are used in interaction (Maynard 1993, Nakau 1994) and analyses how learners develop their use of expressions of three types of modality: (1) epistemic modality (a speaker's commitment to the truth value of a proposition); (2) discoursal modality[2] (a speaker's plan of discourse organization); and (3) interactional modality (a speaker's attitude towards interlocutor and interaction). We analyse use of modal expressions in spoken discourse that was elicited spontaneously with a set procedure specified for the American Council on the Teaching of Foreign Languages (ACTFL) Oral Proficiency Interview (OPI). The three types of modality examined here are considered to contribute to learners' enhanced performance in OPIs. The current study sheds some light on the development of use of Japanese epistemic, discoursal and interactional modal expressions in the study-abroad context by quantitatively and qualitatively analysing the modal expressions used by five English-speaking learners of Japanese who spent one academic year in Japan.

9.2 Background

9.2.1 Modality in Japanese

The meaning of a sentence has two dimensions: one is propositional and the other refers to the speaker's psychological state and attitude (Tokieda 1941, Nitta 1989, Masuoka 1991, Halliday 1970). In the example, *Tanaka-san ga kuru yoo da* ('It seems like Tanaka will come'), the proposition is that a person named Tanaka will come.[3] *Yoo da* is a modal element expressing the speaker's presupposition about the proposition based on observation or evidence (Nihongo Kizyutu Bunpō Kenkyūkai 2003: 169; Masuoka this volume). While the proposition denotes how objects and people happen or exist in the world, modality expresses a subjective aspect concerning the speaker's psychological state and attitude towards the proposition and interaction (Miyazaki et al. 2002, Nihongo Kizyutu Bunpō Kenkyūkai 2003, Masuoka 1991, Nitta 1991).

Japanese modal elements can be further classified into subtypes. For example, Nitta (1991) and Masuoka (1991) divide modality into two major types: *genpyoo-zitai meate no modariti* ('the speaker's attitude towards a proposition') and *hatuwa-dentatu no modariti* ('the communicative function and the role that an utterance or sentence bears') (Nitta 1991: 2). Nihongo Kizyutu Bunpō Kenkyūkai (2003) categorizes Japanese modality into four subtypes, consisting of: (1) *hyoogen-ruikei no modariti* ('modality of expression types') that represents the basic function or illocutionary force of a sentence such as a statement, question, speaker's intention, request and invitation; (2) *hyooka/ninsiki no modariti* ('evaluative/epistemic modality') which expresses how a speaker perceives a proposition such as an acceptable act, necessity, surmise and conjecture; (3) *setumei no modariti* ('explanatory modality') that denotes how a sentence is related to the preceding context (e.g. *no da*); and (4) *dentatu no modariti* ('modality of communication') which expresses the manner in which a speaker conveys a message to an interlocutor (e.g. sentence-final particles).

Other linguists include discourse markers in modality. Maynard (1993: 38) proposes the term discourse modality, which 'conveys the speaker's subjective emotional, mental or psychological attitude toward the message content, the speech act itself or toward his or her interlocutor in discourse'. These types of the speaker's attitude are conveyed through various signs, linguistic and non-linguistic, that operate at the sentence and discourse levels. For example, a variety of sociolinguistic style markers such as choice of different verb-ending forms and lexicon express speaker's attitudes towards the interlocutor and/or the situation, and such linguistic elements operate at a discourse level. Nakau (1994) too recognizes discourse markers as a modality device. He argues that there are two levels at which modality operates. He categorizes modality into S modality (which specifies the proposition only) and D modality (which indicates the manner in which discourse occurs) (Nakau 1994: 53). Adopting an inclusive notion of modality proposed by Maynard (1993) and Nakau (1994), modal expressions in this chapter are defined as linguistic elements that express the speaker's psychological state and/or attitude towards the proposition, as well as how the communication is intended, the speaker's feeling towards the interlocutor, and plans for discourse organization.

Although there are differences among researchers concerning what linguistic features are included in modality and how modality is categorized, many of them seem to share the view that Japanese speakers use explicit linguistic codes to convey their attitude towards or evaluation of a proposition, as well as the speaker's subjective attitude towards how to interact with the interlocutor and to organize the unfolding discourse (Maynard 1993, 1997, Masuoka 1991, Nihongo Kizyutu Bunpō Kenkyūkai 2003). Maynard (1993) points out that while in English the speaker's attitude and feeling are often expressed through paralinguistic features such as emphatic stress and rising intonation, in Japanese they are expressed through linguistic elements. Maynard (2005: 34) states that '[i]n Japanese, the importance of rhetoric is often placed on *pathos* and on the play of emotion in the partner's feelings'.

Kurotaki (2005: 19–23) suggests that differences between Japanese and other languages may be found in the development of modal expressions in first language (L1) and second language (L2) acquisition.[4] She points out that the developmental order for European languages as L1 and L2 tend to be from deontic (i.e. modality indicating the speaker's intention and desire) to epistemic (i.e. expressing the speaker's knowledge and conjecture). However, Kurotaki (2002) found that Japanese learners of English acquired epistemic modality earlier than deontic modality.

Based on this finding, Kurotaki (2005) suggests that while the prototype of English modality is deontic, that of Japanese is epistemic. Kurotaki's argument is indicative of the challenge that English-speaking learners of Japanese may face when mastering Japanese modality.

9.2.2 Modality and second-language acquisition

L2 pragmatics research is primarily concerned with how L2 learners acquire knowledge of 'how to do things with words' in their L2 (Kasper 1998). Accordingly, many studies have focused on learners' realization of speech acts by comparing it to how native speakers achieve the same speech acts. In other words, *hyoogen-ruikei no modariti* ('modality of expression types') (Nihongo Kizyutu Bunpō Kenkyūkai 2003) is the very target of the research. In the process of speech-act realization, modal expressions are viewed as linguistic elements that learners use in order to achieve a variety of speech acts effectively, and researchers have examined the use of modal expressions as one of the strategies employed to perform a particular speech act in contexts with differentiated variables (e.g. intimacy and status).

A few researchers have directly investigated development of modal expressions. Using a corpus of task-oriented conversations between an English native speaker (NS) and a Finnish student of English (NNS), Kärkkäinen (1992) focused on English epistemic modal expressions and compared the NS and NNS in terms of frequency of use and types. One of the major findings was that the NS used far more adverbials such as *really* and *maybe* than the NNS. The Finnish students of English relied on the modal expressions *I think* and *I know*, and their use of modal auxiliaries such as *might* and *could* was far less than the NS. Kärkkäinen (1992: 203) speculates that these modal expressions (*I think* and *I know*) may be used 'as a kind of compensatory strategy for both modal verbs and adverbs'. Similarly, in Salsbury and Bardovi-Harlig's study (2000), low-level learners used *think* and *maybe* rather than modal expressions such as *would* and *could* in oppositional talk. These findings suggest that mastery of English modal expressions that are used to mitigate illocutionary force, in contrast to lexical means and pragmatic routines, is difficult to attain for learners.

Little research has been carried out on L2 Japanese modality acquisition (Kurotaki 2005), but there are a few studies that relate to the development of epistemic modality. Ono (2001) examines L2 learners' errors on the use of *to omou* ('think') and reports that they make errors due to a lack of understanding as to what is expected to be shared with the interlocutor. Using a questionnaire, Oshima (1993) investigated Chinese and Korean learners' understanding of nine Japanese modal expressions including *daroo* ('probably'), *ka mo sirenai* ('may/maybe'), *yoo da* ('seem') and *rasii* ('apparently/look like') and compared their judgements with those of native Japanese speakers. She found that more learners than Japanese respondents judged the use of *yoo da/mitai da* as inappropriate to express indirectness. She suggests that the differences between the learners and native Japanese speakers could be attributed to cultural differences in the need for expression of empathy towards an interlocutor. Siegal (1995, 1996) conducted a study of four women studying Japanese in Japan and reported one woman's difficulty with the epistemic modal *desyoo* ('probably'). Although she used *desyoo* to be polite with the understanding that it displays a polite demeanour, she often used it in inappropriate and potentially face-threatening ways in her interactions with a professor.

There are also scattered reports on such pragmatic elements as sentence-final particles, and these are pertinent to our broader definition of modality. For example, it has been reported that L2 Japanese learners rarely use the sentence-final particle *ne* (the empathetic tag 'isn't it/s/he?') after completing one year of Japanese study (Sawyer 1992). Yoshimi (1999) found that the *ne* used by English-speaking L2 learners who had had at least one year of formal, college-level study was often inappropriate. It can therefore be speculated that since the use of *ne* requires an intricate knowledge of shared information and background that may fluctuate depending on the context, it is difficult for learners to develop the ability to use this sentence-final particle appropriately.

9.2.3 Study abroad and L2 acquisition

It has been suggested that the learning environment plays an important role in L2 acquisition of pragmatic competence because classroom input may not be sufficient for such development. Bardovi-Harlig and Dörnyei (1998) found that while those who learn English as a foreign language in non-English-speaking countries and their teachers found grammatical errors more salient, those who learn English as a second language in English-speaking countries found pragmatic errors more serious. This finding suggests that the learning environment may play a role in the development of pragmatic sensitivity and that experience in a target language community may help learners to be more aware of pragmatic rules. However, despite the seeming potential of a study-abroad setting,

Barron's examination (2003) of the study-abroad context and its role in the development of L2 (German) pragmatics showed that development was rather limited. She found that the learners developed only some aspects of pragmatic competence, such as target-like discourse structure and an increased reliance on pragmatic routines (e.g. 'Are you sure?' and 'It's okay').[5] With regard to syntactic structures used to minimize an imposition in standard request situations, learners did not downgrade syntactically as much as the German native speakers (Barron 2003: 240).

A few studies have examined the development of L2 Japanese in a study-abroad context (Siegal 1995, Dewey 2005, Huebner 1995, Iwasaki 2005, 2007, Marriott 1995). However, little research has been conducted on the development of Japanese modality in the context of study abroad. Marriott (1995) compared Australian high school students' use of Japanese speech styles in an interview setting before and after their study abroad. One finding relevant to pragmatic competence is that while the students used the plain style minimally prior to the study abroad, the plain style became the dominant style for four of the eight students after study abroad. Marriott attributes the lack of sophistication in their use of polite style post-year abroad to the fact that the students were exposed to settings where the plain style was prevalent and also to a lack of adequate corrective feedback. Iwasaki (in press), however, found that even those learners who no longer used the polite style most of the time when addressing their former teacher in post-study-abroad OPIs did gain some understanding of social meanings of the plain and polite styles and that they were making choices as to which style to use.

In sum, most studies that explore Japanese learners' pragmatic competence are concerned with a limited selection of modality markers such as epistemic modal expressions and sentence-final particles. Furthermore, research that investigates the development of Japanese modality in the study-abroad context is limited to the examination of speech styles. Thus, this study aims at filling this gap by examining the development of Japanese learners' use of three types of modal expressions mentioned above in a study-abroad context.

9.2.4 Modal expressions examined in this study

The current study examines epistemic, discoursal and interactional modal expressions. Epistemic modality represents the speaker's perception about presuppositions, conjectures and estimations. It includes linguistic markers such as *hazu* ('is supposed to'), *mitai* ('seem'), *yoo* ('seem'), *rasii* ('apparently', 'seem') and *to omou* ('think').

The conjunction *kedo* ('but') is included in discoursal modality in this study because *kedo* is used to indicate cohesion, that is how the speaker organizes discourse rather than the actual conjoining of two units/sentences. Maynard (1993: 53) and Nakau (1994) include cohesive devices contributing to the formation of discourse in discourse modality. Nagata and Ohama (2001) identify six ways in which *kedo* is used, three of which ('preliminary remark', 'topic raiser' and 'insertion') express the significance of the proposition marked by *kedo* in relation to an entire discourse, revealing the speaker's intention as to how the discourse will unfold. Nakayama and Ichihashi-Nakayama (1997) point out that *kedo* in narratives functions to convey background information. *Kedo* in conversation when used in the sentence-final position, on the other hand, is similar to final particles reflecting 'the speaker's interpersonal concerns' (Nakayama and Ichihashi-Nakayama 1997: 613). Mori (1999) reports on the use of *kedo* as a self-qualification in opinion–negotiation sequences. In stating an opinion, a speaker inserts a comment that qualifies the opinion. According to Uchida (2001: 48), the speaker's feelings conveyed by *kedo* include 'empathy toward the interlocutor, evaluation of the content, and attitude toward the exchanges', suggesting that *kedo* can be used to express the speaker's attitude towards the interlocutor and how communication is to be taken. In this study, *kedo* is examined when used at a mid-point in a sentence as well as at the sentence-final position, as we assume that the functions of *kedo* extend from the semantic level (conjunctive) to discoursal levels.

The second discoursal modal expression investigated here is *n desu* ('it's that'). In the study of Japanese modality, *n desu* is termed *setumei no modariti* or explanatory modality (Nihongo Kizyutu Bunpō Kenkyūkai 2003, Miyazaki et al. 2002) and functions to present the proposition as a background, a reason, a rationale or a conclusion by connecting the content bracketed by *n desu* to a state or to information introduced in a preceding discourse or context. *N desu* may encompass interactional modality that expresses a speaker's feeling towards how a message is conveyed to an interlocutor as it 'can create a feeling of closeness, empathy, understanding, and warmth' (Jorden and Noda 1987: 242). However, *n desu* is categorized under discoursal modality in this study as its primary function is to relate the proposition to something included in a preceding discourse. Mastering the functions of *kedo* and *n desu* is important for Japanese learners as they strive to achieve text cohesion in an extensive discourse, as well as to perform the functions of narrating, describing, explaining and stating opinions as specified in the ACTFL Proficiency Guidelines (Breiner-Sanders et al. 2000).

Lastly, interactional modality includes linguistic elements that express a speaker's sentiment and attitude towards interaction. Sentence-final particles such as *ne* ('isn't it') and *yo* ('I tell you') belong to this type of modality. The sentence-final particles are used frequently in Japanese casual conversation and play an important role in relation-building in Japanese society, as pointed out in Maynard's (2005: 286) statement that 'in spoken Japanese, interactional particles frequently appear, and they are important in making conversation go smoothly and comfortably'. Although mastery of sentence particles helps learners to communicate with native speakers more smoothly and participate in social interaction effectively, this is a challenging problem for learners, as reported above.

The current study aims to shed light on the development of Japanese learners' use of three types of modality: epistemic modality, discoursal modality (*kedo* and *n desu*) and interactional modality (sentence-final particles). We do so by first quantitatively examining the use of various predicate-ending modal expressions of the three types that are found in the pre- and post-study-abroad OPIs to give an overall picture of how often L2 learners use such expressions. We then focus on the two modal expressions *to omou* and *kedo,* and examine how the learners use such elements. The expression *to omou* is the epistemic modal expression most frequently used by L2 Japanese learners, and its English equivalent 'I think' has been reported to be overused among L2 learners, as discussed in section 9.2.2 (Kärkkäinen 1992, Salsbury and Bardovi-Harlig 2000); likewise, the discoursal modal expression *kedo* is a frequently used marker among L2 Japanese learners. As such, it is important to examine how L2 Japanese learners use them.

9.3   Methodology

9.3.1   Participants

In order to examine the effects of the study-abroad experience on L2 acquisition, an OPI was administered to five students enrolled in a North American university before and after their study abroad by an ACTFL certified OPI interviewer. They were all male, native speakers of English, and they were given the pseudonyms Peter, Alan, Henry, Sam and Greg. When they started their study-abroad programme, their ages ranged from 19 to 21. Four of them (Peter, Alan, Henry and Sam) had studied two years of Japanese with six hours of instruction per week (approximately 360 hours in 52 weeks) before going abroad. Greg had studied Japanese for one year (approximately 180 hours in 24 weeks). Peter, Henry, Sam and Greg majored or double-majored in Japanese, and Alan minored in Japanese.

9.3.2 ACTFL oral proficiency interview and rating of the participants

The ACTFL OPI is a criterion-referenced assessment utilizing a set of standardized procedures to elicit speech samples. A speaker is rated according to the four-level scale based on the criteria established in the ACTFL Proficiency Guidelines (Breiner-Sanders et al. 2000). The four major levels of proficiency are Novice, Intermediate, Advanced and Superior. Each of these first three levels further breaks down into the three sub-levels of Low, Mid and High, and ratings consist of a major level and a sub-level such as Intermediate High and Advanced Mid, except for Superior. The Guidelines describe what the speaker at each major level is expected to do with the language (Global Function), as well as what discourse units a speaker is expected to manage (Text Type). Unlike the Discourse Completion Task (DCT) employed in many L2 pragmatic studies, in OPI the interviewee is not asked to perform speech acts during the interview phase.[6] Rather, the interviewee is asked to carry out simple conversation, describe something (a place, people, etc.), relate past experiences, state and support opinions and/or hypothesize. A rating is assigned based on the interviewee's performance of the level-specific global functions, along with the accuracy and text type criteria. Table 9.1 shows some key elements of the Global Function and Text Type for each major level.

Figure 9.1 shows the OPI ratings of the five students before and after studying abroad. All but one student received a higher rating post-study abroad than before going to Japan. Before going abroad, four were

Table 9.1 ACTFL proficiency levels and key criteria

Levels	Global Function	Text Type
Superior	State and support opinions, hypothesize	Extended discourse
Advanced	Describe, narrate and explain	Paragraph
Intermediate	Create with language, carry on basic conversation, ask and answer questions	Sentences
Novice	Formulaic expressions, list and enumerate	Words

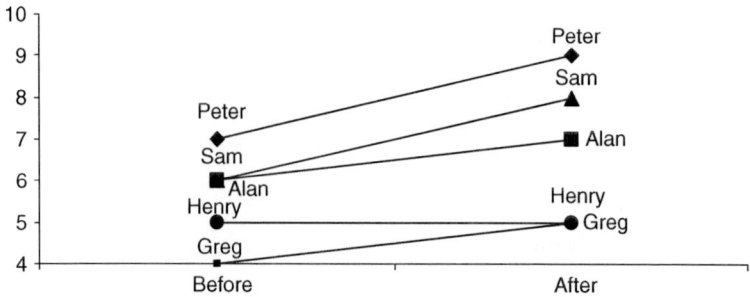

Figure 9.1 ACTFL OPI ratings of five students. Note: The numbers refer to proficiency levels (Novice Low to Novice High are not shown since all participants were above these levels). 4 = Intermediate Low, 5 = Intermediate Mid, 6 = Intermediate High, 7 = Advanced Low, 8 = Advanced Mid, 9 = Advanced High.

rated at the Intermediate level. After the study abroad experience, only two students remained at the Intermediate level. One student (Henry) received the same rating of Intermediate Mid before and after the study abroad programme, but the other four students improved one or more sub-levels.

9.3.3 Data analysis procedure

The speech samples in the OPIs were all transcribed, and based on criteria established by Watanabe (2003), both embedded and sentence-final predicates were identified. The exchanges elicited by role plays were excluded from the analysis because the tasks/functions of each varied greatly depending on the participants' proficiency level. Formulaic expressions such as greetings, noun phrases with omitted copula, unintelligible expressions, repetitions and corrections were excluded from the analyses.

Among the predicates that were identified, the following modal expressions are examined:

1. Epistemic modality that expresses the speaker's awareness, conjecture, and attitude towards a proposition or fact: *desyoo* ('probably'), *hazu* ('is supposed to'), *ka mo sirenai* ('maybe'), *-soo* ('look like'), *mitai* ('seem'), *rasii* ('apparently', 'seem'), *yoo* ('seem'), *to omou* ('think').
2. Conjunctive connector *kedo* and its variants.
3. *N desu* ('it's that …')
4. Sentence-final particles: *ne* ('isn't it?'), *yo* (assertion or 'I tell you'), *yo ne* ('isn't it?', 'right?'), *ka na(a)* ('I wonder'), *mitai na* ('or something

like that'), *to ka* ('and the like'), *kke* (interrogative sentence-particle in recall), *–zya nai ka* ('Surely you'd agree that –'), *ka ne* (question with deliberation or assumed agreement).

In the following section, we will present the results from the quantitative analyses of (1)–(4). As the total numbers of predicates differ greatly among the five students, proportions, instead of frequency counts, are presented. It should be noted that we assume that even native speakers do not use modal expressions on each predicate, so the proportions of sentence-final modal expressions are not expected to approach 100 per cent.[7] We assume that the emergence of modal expressions can be interpreted as the development of modality, but we do not consider the greater proportions as necessarily greater development. After presenting the quantitative analyses, we will present the qualitative analyses of the selected modal expressions *to omou* and *kedo*.[8]

9.4 Analyses and discussion

9.4.1 Quantitative analyses

Figure 9.2 presents comparisons (of pre- and post-study abroad) for the predicates that contain modal expressions. No particular tendency is observed within the group. Figures 9.3–9.6 show comparisons of epistemic modal expressions, *kedo*, *n desu* and the sentence-final particles, respectively. Whereas Greg and Henry, rated Intermediate in the post-OPI, exhibited increases in the use of epistemic modal expressions and the discoursal modal expression *kedo*, Alan and Peter, who were rated Advanced, decreased the use of these modal expressions (Figures 9.3 and 9.4). As for *n desu* and the sentence-final particles, only the most advanced speakers, however, Sam and Peter, increased their use (Sam, *n desu*, Peter, the sentence-final particles) (Figures 9.5 and 9.6).

Although the quantitative analysis of overall modal expressions (epistemic modal expressions, *kedo*, *n desu* and sentence-final particles) revealed no particular tendency towards increase or decrease within a group, there was a difference in the type of modality the learners developed between the Intermediate and Advanced levels. Those at the Intermediate level seemed to show emerging use of epistemic modal expressions (which expresses the speaker's psychological state concerning the proposition). Those at the Advanced levels tended to show more development in interactional modality (as seen in the increased use of sentence-final particles) than they did in epistemic modality. Likewise,

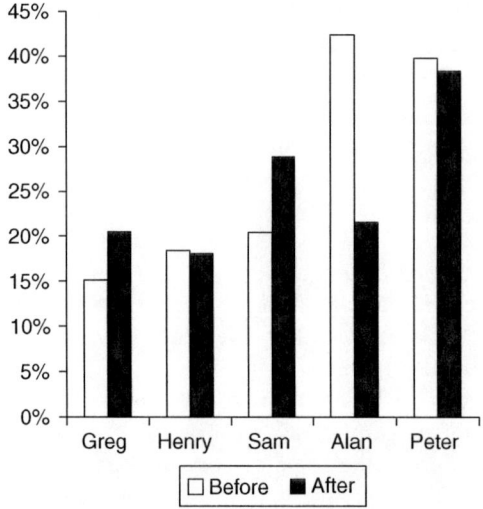

Figure 9.2   Proportion of predicates with modal expressions

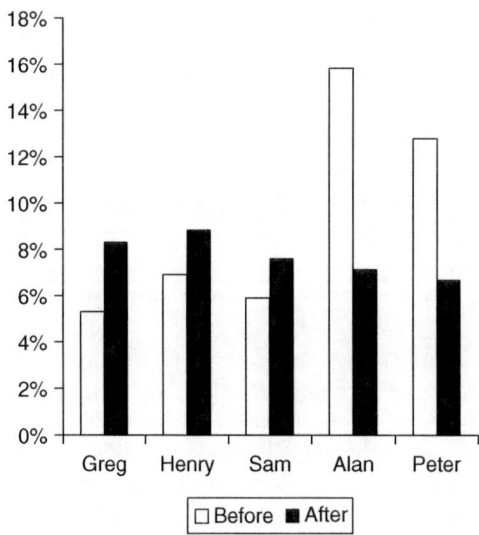

Figure 9.3   Proportion of epistemic modal expressions

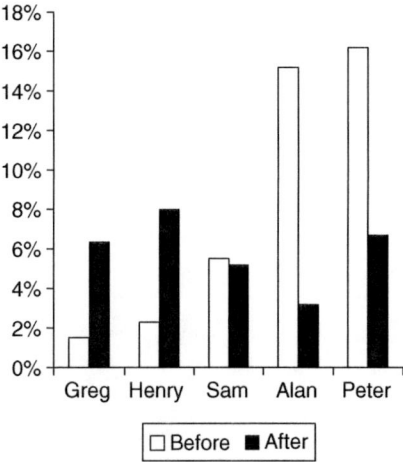

Figure 9.4   Proportion of *kedo*

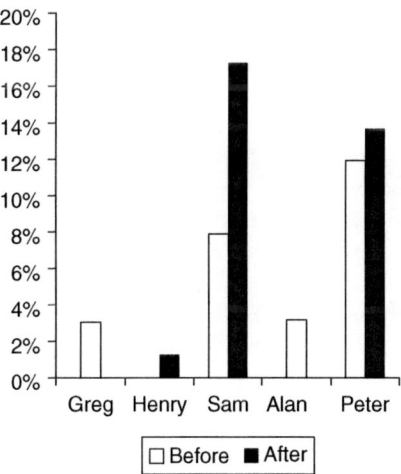

Figure 9.5   Proportion of *n desu*

different patterns of development were observed between the Intermediate and Advanced groups for discoursal modality, *kedo* and *n desu*. While the Intermediate learners (Greg and Henry) exhibited a solid increase in *kedo*, two Advanced learners (Alan and Peter) showed a drastic decrease. In contrast to *kedo*, the two Intermediate learners showed little to no

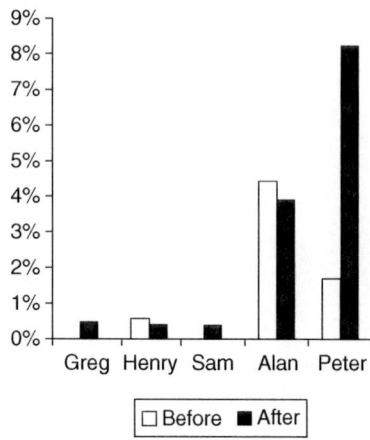

Figure 9.6 Sentence-final particles

gain in the development of *n desu*, and two Advanced learners (Sam and Peter) seemed to have solidified their use of *n desu*, showing that over 12 per cent of the entire predicates counted ended in *n desu*.

The quantitative results suggest that among the five participants examined here, development of epistemic modality emerged at the Intermediate level, at a relatively earlier stage, when learners spent an extensive period of time in the target country. Between the two discoursal modal expressions, *kedo* and *n desu*, the former started to be used at an earlier stage than the latter. Although it is impossible to make generalizations from the current study due to the limited sample, the discoursal modal expression *n desu* appears to be a challenging modality marker to develop for learners. One explanation for this is that compared to *kedo* ('but'), the English phrase 'it's that' is different from *n desu* both in the frequency of use and in its significance in Japanese interactions. It is not used nearly as often or as commonly in English as *n desu* is in Japanese. Thus, learners may not always recognize the need to use *n desu*. Furthermore, it is difficult to grasp the function of *n desu* (relating the proposition to the speaker's subjective construal of observed phenomena or facts). This connection requires sociocultural knowledge. Finally, the interactional modality may not be fully developed before the Advanced level. The result regarding the interactional modality first confirms Sawyer's (1992) and Yoshimi's (1999) findings that the sentence-final particle *ne* is difficult to master for learners of Japanese, but it also indicates that the interactional modal expressions can be developed at the Advanced level in a study-abroad context.

9.4.2 Qualitative analyses

9.4.2.1 To omou

A closer look at the uses of *to omou*, one of the epistemic modal expressions examined in this chapter, in the five students' speech reveals that their use improved after a year in Japan in terms of accuracy and appropriateness, even though the improvement was not across the board.

Before studying abroad, Sam used *to omou* not only to express his judgement or evaluation, but also to describe his usual activities for which evaluation and conjecture are not necessary. Excerpt 1 exemplifies the use of *to omou* when stating routine activities:

Excerpt 1   [Sam-Pre-T29][9]
[Interviewer asked what Sam does on weekends.]
Sam: *Eto, hima na toki, tomodati ni attari, a::, konpyuutaa sitari,*
              eto, nihongo o, nihongo o benkyoo-sitari suru <u>to omoimasu.</u>

[English]

Sam: Uhm, when I have free time, <u>I think</u> I do things like
              seeing my friends, uh, doing things on a computer, and
              studying Japanese.

As Sam added *to omoimasu* to his own leisure activities on weekends, it sounds as if the activities were someone else's. Upon return, he no longer used *to omou* in this manner, but rather to express his evaluation and the basis for decision making.

Peter also used *to omou* in an awkward way before studying abroad. Excerpt 2 is Peter's use of *to omou* before he went to Japan, in which its use, combined with a few other modal expressions, obscures the intended message:

Excerpt 2   [Peter-Pre-T112]
Peter: *Nihon no bunka nara, hutuu no amerika-zin ga, nan to*
              ka, hen da to omotte iru, e:: ten ga, e:: boku ni totte amari
              okasiku nai <u>mitai to omotte iru rasii</u> n desu kedo.

[English]

Peter: If it is Japanese culture, it <u>seems</u> that I am <u>thinking</u> the
              points that normal Americans consider strange <u>seem</u>
              not so weird but.

While the first use of *to omou* in '*Hen da to omotte iru ten*' ('the point that normal Americans consider strange') is appropriate, its second use is not effective because *mitai* ('seem') and *rasii* ('seem') overlap. The phrase *'boku ni totte'* ('for me') may be compatible with *-mitai* or *-rasii* as in *'Boku ni totte okasiku nai mitai/rasii desu'* ('It seems/is apparently not so weird to me'), although it may be uncommon, but it does not go well with *to omou*. *Rasii* following *to omotte iru* makes the entire message sound as if Peter is talking about someone else's view.

Moreover, in Peter's pre-study-abroad OPI, there are two cases in which he added *to omou* to a seemingly completed predicate in *masu/desu* style as in Excerpt 3:

Excerpt 3   [Peter-Pre-T78]
Peter: (...) *A: zyaa daigaku de anmari hoka no koto anmari*
             <u>*benkyoo-sitaku nai n desu nee*</u> *to omotte ita kedo*

[English]
Peter: (...) Yeah well then it's that I <u>don't want to study</u>
             much about other things at college, <u>you know</u>, I was
             thinking, but

Peter added *to omou* immediately after completing a sentence in *masu/desu* style, which suggests his emerging, yet not fully developed, use of *to omou*. However, such use disappeared in his post-study-abroad OPI, and it may imply that full integration of *to omou* in his utterance matured after a year in Japan.

Compared to the improvement in appropriate use of *to omou* by Peter and Sam, Henry improved his use of the copula *da* before *to omou*. Among the 11 tokens of Henry's *to omou* in the pre-departure OPI, five of them were preceded by a noun phrase such as *mati* ('town') or *zyuu-nin gurai* ('about ten people'). He never used the copula *da* between a noun phrase and *to omou* in these five tokens (e.g. '...*mati to omou*' ('I think it is a town ...')). In his post-study-abroad OPI, however, such omission of the copula was observed in three out of ten tokens, and he appropriately used the copula *da* before *to omou* in seven out of ten tokens as in '...*onazi da to omou*' ('I think it is the same...'). In other words, Henry's use of *to omou* in combination with noun–copula predicate became more target-like than it was a year previously.

While Alan's use of *to omou* drastically increased from 9 to 20 times, it is also true that his usage after a year in Japan is not as appropriate as it was prior to the study abroad. Alan's use of *to omou* after a year of studying in Japan included adding *to omou* to a complete sentence or a fragmented predicate. This is similar to Peter's usage seen in Excerpt 3.

Excerpt 4 presents the case where Alan adds '*To omoimasu*' ('I think') after he has completed his sentence, '... *narimasita*' ('I became...'):

Excerpt 4 [Alan-Post-T70]
Alan: (...) *Ano::, zannen desu kedo, boku wa tabun, ano::,*
            hoka no koto yori mo tyotto meewaku ni <u>narimasita</u>,
            to omoimasu.

[English]
Alan: (...) Uhm, I feel bad but I probably
            became a nuisance more than others,
            <u>I think.</u>

Adding *to omou* as an afterthought was observed only once in his pre-study-abroad OPI. One possible explanation for his increased use of *to omou* as an afterthought may be an increased exposure to casual speech in Japan. As indicated in features of spoken language (Chafe and Danielewicz 1987), casual speech is filled with fragmented utterances such as those that end with a nominal (omitting the copula *da*), which are followed by additional elements such as *to omoimasu* and *tte (iu) kanzi desu* ('It's the feeling like'). Thus, Alan's seemingly ungrammatical use of *to omou* may be considered as part of the learning process where he is trying out some features typical of spoken language that are different from grammatical sentences often found in textbooks. Another explanation may be that similar to Peter's use of *to omou* as if an afterthought, Alan's addition of *to omou* indicates an interlanguage stage where a learner is in the process of integrating the modal element in rendering L2 production.

The close examination of the use of *to omou* has demonstrated that accuracy, appropriateness and integration of *to omou* into one full sentence improved among three students. The frequent use of *to omou* among Japanese native speakers may have provided abundant input facilitating improved use of *to omou*.

9.4.2.2   Kedo

As was mentioned earlier, while the two Intermediate speakers increased the use of *kedo*, two of the three Advanced speakers' use of *kedo* decreased drastically. However, a qualitative analysis of their use reveals that accuracy in use improved and a variety of functions expanded. We begin our analysis of *kedo* with Henry, whose performances show that the functions expressed by *kedo* in his post-study-abroad OPI became more diverse, even though his OPI (IM) rating remained the same. He used *kedo* four times in the pre-study-abroad OPI and 19 times after a year in Japan. All four instances of *kedo* in the pre-study-abroad OPI were used to connect two predicates to express a contrasting relation. For example, commenting on how many members belong to his extracurricular group, Henry said, '... *takusan hito zya nai to omou kedo taisetu na hito da kara ...*' ('... I think that that is not many people, but they are important people, so ...') [Henry-Pre-T50]. In his post-study-abroad OPI, the function of *kedo* expanded to include the use of *kedo* to indicate reservation/qualification at the end of a sentence (i.e. quasi-sentence-final particle), as shown in Excerpt 5, and *kedo* as a discourse marker. In Excerpt 5, Henry responds to the interviewee's question about whether he preferred more frequent train service:

Excerpt 5   [Henry-Post-T156]
Henry: *U::n, anmari <u>omoimasen kedo</u>.*

[English]

Henry: U::n, I <u>don't think</u> so that much, but.

Henry's answer in this excerpt is negative, '... *omoimasen*' ('I don't think so'), followed by '*kedo*' ('but'). This *kedo* eases the impact of the negative statement. Henry successfully tones down the negative impact of his disagreement on the listener. *Kedo* in this type of use expresses the speaker's intention as to how the message should be conveyed (Uchida 2001). There was also a case in which Henry used *kedo* as a discourse marker to insert background information at a mid-point while talking about his past experience.

Greg's use of *kedo* also shows notable development after a year in Japan. Before going to Japan, his use of *kedo* was mainly for adversative purposes as shown in Excerpt 6:

Excerpt 6   [Greg-Pre-T28]
Interviewer: *Ano unten-suru no wa suki desu ka.*
Greg: *A::, n::, a::n, tikaku, a::, unten-suru no ga <u>suki desu kedo</u>, a::, otoku[10], an, unten-suru a::, no ga kirai desu.*

[English]

Interviewer: Uhm, do you like driving?
Greg: A::, n::, a::n, I like driving nearby <u>but</u> a::, I hate driving far away.

In Excerpt 6, the predicates are connected with *kedo* to highlight an adversative relation between two contradictory propositions: *suki* ('like') and *kirai* ('hate').

After the study abroad, Greg also used *kedo* to mark his attitude towards a proposition he was about to present and his remark about his linguistic ability. In Excerpt 7, Greg was asked if there were any differences between his host family in Japan and his own family. He started by saying that it was difficult to explain the differences (or lack thereof), which he marked by *kedo*. This *kedo* indicates that the preceding clause is a preliminary part of his response and the main point is to follow:

Excerpt 7 [Greg-Post-T52]
Greg: N::, *etto::*, <u>*setumee .. si-nikui*</u>, *kedo, etto,*
           watasi no hosuto famirii to, eto::, watasi no honto no kazoku,
           wa, mattaku onazi da to omou.

[English]

Greg: N::, well, <u>it's hard to explain</u>, but well,
           my host family and uhm my real family are exactly the
           same, I think.

Excerpt 8 is a segment from Greg's narrative about the trouble of picking up a package in Japan. He uses *kedo* when he adds his evaluative comment to the fact that he explained the situation all in Japanese. According to Labov (1972), an evaluative comment is not a required element in a story as it is not part of the event that actually occurred, but it is added once the protagonist gets out of the situation and is able to reflect upon what happened. Nakayama and Ichihashi-Nakayama (1997: 612) report on the multiple functions of *kedo*, stating that *kedo* in narratives functions to convey background information that is 'not directly incorporated into the sequence of main events'.

Excerpt 8   [Greg-Post-T92]
Interviewer: *Zenbu nihongo de?*
Greg: *Un, zenbu, zenbu nihongo de.* <u>*Honto ni muzukasikatta*</u>
               <u>*kedo.*</u>
               Eto::, na-, nan-kai mo moo haratta to iu, eto, syutyoo,
               <u>*o itta.*</u>
               N::, sono tenin[11] *wa, eto, tabun tabun,*
               katyoo ni denwa-site, etto::, watasi no nimotu o kureta.

[English]

Interviewer:	All in Japanese?
Greg:	Yeah, all, all in Japanese. <u>It was really difficult though.</u>
	Uhm, many times I made the claim that I had already paid,
	Uhm, the sales person, probably, probably,
	called the boss, uhm, and s/he gave me my luggage.

Greg responded to the interviewer's surprised enquiry about speaking all in Japanese first with *'Un, zenbu, zenbu nihongo de. <u>Honto ni muzukasikatta kedo'</u>* ('Yeah, all, all in Japanese. <u>It was really difficult though'</u>), and then continued to explain what happened. *Kedo* marks an insertion of Greg's evaluative comment.

In Alan's case, the frequency of *kedo* decreased from 15.2 to 3.2 per cent after a year in Japan. Before study abroad, although Alan did use qualifying *kedo*, contrastive use was also frequent. Ineffective use of *kedo* was frequently observed, as in Excerpt 9:

Excerpt 9	[Alan-Pre-T14]
Interviewer:	*Mainaa tte iu ka, moo hitotu benkyoo-site iru koto ga aru n desu ka.*
Alan:	*Ano, a::, ima wa ano, kono nihongo no kurasu ato de, a::, nihongo no mainaa ga ima, aru to omoimasu, <u>kedo</u>, ano::, ima,*
	ano, a::, suugakuno no meezyaa mo su, suugaku no se senkoo mo,
	a::, a::, suru:: to omoimasita <u>kedo</u>, ima wa, moo su, a::, moo suugaku o senkoo-suru ka wakarimasen.

[English]

Interviewer:	Do you have a minor or rather one more thing that you are studying?
Alan:	Uhm, uh, now after this Japanese class, uh,
	I think I have a Japanese minor, <u>but</u>, uhm, now,
	uhm, uh, I thought I was going to major in
	math major, math major too, <u>but</u>, now, I no longer, uh,
	know if I would major in math.

In this excerpt, the first *kedo* after mentioning the Japanese minor guides the hearer to expect something contrastive in the following sentences.

For example, *suugaku* ('mathematics') is actually Alan's minor or major instead of Japanese or he is changing his mind about getting a Japanese minor. Contrary to this expectation, however, he does not come back to the topic of a Japanese minor.[12] Instead, he uses another *kedo* to contrast the fact that he was going to major in mathematics and the current status that he was having second thoughts about the mathematics major. Thus, the first *kedo* erroneously sets up an expectation of the direction in which Alan's discourse will unfold. The inappropriate use of the first *kedo* obscures the entire message.

While qualifying *kedo* and contrastive *kedo* were observed in Alan's pre-departure OPI, the use of *kedo* as a discourse marker increased in his post-study-abroad OPI. Alan prefaced a story he was about to tell with *kedo* by saying, '*Kore wa omosiroi hanasi desu kedo*' ('This is an interesting story, but …') as if it were an abstract that contained the point of the story (Labov 1972). Although the proportion of *kedo* in Alan's post-study-abroad OPI drastically decreased, his use became more effective.

Unlike Henry, Greg and Alan discussed above, Sam used *kedo* in various functions even before he departed for study in Japan. In his post-study-abroad OPI, he used *kedo* to acknowledge an opposing view before stating his own opinion and to provide an evaluative comment. Excerpt 10 exemplifies the use of *kedo* to indicate acknowledgement of an opposing opinion:

Excerpt 10   [Sam-Post-T75]

[The interviewer asked which system is better: life-long employment or ability-based employment.]

Sam: (…) *Sono hito no nooryoku, e::, o zyuusi-suru hoo ni katamuite iru to omoimasu.*

Interviewer: *A::, soo desu ka.*

Sam: *Hai. De mo, sono nihon no, e::to, huruku, kara no, e::to, nooryoku to ka, e::to onazi kaisya de, a::, hataraku koto mo, sono, e::, syuukan wa, a:: hontoo ni, un sonkee suru beki koto da to omoimasu.*
                 Ho, sore wa hontoo ni ii koto da to wa omou n desu kedo, kono amerika no, e to, sono hito no, kozin no sainoo o zyuusi-suru syuukan ni narete masu no de, yappari, sore wa motto . . boku, motto mizika na koto desu.

[English]

Sam: (…) I am leaning toward the system that values individual ability, I think.
Interviewer: Is that so.
Sam: Yes. But I think the Japanese traditional custom to work at the same company is something that we should really respect.
              I really think that it's a good thing, but
              I am used to this American custom that values individual talents, so as you'd expect, it is more…a familiar thing for me.

In the beginning, Sam states that the Japanese employment system deserves respect. Then, he acknowledges the value of the system and adds *kedo*, which turns the direction of his discussion towards ability-based employment. *Kedo* signals that what follows is his opinion. This use of *kedo* is reminiscent of *kedo* as a self-qualification in an opinion–negotiation sequence in Mori (1999). This type of *kedo* to acknowledge an opposing view when stating an opinion has been found to be characteristic among Superior speakers in Watanabe's study (2003).

Although the quantitative changes in the use of *kedo* differed among individual students before and after study abroad, the qualitative analyses of its use show increased diversification in its functions among all five students, enabling them to be effective in discourse formation. Before study abroad, *kedo* was used predominantly to indicate an adversative relation and/or contrast between two predicates. A number of instances as an insertion to indicate qualification for the following proposition were observed in some learners. After the study abroad, the use of *kedo* expanded to include preliminary remarks, insertions and quasi-sentence-final particles. *Kedo*, when used as an insertion or a preliminary remark, functioned as a discourse marker to indicate discourse organization and a change in the speaker's stance when talking about past experiences. *Kedo* also marked a proposition with a hedge in the predicate-final position to soften the impact of a statement.[13]

The ACTFL Proficiency Guidelines (Breiner-Sanders et al. 2000), on which OPI is based, assume that as a level advances, text type – that is, a unit of discourse – gets expanded (see Table 9.1). In order to perform at the upper-range levels, learners are expected to be equipped with discourse management strategies. The evolving functions of *kedo* as a discourse marker play an important role in the development of text type.

9.5 Summary and conclusion

9.5.1 Summary

In this chapter, the development of modal expressions after a year of study in Japan was examined using the speech samples obtained through OPI administered to five Japanese learners. The quantitative analysis showed that the kind of modality that increased after a year in Japan differed depending on (the proficiency level of) the learner. The qualitative analysis of the uses of *kedo* and *to omou* revealed that accuracy and appropriateness improved in the use of *to omou* and that the variety of functions of *kedo* expanded.

The two Intermediate speakers, Greg and Henry, showed increases in use of epistemic modal expressions. Among the three Advanced speakers, Alan and Peter increased their use of sentence-final particles and Sam and Peter their use of *n desu*. Moreover, the Advanced speakers, despite their decreased use of *kedo*, showed a diverse and more accurate use of *kedo*. These results indicate that depending on the proficiency level of the learner, the type of L2 modality that develops during the study abroad is different. On the one hand, the increase in the use of epistemic modal expressions among the Intermediate speakers indicates that their level of awareness about the proposition becomes higher. On the other hand, the fact that Advanced speakers made progress in their use of *n desu* and sentence-final particles indicates that they developed linguistic elements that are concerned with interaction – the kinds of modality that convey the speaker's concern as to what is shared and how the message is communicated with the interlocutor.

9.5.2 Conclusion

We acknowledge that there are limitations to this study. For instance, the amount of time spent and the number of times each participant was given opportunities to describe, narrate and explain differed depending on their proficiency level. Because the type of function (narrative and instruction) may affect the type of modality (Dittmar and Terborg 1991), a more controlled study with equal opportunities to perform the same functions is desirable. Moreover, as the learning environment is likely to differentially affect acquisition, a more fine-grained analysis of contact situations is likely to shed more light on the dynamics of the acquisition process.

Nonetheless, the speech elicited by OPI is natural and spontaneous, and is more similar to conversation than the speech elicited in a controlled format such as a Discourse Completion Task, which is a typical data collection approach in L2 pragmatics research. Although tasks required for each proficiency level were somewhat different, the modal expressions examined in this study are not restricted to certain task types as demonstrated in the qualitative analyses. For example, expressions that Advanced speakers used more often, namely sentence-final particles and *n desu*, can be used in any tasks in the interview. Furthermore, a qualitative analysis was found useful and essential in the investigation of the development of pragmatic competence as the evaluation of pragmatic appropriateness involves how and in what context language is used.

In this study, we adopted a broad definition of modality that includes epistemic, discoursal and interactional modality. From the pedagogical point of view, this broader conceptualization of modality is more beneficial because language learners are expected to attain communicative competence that enables them to convey their intended meaning in a way that is deemed appropriate to the target speech community. Moreover, as a discourse unit expands, language learners need to organize discourse in a cohesive and coherent manner. Narrowly defined modality (as in English verb auxiliaries) consisting of a limited set of forms that operate at a sentential level is less useful in exploring L2 development of modality. As the results of this study suggest, as the proficiency level as measured by OPI advances, the development of modality appears to shift from the modality concerning proposition to the modality concerning discourse and interaction. The broadly defined notion of modality adopted here enables researchers to follow the development of L2 pragmatic competence, as evidenced by more frequent and/or sophisticated appropriate use of modal expressions. Further research is called for to explore what linguistic resources are used by native speakers in expressing plans for discourse organization and attitudes towards interaction as well as how they are used in natural settings.

Notes

1. We are grateful to the editors of this volume, Barbara Pizziconi and Mika Kizu, who provided editorial assistance and valuable comments on our manuscript. We would also like to thank Patricia Wetzel and Tammy Gales, who helped edit earlier and recent drafts of this chapter. However, all remaining errors are ours.

2. In order to avoid confusion with discourse modality proposed by Maynard (1993), we use 'discoursal modality' to refer to *kedo* and *n desu* as discussed in section 9.2.1.
3. In this study, Jorden and Noda's (1987) romanization (similar to Kunrei-shiki) and conventions as to word division and hyphenation have been adopted.
4. For historical development of modality, see also Moriya and Horie's chapter in this volume.
5. According to Barron (2003), Irish English speakers tend to repeat an offer a few times even after an initial declining, while German speakers tend to stop offering after the first declining. Thus, the fewer the number of offers performed by Irish English-speaking learners of German, the closer they get to a German native speaker's model.
6. At the Novice High to Advanced Mid levels, a tester is required to give a role play in order to elicit a speech sample that cannot be elicited in the interview mode (Swender et al. 1999). Performance of certain speech acts may occur in a role-play phase, but dialogic interaction takes place for most of the time during an OPI.
7. Although it would be ideal to compare L2 learners' proportions with those of native speakers, such data were not available.
8. In terms of the appropriateness of the use of *n desu* and sentence-final particles, we did not conduct close examination for this study. Overall, there were no serious errors in the usage of *n desu* and sentence-final particles, except for Alan's use of the *masu* form before *ka naa*.
9. The information in the square brackets denotes the student's first name (pseudonym), whether the OPI was conducted before or after the study abroad, and in which turn an utterance appears in the data set. The transcript conventions are as follows:

:	Lengthening of a vowel or *n*
-	When followed by a space abrupt cutting off of sound
?	Rising intonation
,	Break in rhythm
..	Noticeable pause
(…)	Preceding sequence within a turn has been omitted
___	Highlight of the analysis

10. The mispronounced word *otoku* is interpreted as *tooku*, which means 'far'.
11. Although Greg mispronounced the word as /te-ni-n/, we have interpreted it as /teN-in/ meaning 'salesperson'.
12. It is possible that the sequence shows that Alan changed his course of exposition after the first *kedo*. However, as far as the recorded speech data are concerned, there were no linguistic elements such as discourse markers (e.g. 'A (Oh)') or a noticeable pause that indicate such a change.
13. In this study, *kedo* as a topic raiser (e.g. '*Kaigi desu kedo, ikimasu ka?*' ('It's about the meeting, but are you going?')) was not observed. It may be due to the nature of the interaction in OPI, where the learners responded to the interviewer's questions most of the time as the interviewer initiated new topics.

References

Bardovi-Harlig, K. and Z. Dornyei (1998). Do language learners recognize pragmatic violations? Pragmatic versus grammatical awareness in instructed learning. *TESOL Quarterly* 32(2), 233–62.

Barron, A. (2003). *Acquisition in Interlanguage Pragmatics: Learning How to do Things with Words in a Study Abroad Context*. Amsterdam: John Benjamins.

Breiner-Sanders, K., P. Lowe, Jr, J. Miles and E. Swender (2000). ACTFL Proficiency Guidelines – speaking, revised. *Foreign Language Annals* 33(1), 13–18.

Chafe, W. and J. Danielewicz (1987). Properties of spoken and written language. In: Horowitz, R. and Samuels, S. J. (eds), *Comprehending Oral and Written Language*. New York: Academic Press: 83–113.

Dewey, D. P. (2005). Maximizing learning during study abroad: some research-based programmatic suggestions. *Study Abroad: Rethinking our Whys and Hows. Occasional Papers, Association of Teachers of Japanese*, 7, 3–11.

Dittmar, N. and H. Terborg (1991). Modality and second language learning: a challenge for linguistic theory. In: Huebner, T. and Ferguson, C. A. (eds), *Cross-Currents in Second Language Acquisition and Linguistic Theories*. Amsterdam: John Benjamins: 347–84.

Freed, B. F. (1995). *Second Language Acquisition in a Study Abroad Context*. Amsterdam: John Benjamins.

Halliday, M.A.K. (1970). Functional diversity in language as seen from a consideration of modality and mood in English. *Foundations of Language* 6, 322–61.

Huebner, T. (1995). The effects of overseas language programs: report on a case study of an intensive Japanese course. In: Freed, B. F. (ed.), *Second Language Acquisition in a Study Abroad Context*. Amsterdam: John Benjamins: 171–93.

Iwasaki, N. (2005). A year abroad in Japan: participants' perspectives. *Study Abroad: Rethinking our Whys and Hows. Occasional Papers, Association of Teachers of Japanese*, 7, 12–23.

Iwasaki, N. (2007). Assessing progress towards the advanced level Japanese after a year abroad: focus on individual participants. *Japanese Language and Literature* 41(2), 271–96.

Iwasaki, N. (In press). Style shifts among Japanese learners before and after study abroad in Japan: becoming active social agents in Japanese. *Applied Linguistics*.

Jorden, E. H. and M. Noda (1987). *Japanese: the Spoken Language, Part 1*. New Haven, Conn.: Yale University Press.

Kärkkäinen, E. (1992). Modality as a strategy in interaction: epistemic modality in the language of native and non-native speakers of English. In: Bouton, L.F. and Kachru, Y. (eds), *Pragmatics and Language Learning* (Monograph Series 3). Urbana, Ill.: University of Illinois at Urbana-Champaign, Division of English as an International Language: 197–216.

Kasper, G. (1998). Interlanguage pragmatics. In: Byrnes, H. (ed.), *Learning Foreign and Second Languages: Perspectives in Research and Scholarship* (Teaching Languages, Literatures, and Cultures 1). New York: Modern Language Association: 183–208.

Kasper, G. and S. Blum-Kulka (1993). *Interlanguage Pragmatics*. New York: Oxford University Press.

Kurotaki, M. (2002). Chuukan gengo to shite no Epistemic Modality ni kansuru ichi koosatsu: Bunpooka no hookoosei to shuutoku junjo to no kakawari kara [A Study of Epistemic Modality as Interlanguage: Direction of Gammaticalization and Acquisition Order]. *Eigo Hyoogen Kenkyuu* 19, 37–49.

Kurotaki, M. (2005). *Deontic kara epistemic e no huhensei to sootaisei: Modariti no nitiei-taisyo kenkyuu* [Universality and Relativity of the Developmental Order from Deontic to Epistemic: a Comparative Study of English and Japanese Modality]. Tokyo: Kurosio.

Labov, W. (1972). *Language in the Inner City*. Philadelphia, Pa: University of Pennsylvania Press.

Marriott, H. (1995). The acquisition of politeness patterns by exchange students in Japan. In: Freed, B. F. (ed.), *Second Language Acquisition in a Study Abroad Context*. Amsterdam: John Benjamins: 197–224.

Masuoka, T. (1991). *Grammar of Modality*. Tokyo: Kurosio.

Maynard, S. (1993). *Discourse Modality: Subjectivity, Emotion and Voice in the Japanese Language*. Amsterdam: John Benjamins.

Maynard, S. (1997). *Japanese Communication: Language and Thought in Context*. Honolulu, Hawaii: University of Hawaii Press.

Maynard, S. (2005). *Expressive Japanese: a Reference Guide to Sharing Emotion and Empathy*. Honolulu, Hawaii: University of Hawaii Press.

Miyazaki, K., T. Adachi, H. Noda and S. Takanashi (2002). *Modaliti*. Tokyo: Kurosio.

Mori, J. (1999). Well I may be exaggerating but ...: self-qualifying clauses in negotiation of opinions among Japanese speakers. *Human Studies 22*, 447–73.

Nagata, R. and R. Ohama (2001). The relationships among uses of the Japanese conjunction *kedo*. *Nihongo Kyoiku* 110, 62–71.

Nakau, M. (1994). *Ninchi imiron no genri* [Principles of Cognitive Semantics]. Tokyo: Taishukan.

Nakayama, T. and K. Ichihashi-Nakayama (1997). Japanese *kedo*: discourse genre and grammaticization. In: Sohn, H. and Haig, J. (eds), *Japanese/Korean Linguistics*, vol. 6. Stanford, Calif.: CSLI Publications: 607–18.

Nihongo Kizyutu Bunpō Kenkyūkai (2003). *Gendai Nihongo Bunpoo 4, No. 8 Modality*. Tokyo: Kurosio.

Nitta, Y. (1989). Gendai nihongobun no modariti no taikei to koozoo. In: Nitta, Y. and Masuoka, T. (eds), *Nihongo no modariti* [Modality in Japanese]. Tokyo: Kurosio: 1–56.

Ono, M. (2001). The communicative function of *to omou*. *Nihongo Kyoiku*, 110, 22–31.

Oshima, Y. (1993). Chuugokugo/kankokugo-wasya ni okeru nihongono modariti shuutoku ni kansuru kenkyuu [Acquisition of Japanese Modality by Chinese and Korean Learners]. *Nihongo Kyoiku*, 81, 93–103.

Salsbury, T. and K. Bardovi-Harlig (2000). Oppositional talk and the acquisition of modality in L2 English. In: Swierzbin, B., Morris, F., Anderson, M.E., Klee, C. A. and Tarone, E. (eds), *Social and Cognitive Factors in Second Language Acquisition, Selected Proceedings of the 1999 Second Language Research Forum (SLRF)*. Somerville, Mass.: Cascadilla Press: 57–76.

Sawyer, M. (1992). The development of pragmatics in Japanese as a second language: the sentence-final particle *ne*. In: Kasper, G. (ed.), *Pragmatics of Japanese: a Native and Target Language*. Honolulu, Hawaii: University of Hawaii Press: 83–125.

Siegal, M. (1995). Individual differences and study abroad: women learning Japanese in Japan. In: Freed, B. F. (ed.), *Second Language Acquisition in a Study Abroad Context*. Amsterdam: John Benjamins: 225–44.

Siegal, M. (1996). The role of learner subjectivity in second language sociolinguistic competency: Western women learning Japanese. *Applied Linguistics* 17(3), 356–82.

Swender, E., K. E. Breiner-Sanders, L. M. Laughlin, P. Lowe, Jr and J. Miles (1999). *ACTFL Oral Proficiency Interview Tester Training Manual*. New York: ACTFL Inc.

Tokieda, M. (1941). *Kokugogaku genron* [The Principles of Japanese Linguistics]. Tokyo: Iwanami.

Uchida, A. (2001). A study on sentences ending with *-kedo*: the relation between their characteristics and discourse function. *Nihongo Kyoiku* 109, 40–9.

Watanabe, S. (2003). Cohesion and coherence strategies in paragraph and extended discourse in Japanese Oral Proficiency Interview. *Foreign Language Annals* 33(4), 555–65.

Yoshimi, D. R. (1999). L1 language socialization as a variable in the use of *ne* by L2 learners of Japanese. *Journal of Pragmatics* 31, 1513–25.

10
The Interactional Consequences of Epistemic Indexicality – Some Thoughts on the Epistemic Marker -*kamoshirenai*

Barbara Pizziconi

10.1 Introduction[1]

While the grammatical and semantic dimensions of modality have been studied extensively, only a few works have explored its role in actual communication and in social interactions. The amount of research from this perspective has been scarce in comparison to other approaches to modality and even scarcer in the field of Japanese modality. This chapter reviews and summarizes some important works carried out in disciplinary perspectives with an interest in discursive, functional and interactional aspects of language use, and tries to illustrate their arguments through Japanese data. The limited scope of this chapter aims mostly at testing our current understanding of the meaning and function of Japanese modal markers against actual instances of use, and at exploring the potential of qualitative analyses of conversation. The rather cursory discussion I present here is mainly a call for more extensive inquiry into the discursive functions of Japanese modal markers, in socially embedded contexts of use. Three decades ago van Dijk (1981: 132) noted the profitless disciplinary segregation of cognitive psychology (which deals with knowledge and belief) and social psychology (which deals with opinions and attitudes). Indeed, with a few exceptions, the study of attitudes in the field of modality has addressed mostly the 'psychological' but not the 'social'. Much more work is to be done regarding how the use of modal markers is constrained by sociocultural norms and practices.

While it is probably easy to recognize the interactional or social effects of the so-called 'deontic' modality, because of the fairly obvious relevance of notions of obligation and permission to issues of authority as well as morality (Saeed 2003: 137), it is less easy to do so in the case of epistemics (cf. Palmer's definition of deontic modality as concerned with 'language as action', epistemic modality with 'language as information', 1986: 121). Nevertheless, the need to do so has been recognized in various pragmatic and cognitive studies,[2] as well as in the lifelong work of Akio Kamio that I will refer to below. This chapter pursues this point further, and uses the analysis of an actual conversational encounter to explore the ways in which claims about knowledge enact social positioning.

In the following section (10.2) I illustrate the theoretical apparatus (my characterization of modality and some related key concepts), which underlies the analysis of the epistemic marker -*kamoshirenai* in a discursive encounter, carried out in section 10.3. Sections 10.4 and 10.5 summarize my findings and sketch out some implications for future research.

10.2   Characterizing modality in this study

The very definition of modality is a contentious issue that reflects differences in disciplinary horizons and interests. In order to focus on the insights and achievements of interactional approaches, I shall only very briefly state the reasons for my own allegiance and refer the reader to Narrog (2005a, this volume) for a comprehensive review of definitions and conceptualizations of (Japanese) modality.

I concur with a semanticist position that defines modality in terms of 'factuality'. As Narrog (2005a) eloquently argued, this perspective provides a more rigorous definition, compared to definitions based on language-specific syntactic categories (which preclude cross-linguistic generalizations) and definitions based uniquely on the 'subjectivity' feature (which is fuzzy and ultimately undiscriminating). Indeed, 'subjectivity' does not discriminate much – some researchers point out that it is hard to find anything in language that does not exhibit some sort of subjective positioning (Stubbs 1986: 1, Traugott and Dasher 2002: 20). A semantic definition based on factuality allows us to demarcate modality more accurately (and distinguish it from, for example, illocutionary force or honorifics), but subjectivity is a property that pertains to it nevertheless, as I will argue below. Thus for the moment, I shall define the object of this study, epistemic markers, as grammaticalized devices *typically interpreted as indicative of the speaker's attitude or stance, at the time of utterance, towards the factuality of the proposition.* A few qualifications are in order here.

While the notion of 'factuality' refers to the semantic trait that defines and delimits this domain, other terms in the definition offered above refer to the properties of a deictic system. A deictic expression 'makes variables of utterance denotation dependent on variables of interaction' (Agha 2007: 40). In other words, an epistemic marker makes utterance denotation (for example, that the speaker is making a guess and not a statement) dependent on the (non-)factual status of the information in the context of utterance.[3] The phrase 'typically interpreted' in the definition of epistemic markers above refers to the fact that although epistemic markers may exhibit a typical, 'default' interpretation, they may yield variable interpretations under different contextual conditions.[4] The 'speaker's attitude or stance' refers to the speaker's interactional positioning achieved through the indexing of information as more or less 'factual'. The use of the two terms 'attitude' and 'stance' as synonyms here is due to the preference of one or the other in different disciplinary traditions: while most works on modality use the term 'attitude', many recent studies on subjectivity use the term 'stance'. In my view, for the purpose of a definition of modality, the two notions are very much interchangeable, but I prefer 'stance' for its denoting also physical, embodied acts of positioning, a denotation that the more mentalistic term 'attitude' does not allow. In the 'constructivist' conceptualization of modality such as the one I wish to pursue here, the act of 'stance-taking' is not a speaker's passive reflection of an (objective) state of affairs regarding information or knowledge, but a subjective, active and dialogic (Maynard 1993, Du Bois 2007, Kärkkäinen 2006) act of orientation towards, and constitutive of, social reality.

In the following sections I present some key theoretical issues and terminology that will clarify the premises upon which the subsequent discussion of empirical data rests: my conceptualization of attitude/stance (10.2.1), the notion of 'truth' vis-à-vis 'subjective certainty' (10.2.2) and finally the notion of 'epistemic indexicality' (10.2.3).

10.2.1 The speaker's attitude/stance

In spite of the popularity of Lyons' definition of modality as the speaker's 'opinion or attitude towards the proposition that the sentence expresses, or the situation that the proposition describes' (Lyons 1977: 45, Nitta 1989, 2000, Masuoka 1991), even a minimal definition of what such subjective 'attitude' amounts to is rather hard to find in the literature on modality. Maynard, the proponent of a broad, discursive conceptualization of modality, qualifies it slightly more in detail when she defines it as 'the speaker's *subjective emotional, mental or psychological* attitude towards the message content, the speech act itself or towards his or her interlocutor in discourse' (1993: 38, emphasis added). Notable in this definition is the notion of 'attitude' as a cognitive, but importantly also affective, kind of 'posture' or 'stance'. Although not fully perceivable in this definition, Maynard's gaze, in this and later studies, focuses on social actors rather than utterance-producers (cf. 1993: 8ff., 26ff.),[5] a perspective also rather prominent in the construct of 'stance', that can be found in studies on subjectivity.[6]

Kärkkäinen (2003, 2006) uses the term 'stance' to refer to an interactional *practice*, rather than an isolated mental *state* of the speaker, and as an *emergent* property of dialogic interaction. To state that stance is a phenomenon sensitive to interactional factors is not merely a matter of capturing pragmatic effects of the use of this or that modal marker, but observing that its articulation is the outcome of joint activities, it involves the recipients' co-participation, and is responsive to aspects of interaction such as recipient design, or turn completion (Kärkkäinen 2006: 718). This conceptualization of stance entails that any indexical act revealing the speaker's orientation towards a proposition involves the speaker's revealing his/her orientation towards other event participants (other stance-takers) as well; consequently, even the expression of an attitude/stance towards the factuality of the proposition (as a form of evaluation) is assumed to have interactional consequences. In this sense, 'subjectivity', or the speaker's subjective orientation to information, is no more than a device exploited to create interactional (mis)alignments, hence fundamentally *inter*subjective in its functional motivation (cf. Kärkkäinen 2006: 723, Traugott and Dasher 2002: 19).

Du Bois defines stance as 'an act of evaluation owned by a social actor' (2007: 173); not just the private opinions people have, but something people do. Stance is realized through a coordinated orientation of two subjects, co-participants in a communicative event, to a common object (hence the reference to a 'stance triangle'), and therefore it is said to exhibit a dialogic structure. As participants jointly orient to an object, they consequently also adjust their orientation to each other. Moreover, stance 'has the power to assign value to objects of interest, to position social actors with respect to those objects, to calibrate alignment between stancetakers, and to invoke presupposed systems of sociocultural value' (2007: 139). The existence of modality systems demonstrates the noteworthiness not only of information, but also of how information is derived, the nature and legitimacy of the evidential source, the degrees of speakers' confidence about, or commitment towards it (Stubbs, 1986). Within limits that constrain what is logically or conventionally (including language specifically) 'knowable', speakers routinely qualify such knowledge – hence carry out acts of evaluation – in ways that partially involve assessments of appropriateness, as well as self-presentation: 'we adjust stance use for context and audience, and to frame the way others perceive us' (Precht, 2003: 240).

Stance orders phenomena at the structural, affective and social level simultaneously, and therefore all levels of linguistic analysis should be called on in its study.

10.2.2 Truth vs 'subjective certainty'

Many works in an interactionist perspective cite as a seminal theoretical reference Givon's 'revisionist epistemology' (1982: 24). According to this, the notion of 'objective truth' is far less important than the notion of 'subjective certainty';[7] also, the notion of an independently measurable 'speaker's knowledge' is less explanatory than the knowledge that a speaker assumes to be acceptable or challengeable by the hearer. For Givon, the notion of 'certainty' is not just cognitive, but derives from a kind of implicit social contract, whereby taken-for-granted, conventional and widely shared world knowledge and beliefs can achieve the same 'certain' status as objectively experienced events. In this way, propositions that can be accepted by others as taken for granted do not require any specific evidential marking; neither do those that are explicitly asserted with doubt and are to be considered 'beneath challenge'. Only propositions that can be challenged will require some sort of evidential marking.

In this conceptualization, speakers are not so much concerned with the status of the information in terms of their degree of confidence over it (which may justify the distinction between more 'subjective' and more 'objective' types of epistemic uses) but rather with its 'challengeability' by other participants to the interaction. By extension, we can assume that speakers will also be concerned with issues of authority (Fox 2001), and the associated notions of responsibility (e.g. the *obligation* to mark factuality) and entitlements (e.g. the *right* to do so)[8] (see section 10.2.3).

Widening the spotlight to include the hearer in the speaker's assessments of the information is a crucial development not exclusive to full-fledged interactionist perspectives: Takubo's (1990) and Takubo and

Kinsui's (1997) Theory of Discourse Management (*Danwa Kanri Riron*) argues that an S's linguistic behaviour in discourse mirrors his/her monitoring of the different 'mental spaces', or areas of direct/indirect experience in speakers' and hearers' memory, to which information potentially belongs. The work of Akio Kamio from the late 1970s onwards (cf. 1990, 1994, 2002[9]), the Territory of Information Theory (*Johoo Nawabari Riron*) similarly aimed at showing the sensitivity of Japanese grammar to speakers' as well as hearers' 'ownership' of (or entitlements over) information,[10] i.e. whether information is considered to lie within the speaker's own territory, the hearer's, or shared in some common or public territory.[11] Maynard (1993: 193ff.) refers to a concept of 'Relative Information Accessibility and/or Possessorship', which regulates speakers' choices not only on the basis of the location of the information, but its accessibility to or possessorship by a speaker and his/her interlocutors. Building on these theories, Nobuko Trent (1997) claims that modal markers in Japanese are used much more creatively than acknowledged previously, if normative epistemic marking can be systematically manipulated in order to achieve interpersonal and affective effects in actual instances of use. Indeed she finds that the degree of intimacy/formality of a situation affects the use of evidentiality markers (1997: 267–8). This suggests that the very notion of territory is subject to contextual 'measurements', i.e. that what is presented as one's own territory in one context may well be presented as someone else's in another.

In these models a shift is evident from an absolute and subjective, to a relative, dynamic and intersubjective concept of information status. This perspective entails that epistemics (and other modals) cannot be exhaustively described by analyses at the sentence level, because this does not take into account either the speaker's assessment of the hearer's knowledge, or communicative moves that may develop over a stretch of discourse, be it by the speaker or other participants. It presupposes that modal marking is at least partially sensitive to the particular relationship ensuing, at the time of utterance, between participants, which suggests that the very manner in which information is presented will be of some immediate interactional significance. In other words, epistemic markers receive meaning from, and have the potential to reveal something about, the (speaker's assessment of the) social relationships at play at that moment. Characterizations of factuality respond not only to the speaker's evidence for an epistemic judgement, but also to the evaluation of such evidence from the perspective of interaction partners in the situation (Nuyts 2001: 393) and the speaker's assessment of the social appropriateness of any claims to such evidence (e.g. the relative authority of the speaker or the hearer about the information, the social 'acceptability' of certain 'truths', etc.). Hence although the feature of subjectivity does not discriminate modality from other indexical systems (e.g. politeness, or illocutionary force), it must be considered a very constitutive property of modal markers. Based on this interactional conceptualization, the notion of 'subjectivity' needs to be accordingly recharacterized as '*inter*subjectivity'.[12]

10.2.3 Epistemic indexicality and the social value of information

Lyons stated his view of modality as an indexical system very clearly when he wrote: '... modality, as it operates in a good deal of everyday language-behaviour, cannot be understood, or properly analyzed, otherwise than in terms of the indexical and instrumental functions of language, to which its descriptive function is, at times if not always, subordinate' (1977: 849).

When speakers join a conversational encounter, they normally have assumptions about what other participants know about certain topics, people or events, maximally so in the case of intimate interlocutors, minimally so in the case of strangers. More or less in the same way that we make assumptions about people's social standing (which is, for example, a key to estimates of the appropriate politeness register) based on visual, reported or other evidential information about the speaker's identity, we tend to make assumptions about the amount of information people have, are supposed to have, or have the right to have (is s/he a specialist of a certain professional domain, is s/he familiar with the person talked about, etc.), and we expect them to index that appropriately. Lyons (1977: 808) observes: 'It is a general principle, to which we are expected to conform, that we should always make the strongest commitment for which we have epistemic warrant.' This echoes a Gricean conversational principle, but (in spite of Lyons' definite interest in issues of appropriateness rather than epistemic precision), it does not fully account for the social role of knowledge. Kamio addresses this issue when he amends the Gricean maxim of quality ('don't say what you believe to be false', 'don't say that for which you lack adequate evidence') so as to include a notion of 'territory of information': 'in speech, abide by the relation of information to territory' (Kamio 2002: 111). His notion of 'territory' is the cognitive or psychological correlate of a 'space' in human and animal social behaviour (2002: 7), over which individuals feel entitled to have control. In his framework, this is what variably regulates (lingua-culturally specific) constraints on, for example, psychological predicates. Hence knowledge is seen as a metaphorical extension of authority over a physical domain, for which we are, and demand others to be, accountable. This suggests that we could think of information of a private or exclusive nature as a kind of inviolable possession; information that is public as a kind of shared commodity; and information that falls in between these poles as subject to careful assessments of ownership, privileged access or transactional rights. It follows that 'zero evidential marking represents a claim to a greater authority, responsibility and entitlement than does overt evidential marking' (Fox 2001: 170). An entitlement gives speakers authority over the information, and responsibility entails that speakers cannot decline such authority without a good reason.

Several studies embrace these assumptions in their modelling of epistemicity and consider the social instrumentality of epistemic marking (Du Bois 1986, Trent 1997, Fox 2001, Kamio 1990, 2002). Importantly, freeing the analysis of epistemics from sentential constraints and broadening the observation to interactional and social variables is of particular significance in view of language's potential for constituting, rather than merely reflecting, stances, activities, relationships or identities (Ochs 1996). This warrants an analysis of epistemic indexicals as one of multiple resources that speakers deploy in carrying out social positioning.

In the preceding three subsections I argued that any characterization of the speaker's orientation to information is not merely a sign of his/her subjective assessment of the epistemic nature of the information, but an intersubjective act of stance-taking with interactional consequences. This is because information is never socially neutral, knowledge is a socially valued entity, and its display is construed as a display of social power. In the following section I will substantiate these statements by examining the use of the epistemic marker -*kamoshirenai* in a conversational encounter.

10.3   Epistemic markers in conversation

Epistemic indexicality is a way of characterizing the speaker's relationship to information and knowledge, including the speaker's qualification of the probability of some state of affairs, and in Japanese this can typically be done, among other things, through the following markers: -*hazu*, -*ni chigainai*, -*daroo*, -*kamoshirenai*, only the last of which – for reasons of space – will I use as an illustration. Given the considerable amount of scholarly inquiry carried out on these forms, we should be able to provide exhaustive descriptions of their meanings and functions. In reality, this is not yet the case, as we will see below; perhaps the reason is precisely the deictic nature of epistemic (as well as other) modal forms. A property of a deictic system is to 'anchor' specific variables (i.e. time, space, social rank, degree of certainty/commitment to information, etc.) to the time and contextual circumstances of utterance, only in relation to which can they be interpreted. When sentences are removed from the context of utterance, part of their 'meaning' is lost (as Lyons put it: 'deixis sets limits to the possibility of decontextualization', 1977: 646).

Before I present two brief excerpts of group conversations, I will review a few relevant studies in order to compare our current understanding of their meaning, with meanings emerging from situated contexts of use.

10.3.1 The characterization of *-kamoshirenai*

For Teramura (1984: 235) *-kamoshirenai* expresses the low degree of certainty over the legitimacy of the speaker's supposition; for Masuoka (2002: 7) it expresses 'possibility', a type of modality marking the 'qualified judgements' *(teihandan)* that a speaker makes when unable to make an assertion.[13] In his subjectivity-based analysis, Nitta (1991: 61–2) categorizes *-kamoshirenai* as 'pseudo-modality' (but with 'true' modality uses), since as well as the attitudes of the speaker at the time of utterance, it can be used to express a third person's attitudes and tensed utterances. Also, because it can indicate pure guesses on the part of the speaker, as well as speculations based on facts expressed in the external world, it is said to have a hybrid subjective/objective character (1991: 62).[14] Finally, he notes that expressions including *-kamoshirenai* display the tendency to change from mere suppositional expressions to 'euphemistic' or 'mitigating statements' (*enkyokutekina nobetate, dangen wo hikaeta nobetate,* 1991: 102).

In contrast, Johnson (1999), based on semantic/syntactic arguments, describes *-kamoshirenai* as a maximally modal form, i.e. one that indicates the speaker's weakest confidence in the possibility of realization of the proposition.[15] She maintains that the more a proposition indicates an *irrealis* world, the more it needs to be modalized, and then illustrates the distribution of various Japanese modal auxiliaries along a continuum between the notions of 'necessity' (worlds close to reality) and 'possibility' (*irrealis* worlds). In such a curve (excluding from the current discussion the evidential markers *-soo, -rashii, -yoo*) *-kamoshirenai* occupies the highest level of modality, followed by *-daroo, -ni chigainai* and *-hazu* (at increasing levels of 'objective' flavour).

Kawaguchi (2003, 2005) observes how received definitions of *-kamoshirenai* as a marker indicating relatively low probability of occurrence that one finds in traditional sentence-level analyses have recently been revised towards a more 'pragmatic' (and, for her, more accurate) understanding of the meaning of this form. This plays down the meaning of 'judgement of (low) degree of probability', to emphasize instead the meaning of 'possibility that the proposition is true' (Kawaguchi 2003: 58). Kawaguchi concludes that the fundamental meaning of this form should be described as 'an indication of a definite possibility' (2005: 46). Moriyama (2002: 17) notes that this form, 'within a question of possibility or non-possibility that the proposition is true, focuses on its being possible', 'even when that possibility is low'. Nitta too defines it as a form indicating that a possibility (although no more than an uncertain possibility) exists of the proposition's occurrence, but through which, together with the possibility of occurrence, the possibility of non-occurrence is also entertained (Nitta 2000:130).[16] Indeed, the latter is a very important semantic trait[17] whose rhetorical effects are, as we will see, fully exploited in discourse.

The definitions above, although not necessarily incompatible with each other when the different terminological conventions are considered, show the difficulty of defining the meaning and functions of this form with satisfactory precision.[18] To anticipate my point, I take this 'elusiveness' to be precisely what characterizes a deictic marker. *-Kamoshirenai* provides no more than a speaker's qualification of the status of information (e.g. his/her commitment to (non-)factuality), but the functional definitions of 'suspension of judgement', 'mitigating assertions', 'judgement of low probability', etc. can only be evinced from and be disambiguated by its interaction with other co-textual and situational variables.

10.3.2   A case study

I stated before that a property of an epistemic marker is to provide evidence of the speaker's epistemic stance, but that utterance interpretation is crucially dependent on the contextual (and volatile) factors co-present at the time of utterance, among which relative positions of authority between participants come to have a bearing. Based on an intersubjective characterization of markers of factuality, I think that at least the following factors are of particular relevance: the nature of the participants' relationship prior to an encounter (including knowledge of others' knowledge, personal knowledge of each other's rhetorical styles, claimed or attributed identities, etc.), participant goals, and their framing of the encounter (cf. Pizziconi, forthcoming).

The encounter that I describe here involves four participants, the only non-Japanese of whom is the author (an Italian working in London). Yuri is an old friend of the author from university days, slightly younger than the author. She is the connection between the author and the other two participants: Aki, her colleague, and Kyo, their line manager, male and slightly older than the rest of the group. All of them work closely in the same department of a quasi-governmental institution, have spent several years abroad during their studies and/or in a professional capacity, and have a relatively cosmopolitan background. The participants have kindly agreed to help the author's research project (whose real nature – the cultural basis of affective/social evaluations – was not disclosed at the time), by allowing the recording of a dinner conversation. This activity can therefore be characterized as a group discussion, in which participants have been asked to freely express personal views and opinions. As such, we can expect to observe acts of interpretation and evaluation. The author's connection to Yuri is a long-standing (but also mostly long-distance) friendship; the connection to Kyo and Aki is via Yuri's introduction. The conversation is lively and engaging, ranging from linguistic to cultural, general to private topics, in a relatively free-ranging, informal, casual manner.

In what follows, for reasons of space, I will only analyse instances of *-kamoshirenai*, and refer to other forms in footnotes, or *en passant* as they become relevant in the discussion.

Background to Excerpt 1: The group is talking about 'conventionalized hints' in Japanese (i.e. the extent to which the indirect speech act of hinting is recognized as a conventionalized form of request), and commenting on my inability to recognize speakers' intentions in my early years of Japanese language study. I am recalling an episode in which my landlord came to fix a television cable in my flat, and while working on it remarking that the room was very dark. This I initially read merely as a comment on my preference for a small table lamp instead of the customary neon lights fitted in the room, but after several repetitions of the same remark, and a final explicit statement, I realized that from the outset it may have been a hint to request that I provide more lighting. At this point in the interview, we are discussing whether my landlord would have regarded me simply as slow on the uptake, or outright inconsiderate.

EXCERPT 1 (1Aa; 30′06″)[19]

bp 1. *...demo tashika   kurai desu nee   toka nankai   kurikaeshitemo, watashi*
      ...but   certainly   dark COP FP   HED many.times   repeat -CONC   I
   2. *tsuujinakatta   n   desu yo,   ito   ga.*
      understand NEG-PAST NM-   POL FP   INTENTION   SUBJ
      '...but certainly I didn't understand even when he repeated
      "but it's really dark [in here]!" several times...'

Kyo 3. *aa naruhodo naruhodo*
      oh indeed   indeed
      "I see, I see.'

bp 4. *soredemo osoraku juppun-gurai   kocchi bakari no   hanashi o   shite demo*
      CONC   maybe   10 min.about   my   only GEN talk   OBJ do   but
   5. *watashi ga   mienai   to   iwa...@@@..iwanakya ikenaku natte,*
      I   SUBJ see-NEG QUOT say   say.must   become-SUSP
      'Even then I went on and on for about ten minutes talking
      only about myself, and he had to say "but I can't see
      anything"!'

Kyo 6. *naruhodo //naruhodo//*
      indeed   indeed
      'I see, I see.'

bp 7. *//sono toki// ikinari   hirameita n desu kedomo. nanka yappari chotto jibun ga*
      that.time   suddenly   flash   NM POL but   HED   in fact a.little self-SUBJ
   8. *baka da   na to   omotte, isshookenmei nanka itte kudasaru no ni   ano...//*
      silly COP FP QUOT think   very.hard   HED   say BEN   in.spite well
   9. *kocchi wa   tsuujinai //*
      I   TOP understand-NEG
      'And then it hit me, and I thought: "I'm really silly!" He
      goes to all that trouble to tell me, and I don't get it.'

Kyo 10. *//iya sorewa...// nn, demo ma fuhentekina jookyoo da yone. maa, ano nihonjin*
      no that   umm but HES universal situation COP FP HES HES Japanese
   11. *daitai wa   akarui nowa   suki dakara soiu koto   shinai kedo soiu no wa*
      generally-TOP bright NM-TOP like because such things do-NEG but that NM-TOP
   12. *kiga tsukanai tte iu no wa   ariuru...*
      realize-NEG   QUOT-NM-TOP possible-MOD
      'But that...umm, that is a universal situation though. Well,
      Japanese normally prefer well-lit [rooms] so it wouldn't
      happen to them, but that one would not realize [that
      meaning/intention] is still possible.'

Yuri 13. *ato soo, dakara ooyasan mo saisho   kara kansetsutekini iyoo   toka*
      then yes because landlord TOP beginning from indirectly   say-VOL HED
   14. *omotte ita   n   ja nakute, honto ni kanji   toshite kurai naa toiu   no o*
      think-PAST NM NEG-SUSP really   feeling as   dark FP QUOT NM OBJ
   15. *koo   // kuchini dashite iru uchi ni...//*
      like this   speak   while
      'And also, well, [it is not that] the landlord meant it as a
      hint from the beginning, [he just] felt "it's dark in here"...
      and while he was saying this...'

bp 16. *// a soo? demo yappari saigo ni wa // de mo watashi mienai...*
      really but in.fact end at TOP but I   see-NEG
   17. *[to iu kara],   yappari nanka saisho   kara kitai shite irashita n*
      -QUOT say because in fact HED beginning from expect-POL-PAST NM

18. *janai   kana to   // watashi ga omotte //*
    COP-NEG Q-FP QUOT   I   SUBJ think-SUSP
    'Ah, do you think so? But he said "but I can't see [a
    thing]", so I thought that maybe from the outset he was
    expecting me [to get it].'

Yuri 19. *// soo datta   no   kanaa... //*
    that COP-PAST NM   Q-FP
    'I wonder...'

bp 20. *a soo? kanarazushi mo soo janai   to   // omotta   n //*
    really necessarily so COP-NEG QUOT   think-PAST NM
    'Really? You thought it wouldn't necessarily mean this?'

Yuri 21. *//saisho // nanka kurai na to   omotteita   no **kamoshirenai**... //ne... nn.//*
    start   HED dark FP QUOT think-PAST NM MOD   FP   HES
    at the beginning he **may** have thought it was
    dark...//right? ...yes//.

bp 22. *//nn. sore dake// no koto de... de sore o yappari watashi no   zemi no anoo...*
    HES that only NM thing-COP that OBJ in fact I   -GEN seminar-GEN HES

23. *kurasumeeto ni hanashite itara, sore wa   maa gaijin   dakara yuruseru*
    classmates to speak   COND that-TOP HES foreigner-COP because excuse.can

24. *kedo, yappari ano... aruiwa kikokushijo dattara   yuruseru   kedo yappari hutsuu*
    but in.fact HES or   returnees COP-COND excuse.can but in.fact normal

25. *no nihonjin nara... yappari sokode ito   o yonde kureru no o kitai*
    -GEN Japanese COND in.fact there intention OBJ read BEN   -NM-OBJ expect

26. *shite iru... tteiu   hanashi ni natte...*
    QUOT talk   become
    '//I see, only that [meaning]//.... Well, I discussed this
    with the classmates at the seminar, and we started talking
    about the fact that if you are a foreigner, or even perhaps
    a [Japanese] returnee, you would be excused, but if you are
    just a regular Japanese you would be expected to 'read' those
    intentions...'

Kyo 27. *soo, donkan   toka soo iwarechau   **kamoshirenai**.*
    yes insensitive QUOT so tell PASS-COMPL MOD
    'yes, you **may** be thought of as insensitive/unperceptive'

bp 28. *soo... kitto soo omowareta n   dato omoimasu yo*
    so surely so think-PASS-NM QUOT think   FP
    'Yes, I think that's precisely what he thought of me...'

Kyo 29. *nn gaikokujin dattara   soo wa omowanai kedo...*
    HES foreigner COP-COND so-TOP think-NEG but
    'Mhh, I don't think a foreigner would be considered so...'

Based on previous accounts of *-kamoshirenai*, we could say that what
Yuri does in line 21 is merely '*stating* the possibility (and low probability)' that the landlord's intention was not to make a hint. However, if we
look at the discursive genesis of line 21, we see that this line is a conclusive move in a sequence configuring an OBJECTION: she is objecting to
my implicitly self-deprecatory belief that I was slow on the uptake, and
her modalized utterance is one that reiterates the point that the alternative interpretation (i.e. that there was no expectation that I should
understand the hint straightaway), is possible.

I suggested that my response to the landlord's hint had been unperceptive (up to line 5), to which Kyo, in a rather categorical way, responds that even other native speakers may have similarly failed to see the hint as a request (lines 10–12; I will comment on these below). Yuri additionally suggests that the landlord himself may have not meant it as a request in the first place, at least the first time (lines 13–15). When I still express some doubts (lines 16–18), Yuri questions them again indirectly (in line 19), finally reiterating her opinion with the statement containing -*kamoshirenai* in line 21.

Objections can be interactionally sensitive; Yuri's is potentially problematic on the illocutionary level, but effectively supportive on the interactional level.[20] In fact, because she is objecting to a possibly negative belief about myself entertained by me (i.e. that I was being slow-witted), a strong objection would have had a more 'positive' effect, i.e. a more favourable interpretation than a weak one. So we could argue that if her main interactional goal was to display a supportive stance (i.e. to make manifest a 'courteous belief', in the sense of Leech 2007), she could have 'reassured' me more forcefully with another modal, indexing stronger subjective certainty, and so enhancing the sympathetic objection; she could, for example, have said '*I think* he just meant to say it was dark' (with -*to omou* [*yo*]),[21] or something along these lines. In that case however, she would have had to justify her entitlement to a more authoritative statement: as a native speaker of Japanese she is arguably unchallengeable by me (but not the others) regarding linguistic interpretations, but she had never met the landlord and could not claim knowledge of his ordinary rhetorical style, so she was challengeable by me as a personal acquaintance of the landlord. Overstating her confidence in the proposition could have backfired and generated some misalignment (a challenge of the type: 'how do you know that that is the case?'). Indeed it has been argued that Japanese is 'stricter' than English with regards to the S's entitlement to 'objective' statements about other people's psychological states and intentions (Kamio 2002: 67,[22] Shibatani 1990: 383), and this strong cognitive constraint could be seen as setting an upper limit to her ability to assert her opinion with certainty. Thus with -*kamoshirenai* she has arguably produced an optimal solution to the tension created by the multiple, overlapping goals of objecting to my statements but with a minimal amount of face threat, and asserting her opinion without overstating her authority over the information. This shows modalization to be motivated by both interactional and cognitive considerations.

In a discursive context in which the speaker is making an objection and trying to make a point, using -*kamoshirenai* in order to indicate 'low probability of the proposition' would be off the mark. Yuri uses it instead to *assert the very likelihood* of her interpretation, albeit not to the detriment of other interpretations.[23]

Now let us compare this with Kyo's objections to my self-deprecatory statements. In lines 10–12 Kyo expresses his views about Japanese norms and preferences with at least three epistemically unmodalized phrases: '*fuhentekina jookyoo da*', '*nihonjin daitai wa akarui no wa suki da*' and '*soiu koto shinai kedo*', all of which could have been modalized (e.g. '*shinai kamoshirenai/deshoo/hazuda kedo*') in view of the fact that he cannot possibly have an absolute certainty of their truth. Moreover, even the final predicate he chooses borders on the 'objective' end of the epistemic scale: *ariuru* ('it is possible', in which -*uru* is a lexicalized epistemic verbal morpheme).[24] Altogether, unlike Yuri's earlier objection, Kyo's statement that I may be wrong (effectively indicating a positive belief about me) is expressed with a certain degree of commitment. Note, however, that while Yuri's objection was possibly constrained by her not knowing the landlord personally (or being more 'distant' from him than I was, and hence not having sufficient authority on his intended meaning), Kyo's objection refers more broadly to the 'Japanese'. Of course, the Japanese as a whole are not more 'knowable' to Kyo than one individual, but arguably he could more authoritative over this information precisely because it is generic, refers to an idealized standard arguably shared by many, with which he can claim familiarity as a full-fledged member of the same community. However, more importantly, I think that this is a piece of information on which he can confidently (and safely) claim to be more knowledgeable than me. Similarly, the definite negation *iya*, as well as the unmodalized predicates in the same utterance (*sukida kara*, *shinai kedo*), convey the same 'subjective certainty', legitimate in respect to my rights to authoritative knowledge, compared to, say, those of an interlocutor who had just carried out a quantitative study of Japanese preferences for degrees of lighting. Moreover, in uttering these categorical statements, Kyo (unlike Yuri) could possibly discount any likelihood of challenge from the other native speakers present, who are after all his subordinates in the workplace.

We then come across again, in my lines 22–26, some generic comments about Japanese attitudes to natives' and non-natives' responsiveness to hints. Kyo confirms my remarks, but this time (although he is still commenting, as before, about Japanese people in general) he

modalizes his statement with -*kamoshirenai*. Here Kyo is not just confirming what I said, or making relatively neutral generalizing statements,
but crucially also adding an explicit evaluative judgement (*donkan
to iwareru*) of my previous, neutral statement. The implied assertion
exposes his personal opinion (which may or may not be ratified by other
participants) and with it, his stance. That this carries a potential risk
of misalignment with other participants is evident from the fact that
when I take the evaluation of 'unperceptiveness' to be indeed applicable to my case (line 28), he denies it more categorically (line 29).[25] The
sudden clear-cut positioning generated by the evaluative term demands
to be 'blurred' (which he does by deploying -*kamoshirenai*'s distinctive
trait of hinting at a 50 per cent possibility that things are otherwise),
so the modal marking transforms a potential JUDGEMENT into a mere
SUGGESTION.

Yuri's whole contribution (note also the omission of a predicate
in line 15, although this is possibly due to overlapping), including
the final -*kamoshirenai*, reveals her reluctance to commit to a definite
stance towards her interpretation of the information, and by doing so,
she manages to maintain a relatively friendly and cooperative stance
towards me, while expressing her views on the matter at hand. In contrast, Kyo displays relative authority over generic opinions, and resorts
to an epistemic 'hedging' when volunteering a personal and very specific
evaluation. In both cases, we can certainly say that -*kamoshirenai* indicates the speaker's lack of certainty about, or unwillingness to commit
to, the factuality of the proposition. In both cases, the marker indicates
a 50 per cent possibility that something is the case. But this semantic resource assists Yuri in carrying out an (other-oriented) supportive
move, i.e. a mild OBJECTION to my insistent opinions; and assists Kyo
in CONFIRMING, but also further qualifying a previous evaluation, cau-
tiously expressing it as a SUGGESTION. These are not inherent meanings
of the modal, but meanings emerging from the interaction of the modal
with other textual (lexical items, compositional features, sequences of
discursive moves by the speaker as well as other participants) and
non-textual factors (their knowledge of Japanese norms or the specific
individual in question vis-à-vis mine and that of other participants,
the psychological and affective distance perceived at the time of the
encounter, etc.).

Background to Excerpt 2: I am recalling an episode at a restaurant
with a Japanese friend. The girl waiting on us had mistakenly brought
us a dish we did not order, but when we pointed this out she reacted

quite unexpectedly: she did not take the dish away, nor suggested to replace it with another, or any other alternative course of action; she stood in front of us speechless and motionless, obviously troubled but seemingly oblivious to our repeated questions. My friend and I reacted to this in very different ways: my friend felt sorry for the girl, assuming her reaction to betray a lack of training and possibly fear of the possible consequences (including dismissal). In contrast to my friend's compassionate reaction, I had felt rather annoyed, as her refusal to respond to our questioning or to even make eye contact felt to me not just unprofessional but also bad-mannered. I am now discussing with Kyo, Aki and Yuri the possibility that the dynamics of the episode, including the participants' contrasting reactions, had a culture-specific dimension, with regard to the role of self-expression in the cultures of Europe and Japan (note that all my interviewees have lived and worked in Europe).

EXCERPT 2 (2A; 22'18")

bp 30. *yappari nanka mitomete   moraenai tteiu   no wa...*
    In.fact HED acknowledge BEN-NEG QUOT-NM TOP
    'but after all the fact that she wouldn't acknowledge [our presence]...'

Kyo 31. *a, da kara arienai   to   omou ne... yappari... hokano kuni...   ma...*
    because possible-MOD-NEG- QUOT think FP   in.fact   other   countries HES
    32. *yooroppa toka no kyooiku ...no nakade wa, sooiu hito dete konai   desu yone...*
    Europe HED-GEN education GEN in   TOP such people come.out NEG-POL-FP
    33. *nande mo iikara   //iwanakya ikenai desu yo ne...*
    anything fine because   say-must-POL-FP
    'Oh well, I don't think (something like that) could happen in other countries...a person like that could simply not come out of a European education...you'd have to say something, anything at all.'

bp 34. *// nn, nn, nanka machigatte te...demo iu to   omou//*
    HES   HED mistake.make-CONC say QUOT-think
    'Yes, you would say something...even something wrong...'

Kyo 35. *//soo desho//*
    so POL-MOD
    'right?'

Aki 36. *docchikatte ittara   uso demo   iikara   nandemo iikara   jibun o*
    either-QUOT say-COND lie-CONC good.because anything good.because self-OBJ
    37. *yoogo suru hooga   mada ii   toka...*
    defend rather –SUBJ still better HED
    'It is always better to say something, even something untrue, so you can defend yourself?'

Kyo 38. *//soo soo soo//..dakara nihon wa soo janai no ne,   dakara   sakki ano*
    so   therefore Japan-TOP so COP-NEG-NM-FP therefore before HED
    39. *uchinoko   ga itteta   mawari mite kara te o ageru toka ...souiu*
    my.daughter-SUB say-PAST others look after hand-OBJ raise HED   such

40. *bunka dakara ... chigau n desu yone, dakara   gyakuni iikagenna koto o*
    culture because   differ NM-POL FP   therefore instead random thing-OBJ

41. *iccha ikenai   toka ... kara   sono ko wa so ... sore no   giseisha nano*
    say-must.not HED   therefore that girl-TOP   that-GEN victim COP-NM

42. **kamoshirenai**
    MOD

    'Yes, indeed, but Japan is not like that. Like my children
    said before, it is a culture in which you look around before
    you raise your hand (in class), so it's rather different.
    If anything, you would never just open your mouth and say
    something random; I think that that girl (waitress) **may** be a
    victim of this (culture).'

bp 43. *hontoo mitete kawaisoo datta   ndesu   kedo kocchi ga sakki ni jibun ga*
    really looking pitiable COP-PAST NM-POL but I   -SUBJ before self-SUBJ

44. *okotte iru koto .sore dake ... bakari kangaete ite, kanojo wa kawaisoo da*
    be.angry NM that only   only think-SUSP she -TOP pitiable COP

45. *toka ... omoete konakatta shi..ano kata ni   kiite kara, a yappari soo datta*
    HED   think -NEG -PAST and that.person-to hear after in.fact so COP-PAST

46. *kamoshirenai to   omotta n // desu ke...//*
    MOD   QUOT think-NM -COP-POL

    'Yes, I thought she appeared troubled, but I was just
    focused on my own irritation, and didn't feel sorry for
    her, until my friend pointed it out and made me realize that
    maybe I should have.'

Kyo 47. *//a soo desu ka // sore wa yappari kyooiku   toka bunka   shakai no*
    SO INT-POL-Q   that-TOP in.fact education HED culture society-GEN

48. *tokuchoo ga nyojitsu ni arawarete iru no **kamoshirenai ne..***
    feature-SUBJ truthfully emerge -NM MOD   FP

    'Oh I see. **Perhaps** one's education or cultural and social
    mindset/background are revealed more truthfully in these
    judgements/responses/situations?'

Line 30 concludes my explanation of why I felt offended by the waitress's lack of response. Kyo follows this up with a sequence of relatively
categorical interpretive statements minimally mitigated by (*ari-enai*) *to
omou* (line 31),[26] about the European educational system and how a
member of such cultures is expected to react (lines 32–33). In this way,
he is construing his position vis-à-vis the European context rather confidently, in spite of the fact that my background possibly entitles me
to challenge it. He continues to do so in lines 38–42 where he contrasts that with the Japanese culture, on which surely he can claim
some authority. So after several lines of unmodalized and authoritative-
sounding statements, why does Kyo bother to use a modal marker
(line 42)? I argue that although he has been expressing a subjective
interpretation all along, his remarks had been of a relatively general
nature, whose relationship with myself was rather indirect. However,

the statement in line 42 marks a shift in his discursive positioning, in which from relatively neutral comments he takes a more explicit evaluative stance. Qualifying the waitress as a victim potentially deflects blame from her, consequently undermines the legitimacy of the stance I have taken through my prior contributions (I had declared to have felt offended), and it is therefore a rather argumentative move. The modal mitigates (by reference to a mere 'possibility') the force of the judgement, transforming a potential DISAGREEMENT into a SUGGESTION, and minimizing the potential implication that I had been blind to the waitress's predicament (an implicit act of BLAME). Note that again the interpretation outlined here is triggered by the modal but only accrues from the interaction of epistemic deixis with discursive considerations, i.e. the preceding contributions. Decontextualizing this utterance does not allow this reading, and indeed can only describe S's enunciation of a possibility.

The sensitivity of modals to emerging discursive positions is evident, I believe, also in Kyo's next modalized statement in line 48. I make the point that until my friend (a Japanese) had pointed out to me that the waitress should have deserved our sympathy for having received little training, that possibility had not occurred to me. Hence Kyo's uptake of this statement (lines 47–48), attributing this to different cultural mindsets, is effectively a comment about me (a judgement), and hence a sensitive act of stance-taking, that once again he demotes from the status of a categorical assertion. This mitigates his claim to authority and allows him to display an unassuming stance.

10.4 Summary

I hope this analysis has shown how modals respond to interactional needs and how they can shape interactional stances. Within limits set by language-specific parameters (i.e. the comparatively more stringent constraints upon Japanese modals and psychological predicates), modals allow speakers to moderate their stance-taking and negotiate discursive (mis)alignment. This supports a view of modals as arising from intersubjective, rather than purely subjective, concerns and suggests that we should focus on *joint* activities to fully account for the use of factuality statements to achieve interactional goals.

With regards to -*kamoshirenai*, we have seen how it assists speakers in carrying out interactionally sensitive communicative acts (objecting, confirming, submitting evaluations, opinions, etc.), by 'qualifying' (via specific epistemic stances) the particular interactional stances speakers adopt while doing that. Because such interactional stances are partially a product of volatile contextual factors, generalizing a modal marker's discursive function and deriving a 'predictive' definition is not possible. While syntactic analyses specify sentential constraints, and semantic analyses the potential that speakers strategically deploy in conversation, contextual (interactional) considerations also play an indisputable role. Thus the best generic qualification we can provide of a modal like -*kamoshirenai* is that of a marker of non-factuality, which indexes the speaker's belief about the possibility of existence/occurrence of a certain state of affairs, while admitting alternative possibilities as well. Whether its prominent meaning is the very *statement* of such possibility or the statement of a *mere possibility*, cannot possibly be established in the absence of a qualifying context. Likewise, whether it will qualify advice, objections, evaluations, etc. cannot be established pre-contextually (and moreover, could be assigned different meanings by different participants).

In the context of the interview I presented, modals helped speakers to display *aligning* stances (through various collaborative communicative moves). The interactional stance that my interlocutors arguably seemed intent on construing (albeit in different degrees in Yuri's and Kyo's stances) was that of knowledgeable, informed and articulate, but also considerate, unostentatious and unassuming informants and commentators (unassuming, but not hazy or vague: cf. Pizziconi, in press). But of course different interactional contexts (participants' expectations, goals) could transform the same acts into *misaligning* stances – for example, when the notion of 'possibility' is more detrimental or unfavourable to the hearer's position than one of 'certainty'.[27] This demonstrates the role of epistemic marking in the constitution of social relations through discourse.

10.5 Conclusions

An ethnographic approach to discourse analysis enables us to foreground the interactional function of factuality, and its instrumental role in shaping interpersonal stances through indexical reference to claims to knowledge (hence to authority and power), and the associated notions of information-territorial rights and duties. The clear functional affinity of modal markers and politeness markers has not gone unnoticed: Shibatani (1990: 374ff.), for example, explicitly links Japanese honorific, spatial and epistemic deixis through the common trait of a notion of 'distance'. Some categorizations of modality include honorifics *tout court* (e.g. Nitta, 1991; Nakau 1994),[28] others only some of them (e.g. 'performative' honorifics, as Masuoka, this volume); others consider modality as a regulating principle in honorific marking (Kamio 2002: 59). But some other studies consider modality as a tool to express polite attitudes over and beyond honorific marking (Pon 2004: 12, Maynard 1993; in particular on evidentiality Hirata 2001, Trent 1997, Ohta 1991). These and other studies understand modality marking in terms of strategies oriented to (Brown and Levinsonian) notions of 'face'. Some of the uses presented here can certainly be accounted for by an overarching notion of 'facework' (leaving aside the considerable lack of consensus on the definition of 'face'; cf. O'Driscoll 2007). But this macro-notion is somewhat 'coarse' in order to account for the mechanisms involved in very many different types of communicative acts and interactional orientations: to mention but the few that we have observed here, assisting the speaker's objections or the speaker's evaluations, deflecting potential blame, constituting unassuming identities, and so on. More useful, although not entirely unrelated, is the notion of speaker 'authority' (Fox 2001). When knowledge is characterized as a socially valued good, its ownership is symbolically conceptualized as power, which comes with entitlements and responsibilities. These are not absolute, but vary with the relationship to others, and hence (like power) are to a certain extent subject to social negotiation, challenge and expectations. Epistemic authority over knowledge can be thought of as the social reflex of the semantic notion of factuality – declarable only under certain conditions.

As a socially embedded practice, the use of epistemic markers is arguably shaped by sociocultural norms and customs (Precht 2003: 240, Wierzbicka 2006, Traugott and Dasher 2002: 21) in both their diachronic development and their synchronic use. The extraordinary body of scholarship on Japanese modality from syntactic, semantic and cognitive perspectives urgently needs to be complemented from social psychological, historical, discursive perspectives that restore attention to 'language in culture'. We need descriptions of epistemic markers in situated contexts of use, of epistemic stances that are valued or proscribed in specific interactional contexts; ways in which claims to authority are received or disputed, and the ideological or sociocultural systems that these stances sustain.

The wealth of research in the field of Japanese modality studies suggests we have sufficient resources to face this challenge.

Acknowledgements

I wish to express my gratitude to the Japan Foundation, for providing generous funding of the fieldwork in Tokyo in the autumn of 2005 which provided the data presented here, and to the friends and new acquaintances whose interview I reported, for their generous gift of time and interest.

Notes

1. This chapter follows the Hepburn romanization conventions.
2. See Caffi (2007: 222ff.) for reference to the Leechian maxims of modesty that links status and display of knowledge, Givonian gradations from epistemic to 'actional' modes, etc.; also relevant is Du Bois's (1986: 323) discussion of evidence in acts of persuasion.
3. Insofar as modal markers can index a schema of 'default' location of information (cf. Kizu in this volume on 'person restriction' on the subjects of modal predicates, and notions of information territory that I will describe below), they can be thought of as a type of deictic, indexing patterns of participant roles (Agha 2007: 37), a point on which however I will not elaborate in this study.
4. At the level of textual conditions, relativization, for example, may impose constraints on the degree of 'subjectivity' perceived in a certain form, as in *iku kamoshirenai hito* ('those who might go/are likely to go/are thinking of maybe going') vs *iku kamoshirenai* ('they might go'). Past tense imposes a similar constraint. The rest of this study concerns itself with social, situational conditions.
5. Maynard maintains that her 'discourse modality indicators' cannot be examined in a 'social vacuum' (1993: 41), and her analysis of conversational data focuses on both co-textual and situational aspects.
6. Just like the term 'subjectivity', the term 'stance' has been called to account for a myriad of different phenomena (cf. Precht 2003: 242), but several studies offer considerably detailed analyses of this construct and its workings. A useful discussion from an interactional perspective is provided by Englebretson (2007) whose review of ordinary language users' data reveals that 'stance' is commonly characterized as a public act, a relational, interactional phenomenon, a physical embodied action, a personal belief/attitude/evaluation or social morality, socioculturally embedded, and consequential for stance-takers.
7. Givon directly criticizes a philosophical and linguistic tradition mainly concerned with 'sentential modalities', which thus 'appear to be an *objective* matter, to which neither the speaker nor the hearer – the two participants in the *communicative transaction* in which human language is actually used – bear any relevance' (1982: 24). Thus he considers the speaker's *subjective certainty* an 'inferential by-product of the evidentiary, *experiential* aspect of knowledge' (1982: 25). He concludes that the logician's 'truth'

'is a peculiar concept that seems to have no empirical, behavioural attestation in psychology' and in linguistics, 'it is confined to a narrow band of "marked" phenomena, overblown beyond proportion by millennia of traditional epistemology' (1982: 46).

8. Variable interpretations of such rights and obligations by conversational partners explain why the modal characterization of an utterance can be disputed. Indeed speakers can 'feign' certainty when they have none (and be challenged as liars or presumptuous, cf. Trent 1997: 106, 177–8), and 'feign' uncertainty when they have sufficient information (and be accused of irresponsibility, Moriyama 1992: 106).

9. As stated by the same Kamio (2002: 35), the main difference between the theory presented in 1990 and in 2002 lies in 'technicalities' such as more subtle, graded differences between information within and without one's territory, and in information obtained from outside sources.

10. Note the implicit distinction here, which I also make, between 'information' and 'knowledge', conceptualized as 'ownership' of information.

11. Kamio focuses on Japanese, but also offers some generalizations to English. For a treatment of English in terms of a comparable notion of territory see Labov and Fanshel (1977: 100).

12. Based on this argument, Nuyts (2001) suggests we redefine Lyons' distinction between 'subjective' vs 'objective' modality, as 'subjective' vs 'intersubjective' evidentiality (where 'evidentiality' is used in a general epistemic sense). This is consistent with Givon's notion of 'subjective certainty' and the disputedness of certain truths.

13. Masuoka (1991: 116) qualifies it as 'secondary-modality' in view of its derivative 'secondary' meaning of 'suspension of judgement' from a 'primary' meaning of 'statement of possibility'.

14. Unlike -*nichigainai*, in which an inference has to have some sort of external validation (Nitta 1991: 102), -*kamoshirenai* can be based also merely on internal conjectures as to the uncertainty of some proposition. Arguably however, both the attribution to external sources, or internal conjecture, are also manipulated on the basis of *inter*subjective assessments of participants' territories (Nuyts 2001: 386).

15. Johnson discusses modality from the viewpoint of the speaker's judgement of a proposition's 'necessity' and 'possibility', and based on semantico-syntactic parameters, shows the relative distribution of Japanese epistemic and evidential auxiliaries. She claims (1999: 158) that propositions describing facts of high possibility of realization (i.e. close to the real world) do not require much modal marking, and vice versa, those with lower possibility of realization (i.e. *irrealis* worlds) require various degrees of modalization, whose differences she shows by a continuous curve along the intersecting axes of 'degree of modality', and 'necessity–possibility'. Cf. this statement with Larm's analysis, in this volume, that shows -*kamoshirenai* as a marker of 'low subjectivity'. This exemplifies the point I will make below about the elusiveness of indexicals, and their sensitivity to the particular analytical parameters adopted.

16. This has the nature of a logical implication: possibility implies non-possibility. Thus -*kamoshirenai* can refer to two contrastive (including mutually exclusive) possibilities (e.g. *kare ga kuru kamoshirenai shi, konai*

kamoshirenai = 'he may come, he may not'; Nitta 2000: 130); in contrast, *daroo* requires that the events referred to are compatible.

17. This is derivable from the relative transparency of its constituents: while the dubitative particle *ka* and the predicative *shirenai* (lit: cannot be known) imply uncertainty, *mo* (lit: too, even) refers to the existence of something else (Harima Keiko 1998 'Kamoshirenai' no naritachi ni tsuite [On the development of *kamoshirenai*], *Nihon Bungaku kenkyuu 33* Baiku gakuin daigaku, quoted in Jiang 2009).

18. See for example Kawaguchi (2003: 60) for very sensible observations about the distinction of 'basic meanings' and 'communicative functions', the latter of which are derived from contextual factors: e.g. the function of *gijiteki dooi*, or 'pseudo-agreements' like *tashikani ossharu toori ka mo shiremasen ga*, 'it may be as you say, but', which Hirata (2001) maintains to be a derivational euphemistic 'meaning' of the form.

19. The glosses are very concise for reasons of space, and omit prosodic features. The author's contributions (as she is not a native speaker of Japanese) are not analysed. Legenda: ADV adverbial; COMPL completive auxiliary; CONC concessive; COND conditional; CONJ conjunction; COP copula; FP sentence final particle; GEN genitive particle; HED discourse hedge (mostly refers to *nanka*, or the bound morpheme *to ka*, discursive markers of uncertainty); HES hesitation marker; MOD modal marker; NEG negative; NM nominalizer; OBJ object particle; PAST past tense; POL polite form; SUSP suspensive form; QUOT quotative particle; SUBJ subject particle; TOP topic; VOL volitive; @ laughter; // overlapping turns.

20. In other words, while on an illocutionary level she is negating my suggestions, which is a potential 'misaligning' move, on an interactional level she is orienting herself to a sympathetic position in relation to mine, a stance interactionally supportive of my face in that context. Her 'alignment' is therefore an emergent 'meaning' contingent to this interaction, and not one conveyed by the specific speech act.

21. Cf. note 25 on *omou* (think). -*Kamoshirenai* constitutes a suspension of the preparatory conditions of an assertion (that the speaker has grounds for the truth of *p*); it therefore at best constitutes a (quasi)-assertion (cf. McDowell 1991).

22. Kamio argues that psychological predicates (in the present tense) are a pragmatic phenomenon in English but a grammatical one in Japanese. This means that utterances which are unacceptable in Japanese may be variably acceptable, unnatural or simply inappropriate in English (Kamio 2002: 67). In contrast, Masuoka (1997: 9) claims that modality does not need a cognitive theory to be explained, but just a pragmatic principle of 'private territories'.

23. Note, incidentally, the different levels of interpretation: referential, functional, interactional. Line 21 simultaneously establishes reference (who did what), responds to the previous turn (my questions), and does interactional work (by mitigating an objection). Cf. Agha (2007: 86) on progressively more encompassing levels of text structure, which incorporate wider amounts of context.

24. -*Uru* differs from -*kamoshirenai* in many respects: it admits negation, question, can co-occur with other suppositional markers (*suiryoo*); it suffixes

intentional verbs; with non-intentional verbs it requires nominalization (**boo wa ore-uru* vs *boo wa oreru koto wa ariruru,* = the stick could break)*;* it indicates that something will happen, given the right conditions. Its distinctive trait is its reference to the existence of a real (rather than potential) possibility that something will happen, independent of the speaker's assessment of its likelihood, hence closer to factual worlds than *-kamoshirenai* (Moriyama 2002: 20).

25. In line 29 Kyo uses the negative form of the verb *omou*, 'to think' (followed by the mitigator *kedo*). For Lyons (1977: 795) this verb is a non-factive predicator: it commits S to neither the truth nor falsity of the proposition in the complement clause; it therefore suspends commitment. Likewise for Wierzbicka (2006: 38) it is a 'downtoner'. 'I don't' think Ø/that…' means: 'I don't say: I know'. However, it can be ambiguous as to whether it indicates the speaker's internal cognition or a mitigation of commitment, and possibly interpreted as the former when the proposition is not empirically verifiable (Stubbs 1986: 18). In some cases the meaning of 'uncertainty' seems indeed rather feeble: *Nihon no ima no iryoo seido wa machigatte iru to omou* ('I think that the current health service in Japan is wrong'), according to Moriyama (1992: 110), merely 'transmits the speaker's opinion'. It is no mere coincidence that in the utterances in question the complement clause contains an evaluative judgement rather than a fact (and that some structures such as first person desiderative + *omou* convey the same assertive force: *kampai shitai to omoimasu* ['I wish to propose a toast']), Moriyama (1992: 113). Unlike *-kamoshirenai*'s inability to reach the force of a statement (it is a quasi-statement) *-to omou* (attached to evaluative terms) fully constitutes one, and hence approaches the realm of 'factuality'.

26. See the previous two footnotes on *omou* (think) and *-uru* (of which *-enai* is the negative form).

27. We saw this potentially in Yuri's first modalized statement, which, as far as degrees of H's support is concerned, is less forceful than more categorical statements could have been.

28. This chapter, however, does not subscribe to this position, as stated in section 10.2. To be more precise, following Shibatani (1990) and particularly Agha (2007: 39), I consider both honorifics and modal markers deictic systems that take the speaker as the origo of reckoning. The first indexes the speaker's stance towards a particular socio-affective interactional 'schema', and the second the speaker's stance towards information. However, while modality has to do with 'factuality', honorifics do not.

References

Agha, Asif (2007). *Language and Social Relations.* Cambridge: Cambridge University Press.

Caffi, Claudia (2007). *Mitigation.* Amsterdam: Elsevier.

Du Bois, John W. (1986). Self-evidence and authority in rituals. In: Chafe, Wallace and Johanna Nichols (eds), *Evidentiality: the Linguistics Coding of Epistemology.* Norwood, NJ: Ablex Publishing: 313–16.

Du Bois, John W. (2007). The stance triangle. In: Englebretson, Robert (ed.), *Stancetaking in Discourse – Subjectivity, Evaluation, Interaction*. Amsterdam: John Benjamins: 139–82.

Englebretson, Robert (2007). Introduction. In: Englebretson, Robert (ed.), *Stancetaking in Discourse – Subjectivity, Evaluation, Interaction*. Amsterdam: John Benjamins: 1–25.

Fox, Barbara A. (2001). Evidentiality: authority, responsibility, and entitlement in English conversation. *Journal of Linguistic Anthropology* 11(2), 67–92.

Givon, Talmy (1982). Evidentiality and epistemic space. *Studies in Language* 6, 23–49.

Hirata, Mami (2001). *Kamoshirenai no imi – modariti to goyooron no setten o saguru* [The meaning of *kamoshirenai* – pursuing the connection of modality and pragmatics]. *Nihongo Kyooiku* 108, 60–8.

Jiang Jiayi [蒋家義] (2009). *'Kamoshirenai' no shosoo* [Aspects of *kamoshirenai*], *Kyorin Daigaku Daigakuin Kokusai Kyooryoku Kenkyuukai Daigakuin Ronbunshuu 6* [Graduate School of International Relations Journal of Master Degree] (available at http://www.linguistics.com.cn/jiang/dxy05.pdf).

Johnson, Yuki (1999). *Modariti riron no meikakuka wo motomete* [A plea for clarification in Modality theory]. In: Aramu Sasaki Yukiko (ed.), *Gengogaku to Nihongo Kyooiku* [Linguistics and Japanese Language Learning]. Tokyo: Kuroshio: 145–60.

Johnson, Yuki (2003). *Modality and the Japanese Language*. Ann Arbor: University of Michigan: Centre for Japanese Studies.

Kamio, Akio (1990). *Joohoo no Nawabari Riron* [The theory of territory of information]. Tokyo: Taishuukan.

Kamio, Akio (1994). The theory of territory of information: the case of Japanese. *Journal of Pragmatics* 21(1), 67–100.

Kamio, Akio (2002). *Zoku Joohoo no Nawabari Riron* [The theory of territory of information continued]. Tokyo: Taishuukan.

Kärkkäinen, Elise (2003). *Epistemic Stance in English Conversation*. Amsterdam: John Benjamins.

Kärkkäinen, Elise (2006). Stance taking in conversation: from subjectivity to intersubjectivity. *Text and Talk* 26(6), 699–731.

Kawaguchi, Sachiko (2003). *Kamoshirenai no 'kanoosei meiji' – 'imi' 'bunmyaku' 'kinoo' no kijutsu*, [The 'expression of possibility' in *kamoshirenai* – a description of 'meaning', 'context' and 'function']. *The Journal of Seigakuin University* 15(2), 69–99.

Kawaguchi, Sachiko (2005). *Nihongokyokasho ni okeru kamoshirenai- 'Bunmyaku' to 'kinoo' ni yoru kyoozai bunseki* [*Kamoshirenai* in textbooks of Japanese as a second language – a textbook analysis through 'context' and 'function']. *The Journal of Seigakuin University* 17(3), 37–48.

Labov, William and David Fanshel (1977). *Therapeutic Discourse: Psychotherapy as Conversation*. New York: Academic Press.

Leech, Geoffrey (2007). Politeness: Is there an East–West divide? *Journal of Politeness Research* 3(2), 167–206.

Lyons, John (1977). *Semantics 2*. Cambridge: Cambridge University Press.

McDowell, Joyce P. (1991). Quasi-assertion. *Journal of Semantics* 8, 311–31.

Masuoka, Takashi (1991). *Modariti no bunpoo* [The grammar of *Modariti*]. Tokyo: Kuroshio.

Masuoka, Takashi (1997). *Hyoogen no Shuukansei* [The expression's subjectivity]. In: Takubo, Yukinori (ed.), *Shiten to Gengo Koodoo* [Perspective and Linguistic. Behaviour]. Tokyo: Kuroshio: 1–11.

Masuoka, Takashi (2002). *Handan no modariti – Genjitsu to higenjitsu no tairitsu* [Modality of Judgment – the *realis/irrealis* opposition]. *Nihongogaku* 21, 6–16.

Maynard, Senko K. (1993). *Discourse Modality*. Amsterdam: John Benjamins.

Moriyama, Takuro (1992). *Bunmatsu shikoo dooshi 'omou' wo megutte* [On the sentence-final mental verb *omou*]. *Nihongogaku* [Japanese Linguistics] 11(8), 105–16.

Moriyama, Takuro (2002). *Kanoosei to sono shuuhen – 'kanenai', 'ariuru', 'kanoosei ga aru', nado no ugenteki hyoogen to 'kamoshirenai'* [Possibility and its surroundings – *kamoshirenai* and the circumlocutions *kanenai, ariuru, kanoosei ga aru*]. *Nihongogaku* [Japanese Linguistics] 2, 17–27.

Nakau, Minoru (1994). *Ninchi imiron no genri* [Principles of Cognitive Semantics]. Tokyo: Taishukan.

Narrog, Heiko (2005a). On defining modality again. *Language Sciences* 27(2), 165–92.

Narrog, Heiko (2005b). Modality, mood, and change of modal meanings – a new perspective. *Cognitive Linguistics* 16(4), 677–731.

Nitta, Yoshio (1989). *Bun no Koozoo* [Sentence structure]. In Kitahara, Yasuo (ed.), *Koza nihongo to nihongo kyouiku* [A course in Japanese and Japanese language education] 4, Tokyo Meiji Shooin: 25–52.

Nitta, Yoshio (1991). *Nihongo no modariti to ninshoo* [Japanese Modality and Person]. Tokyo: Hitsuji shobo.

Nitta, Yoshio (2000). *Ninshiki no Modariti to sono shuuhen* [Epistemic modality and its surroundings]. In: Moriyama, Takuro, Yoshio Nitta and Hiroshi Kudoo (eds), *Modariti*. Tokyo: Iwanami Shoten: 79–159.

Nuyts, Jan (2001). Subjectivity as an evidential dimension in epistemic modal expressions. *Journal of Pragmatics* 33(3), 383–400.

Ochs, Eleanor (1996). Linguistic resources for socializing humanity. In: Gumperz, John J. and Stephen Levinson (eds), *Rethinking Linguistic Relativity*. Cambridge: Cambridge University Press: 407–38.

Ohta, Amy Snyder (1991). Evidentiality and politeness in Japanese. *Issues in Applied Linguistics* 2(2), 211–38.

O'Driscoll, Jim (2007). Brown & Levinson's face: how it can – and can't – help us to understand interaction across cultures. *Intercultural Pragmatics* 4(4), 463–92.

Palmer, Frank R. (1986). *Mood and Modality*. Cambridge: Cambridge University Press.

Pizziconi, Barbara (in press). Stereotyping communicative style in and out of the language and culture classroom: Japanese indirectness, ambiguity and vagueness. In: Gómez Morón, Reyes, Manuel Padilla Cruz, Lucía Fernández Amaya and María de la O Hernández López (eds), *Pragmatics Applied to Language Teaching and Learning*, Cambridge: Cambridge Scholars Publishing: 221–54.

Pon Fei [Peng, Fei] (2004). *Nihongo no 'hairyo hyoogen' ni kansuru kenkyuu: Chuugokugo to no hikaku kenkyuu ni okeru shomondai* [Studies in Japanese 'considerate expressions': a few problems in Japanese–Chinese contrastive studies]. Osaka: Izumi Shoin.

Precht, Kristen (2003). Stance moods in spoken English: evidentiality and affect in British and American conversation. *Text* 23(2), 239.

Saeed, John I. (2003). *Semantics*, 2nd edn. Oxford: Blackwell.

Shibatani, Masayoshi (1990). *The Languages of Japan*. Cambridge: Cambridge University Press.

Stubbs, Michael (1986). Towards a modal grammar of English: a matter of prolonged fieldwork. *Applied Linguistics* 7(1), 1–25.

Takubo, Yukinori (1990). On the role of hearer's territory of information. In: The Japan Cognitive Science Society (ed.), *Ninchikagaku no Hatten – Mentaru Supe-su* [Advances in Cognitive Science – Mental Spaces] 3. Tokyo: Kodansha: 67–84.

Takubo, Yukinori and Satoshi Kinsui (1997). Discourse management in terms of mental spaces. *Journal of Pragmatics* 28(6), 741–58.

Teramura, Hideo (1984). *Nihongo no Sintakkusu to Imi* II [Syntax and Semantics of Japanese II]. Tokyo: Kuroshio Shuppan.

Traugott, Elizabeth C. and Richard B. Dasher (2002). *Regularity in Semantic Change*. Cambridge: Cambridge University Press.

Trent, Nobuko (1997). Linguistic coding of evidentiality in Japanese spoken discourse and Japanese politeness Unpublished dissertation, University of Texas at Austin, Ann Arbor, Michigan.

van Dijk, Teun A. (1981). Towards an empirical pragmatics. *Philosophica* 27, 127–38 (available at http://www.discourses.org/download/articles/).

Wierzbicka, Anna (2006). *English: Meaning and Culture*. Oxford: Oxford University Press.

Subject Index

abduction, 4, 151, 164, 165, 166, 167, 172, 173
accuracy, 239, 245, 247, 253
adverbial (adverbial form), 2, 118, 122, 127, 140, 170, 234: clause, 100, 101; phrase, 197, 219
  modal, 197
  time, 219
agreement, 241
  case, 199
  syntactic, 4, 91, 184, 195, 196, 197, 202n, 203n
aligning stance, 278
alignment, 262, 277, 282n
  see also misalignment
American Council on the Teaching of Foreign Languages (ACTFL), 231, 238, 239, 240
antecedent, 66, 71, 117, 118, 120, 124, 125, 128, 129, 130, 131, 132, 133, 134, 135, 136, 138, 139, 141, 142, 143, 145, 146, 147n, 155, 156, 224
appropriateness
  pragmatic, 245, 247, 253, 254, 255n, 265
  social, 263, 265
aspect, 12, 14, 21, 40, 41, 48, 118, 140, 147n, 210, 222
  form/marker, 117, 118, 145
aspectual
  auxiliary, 140
  classification, 1
  morpheme, 32, 139
aspectuality, 48, 49, 90
assumptive, 57, 71, 75, 77
attitude, 254, 259, 274, 279, 281n
  of the speaker, 59, 60, 97, 105, 184, 185, 188, 207, 208, 209, 218, 225, 226, 227, 231, 232, 233, 237, 238, 240, 249, 254, 259, 261–2, 267, 279, 280n
  propositional attitude verbs, 66, 82n

subjective, 10, 105, 208, 218, 226, 233
  third person's, 267
authority, 111, 260, 263, 265–6, 268, 272, 273, 274, 276–7, 278, 279

BECOME-language, *see* BE-language
BE-language, 88, 107, 108
boundness, 90, 91

C system, 191, 198, 199, 200
case grammar, 14, 37
c-command domain, 161
certainty, 94, 95, 101, 134, 135, 143, 267, 279
  subjective, 261, **263**, 267, 272, 273, 280n, 281n
  see also uncertainty
chinjutsu [predication], 15, 16, **17**, **18**, **19**, **20**, **21**, **23**, 27, 28, 29, 30, 31n, 62, 87, 97
  ron [predication theory], **14**, **15**, **19**, **24**, 31n
  fukushi [declarative adverbs], 147n
closed-class, 90, 91
cohesion, 237
communicative competence, 254
conditional, **117**, **125**, 141, 145, **150**, 155, 156, 164, 165, 171, 177n, 224
  clause, 4, 109, 118, 128, 134, 141, 145, 146, 147n, 157, 160, **223**, **224**
  construction/sentence, 36, **41**, **42**, 66, 71, 82n, 118, 145, 147n, 150, 160, 177n
  counterfactual, 117, 125, 131, **125**, 131, **141**, **142**
  direct, 118, 119
  epistemic, 117, **124**, **125**, 131, **133**, 135, 136, 145, 146, 146n, 168

Language Index

Name Index

Grammatical Form Index

VG\Like New

£35